Working With Words

A Handbook for Media Writers and Editors

TENTH EDITION

Working With Words

A Handbook for Media Writers and Editors

Brian S. Brooks

University of Missouri–Columbia
Professor and Associate Dean Emeritus

James L. Pinson

Eastern Michigan University
Professor Emeritus

Jean Gaddy Wilson

Position the Future Consultants

bedford/st.martin's
Macmillan Learning

Boston | New York

For Bedford/St. Martin's

Vice President, Editorial, Macmillan Learning Humanities: Edwin Hill
Program Director for Communication: Erika Gutierrez
Program Manager for Human Communication: Allen Cooper
Marketing Manager: Amy Haines
Director of Content Development, Humanities: Jane Knetzger
Developmental Editor: Melanie McFadyen
Senior Workflow Project Manager: Lisa McDowell
Production Supervisor: Robin Besofsky
Media Project Manager: Sarah O'Connor
Senior Media Editor: Tom Kane
Assistant Editor: Audrey Webster
Senior Manager of Publishing Services: Andrea Cava
Project Management: Lumina Datamatics, Inc.
Composition: Lumina Datamatics, Inc.
Text Permissions Manager: Kalina Ingham
Permissions Associate: Allison Ziebka
Director of Design, Content Management: Diana Blume
Text Design: Claire Seng-Niemoeller, Diana Blume
Cover Design: William Boardman
Printing and Binding: RR Donnelley

Printed in China.

1   2   3   4   5   6   24   23   22   21   20   19

For information, write: Bedford/St. Martin's, 75 Arlington Street, Boston, MA 02116

ISBN 978-1-319-20117-3

Acknowledgments

Acknowledgments and copyrights appear on the same page as the text and art selections they cover; these acknowledgments and copyrights constitute an extension of the copyright page.

At the time of publication all internet URLs published in this text were found to accurately link to their intended website. If you do find a broken link, please forward the information to melanie.mcfadyen@macmillan.com so that it can be corrected for the next printing.

Preface

Working With Words had its beginnings in our own work as newspaper copy editors. We found the stylebook and dictionary didn't always answer the questions that came up every day about grammar, usage, punctuation, compound-word spellings and similar issues. Also, cultural and demographic shifts forced writers to be more aware about avoiding racism, sexism and ageism, as well as dismissive language about the disabled, new immigrants, religious group members and so on. We kept a small shelf of books to consult at such times, but there was no single, comprehensive resource a member of the working press could turn to for answers.

Later, when teaching editing to students at the University of Missouri and supervising their work on the daily *Columbia Missourian*, we realized that if professionals needed a book that addressed all of these questions in one place, students needed it even more. Instructors across the country report that students are underprepared in grammar and style, and the changing world requires all of us to catch up and keep up.

Our students often tell us the last time their teachers covered grammar was in middle school or even elementary school. Further, modern technologies such as texting, tweeting, Facebook and other social media introduce a casualness in communication that can confuse students' writing habits. Using these media, as well as the web and broadcast media as major news sources, not only affect student writing but also demand us as writers and editors to adapt, whether we are students learning the ropes or experienced journalists.

Working With Words Today

With news outlets, both print and broadcast, stressing their online presence while continually cutting staff, how do students and seasoned journalists adapt? What skills and principles lead to success with technology and media as they change rapidly?

Although knowing grammar, usage, style, tightening and sensitivity obviously isn't the whole answer, it is an important part of the picture.

The rapid rise of new technology requires students and working journalists to become better self-editors than ever.

Journalists also need to know how different media can influence the way they write: Do traditional language rules still apply? What adjustments help journalists use Facebook, Twitter, Instagram, Snapchat and blogs to promote reader interest without sacrificing integrity or making embarrassing gaffes? As the way readers consume the news has shifted and continues to change, providing them with clear, compelling writing becomes more challenging and all the more important.

The Best Guidance for Writers and Editors

In this book, we offer a number of strategies to use when facing the challenges of writing and editing today. *Working With Words* is more than just an introduction to journalistic writing or a grammar and usage manual. This relatively brief but comprehensive text is a well-rounded resource to use from beginning journalistic training all the way through journalistic careers, no matter the medium.

Part One covers the basics of journalistic writing and of writing concisely—skills essential in all media. It then explains how today's new technologies marry print, broadcast and digital skills, and call on us to learn how to write for different media. Chapters 3–6 cover the keys of writing for print, broadcast and online media, and—new to this edition—strategic communication. With each, we show how word choice, word order, style and even story organization change with the medium.

In this edition, as in previous ones, we've presented the latest advice students need for writing online, including guidance on blogging, search engine optimization, promoting news using social media like Twitter, Facebook, Instagram and Snapchat, and editing your own copy. Finally, we cover the increasingly important topic of "Isms:" sexism, racism and so on. We're proud to say ours was one of the first journalism texts, if not the first, to tackle this issue all the way back in its first edition in 1989. With updates for the new edition, we think we're still on the cutting edge of these global changes.

Part Two focuses on the kinds of usage and grammar issues that were the original impetus for the book, but we have reevaluated and updated our advice for the many changes in language since earlier editions. We think *Working With Words* remains the most concise, complete and up-to-date source of journalism advice on these topics.

As in the Ninth Edition, we have divided chapters in Part Two into two discussions: first, on the most important basic rules to know about that subject, what we call "Solving Common Problems"; and second, on additional, less common and more nuanced points, what we call "Understanding in More Depth." We think this helps teachers and students better navigate the chapters, so that they have a clearer focus on where to start in studying topics for which there may be more rules than can easily be taken in at once.

Part Three then is a compilation of useful reference lists of examples of some of the topics raised earlier in the text, such as AP style, compound words, "Isms," spelling, tightening, trademarks and usage. These lists appeared in previous editions mainly within the chapters, but we decided they would be easier to use as a reference section of their own, which would at the same time shorten and improve the flow of the chapters. Of course, like everything else, these lists have been updated.

Throughout the text we elaborate on appropriate *AP Stylebook* rules most journalists follow and give plenty of examples. But in addition, we provide an appendix that lists the most essential style rules to help beginners get off to a faster start and more advanced students or professionals to fill in a few gaps.

Whatever the subject, we always explain the issues as simply as we can. But at the same time, we haven't tried to make the subjects look easier than they are, as many books do by leaving out the harder, trickier questions that arise when you make your living working with words. Instead, we face these issues straight on in the main text as well as in the Journalism Tip boxes, which provide more specific guidance on challenges confronting journalists on the job.

We've also provided tip boxes specifically on dealing with "Our Changing Language." In the Ninth Edition, we called these "Rules to Retire" because they highlight rules that are either obsolete or we think soon will be. We thought that the new title better addresses how our language is constantly changing and evolving. Just as the chapter on "Sexism, Racism and Other 'Isms'" has to be continually updated in each edition to reflect changes in our culture, we think it's essential to spotlight where the rules of grammar, for example, have already changed or are in the process of changing.

New to This Edition

The Tenth Edition has been revised to reflect a changing media landscape. It is also a time of great cultural change, and we have aimed this text to help journalism students of all backgrounds update their language and methods to find success in today's world.

Those who have used a previous edition of this book will probably notice a variety of changes, all of which we think contribute to make *Working With Words* a more valuable resource with each edition.

A Reorganized Approach. We have reorganized the text's main parts and the placement of some chapters. Part One, "Writing for the Media," now features the chapter on "Sexism, Racism and Other 'Isms,'" which was moved to reflect its importance in the basics of writing for journalism. All of the longer reference lists, formerly located within the chapters whose topics they exemplify, have been moved into Part Three so that students may find them easier to locate and use. These lists offer useful insights on bias-related terms, hyphenated (or not hyphenated) words, spelling rules, ways to tighten your language, trademarks and misused and confused words and phrases.

A New Introductory Chapter.   We have revised and expanded the Student Introduction from the last edition to provide a better overview to the course as the title, "Understanding Journalism and the News," suggests. Chapter 1 provides a broad definition of journalism and explains its differences from opinion, which leads into a discussion of perceptions of media bias, "fake news" and the state of the media industry today. The chapter concludes with a discussion of the importance of newspapers and how, although print newspapers may be declining, journalism continues to thrive with many opportunities for new journalists in print and in media.

New Coverage on Strategic Communication.   Chapter 6, "Writing News for Strategic Communication," explores the opportunities for journalism students within the world of advertising and public relations. This chapter covers the following topics related to strategic communication: the process, the similarities to and differences from news writing, legal and ethical issues to be aware of, and the skills needed to succeed in careers within these fields.

Updates on Sexism, Racism and Other "Isms."   Chapter 7 reflects where we are in today's language, how our futures depend upon the un-learning and relearning of societal assumptions, and how students will need to update their language to fit the new standards of a changing world and media. We provide the latest guidance for our readers on matters of appropriate, sensitive and fair language in our increasingly connected world. The demands of writing with fairness and sensitivity evolve quickly, and writing for larger, more inclusive global audiences requires more sophistication and sensitivity than ever before.

Digital Resources

We want to call your attention to the digital resources that students can use to become better writers and editors. Macmillan's online ***LaunchPad Solo for Journalism*** is an easy-to-use platform that offers digital tools to help students understand the field of journalism and develop writing and editing skills. It contains high-quality multimedia content and ready-made assessment options, including our exercise book keyed to the chapters in *Working With Words* and *Exercise Central for AP Style*. Your book may have come with an access card to LaunchPad Solo at your instructor's request. If not, you can purchase access online at **launchpadworks.com**.

Inside LaunchPad Solo, you'll find:

- *Exercise Book for Working With Words*, **Tenth Edition.** Revised and updated, the exercise book gives students the opportunity to master the writing and editing skills covered in the main text, including grammar and mechanics guidelines, practicing proper copy-editing symbols, rewriting sentences for clarity and conciseness, learning how to write successful leads and recognizing the conventions of wire-service style. Students can download assignments in a PDF format directly from the LaunchPad platform.

- *Answer Key for Working With Words*, **Tenth Edition.** An online answer key, available only to instructors through LaunchPad, provides answers to all the questions in the exercise book.

- **Online Writing and Grammar Help With** *Exercise Central for AP Style*. *Exercise Central for AP Style* contains thousands of interactive grammar and style exercises addressing the most common errors journalism students make in abbreviations, capitalization, numbers, attribution and copy-editing symbols.

- **A Premium Video Collection for the Journalism Classroom.** LaunchPad Solo includes two dozen clips of media insiders like Amy Goodman, Clarence Page, Jim Spencer and David Herzog talking about the latest trends, from convergence to media entrepreneurship to real versus fake news sources, and more. In addition, several clips help students gain valuable insight into the interviewing process.

Acknowledgments

In closing, we again want to thank our families for their love and support. Thanks also to the many faculty, students, professionals and others who have used previous editions of this book. Thanks especially to students, faculty and media professionals who have sent us questions and suggestions for this new edition.

We are further grateful to the following reviewers who graciously offered comprehensive suggestions for this new edition: Donald Bowen, *University of Nebraska*; Scott Brown, *California State University*; Kevin Capie, *Bradley University*; Corey Cockerill, *Wilmington College*; Renee Collins, *Adrian College*; Dana Eversole, *Northeastern State University*; Gina Firenzi, *Santa Clara University*; Marti Harvey, *University of Texas*; Lisa Lenoir, *Stephens College*; Michael Longinow, *Biola University*; Lori McKinnon, *Oklahoma State University*; Derek Moscato, *Western Washington University*;

Raymond Murray, *Oklahoma State University*; and Nicolas Tatro, *University of North Florida, Stetson University.*

Thanks, too, to the staff at Bedford/St. Martin's, who have believed in this book and who have worked with us to make it what it is. We especially want to thank our editor this time, Melanie McFadyen, for her well-considered suggestions for making this, once again, the best edition so far.

Good writing takes good, hard thinking. This book lives because writers, students, educators and journalists send us questions about each edition or suggestions for the next. Please write us with yours. Here are our email addresses:

Brian S. Brooks   BrooksBS@missouri.edu

James L. Pinson   jpinson@emich.edu

Jean Gaddy Wilson   jeangaddywilson@positionthefuture.com

Brief Table of Contents

Preface   v
Useful Lists at a Glance   xxiii

PART ONE   **Writing for the Media**   1

1   Understanding Journalism and the News   3
2   The Basics of Writing for Journalism   17
3   Writing News That's Fit for Print   31
4   Writing News for Radio and Television   47
5   Writing News for Online and Mobile Media   65
6   Writing News for Strategic Communication   79
7   Sexism, Racism and Other "Isms"   88

PART TWO   **Grammar and Usage**   107

8   Choosing Your Words   109
9   Grammar Basics   118
10   Phrases, Clauses and Sentences   136
11   Subjects and Objects   146
12   Verbs   163
13   Making the Parts Agree   192
14   Modifiers and Connecting Words   203
15   Getting Words in the Right Order and Punctuation   215

PART THREE   **Reference Lists**   239

Bias-Related Terms   241
One Word, Two Words or Hyphenated?   255
Spelling   272
Tightening   287
Trademarks and Generics   323
Usage   328

Appendix: Associated Press Print and Web Style Summary   403
Online Resources   413
Index   419
Copy-Editing Marks   438
Overcome These 20 Common Errors   *inside back cover*

Brief Table of Contents

Preface   v

Useful Lists at a Glance   xxii

PART ONE   Writing for the Media   1

1   Understanding Journalism and the News   3
2   The Basics of Writing for Journalism   17
3   Writing News That's Fit to Print   31
4   Writing News for Radio and Television   47
5   Using News for Online and Mobile Media   63
6   Writing News for Strategic Communication   77
7   Slogan, Kicker and Other Uses   88

PART TWO   Grammar and Usage   107

8   Choosing Your Words   109
9   Grammar Basics   115
10   Phrases, Clauses and Sentences   127
11   Subjects and Objects   143
12   Verbs   155
13   Making the Parts Agree   182
14   Modifiers and Connecting Words   205
15   Getting Words in the Right Order and Punctuation   215

PART THREE   Reference Lists   239

Plain-English Style   241
The Right Word with the Right Emphasis   275
Spelling   293
Usages   297
Punctuation and Grammar   323
Usage   325

Appendix: Associated Press Print and Web Style Summary   403
Online Resources   417
Index   419
Correcting Work   438
Overcome These 20 Common Errors Inside Back Cover

Contents

Preface   v
Useful Lists at a Glance   xxiii

PART ONE   Writing for the Media   1

Chapter 1   *Understanding Journalism and the News*   3

What's News? What's Journalism? What's Opinion?   3
    Defining News   3
    Defining Journalism   5
    Defining Opinion   7
Confronting Perceptions of Media Bias   9
The Political Climate and "Fake News"   10
The State of the Media Industry   13
The Importance of Newspapers   14
Newspapers May Decline, but Journalism Thrives   15

Chapter 2   *The Basics of Writing for Journalism*   17

Journalistic Writing Versus Fiction Writing   17
Clarity   18
    A Clarity Checklist   19
    Write Short Sentences and Paragraphs, and Use Common Words   19
    Anticipate Readers' Questions   20
    Include Specifics   20
    Explain Numbers and Statistics   21

Correctness   23
  A Correctness Checklist   23
  Use Correct Grammar, Usage, Spelling and Style   23
  Write to Your Audience and Purpose   23
  Use the Right Story Formula   24
  Maintain Objectivity in Your Writing   24
  Rules of Objective Writing   25
  Modifiers to Be Avoided   28
  JOURNALISM TIP: Writing for Eighth-Grade-Level Readability   30

Chapter 3   Writing News That's Fit for Print   31

Pick the Best Angle   32
Types of News Leads   34
Hard-News Leads   34
  Who Was Involved?   35
  What Happened?   37
  When Did It Happen?   39
  JOURNALISM TIP: Words to Avoid in Attributing Information   39
  Where Did It Happen?   40
  Problems With Hard-News Leads   40
  What Comes After the Hard-News Lead?   42
Soft-News Leads   43
  Soft-News Clichés   43
  What Comes After the Soft-News Lead?   45
Using Paraphrases and Transitions to Build a Story   46

Chapter 4   Writing News for Radio and Television   47

Print and Online Versus Radio and Television News   48
  Use a Conversational Style   49
  Personalize the News   50
  Make It Easy to Understand   51
  Keep It Short   52
  Keep It Timely   52
  Make It Clear   53
Radio and Television Journalists Must Know Grammar   53
Radio and Television Journalists Must Know Pronunciation   54
Radio and Television Hard-News Leads   56
  Starting With the *Who*   57
  What Happened?   57
  Other Points to Remember   58

Radio and Television Story Structure   59
Radio and Television Style Summary   60
    Preparing Your Manuscript for Radio   60
    Preparing Your Manuscript for Television   61
    Editing and Other Symbols   61
    Pronunciation   61
    Abbreviations   62
    Numbers   62
    Punctuation   63
    Names   63
    Spelling   64

Chapter 5   Writing News for Online and Mobile Media   65

Online Media Are Unique   67
    Be Clear   68
    Be Correct (and Credible)   68
    Be Concise   69
Writing and Presenting News Online   70
    SEO: Writing With Search Engines in Mind   73
    Writing for International Audiences   73
    Writing for Blogs   73
    JOURNALISM TIP: Editing Your Own Copy   74
    Promoting News on Social Media   75
    Legal and Ethical Concerns   76
    Corrections   78

Chapter 6   Writing News for Strategic Communication   79

The Strategic Communication Process   81
    Setting Your Goal   81
    Choosing the Target Audience   82
    Designing the Message   82
    Determining Timing of the Project's Launch   83
    Evaluating the Impact of Your Campaign   83
How Public Relations Writing Differs From News Writing   84
    Essentials of a Good News Release   84
    Following Up With Media Contacts   85
Legal and Ethical Issues in Strategic Communication   85
Skills Needed by Strategic Communicators   86

Chapter 7   ***Sexism, Racism and Other "Isms"***   88

Why You Are Where You Are in Today's Language   88

What Does That Mean to You?   90

The Future Arrives on Little Feet   91

A Shifting "Center of Gravity"   93

Language Turns to the Future   94

Update With *Working With Words* Language Triangle   94

   1. New social change—to recognize current reality, look for the action   95

   2. New standards of language—the changing world and social media   97

   3. Resulting new video/content requirements   97

New Players in the New Millennium   98

A Brief History of "Isms" in the U.S.   99

Dealing With Current Reality   100

   Sexism   100

   Racism   101

   Ageism   102

   Other Stereotypes   103

   The Nonbias Rule   103

Seven Ways to Be Up to Date Instead of Out of Date   104

PART TWO   Grammar and Usage   107

Chapter 8   ***Choosing Your Words***   109

Know the Meaning of Words Often Confused   109

Choose Simpler and Clearer Wordings   113

   Use Fewer Words   114

   Use Simpler Words   116

   Use Exact Words   116

   Be Fresh, Not Stale   117

Chapter 9   ***Grammar Basics***   118

Solving Common Problems   118

   1. Use the right word.   119

   2. Make sure your words agree and go together.   119

   3. Make sure your words are in the right order.   120

   4. Use the right form of the word.   121

   5. Punctuate according to sentence grammar.   126

Understanding in More Depth   129

    Using Standard English   129

    Why Don't We Write How We Talk?   130

    Conventional Wisdom   131

    Competing Grammars and Stylebooks   131

    When Is an Error Not an Error?   132

    Grammar and Confidence   133

    Communicating Well   133

    Talking Shop   134

Chapter 10   Phrases, Clauses and Sentences   136

Solving Common Problems   137

    1. Beware of common sentence errors.   137

    2. Know the difference between restrictive versus nonrestrictive elements.   139

    JOURNALISM TIP: Punctuating Nonrestrictive Phrases and Clauses   140

Understanding in More Depth   141

    Phrases   141

    Clauses   142

    Sentences   143

    JOURNALISM TIP: Using Different Types of Sentences   145

Chapter 11   Subjects and Objects   146

Solving Common Problems   146

    1. Choose among *that* or *which,* or *who* or *whom.*   147

    2. Understand how to use pronouns ending in *self* or *selves.*   150

    3. Spell singulars, plurals and possessives correctly.   150

    4. Choose the right pronoun case.   152

    5. Capitalize *proper nouns* (nouns referring to actual names).   155

    6. Know when to capitalize names that are neither clearly proper names nor common nouns.   156

    7. Make nouns and pronouns possessive before a gerund.   156

Understanding in More Depth   157

    Kinds of Subjects   158

    Kinds of Objects   159

    Verbal Nouns: Gerunds and Infinitives   160

    More on Forming Singulars and Plurals of Nouns   160

    More on Forming Possessives of Nouns   161

Chapter 12   Verbs   163

Solving Common Problems   163

1. Know when there should or should not be an *s* at the end of a verb.   163
2. Don't confuse the verbs *can, may, shall* and *will* with *could, might, would* and *should*, or with each other.   164
3. Don't misuse helping verbs—the verbs added to a main verb.   164
4. Don't misuse irregular verbs—those that don't make their past forms by adding *ed.*   165
5. Normally, avoid passive voice.   166
6. Avoid using nouns as verbs that editors dislike.   169

Understanding in More Depth   170

What's the Difference Between a Verb and a Predicate?   170
What Are Helping Verbs and Main Verbs?   170
What Are Transitive Verbs and Intransitive Verbs?   171
Understanding Verb Tenses   173
Principal Parts of Common Irregular and Other Confusing Verbs   177
Sequence of Tenses   179
Keeping Verb Tenses Consistent   182
More on Active Voice Versus Passive Voice   183
What Is Verb Mood?   184
JOURNALISM TIP: Verb Moods   186
What Are Verbals?   190

Chapter 13   Making the Parts Agree   192

Solving Common Problems   192

1. Make sure each subject and its verb agree in number.   192
JOURNALISM TIP: Groups of People in the News   194
2. Make sure each pronoun agrees with its antecedent in number, gender and person.   197
3. Make sure each sentence's words, phrases and clauses have parallel structure.   199

Understanding in More Depth   199

More on Subject-Verb Agreement With Conjunctions   199
More on Subject-Verb Agreement With Uncountable Nouns   200
More on Subject-Verb Agreement With Other Confusing Nouns   200
More on Prepositional Phrases   200
More on Pronoun-Antecedent Agreement   201
More on Making Verbs Parallel   201

Chapter 14   *Modifiers and Connecting Words*   203

Solving Common Problems With Modifiers   203

    1. Use the correct forms of adjectives and adverbs.   204

    2. Don't confuse adjectives with adverbs.   206

    3. Know the difference between *coordinate adjectives* and *compound modifiers*.   207

    4. Know how to use articles correctly.   207

    5. Set off sentence adverbs with commas from the rest of the sentence.   208

    6. Don't use double negatives.   208

    7. Punctuate interjections correctly.   209

Solving Common Problems With Connecting Words   209

    1. Pay attention to how you use prepositions and whether the preposition is necessary.   209

    2. Make sure that you use the correct conjunction to connect equal or unequal parts of a sentence.   211

Understanding in More Depth   212

    More About Other Kinds of Modifiers   212

    More About Participles   213

    More About Interjections   213

    More About Correlative Conjunctions   213

Chapter 15   *Getting Words in the Right Order and Punctuation*   215

Getting Words in the Right Order   215

Solving Common Problems   215

    1. Place modifiers as close as possible to the word they modify.   215

    2. Adverbs require extra attention to placement in verb phrases because different orders are preferable here depending on the meaning.   217

Understanding in More Depth   218

    Understanding Preposition Placement   218

    Understanding Split Infinitives   218

Punctuating for Clarity   219

Solving Common Problems With Commas   220

    1. Know when always to use a comma.   220

    2. Know when never to use a comma.   223

    3. Know when you might want to use a comma.   224

Solving Common Problems With Quotations   225

    1. Know what and how to quote.   225

    2. Know how to attribute quotations and paraphrases.   227

3. Know how to carry quotations across paragraphs.   229

4. Know how to handle these special issues with quotes.   230

Solving Common Problems With Punctuating Pairs of Modifiers   231

1. Use the correct *conjunction* to connect equal or unequal parts of a sentence—a coordinating one for equal parts, a subordinating one for unequal parts—and punctuate them correctly.   231

2. Set off conjunctive adverbs by placing a comma after them.   231

3. Know the difference between punctuating *coordinate adjectives* and *compound modifiers*.   232

Understanding Punctuation in More Depth   234

Semicolons   234

Colons   234

Dashes   235

Parentheses   236

Hyphens   236

Apostrophes   237

Slashes   237

Periods, Exclamation Points and Question Marks   237

PART THREE   Reference Lists   239

Bias-Related Terms   241

One Word, Two Words or Hyphenated?   255

Spelling   272

Spelling Rules   272

JOURNALISM TIP: Spelling and Your Career   274

Hyphenation as a Spelling Problem   276

Words Often Misspelled   280

Tightening   287

What to Tighten, A–Z   287

Trademarks and Generics 323

Former Trademarks Now Also Considered Generic 326
Not Trademarks 327
Trademarks That Pose Other Spelling Issues 327

Usage 328

Usage Differences 328
Misused and Confused Words and Phrases 329

Appendix   *Associated Press Print and Web Style Summary* 403

Abbreviations and Acronyms 404
Punctuation 404
Symbols 404
Dates 404
People and Titles 405
Organizations 405
Places 406
Miscellaneous 407

Capitalization 407
Proper Nouns 407
Geographic Regions 407
Government and College Terms 408
Religious Terms 409
Titles 410
Miscellaneous 410

Numbers 411
Cardinal Numbers 411
Numerals With Suffixes 412
Numbers as Words 412
Other Rules for Numbers 412

Online Resources 413
Index 419
Copy-Editing Marks 438
Overcome These 20 Common Errors   *inside back cover*

Useful Lists at a Glance

Here's a guide to the most commonly referenced lists in the text.

Clarity checklist   19

Modifiers to be avoided   28

Preparing your manuscript for radio   60

Preparing your manuscript for television   61

Writing and presenting news online   70

Nouns to avoid using as verbs   169

Common helping verbs   171

Linking verbs   172

Simple tenses   173

Perfect tenses   174

Principal parts of common irregular verbs   177

Correlative conjunctions   214

Common conjunctive adverbs   232

Vocabulary for nonbiased writing   241

Prefixes generally not hyphenated   277

Prefixes commonly hyphenated   278

Words often misspelled   280

Tightening, A–Z   287

Brand names and their generic equivalents   323

Misused and confused words and phrases   329

Working With Words

A Handbook for Media Writers and Editors

Chapter 1   Understanding Journalism and the News   3

What's News? What's Journalism? What's Opinion?   3
Confronting Perceptions of Media Bias   9
The Political Climate and "Fake News"   10
REFERENCE LIST: Fake News Checklist   12
The State of the Media Industry   13
The Importance of Newspapers   14
Newspapers May Decline, but Journalism Thrives   15

Chapter 2   The Basics of Writing for Journalism   17

Journalistic Writing Versus Fiction Writing   17
Clarity   18
REFERENCE LIST: A Clarity Checklist   19
Correctness   23
REFERENCE LIST: A Correctness Checklist   23
REFERENCE LIST: Modifiers to Be Avoided   28
JOURNALISM TIP: Writing for Eighth-Grade-Level Readability   30

Chapter 3   Writing News That's Fit for Print   31

Pick the Best Angle   32
Types of News Leads   34
Hard-News Leads   34
JOURNALISM TIP: Words to Avoid in Attributing Information   39
Soft-News Leads   43
Using Paraphrases and Transitions to Build a Story   46

Chapter 4   Writing News for Radio and Television   47

Print and Online Versus Radio and Television News   48
Radio and Television Journalists Must Know Grammar   53
Radio and Television Journalists Must Know Pronunciation   54
REFERENCE LIST: Commonly Mispronounced Words   54
Radio and Television Hard-News Leads   56

Continued ▶

Radio and Television Story Structure   59
Radio and Television Style Summary   60
REFERENCE LIST: Preparing Your Manuscript for Radio   60
REFERENCE LIST: Preparing Your Manuscript for Television   61

Chapter 5   Writing News for Online and Mobile Media   65
Online Media Are Unique   67
Writing and Presenting News Online   70
JOURNALISM TIP: Editing Your Own Copy   74

Chapter 6   Writing News for Strategic Communication   79
The Strategic Communication Process   81
How Public Relations Writing Differs From News Writing   84
REFERENCE LIST: Essentials of a Good News Release   84
Legal and Ethical Issues in Strategic Communication   85
Skills Needed by Strategic Communicators   86
REFERENCE LIST: Common jobs in the field   87

Chapter 7   Sexism, Racism, and Other "Isms"   88
Why You Are Where You Are in Today's Language   88
What Does That Mean to You?   90
The Future Arrives on Little Feet   91
A Shifting "Center of Gravity"   93
Language Turns to the Future   94
Update With *Working With Words* Language Triangle   94
New Players in the New Millennium   98
A Brief History of "Isms" in the U.S.   99
Dealing With Current Reality   100
Seven Ways to Be Up to Date Instead of Out of Date   104

CHAPTER 1

Understanding Journalism and the News

What's News? What's Journalism? What's Opinion?

If you're reading this book, it's likely you're either intent on becoming a journalist, exploring the idea of becoming one or already are one. If you already are one, we suspect you understand much of what's in this chapter. But for prospective journalists, the purpose of this chapter is to help you understand what news is—and isn't—and how to produce it. To do that, you need to understand what journalism is, and what it isn't.

Journalism provided by trained journalists is at the heart of our democracy, which is why our Founding Fathers provided for "freedom of the press." So, journalism is all about producing accurate, informed news so citizens can be informed voters. The core product of journalism is news that informs by telling the truth, or, as some would define it, news that is based on "the best obtainable version of the truth." The practice of journalism isn't about producing "fake news," which is a form of fiction. Thus, anything that is fake news is not journalism, and those who produce it are not journalists. Sandwiched somewhere between those two extremes is opinion. So, let's try to explain the difference in those things.

Defining News

To reduce it to its simplest form, news is what's happening today or what has just been revealed to have happened in the past. In the textbook *News Reporting and Writing*, the Missouri Group, professors at the Missouri School of Journalism, list three standards that journalists use to evaluate whether something is news:

- **Relevance.**
- **Usefulness.**
- **Interest.**

Thus, news is information that is relevant to a group of readers, listeners or viewers. The importance of each piece of news is determined by how many people find it relevant, useful and interesting. This also determines whether a story is considered important by journalists, which determines whether it is printed, broadcast or placed online.

Others who attempt to define news have offered additional criteria for determining what's newsworthy and what's not. Here's a typical list:

- **Impact.** How many people are affected by what's happening? Things that affect many people often are more newsworthy than things that affect only a few. The number of people affected can be further broken down into the number of people this happened to, the number of people in your audience likely to care about it and the depth of emotions it is likely to evoke in your audience.

- **Conflict.** Are peoples and nations at loggerheads, or are people battling evil or natural forces (war, hurricanes, tornadoes, volcano eruptions, earthquakes, explosions and other disasters)? Such news almost always interests the public, even if it occurs in faraway places.

- **Novelty.** Is this unusual? Is it a first? Is it the largest? Is it the best? Is it the last? But be careful. Make sure it is indeed the first, largest, best or last.

- **Prominence.** Are famous people involved? Many people are fascinated by the acts of the rich, famous and powerful.

- **Proximity.** Did it happen close to our location? A local story in Keokuk, Iowa, is much more important in Iowa than in Louisiana.

- **Timeliness.** Did it just happen or is it old news? But remember that old news can still be important if it is recently discovered.

It's fair to say that determining what's news is an art, not a science. In the end, determining what's news is one of the many roles of the editor. Usually, it's obvious that something is newsworthy. At other times, it comes down to the editor's gut feeling about whether the public will be interested. Through it all, it's important to help news consumers get as much as possible from your work. Consider these helpful means of doing that:

- **Allow Readers, Viewers and Listeners to Engage.** Do you expect your audience to passively read, watch or listen to your story without reacting? Many *will* want to react, so make it easy for them by allowing two-way communication between the journalist and consumer. There are several ways to do that, and here are a few: Include your email or telephone number at the end of a news story, post a call-in number during your newscast or allow comments on a website. Doing one or more of those helps build loyalty to your news medium.

- **Offer Possible Solutions.** Whenever possible, journalists should interview experts who have solutions to the problems the news uncovers.

Constantly bombarding the public with news of problems and offering no solutions merely serves to annoy the audience. However, find *experts* who can offer proposed solutions, don't offer them up yourself. That's not your role.

Defining Journalism

Simply defined, journalism is the art of producing news that keeps the public informed of current events in a local area, a state, a region, the nation or throughout the world. Performing that service is so important to a democratic society that our Founding Fathers enshrined it in the First Amendment to the U.S. Constitution:

> Congress shall make no law respecting an establishment of religion, or prohibiting the free exercise thereof; or abridging the freedom of speech, *or of the press* [emphasis added]; or the right of the people peaceably to assemble, and to petition the Government for a redress of grievances.

The founders' thinking is clear: To function properly, a democracy must have a well-informed populace that will make good decisions in the voting booth. The people must have access to news, the right to free speech and public assembly and the right to petition government for redress of grievances. And, since newspapers were the primary means of conveying news in that era, the Founding Fathers protected "freedom . . . of the press." The press was privately owned even then, so in writing that clause our forefathers took the unusual step of protecting a private industry from government interference. Their willingness to do so showed just how strongly they felt about the issue.

Today, journalism is about far more than news that appears in newspapers. It includes news that appears in magazines, on radio, on television and on the internet. And, it's important to note that all those media produce far more than just news. They also contain commercial information, including advertising; play a major role in the entertainment industry; and serve as platforms for social media. So, it's important to remember that comics and horoscopes in newspapers; soap operas, drama and comedy on television; and most of what's distributed on social media are *not* journalism. They are entertainment, although they sometimes are *disguised* as news, as we shall learn later.

In their seminal book *The Elements of Journalism*, first published in 2001, veteran journalists Bill Kovach and Tom Rosenstiel explain that "the purpose of journalism is to provide people with the information they need to be free and self-governing." They list 10 principles of journalism that distinguish it from other forms of writing:

- Journalism's first obligation is to the truth.
- Its first loyalty is to citizens.

- Its essence is a discipline of verification.
- Its practitioners must maintain independence from those they cover.
- Journalism must serve as an independent monitor of power.
- It must provide a forum for public criticism and compromise.
- It must strive to make the significant interesting and relevant.
- It must keep the news comprehensive and proportional.
- Its practitioners must be allowed to exercise their personal conscience (but without inserting opinions).
- Citizens, too, have rights and responsibilities when it comes to the news. (Most notably, they owe it to themselves to balance where they get their news, not just find news organizations that share their biases.)

Note the first principle they list: Journalism's first obligation is to the truth. No journalist should ever forget that. No journalist who violates that principle should be entitled to continue calling himself or herself a journalist.

By keeping those principles in mind as they work, journalists are less likely to distort the news or to provide biased work. And notice how those principles conform nicely to the intent of the authors of the First Amendment. Those principles seek to ensure that the news media indeed perform the role our founders intended.

So far, we've described fact-based journalism or **hard news**, which we'd define as fact-based, straightforward reporting of an event. But journalism doesn't stop there. There's also **explanatory journalism**, which often follows an important hard-news story. Following a summit between U.S. President Donald J. Trump and North Korean dictator Kim Jong-un, major media outlets carried factual stories about what occurred during their meeting in Singapore. The next day, many carried stories with headlines like this: "Here's what the historic Trump–Kim summit means for world peace." That's explanatory journalism. Typically, such a story would include quotes from experts who study nuclear disarmament, Asia and North Korea. The story likely would include opinions of those interviewed, but not opinions of the journalist who wrote it. Sometimes this is also called **analytical journalism**.

Then there are stories journalists refer to as **soft news** or **features**. These often are stories focused on people who are famous, interesting or have been recently pushed into the limelight. Here, reporters are given license to describe. If, for example, the subject is interviewed in an office, the reporter might note in the story that the subject keeps numerous photos of her children behind her desk and a basketball commemorating the championship she won with her college teammates. Such description, while innocuous in some ways, adds to the reader's or viewer's understanding of the persona of the interviewee. Reporters also are given license to describe the scenes of accidents, fires and disasters and in other stories where they actually witness an event.

Journalists consider all these legitimate ways of reporting the news. Things become more complicated when the line between fact and opinion is crossed.

Defining Opinion

Earlier, we mentioned that opinion falls in a gray area between truth-based factual journalism and what's lately become known as fake news. Let's look at three definitions of **opinion** that can be found in dictionaries:

- *A view, appraisal or judgment formed in the mind about a particular matter.* That's vague enough to allow two individuals looking at identical facts to draw entirely opposite conclusions because it is not entirely—or sometimes even partially—based on fact. This is the kind of opinion we see most often when political opponents argue their respective positions on an issue.

- *A belief stronger than impression and less strong than positive knowledge.* This is problematic because it is based on impression and a few random facts—not on positive knowledge. This is the kind of opinion a scientist has when launching an experiment to prove or disprove a hypothesis. The scientist hopes to turn opinion into fact—or, alternatively, to disprove it.

- *A formal expression of judgment or advice by an expert.* This is more believable because of the expert status of the person from whom it comes. A doctor, for example, uses various kinds of tests and analyzes symptoms to form an opinion, or diagnosis, of what's wrong with a patient. It's opinion, but it's informed, expert opinion.

Because we often don't know whether an opinion is based on impression, fact or some combination of the two, we'd argue that *all* opinion presented in the news media should be labeled as **opinion** or **commentary** and should be segregated from the news as much as possible. This was always the goal of magazines and newspapers during the 20th century. More recently, we find more and more examples of reporters' and columnists' opinions creeping into articles that pass as hard news.

How does that happen? Sometimes it's intentional and even encouraged by management, especially when it's thought the opinion expressed will appeal to the target audience. At other times it's a case of bias slipping into a story, and that can be either intentional or unintentional. And sometimes even the writing technique employed by the author can lead to problems. A popular form of writing in newspapers and magazines these days is **narrative writing**. In it, a writer employs the descriptive and observational techniques of a novelist. Doing so occasionally transforms writing from mere description into outright bias on the part of the writer. We don't mean to suggest that narrative writing is bad. In fact, it makes articles much more readable. But writers need to take care that their opinions don't creep into the news columns. Whatever the cause or source, bias has no place in news stories.

Here are various forms of opinion ranging from some that are legitimate to fake news, which is not news at all:

Reviews.   U.S. law provides much leeway for the media to review and critique public performances of music, plays, books, restaurants, sports events and similar items offered to the public. This is considered valid criticism of creative content, sports or food, and no matter how negative the review or account, the reporter and media outlet are not subject to most lawsuits. This is known under the law as **fair comment and criticism**. Such material should make clear that it is a review of a public offering.

Editorials.   These should appear on a newspaper or magazine editorial page, not in the news columns. Most often, these are the opinions of publishers or broadcast station managers. Any worthwhile editorial should have facts to support the stated opinion. Opinion alone is not convincing, and the purpose of an editorial is to sway public opinion. Absent facts, it is unlikely to do so. In the case of broadcast editorials, they should be clearly defined to distinguish them from the station's news. Online editorials should be clearly labeled and should state whether the editorial represents the view of the news outlet's management or a single person. If a single person, he or she should be identified.

Commentary.   This usually is the opinion of a print columnist or a broadcast news executive. To be credible, it should be supported by factual information. Again, it should be clearly distinguished from news.

Satire.   In various publications, we've seen satire posing as news. *The Onion* is a hilarious example, but sometimes when people repost stories from it on social media, they consider it serious and factual. And on television, particularly cable television, "news satire" often masquerades as the real thing. But even when it's clear that a show like "The Daily Show" is comedy, polls of young people find they get much if not most of what they think is "news" from late-night comedy programs. Any attempt to provide satire should be clearly labeled as such even when you think it's obvious. And in publications, broadcasts and online media, it should be separated from real news.

Fake news.   You'll find more on this later in this chapter, but for now let's just say this: Fake news is fake. It is slanted, misleading or untruthful and has no place in the news media. It misleads the public rather than informs and has no place in legitimate news organizations. The problem, of course, lies in determining what's true and what isn't. It's also not synonymous with news reporting you disagree with. Labeling something "fake news" for this reason is harmful against not just that story but public perception of journalism as a whole.

We'd weigh in on these items this way: Reviews, editorials and commentary are expected content in respected publications or websites and on good broadcast stations. Journalists may produce such material but should clearly label them for what they are. Satire also can be acceptable if clearly labeled as such. Fake news is *never* appropriate.

Confronting Perceptions of Media Bias

Why are we so insistent on labeling any form of opinion in the mainstream press? And why are we insistent on preventing fake news from entering our columns or polluting our airwaves? The answer is simple: In recent years, trust in the media has declined noticeably in public opinion surveys. Bias and fake news further deteriorate that credibility. As recently as the mid-1970s, about 73 percent of the public expressed a positive level of confidence in the news media. But, according to a late 2017 survey by the Poynter Institute, only 12 percent of the public now has a "great deal" of confidence in the news media, and 37 percent has a "fair amount" of confidence. About 13 percent has "no confidence at all" and 39 percent has "not very much" confidence. That's about evenly divided.

The perception of media bias exists in part because American journalism has built-in biases that are unavoidable. War usually makes for better news than peace. Crime usually makes for better news than a family reunion. Journalists are attracted to anything "new" or "different." Celebrities always get more coverage than the anonymous masses.

It's also true that journalists see it as their duty to afflict the comfortable and serve as comforters of the afflicted. Thus, they regularly reveal warts on our society that many citizens would be more comfortable avoiding.

Journalists also see themselves as the ultimate skeptics — unwilling to accept what they're told at face value. Instead, they're inclined to seek out the other side of the story and in doing so they dig more deeply into a subject. One side or the other inevitably doesn't like that.

It's also true that much of the perception of bias in the press has to do with the increased polarization of U.S. politics. About 74 percent of Democrats, including those who lean Democratic, express a "great deal" or a "fair amount" of confidence in the news media. Only 19 percent of Republicans or those who lean Republican do so. Thus, we have a widening partisan gap in perceptions of media over time.

The perception of Republicans who believe the press distorts the news in favor of the left is at least partially true. Are journalists intentionally biased? There is no doubt that most journalists lean to the left politically, which makes their views far different from those of Republicans. Why are journalists left-leaning? Some studies show that young people are attracted to journalism in hopes of making the U.S. a better place. Many support universal health care, affordable education, and the social safety net represented by Social Security, Medicare, Medicaid and the food-stamp program. They see value in the diversity, and often the skills, that immigrants bring to our country. All those are sentiments with which most Democrats would agree, so it's natural that those who feel that way lean to the left.

The question, then, is whether journalists are capable of reporting as objectively as possible without revealing their biases. Whether they can do that is often questionable, so in some cases Republicans may well have a legitimate beef. Democrats often have the same complaint about things printed or broadcast in more conservative outlets. Is it intentional bias? Most often, the answer is no. Is it subtle, unintentional bias? Too often, the answer is yes, and that bias shows not only in the stories that journalists cover but also in the things they choose not to cover.

This left-leaning bias in the media is nothing new—it has existed for years—but the problem is compounded by the increased movement of Democrats to the left and Republicans to the right. The days when President Lyndon Johnson, a Democrat, would sit down with the Republican Minority Leader of the Senate, Everett Dirksen, for a beer every Friday afternoon are long gone. Today, the two major political parties are farther apart ideologically than ever, and much of the civility that existed in past years has disappeared in favor of political ads and daily discourse that vilify each other and portray the very worst.

Journalists continue to fight the perception of bias with attempts to report "objectively" and with "fairness." In *The Elements of Journalism*, Kovach and Rosenstiel reject the traditional concept of journalistic objectivity. The form of it practiced by journalists throughout most of the 20th century, they write, was seriously flawed: Every effort was made to balance an expert opinion—or a political argument—with an opposing view to achieve "fairness and balance." A much better form of objectivity, Kovach and Rosenstiel argue, is to duplicate the scientific method: Create a hypothesis, then use a variety of techniques to pursue truth and verify facts. The goal should be to find truth, not simply pass along two sides of a dispute, particularly when provable evidence decidedly supports one side or the other. The goal, then, should be to prove or disprove a hypothesis, just as scientists try to do. Why provide "balance," Kovach and Rosenstiel argue, when the best obtainable version of the truth leads us to believe that one version or the other is true?

Undoubtedly, that's a great way for journalists to approach the news. However, there's a potential trap here. Most people, journalists included, confuse the "truth" with what they already believe and therefore rationalize their own prejudices as telling the truth. The best way to prevent that is to follow the exact process that scientists follow—state your opinion as a hypothesis, then try honestly to *disprove* it. Next, view all the evidence on both sides fairly, unwedded to your initial bias, and make a conclusion as a juror does, disregarding any previous ideas you may have had. The truth must be seen as not what you initially thought, but what you honestly, impartially decided after a skeptical but open-minded process.

The Political Climate and "Fake News"

President Trump and other elected and appointed government officials like to rip *The New York Times* and *The Washington Post* as biased, fake news outlets, but most media experts consider those newspapers to be among the best in the world with outstanding reporting staffs.

Do those two papers lean to the left? On their editorial pages, they absolutely do. But along with *The Wall Street Journal*, whose editorial page is slanted hard to the right, the news columns of all three are mostly objective and do a terrific job of chronicling the news of the day. Do their news columns occasionally tilt to the left in the case of the *Times* and *Post* or to the right in the case of the *Journal?* A lot of media critics insist they do. There are charts out there that attempt to rank the political bias of media outlets from left to right and accuracy from top to bottom. The *Times* and *Post* often are shown as left of center and the *Journal* right of center, but all three rank high in accuracy.

The Associated Press and the three major broadcast television networks — ABC, CBS and NBC — produce fact-based news that serves the public well. Public broadcasting, both PBS and NPR, also produces news of high quality and does so with much better objectivity than some would have you believe.

Cable television news is more problematic. MSNBC tilts heavily leftward and *Fox News* tilts heavily to the right. CNN falls more toward the middle with, in many cases, a decided left-leaning bias. CNN does, however, regularly feature conservative guests who provide some balance to the network's news. And some Fox commentators, Shepard Smith for one, often criticize their own network on air when they believe Fox has strayed too far from objectivity.

At the bottom of the heap in credibility are so-called news websites, which often don't provide news at all but rather distorted views supporting one political party or the other. From *Liberal Society* on the left to *Conservative 101* on the right, you can count on these and similar sites to produce distorted — and sometimes wildly distorted — views of the news. According to *Buzzfeed*, it turns out that both of those sites are owned by the same Florida company and exist to produce website clicks, not serious news.

In the end, *Fox News* and *Breitbart* ranked as the most biased news sources among major media outlets in a 2018 survey done by the Knight Foundation and Gallup. Far-left and far-right websites were not included in the survey. The problem with polls, of course, is that they don't do an objective job of evaluating bias. A more objective look at media bias would have to involve a look at how much various news outlets' coverage was weighted in positive versus negative stories on politically divisive issues. Relatively few such studies have been done, and those tend to be outdated and therefore of marginal value.

So, what is fake news and where can you find it? You'll find most of that on the far-right and far-left websites. Can't find them? Try *Facebook*, which is used to drive traffic to them. Indeed, *Facebook* and *Twitter* have faced a torrent of criticism for not doing enough to combat fake news. And it should be noted that some legitimate conservative news websites complain that *Facebook* has greatly reduced their hits by changing algorithms and using more liberal sources as arbiters.

Here are some tips, adapted from an article in *FactCheck.org*, to help you decide whether a news item is fake news:

1. **Consider the source**. Some sites admit quite plainly that they're all about spreading fake news. A website called *WTOE 5 News* masquerades as a television station site but its "about" page says it's a "fantasy news website." *WhatDoesItMean.com* carried a story about former President Obama and his wife purchasing a vacation home in Dubai. That site describes itself as "One of the Top-Ranked websites in the World for New World Order, Conspiracy Theories and Alternative News." Amazingly, many people post such stories to *Facebook* as fact. They apparently want to believe them to be true.

2. **Read beyond the headline**. *FactCheck.org* debunked a claim in a story headlined "Obama Signs Executive Order Banning the Pledge of Allegiance in Schools Nationwide." If those who passed along this bit of fake news had read more of the story, they might have suspected something was amiss when it quoted "Fappy the Anti-Masturbation Dolphin."

3. **Check the author**. The Pledge of Allegiance story appeared on *abcnews.com.co*, which is not the website of ABC as it might appear to be. The author of the story was listed as Jimmy Rustling, whose author page identified him as the winner of 14 Peabody Awards and a handful of Pulitzer Prizes. No one by that name has ever won either of those awards.

4. **What's the support?** The story about banning the Pledge of Allegiance cited the actual number of the executive order. When *FactCheck.org* checked it out, it had nothing at all to do with the Pledge of Allegiance.

5. **Check the date**. Some fake stories aren't necessarily false but instead are distortions of event timing. One site took a 2015 CNN story and slapped a new headline and date on it, proclaiming "Ford Shifts Truck Production from Mexico to Ohio." It credited President Trump with forcing the shift, but the event occurred long before Trump became president.

6. **Is this some kind of joke?** Andy Borowitz has written a satirical column for *The New Yorker* since 2001, but *FactCheck.org* often gets inquiries about whether his column is factual. It's satire.

7. **Check your biases**. People place more stock in things that match their own views. That is, after all, why many people look only at websites or cable television networks that confirm their biases. Readers and viewers would do well to broaden their sources of news and include some of the less-biased, mainstream media outlets.

8. **Consult the experts**. Several sites specialize in letting you know whether news is factual. These include *FactCheck.org*, *snopes.com*, the *Washington Post* Fact Checker and *PolitiFact.com*.

Some of the examples of fake news listed here are not necessarily nefarious, but they become problematic if readers and viewers are unable to identify them as false. Fake news masquerading as real news is the most serious threat.

The problematic environment in which the media operate today make it difficult to find a solution to the problem of perceived bias. When presidents assail the mainstream media as purveyors of fake news, as President Trump has done repeatedly, his supporters increasingly lose faith in the media. And, while President Barack Obama, Trump's predecessor, was not as openly critical of the media, neither was he media-friendly. Obama held far fewer press conferences than most of his predecessors, leading to a lack of transparency and accountability.

While President Trump is likely the most famous person ever to toss around the term "fake news," he certainly didn't invent it. Indeed, one can make a solid case that liberals used it first to describe conservative news outlets like *Fox News*. Regardless of who's using it, this term should not be used to discredit news that you don't agree with just because it represents a different viewpoint. Accurate use of the term comes down to objectivity — the process of checking it out with skeptical open-mindedness.

That seldom occurs in cable television roundtables that far too often result in shouting matches between Democrats and Republicans. Those are not an attempt to arrive at the truth. More often, they are designed to stir up arguments, create fodder for viral videos and drive up drama and ratings.

All this means that today's environment is a difficult one in which the media operate. If your goal is to become a journalist, expect to encounter a skeptical public that has minimal understanding of what you do.

The State of the Media Industry

Newer services are challenging and disrupting numerous older industries. Consider, for example, what Uber and Lyft have done to the taxi business in more than 600 cities in the U.S. and around the world, or how Airbnb has become a series competitor to hotels by offering cheaper accommodations in private homes. No-frills airlines like Southwest and Spirit have also drastically undercut prices of traditional carriers American and Delta on many routes, forcing the latter group to cut prices to compete.

In all those cases, technology played a role. Finding a ride from Uber or Lyft is made possible by smartphones, which are able to quickly find the nearest available driver by using the internet's location services. Without the internet, it would be much harder to locate a room in a private home for rent or the lowest airfare from one city to another.

The news industry is not immune to the internet's disruptive nature, and newspapers, in particular, have arguably been affected more adversely than even taxis, hotels and airlines. Although taxis won't disappear anytime soon, most hotels aren't likely to fail and traditional air carriers continue to make large profits, newspapers are disappearing at an alarming rate. Most afternoon papers have closed, and total daily newspaper circulation is at its lowest level since the 1940s. Newsroom employment at newspapers has plummeted from more than 70,000 to about 40,000 in the last 10 years, and it continues to decline. The salaries of those newsroom employees have remained relatively flat over the last five years thanks to stress caused not only by declining circulation but also a resulting sharp decline in print advertising.

Magazines are similarly threatened. While magazines are extremely attractive because of high-quality white paper and brilliant color, they are expensive to produce and distribute. Many are threatened by online competitors that don't share those high costs. Television, too, is threatened. The proliferation of cable television channels has reduced the audiences of traditional news programs on ABC, CBS and NBC, and the news programs of their local affiliates. When television audiences shrink, so does revenue.

In the end, though, there are some undeniable facts that are reshaping the news industry. People, particularly younger people, now prefer to get their news on computers, tablets or smartphones. Most young people simply don't read newspapers. Nor do they watch television news. Older generations do, but, as they die, younger readers and viewers simply aren't replacing them. As a result, the news industry is being forced to rethink almost everything about the way it does business. It is, to say the least, a challenging environment.

The Importance of Newspapers

Historically, newspapers have been the best source of news. One recent study estimated that 85 percent of all news consumed in the U.S. originated at newspapers. That's right: Much of what you read online or see on television we'd probably never know about if newspapers hadn't reported it first. Why? Because newspapers almost without exception have the largest and best news-gathering staffs in every U.S. city. Make no mistake about it — television stations often scan the morning newspaper to find out what they should cover that day. That leads us to ask this question: If newspapers die, who will report the news?

If a plane crashes or a building burns, television news is all over it. So we wouldn't lose that if newspapers disappeared. But what about coverage of city and county government? What about the local courts? State government? Scientific advancements and medical news? For the most part, television doesn't report news about those things except in the most highly visible cases. Why? Because that news isn't visual, and television thrives on accidents, fires, disasters and other news items that have visual appeal. Without visuals, most television news items are brief and shallow.

So, the decline of newspapers is worrisome not only for newspaper journalists but also for all of us. We depend on newspapers to report the news that may not be visual but is extremely important to our lives and the functioning of democracy. An informed public makes better decisions at the voting booth and understands the issues facing the community.

Lots of folks in the media industry are trying to find solutions to that problem — just in case newspapers continue to decline in importance and fail to find an economic model that will support first-class news-gathering. In some cities, foundations are funding investigative reporting and news-gathering in an effort to replace the declining number of investigative reporters at newspapers. In other cities, entertainment-oriented websites like the *Charlotte* (North Carolina) *Agenda* seek to make enough money to eventually do a better job of covering the news. Stunningly, New Jersey even passed a bill devoting $5 million to the Civic Information Consortium, a nonprofit with a mission of reviving local journalism in the state. It's particularly targeted to projects in underserved communities, low-income communities and communities with people of color. Indeed, all sorts of schemes are being tried to protect the reporting of important news. It remains to be seen how many of these experiments will be successful.

Historically, the best journalism in the U.S. has been practiced at newspapers and news magazines. Print was king for two centuries, and its legacy is that it created the best and most credible news products. As the newspaper industry and news magazines continue to decline, it's fair to ask: Who will do the high-quality reporting?

Newspapers May Decline, but Journalism Thrives

Too many people in the U.S. confuse the decline of newspapers with the decline of journalism in general. While the number of news jobs at newspapers has been cut dramatically during the past decade, job growth at other media outlets has exploded and more than offset those losses. There are literally thousands of news-related jobs at websites like *Politico* and *HuffPost* that simply did not exist 20 years ago. Cable television and the ability of the web to provide news stories with video content have multiplied the market for audio- and video-trained journalists many times over.

Most of the large journalism schools have seen no decrease in the percentage of students getting jobs after graduation. And, most recently, there has been a resurgence of interest in high school students wanting to pursue journalism careers. Some of that has been sparked by President Trump's attacks on the media, much as a similar surge was prompted by President Nixon's criticism of the press during the Watergate investigations of the 1970s.

What has changed is a need for all journalism students to be well-educated in the use of multimedia. No longer is it acceptable to see yourself as a newspaper reporter who writes for print only. Most newspaper websites now carry video, produced almost entirely by reporters who once only wrote. So, while the future of newspapers may be clouded, the future of journalism is not. Now, more than ever, the nation needs journalists — multimedia journalists.

Meanwhile, don't get the idea that newspapers are giving up. They indisputably produce a manufactured product more appropriate for the pre-internet age, but they also are trying to make technology work in their favor. Some are having success. Digital circulation is booming at major newspapers like *The New York Times*, *The Wall Street Journal* and *The Washington Post*. Those publications saw digital circulation rise 10 percent in just one year from 2016 to 2017. Digital advertising revenue also increased from 17 percent of total revenue in 2011 to 31 percent in 2017.

So, newspapers are at last creating strategies to help them survive. And one fact is lost on many observers: There are still about 1,300 daily newspapers in the U.S., and they employ thousands of journalists. It's also true that most weekly newspapers are doing just fine. In many cases, they are the only real source of local news in small towns and rural areas.

CHAPTER 2

The Basics of Writing for Journalism

In this chapter, we'll introduce you to the basic tenets of journalistic writing. In subsequent chapters, we'll study the use and misuse of language and widely used formulas that help journalists write well on deadline for various media. We'll look at getting it right, legally and ethically. And we'll look at getting the smaller details right, including tightening your writing, the basics of usage and grammar, and spelling and punctuation. Just as carpenters must learn to use saws, hammers and nails, journalists must learn these things. They are the tools of our trade.

Journalistic Writing Versus Fiction Writing

Today's journalism makes liberal use of advanced writing techniques more often associated with novels. Never more than today have journalists enjoyed such immense freedom to strut their stuff — to chronicle the news of the day with compelling prose filled with metaphors, similes and good old-fashioned storytelling. Journalists today often refer to that simply as **narrative writing**, but it's writing that borrows heavily from the repertoire of the novelist.

Make no mistake, however: Fundamental differences remain between writing news stories and writing novels, just as differences exist between all kinds of writing. The purpose of journalism is to convey information clearly, correctly and concisely. Literary license to invent fictitious scenarios is forbidden in journalism. As one form of nonfiction writing, journalism has much in common with technical writing—writing reports, manuals and instructions—especially in straightforward news stories aimed at conveying information.

Some journalism, of course, such as features, columns, blogs and reviews, has much in common with creative writing, such as novels, short stories, plays and poems. But for those with literary aspirations, here are some differences between journalistic writing and creative writing:

- **Clear, simple writing.** Straight-news reporting stresses the clear, correct and concise statement of facts, rather than an expression of imagination or vision. Creative writers take license with language for literary effect, and ambiguity is often praised. True, literary critics value writing that is *ambiguous* (which means it has multiple meanings) but usually not writing that is *obscure* (which means readers have no idea what it means). People reading the news, however, want neither obscurity to confuse them nor multiple meanings to puzzle them. Instead, they want the facts, clearly and quickly. Of course, when people read features, columns and reviews, whether in print or online, they also expect to be entertained.

- **Quick, efficient writing.** Hard-news journalism, which we see in objective news accounts, is more formulaic than creative writing is. Other than feature writers, reviewers, columnists and bloggers, journalists place less stress on originality of style and more on knowing story formulas that help them write quickly while covering a subject logically and thoroughly. As we'll see later, however, journalists often use formulas even in soft-news stories.

- **Stress on mechanics.** Journalism places greater emphasis on what English teachers often call mechanics (grammar, usage, spelling, style and tight writing) than creative writing because adherence to such rules keeps the news reader from being distracted by irregularities. The poet e.e. cummings avoided capitalization and punctuation in his poems to develop an original style that could sometimes make use of the double meanings that were created when such guideposts were missing. A journalist, however, would never do that. Using correct mechanics helps to maintain a journalist's credibility. If people find mistakes or inconsistencies of any kind in journalism, they start wondering whether they can trust the accuracy of the news presented.

Good, tight journalistic writing demands that the writer and editor:

- Be clear.
- Be concise.
- Be correct.

In this chapter, we look at the first two rules in detail. We'll discuss the third later in the book.

Clarity

It's especially important for journalistic writing to be clear. News consumers don't want to be confused about what they are reading in print or online or listening to on the radio or television. Here's a checklist of some key reminders about making your writing clear:

A Clarity Checklist

☑   Make sure all sentences flow from one to another without abruptly changing topics. Make sure all points, details or quotes support the main point.

☑   Write for readability. Don't use less common or bigger words than you need to. Don't make sentences or paragraphs longer than can be easily followed by a reader. (See the Journalism Tip on Page 30 and the "Tightening list" on Page 287.)

☑   Make sure all of a reader's likely questions are answered. Explain any jargon or technical terms or any information with which readers might not be familiar.

☑   Include specific details, making sure to illustrate generalizations with examples. Avoid vague and unsubstantiated statements.

☑   Make sure that any numbers in a story are used to make the meaning clearer for the reader. Numbers often intimidate readers, so the writer should tell them what the numbers mean.

☑   Follow the rules of grammar. Keep verb tenses consistent, and construct sentences so that all pronouns, participles and modifiers can be clearly understood. (See Part Two.)

The first point is common to all nonfiction writing. The last point is discussed elsewhere in this book. So, for now, we'll look in more detail at the second through fifth points, which are particularly important for journalism.

Write Short Sentences and Paragraphs, and Use Common Words

Journalists try to write at the eighth-grade level, using short, simple sentences. Sometimes, when people hear this, they're shocked. "Why do journalists 'write down' to people?" they ask. The answer is that writing at the eighth-grade level isn't writing down to most people.

Readability tests, such as the Gunning and Flesch indexes, are mathematical formulas for determining how hard it is to read and understand a piece of writing. The tests work by determining how long or unusual the words are and how long the sentences are. A piece written on the postgraduate level would mean the words in it are so long and unusual and the sentences so long that it's likely to be understood mainly by specialists in the field. That's not necessarily good writing. By contrast, something written at the first-grade level could be so basic that it would bore most adult readers. If a piece of writing is judged to be written at the eighth-grade level, that means it should be understandable and engaging to an average student in the eighth grade or to any adult who reads at or above that level.

Don't think that a piece with a high grade-level rating is better written than one with a low grade-level rating. The eighth-grade level — best for a publication aimed at a general audience—does not mean that the content, format and ideas are simplistic. *The Wall Street Journal* is written at that level. As magazine consultant Don Ranly says, you'll never hear an MBA graduate complain that the WSJ is too easy to read.

Shorter words are usually clearer. Fewer words tend to be, too. But it's not always enough to be brief. Sometimes, it's necessary to say the same thing more clearly in about the same number of words or even to include additional material. Clarity and completeness go hand in hand when it comes to being concise.

Anticipate Readers' Questions

Often, a passage is unclear not because the words are confusing but because the passage raises questions in the reader's mind. In such instances, to achieve clarity requires that you *anticipate what questions the reader might have and answer them.*

If you were an editor and a reporter handed in a story with the following passage, what questions would be raised in your mind?

> A sizable crowd turned out to see the Michigan Wolverines play their baseball opener against the Ohio State Buckeyes.

How about these questions: Who won? What was the score? What's a "sizable" crowd? Where was the game played?

Or consider this final paragraph in an auto-accident story:

> Police said the Paris Road and College Avenue intersection is the scene of many traffic accidents.

How many accidents? Why is this intersection dangerous? Is anybody doing anything about it?

Include Specifics

Providing readers with specifics is closely related to the idea of answering likely questions. Occasionally, writers make generalizations that need to be more clearly explained. Once the specifics are supplied, the generalizations sometimes appear patently false, sometimes more persuasively true. In either case, giving specifics helps clarify the issue.

Here are some examples of the most common kinds of general statements and some questions to ask to draw out detail. As an editor, be on guard for these general statements. As a writer, ask yourself these questions about your own statements:

When a writer makes an abstract statement:

> Some people can't see the forest for the trees.

> Love makes the world go 'round.

Ask, "What do you mean by that?" "What's an example of that?"

When a writer uses a vague modifier:

> Democracy is the best form of government.

> He's a great singer.

Ask, "Compared with what?" "Compared with whom?"

When someone makes a universal statement, one that applies to all members of a group:

> Women aren't good at science.

> Asians are good at math.

Ask, "All?" "Every?" "Never?"

When someone refers to a large, unspecified group:

> Scientists say . . .

> Studies show . . .

Ask, "Who specifically?" "What specifically?" "Which specifically?"

When someone talks about *can't*, *must*, *ought* or *should* (or their opposites):

> You should drink six glasses of water a day.

> You shouldn't swear.

Ask, "Why?" "Who says so?" "What causes that?" "What prevents that?" "What would happen if somebody did?"

When people say that something does something:

> Using spray deodorant just hastens the greenhouse effect.

> Opposites attract.

Ask, "How specifically does it do that?" "What makes it do that?" "Why is that true?" "Could it be done in a different way?"

Explain Numbers and Statistics

Numbers should be used in stories to inform and to clarify, but too often they are used in ways that merely confuse people. Many reporters think they have done their jobs when they pepper their stories with a few figures. But what do those figures mean to readers? Put numbers into a meaningful context, and tell readers what they mean. After all, in today's world, almost everything seems to be quantified. Just don't overdo it.

For example, a business-page story tells readers that the Consumer Price Index rose 1.3 percent in June. If readers don't know enough already to equate that index loosely with the cost of living (that's not exactly what it is), the story probably means nothing to them. Furthermore, is it a good thing or a bad thing for the CPI to have risen 1.3 percent? Readers might automatically think it's a bad thing that prices have risen. But perhaps this was the smallest increase in the CPI in six months.

Big numbers especially tend to lose readers and cease to be real. As the late Sen. Everett Dirksen, R-Ill., once said during a discussion of the federal budget, "A billion here, a billion there, and soon you're talking about real money!"

In addition to supplying the raw numbers, try using analogies to help readers grasp the numbers. For example:

> If you could pick up a dollar a second, it would take you 32 years to pick up a billion of them.

> There's a 1 in 1.5 million chance of being killed in an airplane crash. By contrast, the number of people who die each year of smoking is equivalent to the entire population of Kansas City, Missouri.

Because numbers get so fuzzy for many people, they can easily mislead when thrown about unscrupulously. Former British Prime Minister Benjamin Disraeli is quoted as having said, "There are lies, damn lies and statistics."

For example, it is extremely important for journalists to be able to calculate percentages and to understand them. Otherwise, bias tends to creep into stories, either unintentionally or as the result of some interested person's manipulation.

Which of these statements is correct?

1. One percent milk has half the fat of 2 percent milk.
2. One percent milk has 50 percent of the fat of 2 percent milk.
3. Two percent milk has twice the fat of 1 percent milk.
4. Two percent milk has 200 percent of the fat of 1 percent milk.
5. Two percent milk has 100 percent more fat than 1 percent milk.
6. One percent milk has 1 percentage point less fat than 2 percent milk.

Actually, each statement is just a different way of saying the same thing. Some of the statements, however, sound more or less shocking than others. An advocate of 1 percent milk might choose No. 4 because it makes its point dramatically. A journalist should know enough math to see the statement for what it is.

Although some journalists might have chosen their career partly to avoid one that entailed math, they can't escape dealing with percentages. Percentages come up in every story involving government budgets, charity fundraising and so on. You need to know how to calculate them.

The formula for calculating percentages is $p = a/b \times 100$, where a is the number you want to find to be what percentage (p) of the number b.

To put that in clearer English, divide *a* by *b* and then drop the decimal point. For example, 4 is what percentage of 5? Divide 4 by 5. The answer is 0.80. Multiply by 100 to drop the decimal point, and you're left with 80 percent.

Correctness

Different kinds of writing can approach "correctness" in different ways. Journalism must be correct in at least four senses, as shown in the checklist that follows.

A Correctness Checklist

☑ Make sure you get the facts right. Your writing must be unbiased and accurate, which is what journalists mean by *objectivity*. Particularly in hard-news stories, don't express your opinions. Don't use words such as *claims* that express a value judgment — in this case, implying disbelief. Report only what you can prove to be true. Present all sides fairly.

☑ Make sure your writing is appropriate for your audience and your purpose. They are your guides for what to put in and what to leave out of a story.

☑ Use the right story formula for your news story.

☑ Make sure your writing is correct in grammar, usage, spelling and style.

Use Correct Grammar, Usage, Spelling and Style

The "Spelling" and "Usage" lists in Part Three (See Pages 272–286 and 328–402) cover grammar, usage, spelling and punctuation. Style rules, such as those established by the Associated Press or a particular newspaper, magazine or television station, add consistency and therefore clarity. Use Webster's *New World College Dictionary*, or Webster's *Third New International Dictionary* if you don't find it in New World, to check the spelling of words that are not in the stylebook.

Write to Your Audience and Purpose

Your audience and your purpose help you know when to be formal and when to be informal. The style of writing that is proper for *The Chronicle of Higher Education* might not be right for the *New York Daily News*. Even in the same newspaper or magazine — print or online — different writing styles are permissible. A feature story may make liberal use of slang, but a more formal news story may not. A blog or review might also include words that convey value judgments, but those words should be edited out of a straight-news story.

Use the Right Story Formula

Story formulas constitute a checklist of what must be included in a story of a particular type and in what order generally. That, in turn, helps you know what could be left out. We present in Chapters 3, 4 and 5 some basic formulas for hard- and soft-news stories for print, online and broadcast media. For now, let's just mention as an example the most widely known news formula: In hard-news stories, use the inverted-pyramid formula — the most important news at the top, the least important at the bottom.

Maintain Objectivity in Your Writing

Most editors will tell you that accuracy is the most important characteristic of good news writing. The rules of journalistic objectivity are intended to help us achieve accuracy. They also help us take out words and comments from our work that would be inappropriate in a news account.

One of the most cutting epithets the public hurls at journalists is that we are "biased" or "nonobjective." Most journalists try hard to earn public trust by being objective in their coverage. But the public's perception of objectivity and what journalists mean by it are often quite different.

Most people think their own opinions about the world are correct. They think their view of the world is "the way it is." They will often object if journalists don't take their side, even while trying to be more neutral.

The AP Stylebook, for example, suggests journalists use the terms "anti-abortion" and "abortion rights" as modifiers, not "pro-life" and "pro-choice," except in quotes or names of groups. Some on either side might object, but the idea is that these are more neutral terms than the common ones. Why? People on either side criticize the other for not being consistent. Pro-lifers tend also to support gun rights and various military interventions while opposing various social programs that could be said to make people's lives better. Pro-choicers, on the other hand, tend to support laws that oppose choice on matters other than abortion — for example, opposing school choice while supporting government-mandated health care plans and laws reducing people's choice in things like buying a large bottle of soda without paying a steep tax.

Never mind that the journalist took pains not to present his or her own opinion but rather tried to present both sides fairly, without biased language. What people often mean when they say news is biased is that it doesn't conform to their own view of the world — it doesn't confirm their prejudices. By contrast, journalists typically see their role as that of a judge in a jury trial. The journalist, like the judge, is a sort of gatekeeper for the jury, or the public. The journalist, like the judge, must be objective — meaning impartial, dispassionate and unprejudiced.

Journalists usually don't see their role as that of an attorney for the prosecution or the defense, presenting information to prove one side of a case rather than to get at the truth. Journalists would call playing the attorney's role being "subjective," an activity appropriate for public relations, advertising and editorial columns but not for a presentation of straight news.

Objectivity is a great goal, but achieving it is elusive, and some argue that complete objectivity is impossible in material written by humans. It's important to understand the meaning of objectivity in a journalistic context. We explain it this way: Journalists should follow the same investigative system employed by scientists. They develop a hypothesis and then seek the facts, even if the facts don't support what they originally thought — especially if they don't.

Unfortunately, in the 20th century, journalists developed well-intentioned practices to achieve objectivity that were often misguided. Philip Meyer of the University of North Carolina suggests to journalists Bill Kovach and Tom Rosenstiel in their classic book *The Elements of Journalism*:

> I think (the) connection between journalism and science ought to emphasize objectivity of method. That's what scientific method is — our humanity, our subjective impulses . . . directed toward deciding what to investigate by objective means.

What objectivity isn't, Kovach and Rosenstiel argue, is blind loyalty to the concepts of fairness and balance. Fairness, they argue, can be misunderstood if it is seen as a goal unto itself. Fairness should mean that a journalist is fair to the facts and to the public's understanding of them. It should not mean, "Am I being fair to my sources, so that none of them will be unhappy?" or "Does my story seem fair?" Those are subjective judgments that lead the journalist away from the task of independent verification.

Similarly, balance should not mean that it's necessary to get an equal number of scientists speaking on each side of the global-warming debate, for example, or if an overwhelming number of scientists in fact believe that the Earth is round and historians that the Holocaust killed millions.

Thus, to reduce the meaning of objectivity to the concepts of fairness and balance is a mistake, but that's exactly what some journalists do. Instead, journalists should do their best to determine the truth using the same tried-and-true methods a scientist would use.

Rules of Objective Writing

Here are some typical rules journalists follow in their pursuit of objectivity:

Stick to the facts.

Stick to what you know to be true. Distinguish between fact and opinion. Attribute controversial statements. Don't guess or predict. Don't bend the facts consciously or unconsciously to make a better story.

Be careful to avoid making unwarranted assumptions or writing statements you can't prove. Of course, journalists try to be accurate.

But to see how easy it is to make mistakes unintentionally, read the following reporter's notes:

> Ricardo Sanchez, 10, is dead. The police have brought in three people for questioning. All three of them are known to have been near the scene of the killing. All three have police records. We've been told by a police representative that Leroi "Fingers" Washington, one of the three, has now been positively cleared of guilt in this incident.

If we assume the notes are accurate and true, which of the following statements are true? Consider a statement true if, from the notes, we know it to be true, false if we know it to be false, and questionable if we cannot be sure on the basis of the given information.

1. Leroi "Fingers" Washington was near the scene of the incident.
2. We don't really know anyone is dead.
3. Leroi "Fingers" Washington is probably black.
4. The other two suspects were also near the scene.
5. Three men have been arrested.
6. Only Leroi "Fingers" Washington has been cleared by the police.
7. This is an especially heinous murder because the victim was a juvenile.

Here are the answers:

1. *True.* Leroi "Fingers" Washington was one of three people near the scene who were brought in for questioning.
2. *False.* The reporter's notes state that Ricardo Sanchez is dead.
3. *Questionable.* Someone may surmise from the name that he is black, but we don't know for sure from this information alone.
4. *Questionable.* The other two people brought in for questioning were near the scene, but we cannot assume they are suspects. One or both of them may merely have been witnesses.
5. *Questionable.* First, we don't know the people brought in were all men. Second, the truth of the statement also depends on what is meant by "arrested." We know of no one who has been arrested in the sense that most people would understand the term. Some attorneys say, however, that true to the root meaning of the word *arrest*—"to stop"—anytime the police stop you against your will, it is an arrest even if you are not taken in and booked.
6. *Questionable.* We know for sure that one of them, Washington, has been cleared. That does not necessarily mean that he is the *only* one and that no one else has been cleared.
7. *Questionable.* We know the dead person is a juvenile, but we don't know this is a murder. Although many would associate the word *killing* with an intent to do violence, perhaps it was meant in the sense that

Sanchez was "killed," maybe in an accident. Or Sanchez may have been armed, and someone may have acted in self-defense. Or it may have been manslaughter rather than murder. In fact, in a legal sense we don't know it is actually "murder" unless there is a trial and someone is convicted of murder. And to label this "especially heinous," even if it turns out to be murder, is a value judgment. Don't hesitate to quote someone who says that, but don't say it yourself.

Be neutral. In a news story that's supposed to be objective, keep your own opinions out of it.

Either keep your opinions to yourself or save them for more personal pieces, such as commentaries, reviews and blogs. Don't confuse an opinion you believe to be true with journalistic objectivity. Being neutral doesn't permit you to include a statement you believe to be true unless it's also an objective fact that does not involve a matter of belief or opinion. For example, consider the following statements:

The U.S. is the best nation on earth.

"Deadpool" is a great movie.

You may believe one or both of these statements to be true. But they are not objective statements in the eyes of a journalist because they involve value judgments, opinions or beliefs. Both, however, could be quoted with attribution if someone other than a journalist were making the statement.

Don't use words that express a judgment or an evaluation, such as calling a person *attractive* or a proposal *idiotic*, even when you think most people would agree with you. Some editors might be more permissive about allowing value judgments to go unattributed if they express generally agreed-upon, noncontroversial matters, but they're still nonobjective:

Mozart was a greater composer than Salieri.

Adolf Hitler was a madman.

Choose your words carefully, making sure they convey no *unintentional* bias. Journalists may unwittingly take sides in a controversy if they are not careful about their choice of words. For example:

- To call an official a *bureaucrat* implies the negative connotation of someone who takes joy in binding helpless victims with red tape.
- To say a candidate *refuted* an opponent's charges does not simply mean the candidate *answered* them but rather that the candidate *successfully answered* them.
- To say that the City Council *still* hasn't taken action on a proposal implies disapproval for taking so long.
- To say national health care would cost *only* a certain amount implies that the cost is insignificant—a value judgment.

- To write *She disagrees with the fact that she is wrong* is to take the side of those who say she is wrong and to contradict her in the same sentence as her denial by calling this a fact.
- To use hedging phrases such as *appears to be guilty* or *may be guilty* or *in my opinion, he's guilty* convey value judgments akin to saying *he's guilty*. Such phrases are not fully neutral.
- To write that a news source *claimed* something implies you don't believe it. Stick with nonjudgmental words of attribution such as *said* or *says*.
- To write *Barbara Alcott—a pretty, blond legal secretary—said she has never been the victim of sexual discrimination* is to subject Alcott to sexual discrimination in print.

Unfortunately, newspapers occasionally make statements such as the last one about women. Remember, if you would not say the same of a man, the statement is probably sexist. Such descriptions express value judgments about beauty and have no place in objective news. The following sentence would be neutral: *Legal secretary Barbara Alcott says she has never been the victim of sexual discrimination.* (See Chapter 7.)

In addition to avoiding value judgments and advice, journalists should be careful with the use of adjectives, as well as adverbs, in hard-news reporting. Unnecessary modifiers are one of the most common ways bias creeps into a news story. They also tend to clutter a sentence, making it longer than it needs to be.

Modifiers to Be Avoided

absolutely	crucial	interesting
actually	definitely	ironically
alleged, allegedly	disturbing	least
amazing	dramatic	luckily
archconservative	effectively	major
archliberal	evil	most
astounding	exciting	mysterious
awful	fittingly	obviously
bad	frankly	perfectly
best	good	poignant
bizarre	grim	positively
candid	honestly	predictably
certainly	important	radical (left, right)
complex	inevitable	really
controversial	insurmountable	reportedly

respected	successfully	unprecedented
sadly	suspected	unquestionably
seriously	tragic	unusual
shocking	troubling	very
special	ultraconservative	worst
spectacular	ultraliberal	
still	undoubtedly	
stunning	unique	

Be fair. Present all sides as best you can, giving people a chance to respond to charges or criticism.

If people refuse to comment when given the chance, say so in the story so that readers will know you tried to be fair.

Choose your words carefully so that they are fair to the people involved. Whenever you write a crime story, for example, write it in a way that does not assume the guilt of the suspect. After all, the charges may be dropped, or he or she may be found not guilty at a trial.

For example, to write *Police said Dave Jones climbed through the window and sexually assaulted the woman* is to convict the man in print before he has stood trial. Instead, write *Police said a man climbed through the window and sexually assaulted the woman. Dave Jones was arrested Monday* (*on a charge of rape, and charged with rape* or *in connection with the rape*).

Likewise, don't call the suspect an *alleged rapist* or say he *allegedly raped* the woman. Although many journalists don't know it, the words *alleged* and *allegedly* offer little legal protection from later libel action if the person isn't convicted. Who's doing the alleging? You are when you print that statement.

Stories with possible legal consequences are not the only ones that demand fairness to all sides. For example, although prison officials are not likely to sue you, to write *The food is so bad at the prison that inmates have begun a hunger strike* is to agree inadvertently with the inmates. A neutral statement would be *Inmates say the food is so bad that they have begun a hunger strike*. Attribution is important.

Be impersonal in a hard-news story. Don't try to sound creative or original or to write in your own "voice" unless you're taking a feature or more opinionated approach to a story.

We're not trying to stifle your creativity. It's just that such individuality is out of place in most straight-news stories. Feature stories, reviews and commentaries are a different matter.

Journalism Tip
Writing for Eighth-Grade-Level Readability

To keep your writing clear and easily understood, follow these tips.

- Keep most paragraphs one or two sentences long.
- Make a quotation that forms a complete sentence into its own paragraph.
- Keep sentences an average of 16 words long.
- Make sure that leads are short and uncomplicated.
- Vary sentence lengths and patterns to provide pacing and to avoid monotony and choppiness.
- Avoid compound sentences, especially those that use semicolons.
- Cut out words and phrases that don't add meaning.
- Avoid the passive voice, which by its nature is wordy.
- Use short, simple, common words; these are best for journalism.
- Avoid foreign expressions and jargon.
- Explain difficult or technical terms if you need to use them.
- Use adjectives and adverbs only when they are essential.

By the way, the shortest words are usually also the most common, but there are exceptions. Some longer words, such as *important*, are clear to everyone, and some shorter words, such as *fud*, are not. (A *fud* is a rabbit's butt. Remember how Elmer Fudd was often the butt of Bugs Bunny's jokes?) Given the choice between a short uncommon word and a longer common one, choose the more common one. For more on using the right words, see Chapter 9.

CHAPTER 3

Writing News That's Fit for Print

It's not difficult to find someone willing to bash journalistic writing as pedestrian and devoid of literary merit. While it's true that much of journalism is based on formulaic writing—mostly because of the need to churn it out quickly on deadline—there are plenty of exceptions. Consider this marvelous introduction to a story written by Wright Thompson in *ESPN The Magazine*:

> VERONA, Italy—Right until he started quoting Hitler and dropping N-bombs, my new friend was a great dude. I'll call him The Hooligan. [He] seemed nothing like the Hellas Verona fans I'd read about, the neo-fascist, neo-Nazi, racist thugs. The Hooligan insisted the Veronese just have a dark sense of humor and refuse to wear the yoke of modern political correctness.
>
> . . . Near the entrance to the stands, I ask The Hooligan to translate any chants hurled down at the players. . . . His voice is a sharp blade.
>
> "How about, 'You're a f---ing n-----'?"
>
> —Wright Thompson, "When the Beautiful Game Turns Ugly"

After that introduction, even those who are not soccer fans felt compelled to read more about the racist, neo-Nazi fans of Hellas in Verona, northern Italy. Thompson is one of the great sportswriters of our time, and before going to *ESPN The Magazine* he worked for *The Kansas City Star* and the New Orleans *Times-Picayune*. Now he gets the choicest assignments for his magazine because he's a great writer.

In Kansas City and New Orleans, Thompson did his share of formulaic writing, but his talents with words were recognized quickly. He almost instantly became recognized as someone who possessed extraordinary writing skills, and he parlayed that into his job at ESPN, where he gets to do that kind of writing all the time, not just occasionally. As Thompson's work shows, newspaper and magazine writing does not have to be boring. Nor does it have to be written in a rigid, formulaic style devoid of flair.

Many stories today *are* written in a standardized format, usually using the traditional *inverted pyramid*—storytelling in which the most important facts are presented first and the least important last. Standardized writing is not necessarily bad. Indeed, an understanding of journalistic formulas will help a writer produce lots of stories in a brief period of time. It's a terrific way of delivering the news. Just as a knowledge of grammar—the structure of language—lets us write and edit sentences better, so, too, does a knowledge of news-writing formulas allow us to write and edit stories more efficiently.

Talk of formulas inevitably ignites fears that someone is trying to take away the writer's creativity or turn the writer into a hack. That's not our purpose in discussing the most common newspaper-writing formulas in this chapter. We would never suggest that stories should be written like a paint-by-number picture. We simply note that the experience of thousands of journalists over the years has resulted in typical ways of doing things. You don't have to imitate slavishly these typical methods, but you should understand them as a starting point. Most likely, the sweet spot in journalistic writing falls somewhere between flowery prose and the traditional approach of the inverted pyramid.

To be sure, if you were assigned to the police beat, after covering several accidents you'd figure out there are certain things that always need to be included in that kind of story. You'd also learn there is a typical order of importance—deaths ahead of injuries, injuries ahead of damages unless the injuries were slight and the damages large. And you'd learn that certain pitfalls need to be avoided, such as not assigning someone guilt if that person hasn't yet been convicted of a crime.

That doesn't mean every accident story should be written as a fill-in-the-blank report. Details will vary, and those details could require writing the story in an atypical way. But understanding what typically needs to be included and in what order will help you make sure that the most important elements are covered, that you write or edit more quickly and efficiently and that you know the difference between creative variations that grow organically from the material and variations that are merely the result of ignorance or inexperience.

In other words, news formulas, like the standard chord changes in a blues song, can actually free your writing to be more creative in ways that work.

Pick the Best Angle

Sometimes, journalists have trouble writing a story because they can't figure out what *angle* to take. That is, they're looking for the best overall approach—the best way to focus the story. Once you decide what angle to take, the rest usually comes easily. You can make this decision in several ways.

Use the "Hey, did you hear about . . . ?" approach, in which you simply ask yourself what you would tell a friend about the event.

What you would say after "Hey, did you hear about . . . ?" is the angle to take. Broadcasters strongly recommend this approach, but print and online journalists use it, too.

Focus on basic news values.

Focusing on basic news values works for print, radio, television and online stories alike, and it includes the following news values:

Audience: who your audience is and what news it needs or wants from you.

Impact: the number of people involved, the number affected or the depth of emotion people are likely to feel.

Timeliness: how up-to-the-minute the information is.

Proximity: how nearby the story took place.

Prominence: how rich, famous or powerful the people involved are.

Novelty or oddity: how unusual the news item is.

Conflict or drama: how exciting the news is; the more conflict involved, the more dramatic the news is.

With this method, you ask yourself which of these values is appropriate to the story and lead with it. If there's more than one appropriate value, rank them. Then bring them up in the order of their importance.

Stress the angle you think would most affect or interest your audience.

The strongest angle is always to tell readers, listeners or viewers about something that has a direct effect on them. Look for how this information will have an impact on people, and tell them that. For example, will their taxes be raised, will people be laid off, will the price of meat go down or will the streets be safer? If the story doesn't contain information that directly affects the audience, the next best lead is what would most interest them. Don't bury the most interesting parts where people are less likely to see or hear them. Move them toward the top of the story, where they'll attract more attention.

If a story has neither impact nor interest, you might ask: Why run it at all? Who cares? Often, however, if the story at first appears to fail these tests, it will pass if you rewrite it to stress people doing things rather than the things themselves. Words about a *thing* typically contain less built-in interest than words about a *person*. News is people and what they do or what happens to them. An encyclopedia article about gastropods is not news.

Once you've picked an angle, decide whether to write the story as *hard news* or *soft news*. Different formulas define the usual order of details. Depending on the story, you'll choose a hard-news or soft-news lead and story structure, which we'll talk about next.

Types of News Leads

Most editors classify leads—the introductions to stories—as hard-news leads or soft-news leads. Leads that stress summarizing the story and telling the reader the bottom line are called *hard-news leads* (or *straight-news leads*) because they're typically used for stories reporting "hard" news, such as crimes, accidents, government meetings, and political and economic developments.

On the other hand, leads that stress attracting the reader's attention by using a dramatic grabber are called *soft-news leads*. They are typically used for stories reporting "soft" news, such as personality profiles, sports, reviews, entertainment, lifestyle features and columns.

Hard-news leads are used daily in newspapers and even magazines for short, informative news items. They get right to the facts, often including only basic information such as who, what, when, where, why and even how. Beginners often make the mistake of cramming all those items into the lead, which is sure to lead to ponderous writing. Instead, it's best to pick the most important of those items for the lead and save less important ones for the second or third paragraph. And remember, hard-news leads do not have to be boring.

Soft-news leads are increasingly in demand because of the way they attempt to grab the reader's attention in the most interesting way possible. Today, soft-news leads are increasingly used on stories that once demanded hard-news leads. Newspapers and online sites, in particular, have begun to use soft-news leads as a way of enticing readers into a hard-news story. We call this the *mixed approach*—a soft-news lead on top of what is structured after that in the inverted-pyramid structure of most to least important, like a hard-news story. Still, it's important to understand the differences in these types of leads.

Hard-News Leads

Hard-news leads are found more often in newspapers and online than in magazines, although magazines sometimes use them in brief articles. They get to the bottom line, as people in business say. That is, they tell you the essence of the news in the first sentence. If you read no further—and many readers won't—you'll still have the gist of the story.

As noted earlier, it's a myth that the lead needs to tell the reader *who, what, when, where, why* and *how*. A lead with all that information would probably be too long and hard to read. (A lead should be only a sentence or two long, a maximum of 20 to 30 words.)

Many hard-news stories leave out the *why* and *how* because those elements are often more speculative and less objective. Only when *why* or *how* can be discussed objectively are they likely to appear. (Soft-news leads, as you'll see, stress drama more than information and may leave out even some of the basic four details—the *who, what, when* and *where*.)

The "Five W's and an H" are worth remembering, however, because the order in which people typically recite them — *who, what, when, where, why* and *how* — is almost always their order of importance in a story. That means it's also the order in which details typically should appear in a lead.

For example, the two most important details in a story are usually *who* did *what*, in that order. In some stories — especially crime stories — the *what* may come first if what happened or was said is more important than the person involved. Next most important are *when* and *where*. *Why* and *how* come last in the "Five W's and an H" and are almost never found in the lead.

We suggest you think of the basic formula for the hard-news lead as *who, what, time, day* or *date* and *place* — in that order. This corresponds to the well-known *who, what, when, where, why* and *how*, leaving out the *why* and *how* and breaking *when* into *time* and *day* or *date*. *Place*, of course, is the same as *where*. *Time, day* or *date* and *place* are rarely if ever the most important part of a story, so they should not start the lead. They often come not in the lead itself but in later paragraphs, and, in some stories, one or more of these three elements may not appear at all if unimportant. The most common of these three to appear in the lead is *day* or *date*.

There's been a tendency over the past 25 years to use a soft-news lead on some hard-news stories that have special drama. Take a look at the figure on page 36 to see how a news story might be structured with a hard-news (inverted pyramid) lead as opposed to a soft-news (feature) lead (see Figure 3.1). So, again we say: Don't slavishly imitate the formula. Understand it and appreciate it, but use your discretion — and don't be afraid to try something different when you have a valid reason for doing so. And be aware that some types of hard-news stories often use variations on the formula described here. For example, an obituary should begin with the person's name, not just an identifying label, even if the deceased was not famous, and the *place*, the deceased's address, is often given only as a town to eliminate the risk of a burglary during the funeral.

Here's the formula and how to use it.

Who Was Involved?

Use an *immediate-ID who* if the person is well-known to your audience. If the person should be well-known to your readers by name, simply begin with the person's name.

Taylor Swift sang to a full stadium.

Use a title with the name if the person should be well-known to readers of your publication but still could benefit from identification. Place a short title in front of the name or a longer title following it.

Traverse City Mayor Anne Williams said Monday that . . .

Shaun Donovan, secretary of Housing and Urban Development, said Wednesday that . . .

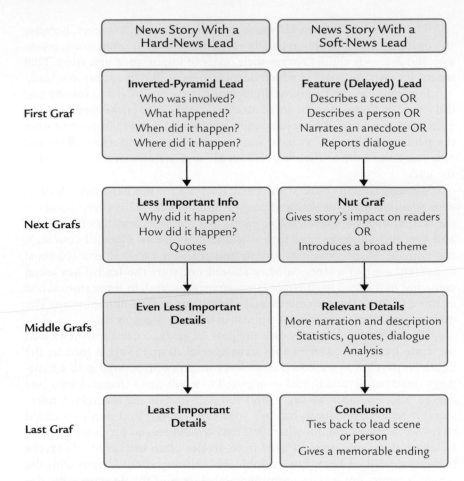

Figure 3.1 Hard-News and Soft-News Leads.

Note that official titles in front of a name are capitalized, but those following a name are not.

Use a *delayed-ID who* if the person isn't well-known to your audience. In the lead, write down a label for the *who*.

An Atlanta man was arrested Friday . . .

An area plumber was killed on Sunday when . . .

After you finish the lead sentence using the delayed ID, start the second paragraph with the name of the person represented by the label in the first sentence:

A Petersburg man died in a two-car accident Thursday on U.S. 23.

Wilbur Jeffers was southbound when . . .

What Happened?

Use the *single-element what* if only one thing happened or is the focus of the story. That way, there's no problem figuring out the *what*. The rest of the story will be filled with extra details about what happened.

> Slain police officer Enrique Montez will be remembered today.

Use the *most-important-element what* if more than one thing happened, but one is more important than the others. This situation is often the case with stories about meetings, but it's used for others as well. The rest of the story is filled with details about the main *what*, then a listing of and details about the other *whats*.

> Police have arrested a suspect in last month's kidnapping of a Springfield girl.

The story may then update the audience on how the girl is doing a month after the ordeal and provide other information, but the focus in the lead is on the arrest.

Use the *multiple-elements what* if more than one thing happened and the events are unrelated and all roughly of equal importance. You're going to have to list them all in the lead before you turn to details about any of them.

The list can be in the first sentence if it doesn't make the sentence too long and unwieldy. Or you may have to list each *what* in separate sentences. Remember to maintain parallel structure:

> The City Council approved Monday night the widening of Main Street but rejected a proposal that would have required city employees to live in town.

In listing the separate elements, try to give them in the order of most impact or interest to your audience, even though they're all important.

Use the *summary what* if more than one thing happened and all the events are of equal importance and have enough in common that they can be summarized without having to list all of them separately. You can summarize all the *whats* in one sentence in the lead.

> Most economic indicators rose in the third quarter.

Consider whether to reverse the *who* and the *what*.

Sometimes, the *what* seems more important than the *who*—as is often the case in a crime story—and the *who* and *what* are reversed in the lead.

> First National Bank in downtown Springfield was robbed this morning by two hooded gunmen who got away with more than $200,000 in cash.

Most readers would not know the names of the suspects in the bank robbery even if police later arrested them. So doing it this way makes more sense, even if it violates a favorite rule of editors—avoid passive voice in favor of active voice (see Chapter 12). Although that's usually great advice because verbs are stronger in the active voice, this example illustrates when to make an exception.

If the *what* involves what someone said—such as in the coverage of a speech, a meeting or an interview—many newspaper writers start with the *what*, then go to the *who*.

> Mesa County needs to spend $1.5 million this year to repair roads and bridges, the public works director told the County Commission at Monday night's meeting.

In beginning with the *what*, however, reporters should avoid presenting a misleading lead that begins with a startling statement that sounds as though it's being presented as a fact, then attributing it in the next paragraph.

AVOID   Odofile Guinn is guilty of killing his wife, Judith Dandridge, and her friend Joseph Goldfarb.

That's what Prosecuting Attorney Elaine Chu told a jury in Los Angeles today.

BETTER   The trial of Odofile Guinn on a charge of killing his wife Judith Dandridge and her friend Joseph Goldfarb began Monday in Criminal Court.

Prosecuting Attorney Elaine Chu told a jury in Los Angeles today that Guinn is guilty of the crime.

State the summary as a thesis, not as a mere topic, in a story where the *what* summarizes a speech, a meeting or an interview.

The lead should make a definite statement, as a thesis does, not just be a word or phrase, like the title of a term paper. One of the worst leads for a story would be one that tells only that someone spoke without giving a clue as to what the person said. Here are four examples of the same lead in order of worst to best:

NO TOPIC MENTIONED   A researcher from the University of Kansas spoke Tuesday night to an audience of local health care providers.

ONLY A TOPIC   A researcher from the University of Kansas spoke Tuesday night to an audience of local health care providers about new developments in cancer treatments.

THESIS   A researcher from the University of Kansas told an audience of local health care providers Tuesday night that there are many exciting new developments in cancer treatments.

THESIS FIRST, WHO SECOND   There are many exciting new developments in cancer treatments, a researcher from the University of Kansas told an audience of local health care providers Tuesday night.

If you have trouble telling a topic from a thesis, here's a hint: *Anytime you've written that somebody <u>discussed</u> something, <u>spoke on</u> something or <u>spoke about</u> something, or <u>talked on</u> or <u>talked about</u> something, what follows is probably* *a topic, not a thesis. If, instead, you force yourself to write that someone <u>said</u> or <u>says</u> something, it's almost impossible to follow that with a mere topic instead of a thesis.*

When Did It Happen?

Time, wherever it appears, should precede *day* or *date*. Remember to avoid redundancy in expressing the time element in a story. You could write *6 p.m.* or *6 this evening* but not *6 p.m. this evening*.

Never use both the day and the date except in a calendar item if local style requires it there.

For an event happening on the day of publication, you may write *this morning*, *this afternoon*, *this evening*, *today* or *tonight*, as appropriate. AP, however, says not to write *yesterday* or *tomorrow*, but rather to use the day of the week instead.

Use the *day of the week* if the *what* will take place (or has taken place) within a week forward (or backward) of the publication date. Use the *date* if the event will take place (or has taken place) further ahead or back than one week. If the event happened exactly a week ago or will happen exactly a week away, some editors say you may use the date or a phrase such as *next Wednesday* or *last Thursday,* but the *next* or *last* are unnecessary.

In some stories, you might mention a general time frame in the lead, with the specifics coming later in the story. For example, a lead might say a fair will be held *this weekend*, with the exact times lower in the story.

If the *what* involved what someone said or reported or what a governing body did, the *when* (either the time or day or date) is often moved up in the sentence immediately following the verb.

> Jerome H. Powell, chairman of the Federal Reserve Board, said today . . .

> The Board of Governors voted Wednesday . . .

Journalism Tip
Words to Avoid in Attributing Information

Good reporters follow the rule that simple forms of attribution are the best. Almost always, that means sticking to *said* or *says*. Failing to do so almost invariably gets reporters in trouble because they seem to lose their objectivity. Here are some words to avoid when attributing information:

- Words that imply the reporter is a mind reader: *believes, feels, hopes, thinks*. How do you know the source believes, feels, hopes or thinks something unless he or she said so?

- Words that suggest the reporter's opinion: *admitted* or *conceded* (imply the person confessed or made a concession), *claimed* (expresses disbelief), *refuted* (expresses agreement with the person answering another's charges), *alleged* (can sound to a reader like disbelief and to an attorney as if the reporter is making the allegation).

Where Did It Happen?

Use a significant identifier for the *where*. The *place* may be the name of a street, a building, an institution, a neighborhood, a town or another location, as appropriate.

> The campus chapter of Women in Communication will meet at 7 p.m. Monday in Room 120 of the Shichtman Student Union.

Notice that this example uses the order of elements recommended for the lead of a story and that the order is based on what's typically most to least important among these five elements.

Problems With Hard-News Leads

Don't make the lead too complicated. Don't load it with too many names, figures or details. Keep the lead sentence short — never more than 30 words and closer to 15 to 20 if possible.

TOO MANY NAMES Gus Gish, manager of Springfield's Downtown Development Fund, said today at a Chamber of Commerce luncheon in Fairfield Village that this year's drive will be co-chaired by Carla Zim, Springfield National Bank vice president, and David Roche, Elmdorf Electronics Corp. general manager.

TO THE POINT The Springfield Downtown Development Fund has named two people to co-chair this year's drive.

Gus Gish, the fund's manager, said . . .

TOO MANY NUMBERS The Springfield Board of Education voted 5–4 Tuesday night to place on the November ballot a proposed property-tax increase of two mills, or $2 for every $1,000 of assessed valuation, up from the 10 mills property owners currently pay, to help cover the school district's budget of $13.2 million, which itself is $350,000 more than last year's.

TO THE POINT Springfield voters will have to consider in November whether to raise their property taxes to pay for schools.

The Board of Education voted 5–4 Monday night to . . .

TOO MANY DETAILS Pete's Brewing — maker of the brown, malty Pete's Wicked Ale — raised about $40 million in its initial public offering Tuesday, as well as an additional $12.5 million for its owners, a total of around 56 times its estimated earnings for next year, as it became the second specialty beer company this year, behind Redhook Ale Brewery of Seattle, to offer its stock to investors.

TO THE POINT Pete's Brewing has become the second specialty beer company to go public this year.

The maker of Pete's Wicked Ale . . .

Don't begin with the *time, day or date* or *place*.

Time, day or *date* or *place* is less important than the *who* and *what*. Hint: If your lead starts with a prepositional phrase, it's probably starting with *time, day* or *date* or *place* and should be rewritten.

WRONG	At 11 a.m. this Thursday, the County Commission will hold a public hearing on allowing fireworks within the county.
RIGHT	The County Commission plans to hold a public hearing this week on allowing fireworks within the county. The meeting will be at 11 a.m. Thursday.

Don't begin with an empty, say-nothing expression or a generality that fails to distinguish this news from other news.

EMPTY	In a report released today . . . [Someone] spoke . . . [Someone] spoke . . .
GENERALITY	Sen. Paul Hogan spoke to the Booster Club here last night. The Student Council acted on four of its most pressing problems Tuesday.

Don't begin with a direct quote if it's a full sentence or longer. Such quotes should first appear in the second or third paragraph of most stories.

WRONG	"This is the happiest day of my life," said the man honored as Chelsea's Man of the Year.
RIGHT	A man who rescued a family of four from a burning home was honored Tuesday night as Chelsea's Man of the Year. "This is the happiest day of my life," said Fred Winston. . . .

Partial quotes in the first sentence are sometimes permissible, especially when a colorful phrase that aptly summarizes the theme can be excerpted from a speech.

Senate candidate Fred Hawkins told a Springfield Auditorium audience last night that "feminazis, compassion fascists and environmental wackos" are on the retreat as more Americans "see them for what they are."

Don't use a form of the verb *to be* in the lead, if you can avoid it.

WEAK	The County Commission was unanimous in approving . . .
BETTER	The County Commission unanimously approved . . .

Writing News That's Fit for Print

Don't overstate the news in the lead, making it more dramatic than it really is.

OVERSTATED	A Springfield woman may have averted a holocaust today when she used her fire extinguisher to put out an inferno in a family's SUV engine.
	[The words *holocaust* and *inferno* overstate the situation.]
REALISTIC	A family of four has a Springfield woman to thank for putting out the engine fire in an SUV this morning.
	[When the lead is thus reduced to reality, we should ask whether this is even worth a news item. It probably would not be except in the smallest of towns.]

For your lead, either state the bottom line—what it all boils down to—or use a grabber that dramatically (but realistically) attracts the reader's attention. Anything else, such as a long history of the problem, won't work.

What Comes After the Hard-News Lead?

A hard-news story is often written in the inverted-pyramid form.

After the hard-news lead, give additional details in descending order of importance.

The advantage of this style to readers is that if pressed for time, they can read only the headline and lead and still get the main information. The advantage of this style to reporters and editors is that it gives them a mutual understanding of what should be cut from a story first when it's too long to fit. Because the reporter puts the information he or she thinks is most important at the top, editors can make quick cuts on deadline by chopping from the end without fear of "butchering" the story.

Any detail that would be of particular interest to the audience should be moved toward the top of a story if it's not there already.

The main mistake reporters make with story structure is simply not putting the items in the best possible order. For example, if a plane crashed and among the passengers was a local family, that detail should be part of the lead, not buried further down.

To take another example, a wire-service story about a man who went to a restaurant and shot 21 people included a detail near the bottom that should have been moved up. The man's wife told police her husband had called a local suicide hotline that morning but had been told to call back later. Because of funding cuts, there were not enough people on duty to answer all the lines.

That detail deserved to be near the top of the newspaper version of the story—although, as we will see in Chapter 4, it could have made a terrific ending for a broadcast version of the story.

Soft-News Leads

Soft-news leads introduce stories dramatically, as Wright Thompson did in the story at the start of this chapter. And, as mentioned before, in addition to using them for soft-news stories, journalists are increasingly using soft-news leads with certain hard-news stories.

Soft-news leads are also sometimes called *delayed leads* or *feature leads*. They take a storyteller's approach by setting the scene, describing a person, starting with dialogue or relating an anecdote before telling the main point. In soft-news leads, it is acceptable to use an *immediate-ID who* even though the *who* may not be well-known.

> The young mother slumped forward in her chair, pressing her hands to the side of her head and weeping inconsolably.
>
> "Gone," she managed to say. "They're all gone."
>
> Andrea Martin, 26, had just learned that her four children all had died in an apartment fire while she was having a few drinks at a nearby bar.
>
> "Let's go, Ma'am," the police officer said. "I've got to take you downtown."
>
> Firefighters were summoned to the scene about 9 p.m. Monday night when a neighbor noticed smoke coming from the apartment. By the time they arrived, much of the building was engulfed in flames. . . .

Soft-News Clichés

Many stories fit into a recognized genre, but that doesn't mean all stories of a given kind should have the same lead.

Clichéd leads often begin life as a clever, new, soft-news lead a reporter gave to a story. But then other reporters who liked the idea stole it and began repeating it often rather than coming up with fresh ideas of their own. After the news audience has seen it or heard it a few times, it's no longer clever, just annoying.

Here are some examples of the most common, most annoying leads.

Avoid the one-word lead, especially when followed by an exclamation point.

> Tired. That's how John Smith felt after winning his first marathon at the age of 56.
>
> Sex! Now that I have your attention, let's talk about birth control.

Avoid the question lead.

> How hot was it Sunday? So hot that Dieter Mann required hospital treatment after walking barefoot on a downtown sidewalk.
>
> What do Bean Blossom, Ind., and Bill Monroe, the father of bluegrass music, have in common?

Notice that in each of these examples, the question lead is phony—the reporter is merely asking a rhetorical question he or she intends to answer.

The one time a question lead isn't phony and clichéd is when the question isn't answered in the story — that is, when the news is that there's an unanswered question.

> What happened to the night clerk at Fred's QuikMart on Friday?
>
> That's what police investigators are asking this morning.
>
> When the early-morning-shift clerk arrived, night clerk Terry Schmidt, 22, was missing, along with all the money from the safe. Police are uncertain whether this is an inside job or a case of robbery and abduction.

In short, don't lead with a question that's answered in the story.

Avoid the dictionary lead.

> Webster's dictionary defines freedom as. . . . But to Denny Davison, freedom means . . .

Avoid the "good and bad news" lead.

> First the good news, then the bad.

Avoid the lead that labels what kind of story this is or isn't.

> This is not another story about street people.
>
> This is a story about people who have survived.

Avoid the "something came early" lead.

> Thanksgiving came early for Diego Ramirez this year.

Avoid the "you might think" lead.

> You might think to look at the Victorian-style house that it's someone's comfortable home, perhaps filled with antiques. But you'd be wrong. The house actually is home to one of the city's high-tech software firms.

Avoid the "one thing's different" lead.

> Like most kids his age, Billy Small goes to school, likes baseball and enjoys ice-cream cones. But one thing about him is different: He's quadriplegic.

Avoid the "what a difference" lead.

> What a difference a day makes. Friday, the Red Sox were in first place. Now, with a loss to the Angels, they've fallen to second behind the Yankees in the American League East.

Avoid the "rain couldn't dampen" lead.

> Rain couldn't dampen the spirits of a capacity crowd at Comerica Park Saturday as Detroit won its season opener against Oakland 5–3.

Writing News That's Fit for Print

Avoid the "all in the family" lead.

> To Brian and Betsy Feintab and their three children, flying is all in the family. Each of them has a pilot's license.

Avoid the recipe lead.

> Take one dash of love, sprinkle in a dash of excitement, and mix with a lifetime of commitment. That's the recipe for a 50-year marriage, say Ted and Ethel Peck, who celebrated their 50th anniversary today.

Avoid the "official" lead.

> It's official: The Ohio State Buckeyes are the No. 1–rated football team in the nation, according to the latest Associated Press sports-writers poll.

Avoid the "funny thing" lead.

> A funny thing happened to Donald Trump on his way to the presidency.

Avoid the "not just for . . . anymore" lead.

> Country music isn't just for country folk anymore. It's one of the most popular segments of the recording industry, even in urban areas.

Avoid the "little did she know" lead.

> When Betty Smith walked up to the ATM at Seventh and Main streets to take out money for lunch, little did she know that a man waiting nearby in his car would force her at gunpoint to withdraw all her money and give it to him.

Avoid the truism lead.

> Everybody has to eat.

Avoid the Snoopy lead (after the famous Peanuts cartoon).

> It was a dark and stormy night.

And one final chestnut we'd like to roast.

> Yes, Virginia, there is a Santa Claus.

What Comes After the Soft-News Lead?

Features, commentaries, analysis pieces and other soft-news stories are not written in inverted-pyramid form. Soft-news stories don't follow the order of most to least important. Instead, they simply try to attract attention in the lead; supply details, analysis or opinion in the middle; and end with a memorable conclusion. For that reason, editors should never shorten a soft-news story by cutting from the end, as they would with a hard-news story.

The Wall Street Journal is excellent at taking abstract subjects such as the economy and personalizing them—showing how they actually affect people. *The Wall Street Journal* formula begins with a person who is affected by the topic under discussion. The lead shows how the topic affects that person.

Then, a *nut graf*—a paragraph that explains why the reader should care about the information in a story—makes a general statement, perhaps about the extent of the problem. Following the nut graf, which typically can be found in the first six or seven paragraphs of the story, the *Journal* presents facts, figures and analysis about the topic in general and then returns in the end to the person with whom it started.

Take a look at a few of *The Wall Street Journal*'s pieces, in print or online, for examples. Notice this construction, and see how effectively it enlivens what could have been a dull abstraction.

Using Paraphrases and Transitions to Build a Story

Paraphrases must be clearly attributed or the reader may think you are editorializing.

The second sentence in the first example (marked as wrong) sounds like a gratuitous opinion offered by the reporter rather than a continuation of what the speaker said. In the second example (marked as right), the sentence is quoted, not paraphrased. Always make sure paraphrases are attributed to someone so that readers don't think you are editorializing.

WRONG   Perez says more than 85 percent of American homes have a computer. But someone needs to worry about those too poor to join the information revolution.

[The second sentence sounds like a gratuitous opinion offered by the reporter.]

RIGHT   "We don't see any compelling reason to change our product line this year," Kuriak said. "Our current models are exceeding our expectations."

[When a reporter quotes someone in one sentence and attribution is provided, it's often clear that the same person is being quoted in the next one, and the attribution is unnecessary for the second sentence.]

Use clear transitions to connect your points.

Don't be afraid to start a sentence with *but* to show contrast. *And* can also be useful at the start of a sentence to introduce something additional. *Meanwhile* and *however*, though, are objectionable to many editors—the first for being overused, the second for being longer and more pompous than *but*. Also, watch for transitions like *as a matter of fact* and *undoubtedly*, which violate journalistic objectivity.

CHAPTER 4

Writing News for Radio and Television

When a duck boat sank with 31 people aboard at Table Rock Lake near Branson, Missouri, 17 were killed, nine of them from one family, and 14 survived. The boat, just minutes from land and safe haven, went under in choppy waters caused by a squall that accompanied a fast-moving thunderstorm. Passengers and crew members of the nearby Branson Belle, a showboat preparing for a dinner cruise, watched in horror as the duck boat sank. Some helped rescue the survivors. Others captured the fateful moments on video with their mobile phones.

Those amateur videos were picked up by nearby television stations and the national media, and almost instantly word of the tragedy spread throughout the world. Soon, television reporters would do their own reporting, interviewing those involved in the rescue and recovery effort while picking up the amateur video. Television is at its best in such moments. No other news medium can cover events of this sort more dramatically.

For decades now, most Americans have said they prefer getting news from television rather than print. The video is often captivating. And, because time is precious for most of us, the prevailing attitude seems to be, "Just tell me what I need to know." Television does that by giving you the news concisely in casual, conversational fashion.

At television stations — and in radio — that means writing the news in a casual way as if the reporter or anchor is speaking directly to you, including the use of nonstandard English that we find common in spoken communication — the widespread use of contractions, colloquialisms and even sentence fragments. Some of that usually wouldn't pass muster in a newspaper or magazine newsroom, but in television they're just fine because they convey the feel of spoken communication.

So, it's fair to say that radio and television journalists don't always organize sentences and stories like their print counterparts. Some of the differences are apparent. Newspapers and magazines stress the written word but may contain illustrations and photographs. Radio stresses the spoken word and has no pictures at all other than the mental ones it stimulates through sound portraits. Television stresses moving pictures and the sound of the spoken word. The web, of course, can do all the above, which means that journalists writing for websites may well use all those techniques.

Less obvious to casual readers, listeners and viewers is that different media *require* news stories to be worded differently. A sentence that reads well in a newspaper or magazine or online might be hard to understand when read aloud on the radio. Likewise, something that might be conversational on radio or television could look wordy or grammatically incorrect in print or on a smartphone or tablet.

Print-journalism students who have received news most of their lives mainly through television and radio often have to learn to adjust to the more formal wording of print. Radio and television students, meanwhile, have to learn how to write for the ear and not for the page, which differs from the more formal, less conversational style they learned while writing term papers in school. Increasingly, however, they have to do both. Their radio and television websites must have stories written more like newspaper articles than scripts. Online journalists have to adjust to the reality that news presented in that medium may well have audio and video as well as text and graphics. The result is that in today's world aspiring journalists must be prepared to write for *any* medium.

Sometimes, when students take classes in print, broadcast and online journalism, they get confused by differing advice they hear in their classes, not realizing that those discrepancies may stem from differences in the media and the kinds of writing they require. Underneath it all, print, broadcast and online news writing have much in common: They all report news that's relevant to their audiences in a manner that's timely and interesting.

Some journalism students choose to learn about writing for other media as a way to expand their job opportunities. Some journalists do it in search of tips from a related field that they may be able to apply to what they're already doing. But most of us have found we need to learn skills outside our medium of choice because online journalism—with its ability to offer multimedia content—becomes more dominant as technology continues to change.

Print and Online Versus Radio and Television News

Print news is written for the eye and is typically longer—and more thorough—than broadcast news, which is written for the ear. Online news stories aren't typically as long as print stories, although they can be, but are mainly designed to appeal to readers in more of a hurry. When you pop the hoods, though, you find that the three vehicles for news have more in common than they have differences. That shouldn't come as a surprise, given that newspaper and magazine journalists pioneered radio and television news writing. They moved to radio and television as new opportunities arose, just as many journalists today are moving to online media.

Radio and television writing requires less knowledge of style rules and editing symbols than do print and online journalism, so people who are considering different careers in journalism should hold themselves, at least as students, to meeting the greater demands of the written media in these areas. But that doesn't mean writing for radio and television isn't as demanding. It can be just as—or even more—demanding of a journalist's knowledge and skills.

For example, radio and television journalists need to pay more attention to how words sound. They must be even more concise and more conversational in their writing. They also need to know in what order details should be presented to be understood best by someone listening—someone who doesn't have the luxury of being able to look back to the previous sentence or paragraph if something important slipped by unheard. Of course, the time constraints of radio and television news, as well as the need to match words with audio and video, place additional demands on radio and television writers.

Even journalism and communications students who are not primarily studying radio and television journalism should take a broadcast class or two and perhaps even volunteer to write news at the campus radio or television station. They'll have the opportunity to hear additional journalists' viewpoints; get practical news experience; acquire audio- and video-editing skills; and learn to write more conversationally, focus their angle on people, tighten their writing and, when necessary, cut stories quickly while keeping them focused on the main points.

Here are some major guidelines for writing radio and television news:

Use a Conversational Style

Radio and television news must be written for the ear. When it's read over the air, it should sound conversational, not stilted. Keep the sentences short—an average of about 15 words, rarely more than 25. Keep the sentence structure as simple as possible, and use active-voice verbs whenever you can. Read your copy aloud (or at least faintly mumbling to yourself) to make sure it doesn't sound awkward or artificial.

Radio and television news should sound informal, not stuffy. The following suggestions are especially useful for those in radio and television, although there is nothing wrong with using most of them in print or online, too—except in the most formal situations.

Note that the examples in this chapter are written in radio and television style, which is summarized on Pages 60–64. Look for the differences in mechanics, such as the treatment of abbreviations and numbers, from the style used for print and online stories, which appears in the appendix.

Try to keep sentences only one thought long. It's usually better not to tack on additional thoughts.

NOT CONVERSATIONAL A local student, Latisha Green, who is one of only 10 students selected nationally, will get to shake hands with the president today.

CONVERSATIONAL A local student will get to shake hands with the president today. Latisha Green is one of only 10 students selected nationally.

Avoid vocabulary or wording that people don't usually use in conversation.

PRINT WORDING The three youths . . .

[Does anyone actually say *youths?* Wouldn't somebody instead say teenagers or something similar?]

PRINT WORDING Judith Cushing, 33, said . . .

(Again, no one would say this. It's just the way newspaper reporters write. People would say something more like *33-year-old Judith Cushing said*. But ages are seldom used in radio and television news, anyway, except in describing children.)

Use contractions — that's how people talk.

TOO FORMAL The president says he cannot attend.

RADIO AND TELEVISION STYLE The president says he can't attend.

It's okay to start a sentence with *and* or *but*.

And that was just in the first game.

But economists are saying next year could be worse.

It's okay to use dashes for dramatic pauses. Some stations prefer ellipses.

CNN reports that since the verdict, ratings have dropped 80 percent — [or . . .] from a rating of three-point-five down to zero-point-seven.

Personalize the News

The faces and voices of television and radio reporters and anchors are familiar to their audience, and part of their success or failure can be attributed to how the audience relates to them personally. By contrast, print and online journalists usually establish far less personal rapport unless they're columnists, bloggers or highly skilled feature writers or sportswriters.

As a result, a radio or television audience may put pressure on newscasters to be personally likable. This can result in more stress on personality in reporting, which can lead to a subtle blurring between news and commentary.

For instance, look at the following statement:

Drivers should use caution today when driving on I-94 near downtown.

This sentence isn't really objective because they are personal expressions offering advice. (See Pages 25–28.)

By contrast, here's a more objective statement, one that might follow such sentences in a radio or television story:

Road work has reduced traffic to one lane in both directions.

[No value judgment or advice is offered.]

But radio and television news generally allows more leeway for expressing personal judgments — especially those that would get little disagreement, such as suggesting that drivers use caution. Such statements have increasingly found their way into print and online news as well.

Make It Easy to Understand

Radio and television news has to be written in an order that lets the audience catch the news in one hearing. We'll go into more detail later about the order of information in a radio and television lead, but here are four general suggestions to help you write news for the listener's ear.

Get to the main point at the start of the sentence, not at the end.

Don't begin the sentence with a dependent clause, prepositional phrase or participial phrase (See Part Two of this book for discussion of grammar terms) that introduces details before we know the subject.

CONFUSING WHEN HEARD Because of reports from the National Weather Service that a thunderstorm is on the way, you may want to take an umbrella along if you're going to the White Sox game.

[The dependent clause at the beginning makes this sentence difficult for a listener to follow.]

CLEARER WHEN HEARD You may want to take an umbrella along if you're going to the White Sox game. The National Weather Service reports a thunderstorm on the way.

Avoiding such details before the subject of the sentence is introduced also fixes the problem of lack of attribution that sometimes creeps in when writers begin with a participial phrase.

NO ATTRIBUTION Believing that Governor Sam Wilson is vulnerable because of his abortion-rights stand, a second candidate has announced she'll run in the Republican primary.

[The reporter is not a mind reader, presumably, but the sentence never attributes how she or he knows what the candidate believes. Similar words that evade attribution include *thinking* and *feeling*.]

SUBJECT FIRST AND STATEMENT ATTRIBUTED A second candidate has announced she will run in the Republican gubernatorial primary. Jill Xavier says she thinks most voters disagree with Governor Sam Wilson's abortion-rights stand.

[Notice that this wording also lets the reporter more easily expand on what before had been the dependent clause.]

Writing News for
Radio and Television

Start with a general statement to attract the audience's attention, putting listeners on alert for what's to come.

> Area motorists are having trouble getting home tonight. Chicago police are reporting 33 fender benders already as the blizzard reduces visibility and makes roadways slick.

Most newspaper editors would cut the first sentence of a lead like that (even if a newspaper could report events as they were happening), as would online editors. In print, that sentence seems to be a delay and, perhaps even more, a comment rather than an objective observation. For most print journalists, the second sentence contains the real lead.

Repeat key information for someone who has just tuned in or who may have caught part of a longer story but missed an essential element.

Especially in a longer or particularly important story, the newscaster may repeat *who* was involved, *what* happened (such as a key sports score) or *where* the event occurred.

Rewrite phrases containing a word that has a *homonym* (a word that sounds like another word) that a listener could reasonably confuse with the intended word.

> *comity* of nations [Or was it *comedy* of nations?]
>
> steel *magnate* [Or was it steel *magnet*?]

Keep It Short

Print, online, and radio and television media all stress tight, concise writing, although radio and television leads are often more general than print and online leads.

The sentences and paragraphs in newspaper, online, and radio and television writing are shorter than those in magazine and book prose. Those in radio and television are even a little shorter than those in newspapers and on websites, especially the sentences.

Newspaper, online, and radio and television stories also tend to be shorter than those in magazines, and radio and television stories average the shortest. Most radio and television stories are told in 20 to 30 seconds. Rarely does a radio or television story go more than two minutes except on noncommercial public radio or commercial all-news television or radio stations.

Keep It Timely

News delivered electronically can be more up-to-the-minute than news that's been set in print and delivered by carriers. As a result, newscasters use different conventions of news writing from what print journalists do when it comes to time elements.

Radio and television journalists write even hard-news stories in the present tense.

Radio and television journalists tend to write about news happening this day, this hour, even this minute. Print news, especially in this age of morning newspaper dominance over afternoon newspapers, is often a day old.

Radio and television journalists also are less likely to report news of events happening days or weeks away than newspapers are.

For this reason, getting verb tenses and time elements straight tends to be easier in radio and television than in print.

Make It Clear

Many entries in the wire-service stylebooks are devoted to getting things right that could appear wrong when a reader looks at them. Radio and television style involves making things *look* clear to the newscaster, who must then make them *sound* clear to the listeners.

Students taking classes in both print, radio and television should note that in some cases, the style rules differ between these fields. See the appendix and Pages 60–64 for summaries of the most common rules for each.

Radio and Television Journalists Must Know Grammar

Don't let the fact that radio and television news is more conversational than print or online news fool you into thinking that the rules of grammar can be ignored.

If students want to improve their writing for radio and television, they should watch their usage and check their subject-verb agreement and pronoun-antecedent agreement. Newscasts demand that the news be written in clear, simple sentences that avoid dependent clauses and that adjectives and adverbs be cut as much as possible. To follow such advice, newscasters must know grammar.

One of the best books we've seen on improving radio and television news copy is *Rewriting Network News* by Mervin Block, a former staff writer for the ABC and CBS evening news shows. His book looks at examples from 345 television and radio news scripts and demonstrates how they could be improved by closer attention to grammar, usage, tightening and order of details. The lessons are useful for print and online journalists, as well.

Good writing means knowing how to put the best words in the best order, and that's what grammar and usage are all about.

Writing News for
Radio and Television

Radio and Television Journalists Must Know Pronunciation

Mispronunciation is to broadcasting what misspelling is to print: It damages your credibility, especially with many educated people.

Many pronunciation problems are common, but as with usage errors in print, pronunciation "errors" sometimes result from regional or dialect differences. This can be a problem, depending on the formality of the broadcast. For example, sports broadcasters often speak the language of players, not necessarily of a social elite, and this has come to be accepted.

Just as we don't have a problem with different levels of formality in the media, depending on the type of communication, we don't really have a problem with dialect differences among broadcasters. Linguists will tell you that no dialect is superior or inferior to another. But Americans often have a prejudice in favor of those they think sound more "elegant" or educated, such as Bostonian or Virginian, and against those they think sound less so, especially South Midland (spoken in many Southern states), African-American dialect or those from New York, such as "Nanny" actress Fran Drescher's Queens accent. There are even language schools for businesspeople to attend to help them lose what might be seen as a less-favored dialect and acquire a more neutral one.

At many if not most stations around the country, broadcasters tend to speak what has been called American "Broadcast Standard English," which we'd describe as essentially the less-identifiable dialect of the American Midwest—especially of the area near where Missouri, Kansas and Nebraska meet—or farther west, that of California (minus the "Valley Girl" dialect).

Here's a list of some of the most commonly mispronounced words. We've also included a few words you might wonder how to pronounce correctly but that have more than one accepted pronunciation. (When looking up pronunciation of words here, as in a dictionary, it's generally better to choose the first acceptable one.) In a few cases, where the pronunciation difference hinges on placement of syllable stress, we've indicated that by capitalizing all of the letters in the stressed syllable.

WORD	WRONG	RIGHT
accessory	a-ses-or-ee	ak-ses-or-ee
advertisement	—	ad-ver-TIZE-ment, ad-VER-tihz-ment
affidavit	af-a-day-vid	af-a-day-vit
ambulance	am-bew-LANCE	AM-bew-luns
Arctic	Ar-tik	Ark-tik
ask	ax	Ask
asterisk	ass-ter-ik	ass-ter-isk
business	bid-ness	biz-ness

WORD	WRONG	RIGHT
cache	cash-ay	Cash
cacophony	car-caf-in-ee	car-cof-in-ee
candidate	can-uh-date	can-dih-date
clothes	cloze	Clohthz
coupon	—	koo-pon, que-pon
decrepit	dee-creh-pid	dee-creh-pit
electoral	elec-TOR-al	e-LEC-tor-al
envelope	—	on(en)-vuh-lope,
escape	ex-cape	es-cayp
especially	ex-speh-shal-ee	es-peh-shal-ee
espresso	ex-press-oh	eh-spres-oh
etc.	ex-cet-er-a	et-cet-er-a
extraordinary	ex-tra-OR-din-ar- y	ex-TROR-din-ar-y
February	Feb-u-ary	Fch-brew-ary
federal	fed-ral	fed-er-al
film	fill-um	Fillm
foliage	foil-ehj	fo-lee-ehj
forte	fort	for-tay
height	high-th	Hight
heinous	hay-nee-us	hay-nus
homogenous	ho-mo-GEE-nee-us	huh-MAH-jin-us
interesting	in-ter-est-ing	in-trest-ing
isn't	id-ent	iz-ent
jewelry	jule-ree	jule-er-ee
just	Jist	Just
Ku Klux Klan	Klew-Klux-Klan	Kew-Klux-Klan
larynx	lair-niks	lair-inks
liable	lie-bel	lie-uh-bel
library	lie-ber-ree	lie-brair-ee
long-lived	long-lihvd	long-lievd
mayonnaise	man-ayz	may-oh-nayz
miniature	mih-ni-cher	mih-nee-uh-cher
mischievous	miss-CHEE-vee-us	MIS-chih-vus
nuclear	new-que-lar	new-clee-er
nuptial	nup-shoo-ul,	nup-shuhl,
	nup-chew-ul	nup-chuhl
often	off-ten	off-en
ordnance	or-din-ance	ord-nance

WORD	WRONG	RIGHT
ostensibly	ah-stens-iv-lee	ah-stens-ib-lee
percolate	per-que-late	per-cuh-layt
peremptory	pree-em-tor-ee	per-emp-tor-ee
perspire	pruh-spire	per-spire
police	POH-lees	poh-LEES, puh-lees
potable	pot-uh-bul	poh-tu-buhl
prerogative	per-og-uh-tiv	pree-rog-uh-tiv
		prih-rog-uh-tiv
prescription	per-skrip-shun	pree-skrip-shun,
		prih-skrip-shun
probably	prob-lee,	PROB-uh-blee
	prob-uh-BLEE	
pronunciation	pro-noun-see-ay-shen	pro-nun-see-ay-shen
prostate	prah-strate	prah-state
realtor	reel-uh-tor	ree-uhl-tor
recur	ree-oh-ker	ree-ker
respite	ruh-spite	res-pit
silicon	sill-uh-kone	sill-uh-kon
strategy	shtrat-uh-gee	stra-tuh-gee
strength	strinth, shtrinth	straynk-th
supposedly	suh-pose-a-blee	suh-pose-ed-lee
supremacist	suh-prem-ist	suh-prem-a-sist
tenet	ten-ehnt	ten-et
Tijuana	Tee-a-wah-nuh	Tee-wah-nuh
triathlon	try-ath-a-lon	try-ath-lon
utmost	up-most	ut-most
verbiage	verb-uhj	verb-ee-uhj
wheelbarrow	wheel-bare-uhl	wheel-bare-oh
zoology	zoo-ol-oh-gee	zoh-ol-oh-gee

Radio and Television Hard-News Leads

Radio and television hard-news leads typically present the same five main elements in the same order as print leads, but the wording of these elements often differs. As with a newspaper lead, the first two items, *who* and *what*, are the most essential. *Time*, *day* and *place* may appear later or even not at all, depending on the nature of the story.

Start with the *Who*

If there's any identification or title with the name, put the ID or title before the name.

> **PRINT STYLE** Dennis Archer, former mayor of Detroit, will speak to the Legion of Black Collegians . . .

> **RADIO AND TELEVISION STYLE** Former Detroit Mayor Dennis Archer will speak to the Legion of Black Collegians . . .

Although many print and online reporters would also write that sentence in the radio and television style, the second example is clearly preferred in radio and television.

Generally, put the attribution at the beginning of the sentence and before the verb.

> **PRINT STYLE** Home sales rose in September to the highest level since the housing-market collapse of 2008, according to a report Wednesday from the National Association of Realtors.

> **RADIO AND TELEVISION STYLE** The National Association of Realtors reports home sales rose in September. They were up to the highest level since the housing-market collapse of 2008.

If the *who* involves a number of people, don't start the lead with the number because readers have not yet heard what subject the number modifies.

> **PRINT STYLE** Five people died and 15 more were injured when an Amtrak train left the tracks near St. Louis this morning.

That lead conforms to the injunction in newspaper journalism that you should lead with what's most important — in this case, that five people died and 15 were injured, not that a train had left the tracks. But newscasters would typically invert the information and write something like this:

> **RADIO AND TELEVISION STYLE** An Amtrak train left the tracks near Saint Louis this morning. Five people were killed and another 15 were hurt.

What Happened?

Use the present tense or present progressive as much as possible, rather than the past tense or present-perfect tense used in newspaper and magazine hard-news stories. (See Chapter 12.)

> **PRINT STYLE** The Republicans *have called* for Medicare cuts.

> **RADIO AND TELEVISION STYLE** The Republicans *are calling* for Medicare cuts.

In this regard, radio and television news is like a print soft-news story. This style point also stresses an advantage radio and television news has over print news: Radio and television can be more timely and up-to-the-minute.

When attributing quotes, don't write someone *said* but someone *says*.

PRINT STYLE Columbia Mayor Bob McDavid said . . .

RADIO AND TELEVISION STYLE Columbia Mayor Bob McDavid says . . .

If the past tense must be used in the lead, include the time element after it.

Speaker of the House Nancy Pelosi said last night. . . .

Put a verb in the lead, as in any other sentence.

Some news directors won't allow any fragments in news copy at their stations. Some permit an occasional fragment if it sounds conversational, but most object to fragments being overused.

For example, many newscasters have overreacted to the common advice that they should avoid the verb *to be* in leads whenever possible and end up with nongrammatical (or we could say headline-style) leads like this:

Owners selling the Tampa Bay Rays.

Without the *are* in front of *selling*, that sentence has just a participle, not a verb. Try this instead:

Owners say they want to sell the Tampa Bay Rays.

Granted, some newscasters occasionally leave out the verb *to be* for some punch.

Another victory in progress at Fenway Park.

But couldn't that fragment have just as much punch if it were recast into a sentence?

It looks as if the Red Sox can chalk up another victory.

Other Points to Remember

Don't say *today* if you can avoid it.

Stress timeliness, and give the story the most up-to-the-minute news peg you can. Say *this morning*, *this afternoon* or *this evening*.

If the news comes from a previous day, it's probably not news in radio and television. An upcoming event more than a week off would probably not be in today's radio and television newscast.

Most references to other days are likely to be within the upcoming week and will simply be referred to as *Thursday*, *Saturday* and so on. An event further off would most likely be referred to as *next week*, in *three weeks*, *next month* and so on.

Street addresses of people or businesses in the news are not used in radio and television in the routine way they are in print.

Radio and Television Story Structure

Radio and television news is typically written to an assigned length of time, often 20 to 30 seconds. So, the journalist writes the average number of words that could be read in the time allotted. After the lead come the most important and interesting details—as many as will fit conversationally in the time slot.

Radio and television stories are like feature stories in print in that they need not only a strong beginning but also a strong ending. In radio and television, the last sentence is called the *snapper*, and, as the name implies, it must have some snap to it.

The snapper may be the punch line for a humorous story, a simple restatement of the main point, a statement putting the story in context or telling the audience what it means, a line quoting a different side of a dispute or a subject stating "no comment" in a controversial story. The one requirement is that the snapper gives the listener a definite sense of closure—that it sounds like an ending. Consider these types of snappers.

Punch-line snapper:

Next time, she says, she'll take the bus.

Restatement snapper:

Once again, Toledo's mayor says he won't run for re-election.

"What it means" snapper:

That would mean property taxes on an average 220-thousand-dollar home would go up 220-dollars a year.

"Other side" snapper:

Pettit says he'll appeal.

"No comment" snapper:

We asked the commissioner to respond to the allegations, but he said he had no comment.

Some snappers have been done so often, they're as stale as the cliché leads we discussed in Chapter 3 (Pages 43–45). Here are a few canned snappers we'd like to see tossed.

The "one thing is certain" ending:

The election results are a week away, but one thing is certain: The winner will be left-handed.

The "only time will tell" ending:

So will it be global warming or global cooling? Only time will tell.

The "riding the elephant" ending:

At the zoo, this is Bill Gahan for Eyewitness News.

[The camera pulls back to reveal the reporter is riding an elephant.]

The late Charles Kuralt, famous for his "On the Road" series, once said this last ending was one of the biggest clichés he noticed in local television news as he traveled the country. That was years ago, but it's still the case that reporters too often think it's clever for the final shot of a feature story to show them good-naturedly participating in an event they are covering, especially if it shows them doing something ridiculous.

Radio and Television Style Summary

Preparing Your Manuscript for Radio

Here are a few guidelines on manuscript preparation at radio stations:

- Most stations want you to triple-space your news copy, although some say double-space.
- Many stations want you to write in all capital letters. We think this is harder to read, but follow your station's conventions on this and other matters.
- In the upper-left corner, type the following information in this order:

    Story's slug (identification) on the first line.

    Time of the newscast.

    Date of the newscast.

    Reporter's name.

    Also at the top, or at the bottom at some stations, you should put a colon followed by the time in seconds it takes to read the story (for example, *:18*), and then circle the time.

- The copy should be typed 70 characters per line — some stations say 60. For the purpose of timing, figure that the newscaster will read aloud about 15 lines a minute on average.
- The story should start 2 to 3 inches from the top of the page and stop at least an inch or two from the bottom. If the story is longer than that, put the word *MORE* in parentheses at the bottom center of the page. At the top of the next page, as the last line of the heading, type *FIRST ADD, SECOND ADD* and so on or *PAGE ONE OF THREE, PAGE TWO OF THREE* and so on. Type *ENDS* or three hash marks (# # #) at the bottom of the last page of a story.
- Don't split words at the end of a line, and don't split sentences across pages.

Preparing Your Manuscript for Television

- As with radio, most stations want you to triple-space your news copy, although some say double-space.

- Again, as with radio, many stations want you to write in all capital letters. We think this is harder to read, but follow your station's conventions on this and other matters.

- Across the top, on one line, write the time of the newscast, the date, the story slug and the reporter's name.

- Set the copy at 40 characters per line in a column on the right side of the page. It should take the newscaster a minute to read about 25 lines.

- To the left of the news copy, type in all capital letters a description of the video and audio, the timed length and any instructions, such as whether the sound should be turned off or a title superimposed.

- If the story goes more than one page, type *MORE* in parentheses at the bottom center of the page. At the top of the next page, under the slug, type *FIRST ADD, SECOND ADD* and so on or *PAGE ONE OF THREE, PAGE TWO OF THREE* and so on. Type *ENDS* or three hash marks (# # #) at the bottom of the last page of a story. (If you're typing this for the teleprompter, this doesn't apply.)

- Don't split words at the end of a line, and don't split sentences across pages.

Editing and Other Symbols

For the most part, newscasters don't use the traditional copy-editing symbols used in the print media.

Instead, they simply mark a line through an error and write the correction above it. If a passage has several errors close together, it's better to cross out and rewrite that whole section rather than make the reader's eyes go up and down between errors.

Some of the few copy-editing symbols that have carried over from print to radio and television are those for deleting and inserting, closing spaces, and separating and connecting paragraphs.

Newscasters don't use the ¢ symbol for *cents*, $ for *dollars* or % for *percent*. They write out the word after the number and use a hyphen between them.

three-cents   25-dollars   13-percent

Pronunciation

Write the pronunciation of any difficult names phonetically in parentheses after the name.

Dmitri Shostakovich (duh-ME-tree shaw-stuh-KO-vich)

To make words easier to pronounce, many news writers add hyphens to words that don't have them in the dictionary.

hydro-electric   wood-stove

To indicate that a word should be stressed in a sentence, either underline it or write it in all caps.

What do you think about <u>that</u>?

Despite the rain, the parade WILL go on.

Abbreviations

In most cases, writers should avoid abbreviations in radio and television copy.

That includes no abbreviations for states, days of the week, months, military titles or countries other than the United States.

Some abbreviations are acceptable.

C-I-A, F-B-I, F-C-C, G-O-P, N-double-A-C-P, U-S
[Note the use of hyphens.]

a.m., p.m., Dr., Mr., Mrs., Ms.

When abbreviations form acronyms pronounced as one word, no hyphens or periods are used.

NATO

Interstate highways are almost always called by their abbreviated form in radio and television, even on first reference.

I-94

Numbers

As is generally the case with newspaper style, write out single-digit numbers. In addition, write out *eleven*, which sometimes poses problems when written as *11*. The numbers *10* and *12* through *999* should be written as numerals. For larger numbers, use a numeral up to three digits long followed by a hyphen and the word *thousand, million, billion* or *trillion*:

6-thousand   160-billion

Write sports scores and stock index numbers as numerals even if they are in single digits.

score of 6 to 4   The Dow Jones index is down 110 points.

Write out fractions in words.

one-half   two-and-three-eighths

Write out decimal numbers in words.

twenty-point-six   one-point-five-trillion

Break street addresses and years into pronounceable units of numerals.

13-0-1 East   William Street the year 20-10

Add *nd*, *rd*, *st* or *th* to the end of numerals whenever the number would be pronounced that way.

July 20th   14th Amendment

Punctuation

The only punctuation marks newscasters typically use are the comma, hyphen, dash, period and question mark.

Newscasters use a dash in place of parentheses, a colon or a semicolon.

Because radio and television copy is written to be performed, it often makes sense to put in dashes or ellipses for longer, dramatic pauses.

At stores like this one, you can buy anything from special hiking shoes . . . to backpacks . . . to canoes. But most sales are of items like sleeping bags and down jackets — items that are practical even for those who only faintly hear the call of the wild.

Most newscasters don't use quotations in their copy because it's awkward to convey in words where a quote begins and ends.

Saying "quote" at the beginning and "unquote" at the end of a quotation sounds too awkward and formal, although some newscasters will say "quote" without the "unquote" or use a phrase such as "to quote the mayor." It's better to use a sound bite, to paraphrase a quote to avoid the problem or, when the exact words are required, to write something like "what he termed," "as she put it" or "in his words" to alert the newscaster that it's a quote.

Use a hyphen between a numeral and the word *cent* or *cents*, *dollar* or *dollars*, *percent*, *thousand*, *million*, *billion* or *trillion*:

20-dollars   three-percent   105-thousand   six-million

Names

Unlike in print style, it's not always necessary to give famous names in their entirety on first reference:

President Trump   Governor Parson

Unlike in newspapers, middle initials should be used only to distinguish someone with a name similar to that of another, and a nickname should be used only with the last name, not following the first name.

George W. Bush [to distinguish him from his father, George H. W. Bush]

Sly Stallone [not Sylvester "Sly" Stallone]

Spelling

Why worry about spelling when your audience will never know whether the words they hear read were spelled the way the dictionary says? Because misspelled words may cause the newscaster to stumble, pause or mispronounce the word. Even if the spellings are recognizable, misspellings will lower the respect your colleagues in the newsroom have for you.

CHAPTER 5

Writing News for Online and Mobile Media

When President Donald Trump met North Korean leader Kim Jong-un for a historic summit in Singapore, the world watched closely to see what would come of it. Arguably, no media organization covered it better than the British Broadcasting Corporation and its website, *BBC News* (www.bbc.co.uk). That's no surprise to those who follow international news closely. When it comes to providing quality international news in depth, the BBC excels. To illustrate, here's a list of the headlines that resulted:

- Trump–Kim summit: What happens next?
- The hidden messages in Trump–Kim gestures.
- Trump and Kim: An on/off bromance.
- Trump and Kim: From enemies to frenemies?
- The moment when Donald Trump and Kim Jong-un shook hands.
- Trump–Kim summit: Win–win or a Kim win?

And those headlines were merely for the news video clips. Stories worthy of the best world newspapers led the package, which, in typical BBC style, showed that its editors possess an amazing understanding of the power of web communication and how to deploy it. Written stories appeared in chunks instead of long, unrelieved newspaper-style stories; photos, charts and graphics abounded; and videos were sprinkled throughout. There was something to match the attention span of all — from those who usually read only headlines to those who want news in depth.

That Herculean effort shows how traditional media companies are beginning to understand the importance of the web in news dissemination. But for every news organization like the BBC, there are still others stuck in the past that simply place on the web the same stories used in traditional media. They make little effort to add value by taking advantage of the web's ability to offer not only text and photos but also audio, video, maps, database access and even interactive graphics.

Slowly, though, even newspapers—among the most traditional media outlets—are investing increasing time and effort into making the web *the* place to visit for the latest news. Among the leaders in that industry is *The New York Times*, a publication often seen as stodgy in its print incarnation. Its website, however, is home to some of the best journalism practiced on the web. The *Times'* graphics department has become the national leader in producing marvelous interactive graphics that engage readers in ways other media cannot. Occasionally, readers are even allowed access to databases of interest.

It's also important to remember that news is increasingly consumed on smartphones and tablets and less frequently on desktop and laptop computers. Many websites now employ software to transform stories for easy readability on such devices, and brevity is of even greater importance when stories are delivered for such formats. Short stories with links to more information are ideal.

Newspapers also are adjusting to the fact that they now need to be digital-first operations that embrace the use of social media sites like *Twitter* and *Facebook*, as well as mobile-based applications such as *Instagram* and *Snapchat*, to drive traffic to their sites.

All this is changing not only the way news and feature information is presented but also how it is written. In this chapter, we look at current best practices for writing online media. But first, let's review the advantages of using online media over those of the traditional media:

- Distribution is instantaneous, like radio and television but unlike newspapers and magazines.

- Information is often thorough and detailed, as in newspapers and magazines, unlike radio and television (except, perhaps, for the cable networks).

- Users not only partake of what editors offer but also sift through original information themselves.

- Users can comment on stories in real time and discuss opinions with other users.

- The web is nonlinear. That is, consumers don't have to follow a story from top to bottom or start to finish. They can jump around to bits and pieces of the story or related material as desired.

- Databases and the capability of delivering animation, audio and video offer a combination possible in no other medium, including radio and television. Television simply cannot deliver database material, and it seldom carries in-depth information on *any* story.

- Readers often skim rather than read, so headlines and leads are even more critical in online and mobile media than they are in print, and short articles—or articles broken into more manageable chunks—are much preferred.

There are, however, a couple of significant problems with using online and mobile media.

- Writers and editors often display an astounding inability to learn the best ways to write for it.
- In a medium in which anyone can become a publisher, there are significant concerns about how to evaluate the reliability of the information being offered.

Let's examine online media in more detail.

Online Media Are Unique

When radio and television came along, the first newscasters simply read news over the air just as it was written for newspapers. That often was the medium from which they came, and they understood the art of crafting a news story for print.

It soon became obvious, however, that the writing formula had to change for radio and even more for television. The way we speak is not the way we write, and broadcast journalism had to make those adjustments. For the most part, they weren't dramatic differences but subtle ones. The tone had to be more conversational, and tough-to-pronounce phrases had to become more casual. When television arrived, the words and pictures had to be melded to tell a story. But through it all, the basics of good journalism—articulated in Chapters 1 and 2— remained: Be clear. Be correct. Be concise.

And just as the arrival of radio and television required journalists to rethink the way news was presented, so, too, has the arrival of the web.

Clarity on the web is the same as in print journalism. It's particularly important for web stories to be complete. Journalists need to anticipate and answer all the questions a reader might ask so that readers don't turn elsewhere for information.

Correctness leads to credibility and, on the web, where there are so many contradictory sources of information, credibility is one of the keys to success. If a source is consistently or even often wrong, its credibility wanes. Credibility keeps people coming back. Correct use of language, grammar and style also tell readers that a site has high professional standards.

Conciseness is a major virtue on the web, where hooking a reader must be accomplished in one computer screen (or, more difficult, one smartphone screen) of information. Links beyond that page provide volumes of depth, or what those who write for the web call *layering*. But if readers aren't hooked on Page 1, they will never get to the rest of the story, no matter how good it may be.

Let's examine each of these issues in more detail.

Be Clear

In the traditional media, clarity refers to conveying a message in ways that are easy to understand and also not contradictory. Lack of clarity creeps into a news report when it fails to answer questions that readers are likely to ask or when fuzzy writing fails to lead the reader from one thought to the next. Even annoying minor errors can cause readers to quit reading, such as when a person's name is spelled one way in the first part of the story and another way toward the end. It also results when numbers don't add up within a story or when we say one thing in the main story and another in a sidebar.

All the guidelines for writing clearly in print (see Chapter 3) also apply to writing for online media. Because of the 24/7 news cycle on the web, though, writers need to be particularly careful to explain emerging details as clearly as possible with each new version of a story and to anticipate readers' questions and responses.

Be Correct (and Credible)

The web is full of false information or information provided by people with a cause to promote. Sorting fact from opinion can be difficult. If the source is a respected organization, such as *The New York Times*, *The Washington Post* or *The Wall Street Journal*, most journalists would consider the information to be trustworthy. But if it is published by an organization promoting a cause or a business promoting a service or product, there is ample reason to be wary.

Online journalists can go wrong in two ways. First, they can use information from unreliable sources. Second, they can provide web links to unreliable sources. Stan Ketterer, a journalist and journalism educator, suggests that journalists evaluate information on the web by following the same journalistic practices they use for assessing the credibility and accuracy of any other information. He developed these guidelines:

Before using information from a web page in a story, verify it with a source.

The exceptions to this rule include taking information from a highly credible government site, such as the Census Bureau, or not being able to contact the source on a breaking story because of time constraints. An editor must clear all exceptions.

In most cases, information taken from the web and used in a story must be attributed.

If you have verified the information on a home page with a source, you can use the organization in the attribution—for example, "according to the EPA" or "EPA figures show." If you cannot verify the information after trying repeatedly, attribute unverified information to the web page—for example, "according to the Voice of America's website." Consult your editor before using unverified information.

If you have doubts about the accuracy of the information and you cannot reach the source, get it from another source, such as a book or a contact person. When in doubt, omit the information.

Check the extension on the site's web address for clues as to the nature of the organization and the likely slant of the information.

The most common extensions used in the U.S. are *.gov* (government), *.edu* (education), *.com* (commercial), *.mil* (military), *.org* (not-for-profit organization) and *.net* (internet administration). Most government and military sites have credible and accurate information. In many cases, you can take the information directly from the site and attribute it to the organization. But consult your editor until you get to know these sites.

Follow accepted standards of evaluating web information.

If college and university sites have source documents, such as the Constitution, attribute the information to the source document. But beware. Personal home pages of students often have *.edu* extensions, and the information on them is not always credible. Do not use information from a personal home page without contacting the person and without the permission of your editor.

Verify and attribute all information found on the home pages of commercial and not-for-profit organizations.

Don't assume information you find on blogs is accurate. Blogs contain plenty of erroneous information.

Check the date when the page was last updated. If no date appears, if the site has not been updated for a while or if it was created some time ago, do not use the information unless you verify it with a source.

The date generally appears at the top or bottom of the first page of the site. Although a recent date does not ensure the information is current, it does indicate the organization is paying attention to the site.

Using the web as a source of information is no riskier than using books, magazines or other printed material, provided you use common sense. Remember, too, that material on the web is subject to copyright laws. Taking care to use only credible sources and to abide by copyright laws will enhance your own credibility.

Be Concise

In addition to making sure their writing is tight, web journalists use a technique called layering to give readers just as much information as they want, without forcing them to read what they don't want.

Typically, the first layer is roughly equivalent to a newspaper headline or magazine article title plus a lead. Often, there is a secondary headline or sentence that gives consumers more information as a tease to read the complete story. If readers are hooked, they will click on the headline to get to the next layer of information, often a complete newspaper-length story (although preferably divided into chunks to make it more consumable online). Then another layer may consist of internal links to earlier stories or stories on the same subject and external links to source material. Links to audio, video, graphics or animations that complete the story may constitute another layer. Readers decide how far into the story to go and jump in non-linear fashion from one item to the next.

Writing and Presenting News Online

When it comes to the actual composition of web stories, writers and editors for digital media often work with storyboards, computerized templates that help them format content for the web. The template organizes the story's layers with items such as the following.

1. Headline or title.
2. One-sentence tease, or lead.
3. First page or quick summary of what happened, not unlike a short radio or television story.
4. Accompanying visuals, usually photos or graphics.
5. Accompanying audio and video, if any.
6. Depth report, likely further layered or divided into chunks.
7. Links—both internal and external.

At a newspaper, magazine, or radio or television station, the work of assembling those items traditionally was parceled out to reporters, graphic artists, photographers, videographers and editors. In a contemporary news-room, one person may well handle most or all of those functions. That's because today's journalist is expected to be adept in handling all aspects of multimedia journalism.

There is no one way to produce a story for the web. A short, quick story may lend itself to the classic newspaper inverted-pyramid writing style. A more complex one may require links to audio, video and still pho-tos with multiple layers of text. Major projects may require even more complex forms of storytelling. Almost without exception, the best way to tell any story on the web is with a combination of media.

The toughest part of preparing such a site is knowing how to prepare the text. Researchers John Morkes and Jakob Nielsen studied just that by taking a website's content and rewriting it. They found that web users prefer writing that is concise, easy to scan and objective rather than promotional.

We've discussed conciseness in this chapter and in Chapter 2, and we covered objectivity in that chapter as well. But what makes a story scannable? John Morkes and Jakob Nielsen found that readers don't *read* a web page—they *scan* it. Readers online—especially mobile readers—are surfers or scanners, much more so than readers of print—perhaps because it takes 25 percent longer to read online than it does in print. Online expert Shel Holtz says you want readers to dive, not to surf or scan. Surfing is what frustrated readers do. Here are some suggestions for writing on the web and for making divers of surfers—at least for holding their attention long enough to get your message across:

Make the story easy to scan.

In most cases, the inverted-pyramid writing style is best for the web because it gets to the gist of the news quickly. Adding links and graphics will also help to attract readers and perhaps cause them to stop and read.

Write concisely.

Use a fraction of the amount of text you would have used in print, perhaps as much as 50 percent less. Web users seldom read extended amounts of text, so make it easy for them by condensing.

Write in chunks.

Break longer stories into chunks that most often do not exceed what will fit on one screen. The chunks can be connected with hypertext links to make it easy for the readers to find and read the related chunk or chunks of most interest. Check longer stories on the BBC website for excellent examples of chunking to prevent lengthy sections of unbroken text.

Save readers' time.

The best way to save readers' time is to be clear. Choose simple words and verbs in the active voice; vary the length of sentences, but keep them short; write short paragraphs. Emphasize keywords by highlighting them or by putting them in color.

Write as if immediacy is a key issue.

It is, of course. Writing online is like writing for the wire services. Readers on the web now consume information the way only a wire-service subscriber used to be able to—as it happens. Keeping readers with you means keeping them informed up-to-the-minute. Update breaking stories quickly and add depth when it is available.

Help readers navigate.

Provide a table of contents, clear headings and useful links for additional information on a topic. Have clear entrances and exits; layer information in such a way that readers can choose the amount of information they need. Creating internal hyperlinks allows readers to click on information elsewhere on your site or find past stories on the same subject. External links lead readers to background information. To find appropriate external hyperlinks, you need to know how to use search engines such as Google *(www.google.com)*, Yahoo! *(www.yahoo.com)* and Bing *(www.bing.com)*.

You may also take readers down one path that branches into several others. Some call this technique "threading." Sports fans, for example, can enjoy seeing a whole gallery of shots from Saturday's championship game after reading about their team's win. They can read interviews from all the stars of the victory—or the defeat. In another example, the story of a plane crash can lead to various threads—the airline and its record of crashes, the plane itself, the record for that type of plane, the place of the accident, the people involved and more.

Use lots of lists and bullets.

Often you can cut copy by putting information into lists. Whenever you can make a list, do so. Lists get more attention and allow for better comprehension and more retention than ordinary sentences and paragraphs. Popular websites such as *BuzzFeed* originally gained momentum because of the quantity of lists they published, which were easy for audiences to read and share with others.

Think visually.

In the past, writers for print thought little about how their stories were going to appear. Television news writers know they must write to the pictures. Good television has good video; a visual medium tries to show rather than tell. Similarly, an online journalist must *think* both verbally and visually. This includes thinking not only about the organization of a page but also about ways to use graphics and icons online; how to make a site interactive; how to incorporate big data as a graph or chart; and how to employ other online tools like animation and video, the use of which is growing exponentially on websites throughout the world. A great example may be found at *Newsy (newsy.com)*, which compares the coverage of news from various traditional media outlets.

Give readers a chance to talk back.

Web readers want a chance to respond, and a big part of being interactive is allowing them to do just that. It's the journalist's job to make sure readers have the opportunity to give feedback. This can be achieved in a number of ways. You can give readers a chance to write directly to you, to your website or to the writer of a piece by including an email address, which is often part of the byline of newspapers like *Miami Herald*. Many radio and television stations, newspapers and magazines also allow readers to respond directly to stories on their websites. Readers also can comment on blogs or engage with others in chat rooms devoted to specific sites or interests.

SEO: Writing With Search Engines in Mind

It's almost impossible to overemphasize one additional consideration in writing for online media: If your online story cannot be found, it won't be read. That's why editors of websites place great emphasis on *search engine optimization*, the process of making sure your story will be found when someone searches for its topic on sites such as Google, Bing or Yahoo!

Newspapers and magazines are notorious for writing baseball stories that never mention the word *baseball* and hockey stories that never use the word *hockey*. That's fine if the story on the web contains *metadata* that include that search term. It matters not at all, though, if the user searches for the team name, such as Texas Rangers. That user will find your story even if the word *baseball* is not included. But what if the user searches for "baseball"? Your story will not be found without that word in the metadata. Understanding this is the key to making sure that possible search terms appear either in the metadata accompanying the story or in the story itself.

Many websites have protocols for ensuring that the proper terms are used, and several companies now offer services to ensure that content is maximized for search engines. That can be a wise investment for a website looking to grow readership.

Writing for International Audiences

Few U.S. media companies operate websites that are bilingual or multilingual, but many users do not speak English, Spanish or French as a first language. Ideally, websites would be multilingual, but providing staff for extensive translation is cost-prohibitive. Fortunately for the English-speaking world, English has become the most commonly used language in international commerce and interaction, so if a site must have only one language, English is usually the best choice.

Still, it's important to remember that the web is a worldwide medium, not a local one. At the least, plain language in writing and the avoidance of colloquialisms allow users throughout the world to better understand content. Simple writing also allows international users to more accurately run a story through online translation programs, such as Google Translate, and make sense of it.

Writing for Blogs

Blogs are an increasingly popular means of connecting with readers, and many traditional media operations have embraced them. If your job—whether as a reporter or an editor—requires you to write and maintain a blog, it's important to remember the difference between writing for traditional media and writing for a blog.

- Traditional journalism is formal, but blogging is informal.
- Traditional journalism is dispassionate, but much of blogging is passionate.

- Traditional journalism is written in the third person ("he," "she," "they"), but much of blogging is written in the first person ("I," "we").

- And while most traditional writing is vetted by multiple editors, much of blogging goes straight from writers to readers.

Not all blogs are written by journalists, of course, but when blogs are sponsored by a newspaper, magazine, or radio or television station, certain standards will apply. Each company sets its own standards, so if you are asked to blog, be sure to understand those limits. There are likely to be constraints on foul language, insults to readers and the like. None of that, however, should limit your ability to connect with readers.

David O'Brien, for example, was until recently *The Atlanta Journal-Constitution*'s beat writer who covered the Atlanta Braves. He has now moved to *The Athletic*, a new online-only, subscription-based publication that employs some of America's best sportswriters. When he wrote for the newspaper, his stories were traditional, but in his blog he wrote in first person, shared inside information about the team and even shared with readers his thoughts on the latest trends in music. Those notes on music closed each of his blogs. It's a totally informal approach that allowed him to connect with readers—almost all of whom were Atlanta Braves fans.

Reading blogs of this type is not unlike participating in a discussion while seated around a large table at a country store or while watching a game at a local bar in Boston. People aired their opinions freely, discussed what O'Brien had written and even got into passionate arguments about the virtues—or lack thereof—of the newest pitcher in the Braves' bullpen. O'Brien's blog was so popular that he had to write a new one every few days so readers were not overwhelmed with thousands of comments.

Journalism Tip
Editing Your Own Copy

One casualty of the rise of web-based journalism is quality editing. Increasingly, writers are asked to place tweets or blog posts on a website without that material being reviewed by an editor.

That's a scary prospect when one considers that a longtime axiom of journalism is this: Everyone needs a good editor. The publication of unedited copy increases the risk of grammatical and spelling errors, libel, slander and all sorts of related disasters.

Most editors would prefer that all such material go through the traditional editing process, but with cutbacks in newsrooms there simply aren't enough editors to make that feasible. Also, in an era where speed to the web is important, delays in getting the news online are unacceptable.

So, the publication of unedited copy is inevitable today. Here are some tips for disciplining yourself to engage in self-editing.

- Read through a tweet, a blog entry or a *Facebook* post at least three times before posting it. All of us miss things the first time or two around. Repeated reading of the item before it is posted can help prevent errors or embarrassment.

- Be sure you are using your word processor's grammar- and spell-checker features. Those aren't perfect, but they help.

- Team with a colleague to read each other's material before it is posted. He or she may spot something you missed.

- Ask readers to help you spot errors in items you post, particularly in blogs. You'll find readers eager to do so, and you can even make a game of it.

- Correct mistakes as soon as they are pointed out to you. Remember that being correct is the key to maintaining your credibility.

So, the best blogs are conversational, full of information and engaging to readers in ways that are fun, provoke discussion and even start arguments. Remember, though, that while some internet writers do not distinguish between fact and fiction, professional journalists must be meticulous about the facts in their blogs.

Promoting News on Social Media

Most journalists today are asked to promote their stories on *Facebook, Twitter, Instagram, Snapchat* or all four. When a writer's article goes live on the website, he or she posts a *Twitter* message with a link to the piece or posts a photo on *Instagram* related to the story along with a link to it in the photo's caption. These posts help drive traffic to the news organization's website. News organizations charge for advertising on their websites by determining how many unique visitors go to their sites each month and how many of those people click on the news stories offered. Driving traffic to those sites has become part of the job for both reporters and editors.

Facebook and *Snapchat* are used in a similar way. Many newspapers, magazines, and radio and television stations have sites on which reporters post links to their stories and readers comment on them. Most, of course, allow such comments on their own websites, too.

Facebook Subscribe is a subservice of Facebook that allows readers to subscribe to the public updates of journalists on *Facebook* without having to add that journalist as a friend. Both *The New York Times* and *The Washington Post* are heavy users of that service.

Journalists use *Twitter* primarily to promote their stories, according to a PEW Research Center study, in much the same way that television anchors use teases before they break for commercials: "After the break, we'll find out when the snowstorm will arrive." A good tease gives enough information to pique readers' interest but not enough to give away the key elements of the story.

Journalists also use *Twitter* to solicit reader suggestions, to talk about the process of news gathering and to break news before they are able to write even a short story for the web.

Because tweets don't go through the editing process, it is important that you read and edit your own tweet before sending it. Journalists who send tweets with spelling, grammar and factual errors are sending damaging messages.

Writing at *Poynter.org*, the website of the Poynter Institute, Jeff Sonderman reported on research by Dan Zarrella, who studied thousands of tweets to determine what led to the highest click-thru rates. Zarrella's advice:

- Write between 120 and 130 characters.
- Place links about a quarter of the way through the tweet (not always at the end).
- Tweet only once or twice an hour.

Zarrella also confirmed earlier research that advised using more verbs and determined that tweets are more effective at night or on weekends.

Legal and Ethical Concerns

As a web journalist, you must be aware that you have the same legal and ethical concerns and responsibilities as other journalists. Libel is still libel, and plagiarism is still plagiarism. Just because you are not "in print" doesn't mean you can destroy someone's reputation or distort the truth.

You also must always be aware that what is on the web is not all yours, even though the very design of it allows you easily to download words and images. If you use someone else's words, photograph or artwork, you must put quotation marks around the quoted text and cite the source for all such items.

Failure to credit a source can have legal repercussions. The web makes it easy to catch someone who has plagiarized. Already there have been several cases where web readers of local columnists or reviewers have turned in a writer for stealing others' work. But plagiarism is not the only danger. The following subjects have stirred up ethical concerns, and some remain difficult for online journalists to solve: privacy, advertising, manipulating photos and concealing your identity.

Privacy

Websites exist that have files and personal information on nearly everyone. Some sites allow you to see what anyone has ever posted in a chat room. What may journalists use, and what might constitute an invasion of privacy? It's often tough to tell. Almost everyone agrees that private email is off limits. But what about material sent to corporate intranets? The experts are divided on that question, and there's really no sure answer. To avoid problems, always exercise caution in such situations.

Advertising

Newspapers and magazines generally try to label advertising as advertising, and they have rules that require ads to use typefaces different from those the publication uses for news and other articles. They also have guidelines about the placement of ads. But online ads regularly break up the copy of news stories or pop up over news stories. There is little separation of ads from editorial content, which can lead to reader confusion as to what is what. Why don't the rules that apply to print apply online? The code of the American Society of Magazine Editors says they should. According to its website, the ASME guidelines state, "Regardless of platform or format, the difference between editorial content and marketing messages should be clear to the average reader."

> The dynamic technology of electronic pages and hypertext links creates a high potential for reader confusion. Permitting such confusion betrays reader trust and undermines the credibility not only of the offending online publication or editorial product, but also of the publisher itself. It is therefore the responsibility of each online publication to make clear to its readers which online content is editorial and which is advertising and to prevent any juxtaposition that gives the impression that editorial material was created for — or influenced by — advertisers.

Others agree that it is the job of the publication to make the distinction between editorial and advertising content for the reader. For example, the code of the American Society of Business Publication Editors says that "care should be used online, as in printed material, to avoid placement of advertisements in a way that could compromise editorial integrity or confuse the reader. Print standards for clear distinction between editorial content and advertising apply here, e.g., labeling and design."

Manipulating Photos

The web makes it easy to digitally alter or manipulate photos, so how can readers tell what is original and what has been changed? How can readers trust what they see? Former *New York Times* photographer Fred Ritchin proposed using an icon to flag a digitally altered photo. Most editors prefer to ban the practice altogether. In news photography, there is no place for alteration.

Concealing Your Identity

It's easy to conceal your identity as a reporter on the web, but usually the time to reveal yourself as a reporter is at the outset of your questioning people online. People have a right to know they are talking with a reporter, and failure to disclose your identity can be a serious ethical violation unless there is good reason to conceal your identity. What's a good reason? Most editors would say that doing so is acceptable only while doing an investigative report and then only if there is no other way to get the information.

Corrections

What happens when a news site makes a mistake? Some act as if they never do; they simply post new stories with updated information. But the best journalistic practice is to tell readers that the story has changed or has been updated with new information and how that was done so that the readers are fully informed. For example, *Forbes.com* erroneously quoted former Disney CEO Michael Eisner as saying he didn't think his company's network, ABC, would be operating "in four to five years." In the update to the story, the changed headline read, "Clarification: Eisner Discusses the ABC Brand and Other Brands."

In addition to correcting the story, *Forbes.com* put asterisks next to the changed sentences and included explanations at the bottom of the story, such as this: "The original version of this story incorrectly stated that Eisner did not see the third-ranked network being around in four to five years." In his column in *The Washington Post*, Howard Kurtz reported that *Forbes.com* editor Paul Maidment said his reporter had "extrapolated" without the "broader context." Unfortunately, such notice of correction or updating is seldom done unless the news site has a clear policy requiring it.

CHAPTER 6

Writing News for Strategic Communication

Starbucks wants you to think the company is socially responsible. McDonald's wants you to know it's concerned about obesity. Exxon–Mobil wants you to know it's searching hard for new sources of energy and is actively engaged in research to find them. All three of these are examples of corporate messaging, and none of them are one-off messages. In each case, the company has carefully researched and defined the audience it wants to reach, honed a carefully designed message and delivered it repeatedly through multiple media outlets and in various forms.

Starbucks, for example, has long sought to create a socially responsible image. Most Starbucks stores, particularly new ones, have messaging inside that point to the company's use of environmentally friendly furnishings throughout. It reinforces that image with campaigns like one recently launched to explain why it is setting a goal of ridding its stores of plastic straws that harm the environment when tossed to the ground or thrown into the trash.

All those companies attempt to present themselves in a positive light to targeted audiences. They do it through marketing and two of its important subsets — advertising and public relations (see Figure 6.1), which we'll focus on here. Those are the main components of what in recent years has come to be known as *strategic communication*. It's a form of *persuasive* communication, unlike most of journalism, which is primarily *informative* communication. There are exceptions. Newspaper and magazine editorials, for example, and perhaps some forms of opinion and commentary, also seek to persuade, not necessarily inform.

We cover writing for strategic communication in this book because it often is taught in schools and departments of journalism and because the writing skills needed by both journalists and strategic communication practitioners are quite similar. Consider, for example, that both regularly write:

- **News stories.** While the work of journalists is usually hard news, strategic communication practitioners write news releases, also known as press releases or public relations releases. Those seek to persuade or

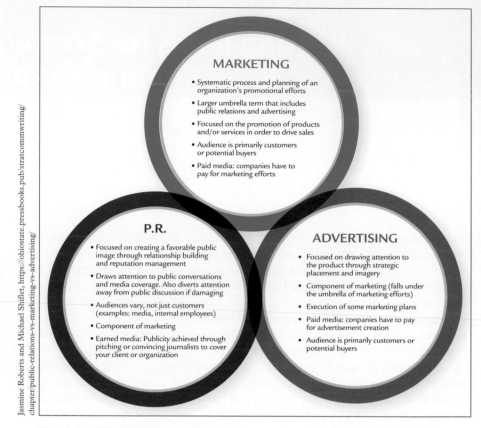

Jasmine Roberts and Michael Shiflet, https://ohiostate.pressbooks.pub/stratcommwriting/ chapter/public-relations-vs-marketing-vs-advertising/

Figure 6.1 The differences among marketing, public relations, and advertising.

positively influence public opinion. The writing form for both is quite similar. In fact, many such releases are written in news style in hopes that media outlets will publish them as is. Many small publications or websites do so. Larger newspapers and magazines would never do so because their higher standards would require additional reporting, not merely news from a single source that may be biased. Still, it's important to note that the primary purpose of *some* news releases, such as many from government agencies, also seek to inform, not necessarily persuade.

- **Feature (soft-news) stories.** The writing style for features in both journalism and strategic communication is also almost identical. It's common to find such articles in magazines or on the websites of corporations, governmental bodies and nonprofits. As with news stories, feature stories from corporations or nonprofits with a cause often seek to persuade or create positive images.

- **Items for social media such as *Facebook* and *Twitter*.** Journalists style these in the form of news briefs, often with links to a news outlet's website. Strategic communication experts try to mimic that style, but the links instead may go to a well-designed corporate message on a company's website.

In today's media environment, both journalists and strategic communicators also must have strong skills in producing audio and video and in web development and production. Strategic communicators often find themselves producing magazines, newsletters and similar printed materials for their own companies or for clients. The skills they employ in doing so are similar to those of a journalist.

There are, however, differences. There's nothing in journalism that equates directly to *advertising copywriting*, which is the art of selling a product, idea or concept in concise written or broadcast form. Conveying a persuasive message in just a few words for an advertisement may well be the toughest form of writing. In journalism, only headline writing comes close.

Strategic communicators, those who specialize in advertising or public relations or both, also must have far more advanced skills in researching and understanding target audiences. That's often referred to as *audience analytics*. Understanding audiences also is increasingly important for journalists, so many larger news organizations have specialists with advanced skills in that area. However, the journalist at a newspaper often needs only a basic understanding of the media outlet's audience, which is general by design. But at a targeted magazine that focuses on the local food scene, knowing both the audience and local restaurateurs is a must.

Finally, strategic communicators also deal in areas such as *media relations*, which is the art of dealing with media to gain placement of messages; *event planning*, which involves organizing events that promote a product or message; and *speechwriting* for corporate, nonprofit or government executives.

Writing News for Strategic Communication

The Strategic Communication Process

Setting Your Goal

The word "strategic" in strategic communication is important. You must determine the goal of your project, think strategically about what you want to communicate and in what form, and design a message with that goal in mind. And the message, of course, must appeal to your target audience. The project goal could be any number of things:

- Increasing brand awareness.
- Introducing a new product.

- Targeting a new demographic.
- Reinforcing a long-standing message.
- Connecting with stakeholders.

Or, it could be something entirely different.

Let's say the goal of your company's strategic communication project is to design and launch an advertising campaign to introduce a new product, a knee brace for soccer players, and sell a million units by the end of the year. That's your project goal, which must be in line with the company's strategic goal of offering the best and most comprehensive line of protective sporting goods available to soccer players at a reasonable price.

Choosing the Target Audience

An all-important part of the strategic communication process involves knowing what audience you want to target and then choosing the right means of getting the message to that audience. Early research shows that those who buy soccer knee braces most often are men. You could target your project to reaching all men, but a message designed to do that probably wouldn't be effective and likely wouldn't be possible within the budget you have available.

So, your target audience needs to be more exacting. You do additional market research using analytics and determine that men 18 to 24 who regularly play soccer in recreational leagues would be those most likely to buy a new, improved knee brace. Analytics also may help you find the right magazines or broadcast outlets to reach the desired audience.

Using audience analytics is a process that requires a lot of number crunching. You might consider running advertisements in 37 magazines, for example, before deciding on eight that would most effectively reach the target audience at a cost that's within the project budget. You also might want to create a television ad for the product while keeping a common theme in both. Messages in multiple media outlets often increase the likelihood of an ad campaign being effective. That means you also have to carefully research where to place the television ads, again using analytics. In this case, you've decided on a print ad to run in eight magazines and a television ad to be targeted to two sports networks, particularly those that carry a lot of soccer programming.

Designing the Message

Here's where the writing comes in. For a print advertisement, that usually means writing a headline and a short block of copy or two to go with a photo, in this case one of a soccer player scoring a goal. That photo might be one of dozens shot by a professional photographer just to get one great shot. Then, it's time to write:

GOOOOAL!!!!!!

Like that sound? Make sure you can score

the next one by protecting your knees.

Studies show that our LevKev Brace reduces the chance of

serious knee injuries by 64 percent. Get it today

at your nearby sporting goods store.

Designing a television commercial to complement the print ad would involve video of a soccer player scoring. However, a completely different approach to the words—in addition to a lot of video—might be needed while retaining the GOOOOAL!!!!!! concept for campaign continuity. Then you would need to prepare news releases in hopes of picking up some mentions of your product, particularly in magazines that appeal to soccer players.

That, of course, is a much-simplified example of an advertising campaign designed in-house for a relatively small company. More often, a team working at a strategic communication agency is contracted to design the campaign. That team may have a dozen or more strategic communicators, each with a different specialty, collaborating on the project. Those likely will include an *account executive*, who sells the campaign to the client and continues to update that client on the status of the campaign; *art directors* who design the ads; *copywriters* who write the ad content; and *analytics experts* who hone in on the targeted audience. A *public relations practitioner* might also seek to place stories about the new product in desired publications.

Throughout the design and execution of the campaign, strategic communicators must be alert to detail. Just one misstep can result in financial losses and an ineffective campaign.

Determining Timing of the Project's Launch

Deciding when to launch a campaign is important. In the case of your knee brace campaign, you might want to launch a month or so before the start of the soccer season. Launching a campaign of that sort just as the harsh winter weather sets in likely will not be as effective in selling knee braces.

Evaluating the Impact of Your Campaign

As your campaign comes to a close, you'll of course have a good idea of how successful it was based on how many knee braces your company sold. Whether successful by that measure or not, you'll want to do a thorough assessment of the campaign, including additional research into who bought the product and why. Assessing the campaign's success with analytics can help you make a follow-up campaign more effective and uncover reasons to alter your sales approach for the next one.

Journalists of today are increasingly focused on their audiences, too, but not nearly to the same extent as those in strategic communication. Even in journalism, it's important to know and understand your target audience.

Writing News for Strategic Communication

How Public Relations Writing Differs From News Writing

Earlier in this chapter, we stated that writing for public relations news releases is quite similar to writing for the news media, newspapers and magazines in particular. We covered news writing in some detail in Chapter 2, so let's focus here on *differences* in the two.

The most fundamental difference is that news writing seeks to inform the audience of both the good and bad occurring in society while a news release seeks to call attention only to things that reflect positively on the client and divert attention from those that are damaging. Again, writing news releases often is a form of persuasive communication. So, news releases seek to tilt public opinion toward a favorable impression of a company or the products it produces. Or, in the case of nonprofits, news releases seek to tilt public opinion toward a positive view of the group's work and in turn assist with fundraising. In government, news releases most often seek to call public attention to the good being done with taxpayers' money. Or, they seek merely to inform:

Headline: **Three City Streets to Be Closed Starting June 9**

Text: Three city streets will be closed starting June 9 for replacement of outdated water lines. Walnut, Oak and Elm streets between Broadway and Eagleton Avenue will be affected. "The old water lines, which were installed in the early 1900s, run right down the middle of the street," said Public Works Director Melody Richards. "As a result, we have to close the streets to complete the work." Richards said . . . .

Essentials of a Good News Release

The most basic of functions performed by strategic communication practitioners is writing a news release to inspire a journalist to follow up and write his or her own story about whatever the company is touting. Here are things that must be included for a news release to be effective:

- *An attention-grabbing headline that summarizes the "news."* But don't write a sales pitch. This should appear to be news, not a sales pitch for a product. It *can* be a sales pitch encouraging a journalist to cover an event or write about something good your company has done.

- *A dateline that shows the city in which the story originated.* If you're sending to local news outlets, this is particularly important because it shows that the news is local. News with a good local angle is more likely to be picked up.

- *A carefully constructed lead paragraph written as a journalist would write it.* In almost every case, the inverted pyramid format is desirable because it gets to the point right away. If you don't grab the recipient immediately, your release is likely to end up in the trash.

- *The body of the text, again written as a journalist would write it.* Your release should be written objectively in the third person. Ensure your release is *grammatically correct* and that all words are *spelled correctly.*
- *Meaningful quotations.* If relatively brief, these always make a release more readable. However, be sure to avoid throwaway quotes of no substance.
- *Boilerplate language.* It's desirable to describe the company, nonprofit or governmental agency issuing the release and perhaps its goal or mission.
- *Contact information.* This tells the recipient whom to contact for more details. It should include, at a minimum, a telephone number and email address.

Above all, *keep it short.* The idea is to attract a journalist's attention and persuade him or her to pursue the story. Length is not a virtue here. One page or less is ideal.

Following Up With Media Contacts

Good strategic communicators also follow up with media people they have met, particularly those who work at major media outlets they are targeting. News releases alone usually don't motivate a journalist to pursue the story, but they often do so if the release is delivered personally. Doing that also gives you a chance to engage the journalist and provide more reasons for pursuing the story.

Legal and Ethical Issues in Strategic Communication

Like journalists, strategic communicators must make sure that what they write or broadcast does not damage or destroy someone's reputation, resulting in a *libel* (written) or *slander* (spoken) defamation lawsuit. Both also must avoid invading someone's *privacy.*

Plagiarism and the resulting *copyright violation* is another legal issue of concern. A public relations professional might be delighted if a reporter picked up large chunks of a press release and dropped it into a story. The reporter's editor definitely would *not* be delighted, and the reporter likely would be fired. Those in both fields should ensure that anything picked up from another source is appropriately credited to that source. And, if the material is a substantial chunk of the original, written permission and perhaps licensing fees are required.

While some ethical issues faced by strategic communicators are similar to those faced by journalists, some are decidedly different. Take, for example, the case of a public relations agency for a resort that is trying to build awareness of a new hotel in the Caribbean. There might be nothing at all wrong with one of the agency's practitioners offering a newspaper's travel writer a free trip to the resort. It would, however, be a conflict of interest for the reporter to accept it. That's because the writer's objectivity about the resort could easily be called into question should she or he write about it.

Strategic communicators occasionally find themselves in the position of trying to restore the reputation of a client company after the company acted illegally or unethically. In 2015, news media reported that Volkswagen had installed a device on millions of cars that detected when they were being tested for emissions. The device then produced false results for those doing the testing. In reality, millions of cars did not meet U.S. admission standards, and the scandal subsequently spread to other nations. Imagine being put in the position of explaining what happened. Volkswagen public relations practitioners were faced with plummeting sales and that very dilemma. In the industry, dealing with something of this sort is known as *crisis communication.*

In such cases, it's always best to tell the truth. Admit the mistake, and explain what the company is doing to fix it and make amends. Lying just digs a bigger hole, and journalists will be all over the story. Eventually, the truth will come out anyway, and it's far preferable for the company to admit its mistake. Obviously, a publicist caught lying to the press would lose all credibility. Reputation matters—in all lines of work.

Journalists abide by the ethics code of the Society of Professional Journalists (*www.spj.org*) while advertising professionals follow the ethics code of the American Advertising Federation (*www.aaf.org*) and public relations specialists follow that of the Public Relations Society of America (*www.prsa.org*). All insist on high standards of ethical behavior.

Skills Needed by Strategic Communicators

We've established that strategic communicators need to learn to write as journalists do. They also must learn to work under deadline pressure and be willing to work odd hours as journalists do. But not all writing done by strategic communicators is akin to news writing. They also must be able to:

- Write copy for marketing materials.
- Write annual reports.
- Write advertising copy.
- Produce corporate magazines.
- Produce employee publications.
- Produce newsletters.
- Manage *Facebook* and *Twitter* accounts.

They also must develop good presentation skills. Pitching an ad or public relations campaign to a client is a common task. So is organizing and facilitating a focus group to assess how members of the public view a product, service or event. Doing well in those roles depends on being comfortable with public speaking and having the ability to connect with an audience in a compelling way.

And, like journalists, strategic communicators of today need to understand multimedia production. They must have the skills to produce audio and video, maps, charts and other forms of information graphics. They even are called upon to organize events that promote a business, product or cause. It's important, then, that those entering the field of strategic communication become well-rounded individuals with a strong set of skills. The more things you can do, the more valuable you will be to your employer.

Here are some job titles common in the field, many of which are open to beginners:

- Account manager
- Art director
- Brand developer
- Communication specialist
- Copywriter
- Event planner
- Government relations specialist
- Marketing manager
- Media buyer
- Press secretary
- Public relations specialist
- Social media manager
- Speechwriter

The *gender revolution* evolves across the world as unspoken agreements are challenged. For example, the day after President Trump's inauguration, the Women's March 2017 protested the anti-immigrant, anti-women, racist and anti-disabled remarks spoken or tweeted by Trump during his campaign. Simultaneous "Sister Marches" took place across every U.S. state and sixty countries, all advocating human rights in legislation and policies for women, immigrants, the disabled, people of color, workers, LGBTQ, people of all religions and the environment.

Mass protest has since become a characteristic of today's communication in civic engagement and keeps growing. The next top three largest protests in the U.S., besides the Women's March 2017, have occurred since President Trump was inaugurated:

- Women's March (annual protest) January 2018;
- March for Our Lives (student-led, protections from gun violence) March 2018; and
- March for Science (evidence-based policy in the public's best interest) April 2017.

These volunteer protests indicate a culture wide demand for democracy's promise: equality for all.

What Does That Mean to You?

Your future depends upon a constant unlearning and relearning of societal assumptions. Most of this chapter is about language changing to catch up with civilization's march to ensure equality to the abused and away from the history of human abuse levied against the less powerful. That's why the list on Page 241 focuses on the remnants of insulting language levied on these groups (a majority of U.S. residents): women, children, racial and ethnic minorities, the disabled, the aging, native peoples, the bullied.

In 2000, the U.S. Census made the historic change of authorizing people to identify themselves according to more than one racial category. The one-race category was becoming irrelevant. The 2020 Census will give U.S. couples the option to define their relationship as either same sex or opposite sex for the first time. These very basic demographic changes signal other important characteristics of the populations for which you create content.

To help you evolve perspective in the content you produce, what can you do to "see" what's shifting?

Think about when the Statue of Liberty was dedicated. Women were barred from Lady Liberty's celebration, forced to hire boats and circle Ellis Island in protest. Today, forbidding the largest segment of a democracy's population from celebrating its democracy seems bizarre and unfair.

Ask yourself: Who today faces a similar lack of access? Women, minorities, the disabled? What are they being blocked from and why? And how can they get that access?

The Future Arrives on Little Feet

Along with massive technology changes that disclose unequal treatment, segments of population shift swiftly. The U.S. Census projects by 2020 "more than half of the nation's children are expected to be part of a minority race or ethnic group." By 2042, more than half the population will be what was formerly "minority." No one racial or ethnic group will dominate.

Simultaneously, you are in the startup stages of the global Evolving World of Words where the individual = media. ("Medium" would be the traditional, but less-used term). As a videomaker and writer, your most important skill lies in your ability to recognize and write about the planet's shifts. New population segments ensured by the Constitution's "We the People" mission bring new possibilities, new actions, new stories.

Before the *hidden information revolution*, individuals were at a terrible disadvantage. You did not have ready access to information about what a used car was worth, nor its past history. You could be manipulated. Cheated. Nor did you have access to background information on someone you might wish to date, go into business with and so forth.

Today, you hold the power in your hand right at the point of transaction. You grab up-to-the minute information on your smartphone.

What does that mean for your present and future? The individual — whether professional journalist or average citizen — is the media.

But not everyone fares the same across the globe. The Kenyan resident's bank is her phone; her family is more advantaged than the 9 million U.S. residents (8 percent of families) who don't have a bank and must spend 2 to 4 percent of their paychecks to get them cashed. That toll costs an unbanked U.S. resident an average of $1,200 a year rather than being available for food, housing, education, transportation, and the building of family health and wealth. New apps now address that need.

At the same time, devices provide documentation of race-motivated discriminatory actions against minorities by those charged with protecting them. Domestic and child abuse evidence now is witnessed by video, voice and pictures on electronic devices. The most important change that 2018 saw was that people who had previously had no voice now move global audiences. Our old assumptions are challenged as the diverse representation of "We the People" publish in distinctive voices, demanding equal treatment. Simultaneously, troll farms, criminals and bullies proliferate. By 2019, it's estimated that more than half the phone calls you receive will be scams.

Sexism, Racism, and Other "Isms"

No matter what your future, your brain needs to juggle even more than just these 5 morphing changes:

- **Demographic shift**—Asian-Americans will outnumber Hispanics/ Latinx by 2065, according to a Pew Research Center report. Important: The report also shows the total U.S. population born outside this country was higher in 1890 than it is today. 2015 was the year the majority of kindergarten students were "minorities."

- **Gender shifts**—Several shifts are occurring. Women, men and children are speaking up about the visible and invisible inequalities the culture forces on females in the culture. A second powerful shift occurs in the use of personal pronouns, she/her/hers, he/him/his and they/they/ their. Transgender individuals, and those whose gender identity does not match that identified at birth, may prefer gender-neutral pronouns.

  Those who do identify with a male or female gender may still choose nongendered pronouns to avoid being stereotyped. Major orchestras now hold tryouts with the vying musicians performing behind a screen so the participants are judged solely on performance. Across all areas of human behavior, new things are tried to make a fairer environment for all.

  Some parents keep their children's biological identity secret. "Theybies" are not a majority . . . yet. The growing use of gender-neutral pronouns allows individuals to choose who they identify as. We expect the discussion to continue as adults and children reshape what was once thought to be binary: male or female.

- **Technology shifts**—Smartphones record real-time action, which leads to civilians recording real-world events and sharing them globally. For instance, crowdsourced videos led to *theguardian.com* reporting that U.S. blacks are more than twice as likely as whites to be unarmed when killed during encounters with police. The study followed individuals' videos documenting several police killings of blacks. The shooting death of Michael Brown in Ferguson, Mo., in 2014 was pivotal in focusing attention to the militarization of U.S. police. The Black Lives Matter movement frames racial injustice through global social media connectedness.

- **Wealth shift**—In 2010, the wealth of the 388 richest people in the world equaled the combined wealth of the poorest half of the human race. In 2016, the 62 richest individuals (35 from the U.S.) in the world had more wealth than the poorest half of the human race. Eighty-two percent of new wealth in 2017 went to the world's richest 1 percent, while the poorest half got nothing.

- **Cultural shift**—The first U.S. same-sex marriage occurred in 2004 in Massachusetts. Eleven years later, the Supreme Court overturned the 1996 federal Defense of Marriage Act, thus legalizing same-sex marriage across the U.S. Women were cleared to serve in any combat area in the U.S. military. Also in 2016, the Department of Defense announced women in the military would get 12 weeks of paid maternity leave in all the services.

Before the media shift, editors were called "gatekeepers," controlling the flow of information audiences received. News relied on the judgment of about 2,000 of these gatekeepers, who were mainly white men. Now, unless you're hooked into cable or network television and print news, there are neither gates nor fences. You can both create and choose content, videos and livestreams among a global outpouring of evolved content, unlike that of even two months ago.

No matter your media venue — facts, opinions, critique, review, persuasion, comedy, curating, games, drama, fiction, nonfiction, public relations, copywriting, marketing, sales, web creation — *nothing is more important than recognizing current reality*. Being up-to-the-second in a fast-moving world gives you a saleable skill, saves you embarrassment and speeds your reputation. Your credibility rests on getting basic reality right. Unless of course, you decide to become a "fake news" producer (see Chapter 1).

Of course, there are myriad and sophisticated problems. In today's globalizing world, basic reality keeps changing. Criminals keep proliferating. Privacy keeps dissolving.

A Shifting "Center of Gravity"

This is your challenge: As media serve a world with more than 7.7 billion inhabitants, global changes require global thinking, writing and editing. China and India are the two most populous countries, comprising 19 and 18 percent of the global population, respectively. India will surpass China around 2024. These large Asian countries have moved on from economic disadvantage, taking on newer, cheaper and better technology than that afforded the U.S., where companies continue to keep legacy infrastructure. On the other hand, across most countries, handheld mobile devices change the balance of power. New ideas spread fast. So do brutal ones.

The point here is that the history of U.S. media coverage has been to assume the U.S. and European countries are the "center of gravity" for the world. If your writing rests on that belief, you set yourself up as a relic of a bygone day.

If you were raised in the U.S., you might think of "Black Friday" or "Cyber Monday" as the biggest yearly e-commerce event. "Alibaba's Singles' Day" on Nov. 11, 2018, earned nearly $40 billion, breaking the 2017 record of $25.3 billion. Global delivery orders surpassed a billion on that one day. The ubiquity of mobile devices, the rise of single adults, the power of the female economy, the blending of online and retail stores, the global supply chain excellence and the fear of missing out were all brought together rather seamlessly — and not by the U.S.

Sexism, Racism, and Other "Isms"

Language Turns to the Future

Unexamined assumptions can make you appear naive. Here are some examples of commonly held misconceptions corrected:

American does not mean *white*. *American* doesn't even mean *a citizen of the U.S.* Instead, *American* refers to *someone from North, South, or Central America*.

Gangs come in all colors. Most teen mothers in the U.S. are white. Since 2005, a majority of adults in the U.S. are unmarried. Muslims are only 1 percent of the U.S. population. More than 90 languages are spoken in the Los Angeles public schools.

The LGBTQ (lesbian, bisexual, gay and transgender) population is an estimated 4.5 percent of the U.S. population, while research shows people consistently assume the LGBTQ population to be 23 percent. While the transgender population is being added to federal surveys, it is generally agreed that the transgender component of society is 0.03 percent. For many employed today in mainstream media, who grew up with "his or her" rules, the coming acceptance of "their" as the singular pronoun seems terribly wrong. Language changes. Get used to it.

Today's everyday language transformations provide one of the best measures of the driving force of social change. Many of the spelling, grammar and punctuation rules covered in this book evolved from Latin, a language that is dead. The concepts discussed in this chapter evolved during the past few decades, many in the past few years. The question, then, is: How does a language grounded in Latin cope with such change?

The answer is that Latin may be dead, but English isn't. Neither are the other main languages in the world: Mandarin is the most used language in the world with 14 percent of the global population. Spanish is second with 5.8 percent, while English is third with 5.5 percent. Just as all living languages, English constantly evolves and changes to fit new, uncomfortable realities. In their classic book, *The Elements of Style*, William Strunk Jr. and E. B. White state: "The language is perpetually in flux: It is a living stream, shifting, changing, receiving new strength from a thousand tributaries, losing old forms in the backwaters of time."

Update With *Working With Words* Language Triangle

1. New social change
2. New standards of language
3. Resulting new video/content requirements

Assume that what you knew—even last year—has changed. An old journalism adage may be more important than at any other time: "If your mother says she loves you, check it out."

1. New social change — to recognize current reality, look for the action.

Language changes to keep in step with power shifts. In a globalizing world, power shifts constantly. For insights, look back at these examples of U.S. social changes in the past few decades.

- 1960s — Civil rights legislation recognized all U.S. citizens had the same rights. One language-related outcome: Labeling an adult black man as "boy" or calling an adult woman a "girl" was recognized as wrong.
- 1970s — Only 22 percent of women in the civilian labor force had attended some college or graduated from college.
- 1980s — As women attended college in greater numbers, advancing society and raising U.S. GDP 20 percent, describing women as "bystanders" and men as "actors" was inaccurate.
- 1980s and 1990s — Coverage of the AIDS epidemic focused disproportionately on gay men, bringing the media heavy criticism. Gay and lesbian groups organized in media companies demanding fair treatment in the news. President George H.W. Bush signed the Hate Crimes Statistics Act into law, requiring the Department of Justice to publish data about crimes motivated by hatred based on race, religion, ethnicity and sexual orientation. Yet, he only advised gays to make behavior changes to avoid HIV/AIDs, rather than mobilizing health care to solve the crisis.
- Early 2000s — Immediately after the Sept. 11, 2001, terrorist attacks on New York City and Washington, news organizations scrambled to develop relevant stylebooks *after the attacks* to avoid racist descriptions of terrorists, Muslims and U.S. citizens born in Middle Eastern countries.
- 2009 — The first African-American U.S. president (Barack Obama) took the oath of office after winning against a white male opponent in his 70s (John McCain) whose running mate was a white woman (Sarah Palin) and after winning a tough primary race against a white woman (Hillary Clinton). His run was big news in the U.S., but even mainline media included racist, ageist and sexist content in their coverage, insulting their core audiences.
- 2011 — The "don't ask, don't tell" military policy was abandoned. DADT prohibited military personnel from discriminating against or harassing closeted gay or bisexual service members or applicants, while barring openly gay, lesbian or bisexual persons from military service.
- 2015 — In the U.S., 23 percent of 25-year-old women and 14 percent of 25-year-old men held a bachelor's degree or higher. Women and minorities owned just more than half of U.S. firms. For women under 30, most births occurred outside marriage. Between the ages of 25 and 54 in the U.S., 70 percent of women and 80 percent of men were in paid employment.

Sexism, Racism, and Other "Isms"

- 2016—The presidential primaries saw what many perceived as continuous slurs against Mexicans, Muslims, women and the LGBTQ segments of the population by candidates in the Republican race. In the months leading up to the national party conventions, 7 in 10 women held unfavorable opinions of Republican frontrunner and real estate/reality television personality, Donald Trump, and he had one Senate endorsement.

- 2017—President Donald J. Trump took office, having won the electoral vote but lost the popular vote by 3 million to former Secretary of State and Sen. Hillary Rodham Clinton.

Perhaps nothing demonstrates the value of journalism in the *longevity, equality, gender and hidden information evolutions* more than four powerful global institutions being called into accountability:

- The 116th Congress—Historical records for members aligning with actual representation of citizens. Women are one-fourth the members of both the House and Senate. More than one-third of them (35) were first voted in in 2018. In the Senate, four Latinos, three African-Americans and three Asian-Americans serve. In the House, African-Americans make up 11 percent of the representatives (and 13 percent of U.S. population), Latinos are 9 percent of the representatives (and 16 percent of U.S. population) and Asians are 3 percent (and 6 percent of U.S. population).

- The global entertainment industry—The #MeToo movement swept across the globe via internet platforms. In 2007, Tarana Burke started a campaign to let other sex-abuse survivors know that they were not alone. Ten years later, her mission became a movement. In response to stories in *The New York Times* and *The New Yorker* disclosing sexual abuse allegations against Harvey Weinstein, movie producer, actor Alyssa Milano took action. She tweeted: "If you've been sexually harassed or assaulted write 'me too' as a reply to this tweet." Within 24 hours, more than 53,000 people had left "me too" comments. The hashtag was tweeted a million times in 48 hours on Twitter. On Facebook, more than 12 million posts took place in fewer than 24 hours by 4.7 million global users. Women in entertainment formed the Time's Up organization, which set a $20 million record for crowdsourcing to fight sexual abuse. More than 200 powerful U.S. men who had not been held accountable for sexual abuse against men and women were fired. U.S. and international companies continue to rid their organizations of sexual predators, both male and female.

- Religious Organizations—Widespread sexual abuse by leaders surfaced with resulting investigations and legal actions. Although 6,721 priests were reported for molesting children to U.S. Catholic Church bishops between 1950 and 2016, with 18,565 victims coming forward, bishops were not held accountable in the church's reforms following the *Boston Globe* Spotlight team's 2002 church abuse report. After a 2018 Pennsylvania grand jury found 300 Catholic Church clergy credibly accused of abusing more than 1,000 children, state prosecutors and the

Department of Justice now investigate decades of alleged molestation and cover-up. Pope Francis dedicated his Christmas 2018 message to abuse, urged victims to come forward, and will convene a global summit on preventing sex abuse in the church in February 2019. The *Fort Worth Star-Telegram*'s investigation in December 2018 discovered more than 400 allegations of sexual misconduct in 187 independent fundamental Baptist churches and their affiliated institutions, spanning 40 states and Canada.

- The Olympics—204 victims of child sexual abuse by the USA Gymnastics team doctor Larry Nassar gave victim impact statements during his 9-day sentencing hearing. His employer, Michigan State University, agreed to pay a settlement of $500 million for 332 victims. The university's president resigned during the scandal and was later charged with lying during the case. USA Gymnastics filed for bankruptcy in December 2018 amid civil lawsuits brought by the young women.

2. New standards of language — the changing world and social media.

The internet makes your audiences global. Mobile and video together shape the future of your individual media platform.

Local is global. One in eight people in the U.S. are foreign-born; they and their children are probably not U.S.-centric. Nor do they have to be. Their individual media along with instant language translation on platforms give them the ability to move geographically, yet stay emotionally connected to their originating country. Reporting, writing, editing and selecting stories now operate worldwide to serve a global web-accessible audience. Therefore, *relevant media writers have a constant struggle to be sophisticated enough in language to serve their diversifying audiences.* Technology is a given. Media upheaval comes from coverage that fails to be current.

3. Resulting new video/content requirements — The world keeps speeding up, but still you must write quickly and accurately.

If you understand what forms today's reality in the *language triangle* (social change, language change, resulting writing changes), you will be able to deliver words, ideas and information in sync with that reality.

Accelerating change sometimes looks and feels like chaos especially to people born *before 2000*. It's your job to think through and then communicate the complex changes in today's language.

The communications device determines audience ages in news consumption. For instance, U.S. network and cable television median-age viewership is 65+ years old and mainly white, so those reports revolve around disappearing white privilege. Mobile devices with internet platforms are used primarily by younger, more diverse audiences – which are now making up the majority of news consumers. No matter what age audience you serve, you must examine your work to see if it underplays or trivializes any of the following groups. They are about 70 percent of your audience.

Sexism, Racism, and Other "Isms"

New Players in the New Millennium

	GROUP	PERCENTAGE OF POPULATION IN 2018
SEX	Women	51
RACE	Hispanics	17
	Blacks	13
	Asian-Americans	5
	Native Americans	1
DISABILITIES	People with disabilities	12
AGE	People over 65	15
SEXUAL ORIENTATION	Gay, lesbian, bisexual, transgender	4
IMMIGRANT	Foreign-born	13

It cannot be stressed enough that women and members of racial, ethnic and immigrant groups continue to move from the sidelines to the headlines. Unprecedented numbers reshape the labor force, higher education and public life. *Multiculturalism now defines the U.S.* Meanwhile, the language and media coverage still carry historic assumptions that people other than males of European descent are inferior. To be accurate, media writing in the U.S. must update to reflect the new multicultural reality.

These five "undercovered" groups of your audience have shifted in power, causing language to shift:

1. *Women* make 80 percent of consumer decisions and earn the majority of college degrees.
2. *Young adults* do not neatly fit the label "millennials." They face a muddy economic future. Although the Great Recession of 2008–2010 has lifted, more than one-third of young adults live with parents.
3. *Racial/ethnic and immigrant groups* are the new entrepreneurs and the future of international business. This will accelerate as "minorities" become the U.S. majority in 2042.
4. *People over 50* are lifetime learners and seekers in the developed world. The U.S. was 34th in life expectancy in the world in 2014, and today it is 43rd, with females expected to live to 81, males to 76. Older women are reshaping the U.S. economy. In 1992, 1 in 12 women over 65 was employed. Projections are that 1 in 5 women over 65 will be in the workforce in 2024.
5. *Children and teens* are the face of U.S. poverty, with endless consequences. The latest U.S. Census Report in 2010 showed more than 31 million children (42 percent) lived in low-income families, with

15.6 million (22 percent) living in poverty. One in 45 children live on the street, and most childhood poverty is not temporary. A century ago, more elders lived in poverty. Today, 9 percent of those over 65 years live in poverty.

All these shifts remold U.S. society. The *society of diminishing white paternalism* brings backlash. Internet trolls threaten violence against women, hate groups rise up and equality legislation is attacked. Why? The power is shifting to include "outsiders."

In resistance to the shift in power, more inclusive language is discounted as being "politically correct" by those losing power. In fact, many of the preferred terms listed later in this chapter have been pejoratively labeled "PC." Pay attention. The voices condemning today's reality and progressive changes are usually from segments losing power. In the conversations leading up to the 2016 presidential primaries, many of the Republican Party's members had complaints about politically correct language and wishes to go back to an earlier time. This contributed to putting Donald Trump in office. Yet, after an over-sampling of white males in media, government, business, technology, et al., new players come forth.

On the advertising side of media, backlash forces companies' actions. In the mid-term elections, the Trump campaign placed orders for an ad that was declined by the majority of news networks because it was deemed racist. After airing the ad multiple times, both Fox News and NBC received backlash from their audiences. Subsequently, NBC and Fox then dropped the 30-second spot a day ahead of the national 2018 midterm election. Facebook had also declined the ad but the content ran on a non-paid status.

Companies in disparate industries continue to dismiss executives and employees when evidence emerges of their racist and sexist comments and/or sexual abuses in their past and present.

At the same time, as this country's population becomes more diverse, those demeaned and/or slandered by racial bias demand fair treatment.

This is just the beginning.

Subtle "isms"—the unconscious use of insults, out-of-date terms, biases and assumptions about whole groups of people or individuals in those groups, also referred to as *microaggressions*—are harder to eliminate than blatant sexism and racism. Why? Although we may hold nonsexist and nonracist beliefs, we may unconsciously fall into the trap of using dated sexist, racist, ageist and dismissive language.

Sexism, Racism, and Other "Isms"

A Brief History of "Isms" in the U.S.

Estimates are that between 8 and 100 million native people in 1492 lived in what is now the U.S. By 1650 there were fewer than 6 million. Today 5.2 million native people, including those of more than one race, live in this country.

As the land mass was colonized by whites, the Pilgrims brought English common law with them. When Blackstone's Commentaries on the Laws of England was used as the basis of the U.S. legal system, women and children (particularly female children) were legally on a par with the male family member's cattle, oxen and dogs. When slavery was institutionalized in the country's laws, black women, men and children were given the same legal status accorded white women and children. All were property belonging to white men.

It can be argued that black men gained citizenship when they got the vote in the 1860s after the Civil War. White women and women of color were elevated to citizen level when they won the vote in 1920. Realistically, men of color and women of all races began to gain equal access to employment, credit and education only in the mid-1960s.

Documents serving as the foundation of this country's government held white males in higher value: "We hold these truths to be self-evident, that all men are created equal."

For those who would argue that *men* was generic then and included everyone, remember that two constitutional amendments were required to bring adults other than white males into the voting process.

Until the civil rights breakthroughs in the 1950s and 1960s, white domination over people of color, as well as male domination over females, was institutionalized and supported in all branches and levels of government. People of color and women were denied their civil rights and opportunities to participate in political, economic and social communities. So, what you are faced with in today's usage is centuries of authoritative language diminishing the roles and lives of women and minorities.

Dealing With Current Reality

Sexism

Sexism is usually thought of as fixed expectations about women's appearance, actions, skills, emotions and "proper" place in society. Sexism also includes male stereotypes.

Instead of adequate and varied portrayals of individual women, five common stereotypes of females emerge in news coverage. These dismissive categories are to be avoided.

1. *Mother/nurturer*: woman as caregiver; examples: grandmother, prostitute with a heart of gold, fairy godmother.

2. *Stepmother/bitch*: woman as non-nurturer; examples: aggressive woman, aloof executive, boss.

3. *Pet/cheerleader*: woman as appendage to a man or children; examples: the little lady, soccer mom.

4. *Tempter/seducer*: woman as sexpot (a term used only for women); examples: gold digger, victim of crime who "asked for it."

5. *Victim*: woman as incompetent; examples: damsel in distress, helpless female, rape victim.

Three common stereotypes for men have emerged in language and should also be avoided.

a. *Macho*: man as battler; examples: financial warrior, political strong-man (no parallel exists for women), master criminal, gang hero.

b. *Wimp/wuss*: man as sensitive; examples: mama's boy, househusband, caregiver, sissy, single father, hipster.

c. *Demon/pervert*: man as "perp"; examples: child molester, rapist, murderer, abuser, predator.

Racism

Racism is discrimination against racial or ethnic groups based on the false assumption that one ethnic group is superior to others. Individuals from any racial or ethnic group can be racist. Avoid common stereotypes.

1. *The secondary*: people who serve the powerful; examples: domestic help, migrant farmworkers, service workers, immigrants.

2. *The ignored or invisible*: people whose achievements are trivialized; examples: slum or reservation residents, servants.

3. *Achievers*: unusual exceptions; examples: model minority, credit to one's race.

4. *The despised or feared*: outsiders, criminals, suspects; examples: welfare cheats, illegal immigrants, drug addicts, "animals."

Often, those outside the white power framework are portrayed as villains without human characteristics attributed by default to whites. In other areas, racial and ethnic groups are overlooked. For generations, history books noted that the only survivor of Custer's last stand at the Battle of the Little Bighorn in Montana was a horse, Comanche. A century after the battle, students at the University of Kansas (where the stuffed Comanche resides in a glass case) pointed out that several thousand Sioux and Crow also survived that day.

What major facts are you getting wrong because of your latent prejudices? When members of racial and ethnic groups are made visible, the reference is sometimes gratuitous and fosters old stereotypes: *Police in Minneapolis are searching today for a black man in his 30s who is suspected of taking part in a convenience-store robbery late last night.*

How many black men in their 30s live in Minneapolis? The report is not a description. If height, weight and distinguishing characteristics such as scars or speech patterns were used, enough information would be given on which to base an identification. Unless you use white as a descriptor, do not use black.

Sexism, Racism, and Other "Isms"

The all-too-common assumption that "minority" issues are the same as "black–white" issues ignores the country's makeup. In today's U.S., immigration is and will be an issue worthy of coverage. But it also is an issue that is multilayered, complex and often emotional. To cover it objectively, you must face facts.

For instance, in the 1995 Oklahoma City bombing, early media reports suggested international terrorists were responsible. Six years later, in September 2001, when terrorists flew U.S. commercial jets into New York's World Trade Center and the Pentagon and attempted to fly into the White House, killing about 3,000 people, news organizations were not prepared to describe the multicultural victims in the attacks, let alone the individuals and groups responsible for them.

Needless stereotyping distorted media reports. The Oklahoma City bomber was a white man, born in the U.S. Today, the major demographic of terrorists committing mass gun violence in the U.S. is white and male.

The Southern Poverty Law Center, which advocates for civil rights, mapped 953 active hate groups in 2018. These groups hold beliefs or practices that attack or malign an entire class of people. The White Nationalist movement, Nazis and conspiracy groups are documented to have inspired violence against minorities and women.

Ageism

Ageism is discrimination primarily against people more than 45 years of age. However, discriminating against someone because of their younger age is also ageism.

In U.S. culture, youth has been idealized and age has been posed as an issue for men and women. But the focus on age is usually not necessary and gets in the way of the greater reality, as in these examples:

> The spry 65-year-old salesman works five days a week in the job he's loved for the past 30 years. [The story later says he founded the company.]

> Grandmother Wins Election as Centralia Mayor [headline]

In the first example, *spry* gives the impression that the salesman is unusually active for his age. The assumption is unfair and ageist. In the second example, *grandmother* is both ageist (it focuses unduly on age) and sexist (it focuses on a woman's tie to her family rather than on an appropriate accomplishment — being elected mayor). You're unlikely to see this headline: *Grandfather Wins Election as Centralia Mayor.*

Today, only Japan, Canada, Europe and a few other developed countries have an older average age than the U.S. (the median age in the U.S. is 36 and going up). The World War II generation and their children, the baby boomers, form large blocs of society. Both groups continue to be active shapers of new power and won't be dismissed easily in language — even with the advent of the Gen Y and millennial age cohorts.

The "young old" of the 70- to 85-year-old group continue to retire but also to be employed, form companies and lead organizations. The "old old," age 86 and older, still vote, subscribe to media sources and make news. Warren Buffett, 88, is considered one of the most successful investors. In November 2018, his net worth of $84.4 billion makes him the third-wealthiest person in the world.

Other Stereotypes

Stereotyping denies the individuality of people or groups by expecting them to conform to unvarying patterns. For example:

> Jones said that after a woman who identified herself only as a "Jewish mother" complained she and her coworkers were upset because of the lack of day care, the company began to survey employees.

Even when a source uses a stereotype, such as *Jewish mother*, it is not your job to perpetuate that stereotype. In this example, it would be a simple matter to drop the offensive labeling. It's hard to imagine that the label is in any way necessary to the story.

Sexist, racist and ageist labels, as well as religious bias, that creep into writing not only are unfair to groups and individuals but also are inaccurate. To repeat the obvious—but obviously neglected, or this chapter would not be necessary—*a media writer's job is to reflect reality.*

The Nonbias Rule

The history of inequality in Western culture has led to language stressing white men as the standard, considering others as substandard. That language is out-of-date. One rule eliminates most language biases.

Ask, "Would my wording be the same if my subject were an affluent white man?"

Sexist reporting occurs when reporters treat men and women unequally, patronizing women by describing them or their clothing or labeling women in emotional or reproductive terms. It's reasonable to expect that old-school media lost credibility as being reliable in the 2008 and 2016 presidential campaigns. Why? Women candidates, women voters, women leaders in both political parties were portrayed in sexist, dismissive language. Women are the majority of media's core audience.

What male candidate's coverage focused on his attire? What male candidate's coverage centered on his abilities as a parent and on his physical attributes? What male spouse of a candidate was critiqued for fashion?

Apply *the nonbias rule* to test whether you write fairly. Writing demonstrates bigotry when it describes female candidates as "shrill" or "emotional" when they raise the volume of their voices on the campaign trail, yet never remark upon male candidates' voices. The lesson? You learned language and assumptions that have centuries of racist, sexist, ageist, dismissive language— *and media attention that primarily pits the changing "We the People" as threats, not positive growth.*

Adjectives and characterizations are always opportunities for derision. Drop as many as possible. Don't label a person as a member of a specific gender, age or racial group.

Seven Ways to Be Up to Date Instead of Out of Date

1. Dump Today's Stereotypes.

There are terms to avoid (many considered slurs) or to include instead when writing or editing stories. *Even when preferable terms are suggested, they should not be used except when germane to the story.* Usually, you should identify everyone, or no one, by race, age, sex, hair color, height, weight, build, and so on.

2. Ask the Source.

Generally, the best way to determine whether a term is prejudicial is to ask the person(s) it covers. For instance, many native people object to the term *Indian*, although some groups retain it. Many prefer being identified by tribal name; some prefer the term *Native American* or *American Indian*. Another example would be transgender or LGBTQ persons who may identify with gender or non-gendered personal pronouns. Ask your sources for their preferences.

3. Eliminate Labels.

Labels stereotype people, annoy audiences and are past their expiration date as language shifts to modernize. Stereotyping all people in a group as acting or being like all others in that group only blinds us to individuals' possibilities and characteristics. Expecting every white man to be like all other white men is just as racist and sexist as expecting all black women to be like all other black women.

4. Be on the Lookout for Unconscious Bias.

Respect all subjects. The most punishing stereotypes are subtle. Medical researchers Michael Lewis, Steven M. Alessandri and Margaret W. Sullivan demonstrate that 3-year-old boys are more encouraged to risk, experiment and fail than are 3-year-old girls. Parents, teachers and others reinforce two different expectations without realizing it. This double standard takes a toll on both boys and girls.

5. Drop Race, Sex, Age or Disability Tags.

Don't provide someone's racial, ethnic or religious background; sex or sexual orientation; or age or disability unless it's relevant to the particular story. The days of the "she's a college professor, but she's black" story were naive because they showed a white–press prejudice. That lack of understanding will push your audience away.

6. Pay Attention.

Remember: Fair, objective language cannot be determined solely by popular usage or rules in books that can have the effect of freezing current understanding. Language changes daily as it responds to an increasingly global culture that changes at an accelerating speed.

The constant revision of language is not easy, as seen by arguments over acceptable and unacceptable language in a globally interdependent society. The controversy over what terms are "politically correct" will grow as the world slouches toward multilevel multiculturalism.

7. Replace Bias-Related Terms.

With the massive shifts both technology and a global communication system bring, language changes speed up.

How to keep current? Be vigilant. Use web resources. Every list, including the one in Part Three of this text is outdated quickly and flawed. Media stylebooks are in constant revision because of society's need for current language.

Speech matters. As minorities and women bring their voices to the national conversation, new perspectives will emerge about what is fair language. See Pages 241–254 for a list of biased terms. *Watch your language.*

Sexism, Racism, and Other "Isms"

PART TWO

Grammar and Usage

Chapter 8 Choosing Your Words   109

Know the Meaning of Words Often Confused   109

Choose Simpler and Clearer Wordings   113

Chapter 9 Grammar Basics   118

Solving Common Problems   118

Understanding in More Depth   129

Chapter 10 Phrases, Clauses and Sentences   136

Solving Common Problems   137

JOURNALISM TIP: Punctuating Nonrestrictive Phrases and Clauses   140

Understanding in More Depth   141

JOURNALISM TIP: Using Different Types of Sentences   145

Chapter 11 Subjects and Objects   146

Solving Common Problems   146

Understanding in More Depth   157

Chapter 12 Verbs   163

Solving Common Problems   163

Understanding in More Depth   170

REFERENCE LIST: Principal Parts of Common Irregular and Other Confusing Verbs   177

REFERENCE LIST: Passive and Active Forms for Simple and Perfect Tenses   183

JOURNALISM TIP: Verb Moods   186

Chapter 13 Making the Parts Agree   192

Solving Common Problems   192

JOURNALISM TIP: Groups of People in the News   194

Understanding in More Depth   199

Chapter 14 Modifiers and Connecting Words   203

Solving Common Problems With Modifiers   203

Solving Common Problems With Connecting Words   209

Understanding in More Depth   212

REFFRENCE LIST: Correlative Conjunctions   214

Continued ▶

Chapter 15   Getting Words in the Right Order and Punctuation   215

Getting Words in the Right Order   215
Solving Common Problems   215
Understanding in More Depth   218
Punctuating for Clarity   219
Solving Common Problems With Commas   220
Solving Common Problems With Quotations   225
Solving Common Problems With Punctuating Pairs of Modifiers   231
REFERENCE LIST: Common Conjunctive Adverbs   232
Understanding Punctuation in More Depth   234

CHAPTER 8

Choosing Your Words

In Chapters 1 and 2, we discussed the importance in journalism of being correct, clear and concise. In this chapter, we'll focus on these topics on the micro or word level rather than on the macro or story level.

Choosing the correct word is often called "*usage.*" This is largely a matter of vocabulary—not so much with the big, unusual words we often think of as vocabulary, but with the smaller, everyday words we think we know but may be using inaccurately or inexactly.

Correct word usage involves understanding the different meanings among words that are often confused and using the right one for what you mean to say. Some of these confused words are *homonyms*, that is they sound alike but mean different things and are spelled differently. Homonyms are a combination usage and *spelling* problem.

But word choice also involves—in addition to correctness—clarity and conciseness. English often gives you a choice of many words that mean the same, or somewhat the same, thing. Choose the ones that are more exactly what you mean, and if more than one means the same thing, choose the words that are shorter and more common. This is often called *tightening* and helps you make sure you communicate as clearly as possible.

Know the Meaning of Words Often Confused

The writer best known for finding just the right word was the French novelist Gustave Flaubert, who spoke of the importance of *le mot juste*, or the exact word. Canadian media theorist Marshall McLuhan, punning on Flaubert's French, said *le mot juste* is the word that gives your writing "the most juice."

Using the right word helps you make your point more clearly so that the reader doesn't have to stop and try to figure out what you meant. People tend to use the wrong word for two reasons: They don't really know what the word they're using means, or they're using a word in a phrase that's not what native or educated speakers would normally use.

An example of both problems is writing *heart-rendering* story instead of *heartrending* story. *Rendering*, which refers to melting down animal fat or salvaging other meat-processing by-products is mistaken for *rending*, a verb meaning "pulling"—as in "pulling at one's heart."

Errors such as *heart-rendering* seem clear-cut: A word has a meaning, or a phrase or common wording, that a writer or speaker is violating. But when enough people make such errors often, the language can change, and what was once wrong becomes right. All you have to do is browse through the historical entries in the *Oxford English Dictionary* to see how the meanings of words have evolved in English usage.

It's also sometimes funny, and more than a little humbling, to see how usage experts of years ago railed against words no one objects to now. For example, in the 18th century, Jonathan Swift thought *communication* and *mob* were horrible new words that should be resisted, just as many editors a few decades ago opposed the use of the term *gay* for "homosexual," a usage that is now preferred by *The AP Stylebook*.

We think it's fine for people who care about language to resist *neologisms*—newly invented words—or new uses for older words when such changes seem ugly or awkward to them. So, for example, some people resisted the term *senior citizens* because it seemed to them a euphemistic and wordy replacement for *the elderly*. But now the term finds little opposition, although *The AP Stylebook* still suggested in 2018 it be used sparingly. But when language changes, eventually stylebooks need to catch up, or we lose credibility when we sound behind the times.

AP, for example, finally gave in several years ago to the use of *hopefully* to mean *it's hoped*, a usage many editors had fought for decades. Likewise, in 2018, it gave in to allowing the use of *collision* for a crash involving only one moving object rather than two or more as it had long required.

Our Changing Language
Conservative Stylebook Rules

That people often ignorantly misuse words is a fact. And sometimes, yesterday's error is today's accepted wording. The problem lies in trying to figure out where we are in the process with any given error. It's easy to label an individual's idiosyncratic variations from the norm as mistakes, but most of the errors listed in any stylebook or usage dictionary are variations that are widely used, or they wouldn't find their way into the book.

For example, almost no native speaker of English uses the verb *lie* in daily conversation to mean "rest" and hasn't for decades. Instead, people tend to use *lay* for that, reserving *lie* only when writing, if at all. Yet, this is widely pointed out in book after book as an error, including AP as of 2018, even though it's almost universally used except in print, where either writers know to use *lie* or editors correct the error. Even in print, this "error" is accepted in dialogue or quotations because that's how people talk.

When we're confronted by nearly universal "misuse" of certain words and phrases and still the majority of stylebooks and usage guides insist on older rules, the language is in the process of changing or has already changed. We also have to admit that something else is going on: a conservative strain among the arbiters making the policies.

Logical or not, agree with them or not, conservative usage rules are a fact of life we must accommodate when we are told to make writing conform to a particular stylebook. But a wise writer or editor should be informed enough both to know the rules and to see through them. As a newer employee, you may not be able to change them, and, in fact, your job might depend on your following them for now. But when you have decision-making power, we'd advise making rules that make sense as much as your knowledge permits.

ESL Tip

The main reason the English language is difficult for speakers of other languages to master is English's huge vocabulary. It has a number of *homonyms* (words that sound alike), *synonyms* (words that mean the same thing) and near synonyms (words with different shades of meaning), as well as a wealth of *idioms* that require a particular word in a phrase rather than a synonym. Of course, vocabulary and idioms often pose problems for native speakers of English, as well.

We hear some words so often we think we know what they mean when we really don't. Then, when we write, we find ourselves using the wrong word for what we intend to say. In Part Three of this book (see Page 239), we provide a long list of words and phrases that are often confused or misused.

Unfortunately, there's not much we can say by way of overall rules to help you remember all that material. But here's a shorter list of some of the most important distinctions to start. Browse first this list, then eventually the longer one to become familiar with the entries. The more you look over the lists, the more points will stick, and the more you'll think to look something up later when you want to use it. Mark the entries that contain distinctions you didn't know. Then concentrate on learning them, perhaps a few a day.

Also, invent associations that can help you remember one item of every pair. For example, if you want to remember the difference between the homonyms *premier* and *premiere*, you might associate the one that ends with an *e* with *entertainment*—an opening of a movie or play. If the word needed in a certain passage doesn't have to do with an opening, you know it should be *premier*—the word without the *e* at the end.

It also helps to focus first on learning the most common words that are confused. We suggest you start with these:

adopt/pass	farther/further	lay/lie
affect/effect	fewer/less	presently
among/between	hanged/hung	raise/rise
burglary/robbery	homicide/murder	set/sit
compose/comprise/ constitute	if/whether	their/there/they're
	imply/infer	while

For the complete list of words that are confused, along with explanations of how these words should be used, see Page 328.

Know which nouns *not* to use as verbs. Some verbs work fine as nouns, but many don't, and certain nouns should only be used as nouns and not as verbs if you're following the most conservative standards. (See Page 169.) Here are a few of the most common nouns editors often tell you to avoid using as verbs:

author   Use only as a noun, not as a verb. Change to *write*.

contact   An "Ask the Editor" at *www.apstylebook.com* (but not the 2018 printed *AP Stylebook*—at least there's no entry for it) now accepts *contact* as a verb. But we suggest it's best to avoid such a usage because it's clearer to change the word to *call*, *write*, *email* or *visit*, depending on whether a street address, email address or phone number follows.

dialogue   Use only as a noun, not as a verb.

debut   Use only as a noun, not as a verb. Don't write that a movie *will debut* but that it *will have its debut*.

host   Use only as a noun, not as a verb. Don't write that someone *will host* a party but that someone *will hold* a party or *be host at* a party.

premiere   Use only as a noun, not as a verb. Don't write that a play *will premiere* but that it *will have its premiere*.

Choose the right spelling for the right homonym or near homonym.

Homonyms are words that sound alike but mean different things and are spelled differently. Here are some of the most commonly confused ones. These are so basic that, as a professional, you should definitely know all of them:

it's, its   let's, lets   their, there, they're   to, too, two

For a more complete list of homonyms and near homonyms, see the list in Part III, Pages 329–402.

Choose Simpler and Clearer Wordings

Writing concisely has long been an important skill for keeping news clear and understandable, and editors have needed to be particularly good at it when trying to fit a story or headline into a limited space. But with the rise of social media, knowing how to say what you want in fewer and simpler words is even more important for more people, especially when trying to get a tweet down to 280 characters (the limit as of 2017).

Trimming unnecessary words makes writing clearer and more effective, saves space and saves the reader's time. As the architect Mies van der Rohe said, "Less is more." Of course, anyone can discard words haphazardly, especially in someone else's writing. What's harder is knowing which words are the dead branches a gardener needs to prune. If you prune too much or the wrong parts, you may kill a tree or other plant. Sometimes, beginning writers and editors don't understand this and snip where they shouldn't.

Writers and editors, like gardeners, need to know what they're doing. So let's be more precise than saying brevity is the sole goal. The real virtue is not so much brevity as conciseness, which is a combination of brevity and completeness. Don't use more words than you need to make your point. But don't use fewer words than you need, either.

The mark of the inexperienced writer is to hold every word sacred, jealously guarding it against deletion as if it were a drop of holy water about to be spilled. Good writing must be concise. That's the most agreed-upon rule of all good writing—journalistic, technical, business or creative. In *The Elements of Style*, William Strunk Jr. and E. B. White write, "A sentence should contain no unnecessary words, a paragraph no unnecessary sentences, for the same reason that a drawing should have no unnecessary lines and a machine no unnecessary parts."

Great writers have agreed. Mark Twain said, "A successful book is not made of what is in it, but what is left out of it." The same could be said of a news story. As a journalist, your job is to tell a story completely but concisely. Editors value those who can do that. Professor Emeritus Don Ranly of the Missouri School of Journalism, one of the all-time great magazine-editing teachers, used to tell students to write papers twice as long as actually assigned then cut them by half. Students might have thought that sounded impossible but usually found their more concise version was much better.

Writing tightly means choosing the fewest, shortest, simplest, most exact and, if possible, freshest words to express your thoughts.

Often, beginning writers think they need to use big words and roundabout phrasing to impress their audiences. Nothing could be further from the truth. The German poet Johann Wolfgang von Goethe once said a common mistake of young writers is that they try to muddy the waters to make them look deep. But good writing isn't writing that confuses people.

Here are some specific suggestions on how to tighten your writing:

Use Fewer Words

Eliminate redundant or irrelevant words, phrases, clauses, sentences, paragraphs, sections or chapters. Get rid of details, examples, quotations and facts or ideas that don't add anything, and use single words rather than phrases whenever possible.

PHRASE TO AVOID	ALTERNATIVE
all of a sudden	suddenly
as a consequence of	because
give consideration to	consider
have a need for	need
put emphasis on	stress

Get rid of the helping-verb forms of *to be* whenever possible. Often, helping verbs just detract from a more active verb.

WEAK	He is hopeful that
BETTER	He hopes

Forms of the verb *to be* often occur in sentences starting with *there*, *here* or *it*. When possible, get rid of them.

WEAK	It was Thoreau who said
BETTER	Thoreau said

Use active voice instead of passive. Passive voice is wordier, less direct and less forceful. (See Pages 183–184.)

PASSIVE	A 13-year-old boy was shot by police.
ACTIVE	Police shot a 13-year-old boy.

An exception is when the person being acted upon is more important than the person doing the acting: *President Kennedy was shot today by an unknown assailant.*

Avoid turning verbs into nouns when the simple verb form will suffice.

WEAK	It is my intention
BETTER	I intend

Avoid vague modifiers, such as *a lot*, *kind of*, *perhaps*, *quite*, *really*, *somewhat*, *sort of* and *very*.

These words are sometimes called "weasel words" because they are favorites of people trying to weasel their way out of speaking precisely. When journalists use them, it's often because they've done an insufficient job of reporting and don't have all the facts. Using such words appears at worst deceitful, at best wishy-washy.

Avoid doubled prepositions (*off of* for *off*) or prepositions that aren't needed (the *up* in *heading up*).

In the sentence *She headed up the largest company in town*, the *up* isn't necessary. But in the following sentence, it is: *They headed up the mountain trail*. Other examples of verbs that usually don't need *up* include *count, divide, drink, eat, fold, free, gather, heat, hoist, hurry, polish, raise, rest, rise* and *settle*.

Avoid whenever possible phrases beginning with *in* or *the* and ending with *of*: (*in*) *the amount of*; (*in*) *the area of*; (*in*) *the case of*; *the concept of*; *the factor of*; (*in*) *the field of*; *the idea of*; (*in*) *the process of*; *in terms of*.

Cut the conjunction *that* if it's unnecessary.

If getting rid of *that* doesn't change the meaning of the sentence, then get rid of it:

WEAK	He said that he would
BETTER	He said he would

But *that* is necessary when:

1. A time element, such as a day, comes between the verb and the dependent clause: *He said Tuesday that he would go.*
2. *That* follows one of these verbs: *advocate, assert, contend, declare, estimate, make clear, point out, propose, state.*
3. *That* comes before a dependent clause beginning with one of the following conjunctions: *after, although, because, before, in addition to, until, while.*

Cut *which are, which is, who are* and *who is* if they are not needed.
Rewrite *the movie, which is a comedy*, as *the movie, a comedy*. Rewrite *the students who are attending* as *the students attending*.

Don't tell us what we already know.

In phrases such as *12 noon, personal friend, sad mourners, blue in color, true fact, armed gunman* and *completely destroyed*, one word implies the other, which is therefore unnecessary. Words such as *famed, famous, renowned* and *well-known* likewise are unnecessary if the person or thing described is indeed famed, famous, renowned or well-known.

Cut the adjectives *both* and *different* if they add nothing.

What's the difference between *both John and Bill* and *John and Bill*? Between *three different views* and *three views*? But leave *both* in if you think it's needed for emphasis: *She said that in 2016 she liked both Bernie Sanders and Hillary Clinton.*

Cut the *or not* after the conjunction *whether*.

Whether includes both possibilities.

Use Simpler Words

Use shorter Anglo-Saxon-derived words rather than longer Latin-derived ones whenever possible.

Say, don't *state*. *Drink*, don't *imbibe*.

Avoid vague nouns.

Substitute something more specific for the following words whenever you can: *area, aspect, concept, condition, consideration, factor, indication, infrastructure, parameter, phase, situation, thing.*

Avoid *ize* verbs.

Words with *ize* are often no more than pretentious jargon. For example, change *finalize* to *end* or *complete; personalize* to *make more personal;* and *utilize* to *use.* But *minimize* means *reduce to as little as possible*, not merely *reduce*, and *maximize* means *increase as much as possible* or *make the most of*, not merely *increase*.

Avoid turning verbs into nouns.

Avoid the following: *activation, fabrication, maximization, optimization, rationalization, utilization.*

Use verbs rather than noun phrases when you have a choice.

Instead of writing *before the committee investigation*, write *before the committee investigated.*

Unless your editor says otherwise, use contractions such as *can't* for *cannot* and *it's* for *it is* or *it has.*

The AP Stylebook permits the use of contractions, provided they're not overused. But they're generally used for all but the most formal writing. They also sound more conversational and save space.

Use Exact Words

Use a specific noun or verb without a modifier rather than a general noun or verb with a modifier.

WEAK	a small city in Utah
BETTER	Cedar City, Utah

Use specific verbs rather than vague ones.

For example, change *go* or *move* to *walk, run, jump, skip, hop* or *gallop.*

Beware of verbs beginning with *re*.

Something is not *reaffirmed, redoubled* or *reshuffled* unless it already has been *affirmed, doubled* or *shuffled.*

In hard-news stories, avoid modifiers that could suggest bias.

Pick words that more closely convey the dictionary meaning (*denotation*) rather than a personal viewpoint (*connotation*). (See Pages 27–29.)

Avoid *euphemisms*, words that say something in an indirect manner rather than confront the truth.

Instead of writing *The maintenance engineer met his Maker,* just say *The custodian died.*

Be Fresh, Not Stale

Avoid clichés

Clichés are phrases that have been used so often they've lost their freshness and power, such as *children of all ages* and *crystal clear.* Some clichés are no longer even understood in their literal sense by most people who use them: *by hook or by crook* or *dead as a doornail.*

Others are more recent — the latest fad media phrases. Some of the words and phrases that are repeated endlessly in the media include *begs the question* (misused to mean *raises the question,* as opposed to its original meaning in rhetoric of *argues in a circle*), *big oil, boots on the ground, cut and run, game changer, man up, the optics* (as in *the optics of the timing look bad*), *perfect storm, shovel-ready, talking points, teachable moment, throw (someone) under the bus* and *what went down.* Many of these, though, are showing signs of sticking around because they're useful or shorter than alternative wordings.

In fact, clichés are often clever and can be succinct, and that's why they catch on. Clichés are such a part of everyday conversation that sometimes it's difficult to imagine how you could express certain thoughts without them. And at some point, some clichés quit being a problem and become a feature of everyday language — the idiomatic way speakers always express an idea whether it makes logical sense or not. For example, instead of saying "Good luck!" Italians say "Into the mouth of the wolf!" and performers say, "Break a leg!"

But whenever you're about to write an expression you've heard before, it's usually a good idea to take the opportunity to try to express your point in a fresher way. For a number of clichés to avoid, see the tightening list in Part Three, Pages 287–322.

Avoid stale story approaches

When journalists approach stories by trying to fit them into a pattern they've seen used many times before, the story not only lacks freshness but also probably misrepresents the truth. Think of these stories as built around clichés of vision. One of the more common stale story approaches is the one that starts, *Christmas came early for* (insert person or place). . . . (See Pages 43–45.)

CHAPTER 9

Grammar Basics

One of the biggest complaints we hear from media teachers and employers is that too many students aren't learning the grammar and usage they need to work at media jobs — whether in print, broadcast or online media, as well as in public relations or advertising. Yet, we're all writing more now: Just think of all the emails and text messages.

But most often, today's writing is informal — personal communications between friends using email and text messaging. Of course, there's nothing wrong with texting someone on your cell phone *TTYL* or *R U there?* Such abbreviations save time and are fine as long as both you and your friend know them. But students wanting a media career need to master a way of writing for mass audiences that's more demanding and less casual than writing to a single close friend, just as you dress more formally for most jobs than you do for hanging out with friends on the weekend.

For people working in the media, knowledge of grammar is one of the most important skills of the trade. Before we discuss in more depth some of the issues of how to communicate clearly and correctly in the media, it's important to remember that it's OK if you haven't studied grammar since middle school or even never. Most students these days haven't been taught much grammar or usage, so you won't be alone. And you've probably successfully mastered subjects far more difficult.

Let's start with an overview of the most common grammar problems we'll be looking at in the following chapters.

Solving Common Problems

There seem to be so many grammar rules that learning them can be intimidating at first. It gets easier, though, once you realize the most commonly violated rules boil down to just five basic ideas:

1. Use the right word.

Many people don't consider usage part of grammar and thus the phrase "grammar and usage." Either way, we looked at usage as part of Chapter 8.

2. Make sure your words agree and go together.

A verb must agree in number with its subject that's doing or acting, and a pronoun must agree with its *antecedent*—the noun to which it refers back—in number, gender and person. Also, similar items and ideas need to be expressed in similar ways, using what is called *parallel structure*. And certain words belong together—when you use one, you also use the other.

Make subjects and verbs agree.

A subject should agree with its verb in number. Singular subjects take singular *predicates* (verbs), and plural subjects take plural predicates. That's called *subject-predicate*, or *subject-verb*, *agreement*. (For a detailed explanation, see Chapter 13.)

One of the prisoners ~~are~~ ^{is} missing.

[*One* is the subject of the sentence. Because it is singular, it takes a singular verb. *Prisoners* is the object of the preposition *of*, so the verb does not agree in number with it. Beware of words coming between the subject and predicate that might confuse you as to the real subject.]

None ~~have~~ ^{has} confessed.

[The pronoun *none* is singular when it means *no one* or *not one*, as it most often does and as it does here. Thus, in this example, *none* takes a singular verb.]

Make nouns and pronouns agree.

Pronoun-antecedent agreement makes pronouns agree with the nouns they refer to in *number* (singular or plural), *gender* (feminine, masculine or neuter) and *person* (first, second or third). (For a variety of situations where this may not be obvious, see Chapter 13.)

Starting in 2018, AP now permits the use of the normally plural *they* or *their* to refer to something singular and gender-neutral when the sentence would be awkward otherwise. This is a move toward how most people use it conversationally, but AP is still a bit more conservative. It suggests that rewording—such as rewriting the antecedent as plural and using *they* or *their* to refer back to it—is often possible and a better choice.

WRONG   A teacher should do *their* best.
              [Except informally, don't use the plural pronoun *their* in place of *his* or *her* when the context means either an individual woman's or an individual man's. *Their* is a good choice from both a grammatical and

nonsexist perspective, however, when there does not need to be an emphasis on individuality and the entire sentence can be recast in the plural. (See the sections on pronoun-antecedent agreement on Pages 197–198 and 201.)]

SEXIST	A teacher should do *his* best. [The problem is, not all teachers are male. So gender-neutral wording is preferred unless the context indicates male or female.]
AWKWARD	A teacher should do *his or her* best.
RIGHT	Teachers should do *their* best.
WRONG	The committee decided *they* would meet again next Monday. [*Committee* is singular—the plural would be *committees*. So a pronoun referring to the singular committee also must be singular.]
RIGHT	The committee decided *it* would meet again next Monday.

Make sure parallel items in a sentence are worded in similar ways.

If you have more than one of anything in a sentence—subjects, verbs, objects and so on—they all usually need to be said in a similar way. (See Chapter 13.)

WRONG	He liked *gathering* information and then *to write* about it. [The gerund (*gathering*) and the infinitive (*to write*) are not balanced.]
RIGHT	He liked *gathering* information and then *writing* about it.

Make sure words that belong together are both there.

With some words, it's important to have the right companion words accompanying them. Following is an abbreviated list. More of these can be found in the list of misused words and mistaken phrases (Pages 329–402).

centers around   Change to *centers on* or *revolves around* because the center is in the middle.

convince that, convince of, persuade to   You're *convinced that* or *convinced of* something, but you're *persuaded to* do something.

different than   Change to *different from*.

forbid to, prohibit from   You *forbid to* or *prohibit from*. Don't mix these verbs and prepositions.

not only . . . but also   *Not only* must always be followed by *but also* later in the sentence.

3. Make sure your words are in the right order.

It can be hard to understand a sentence if the words are out of their proper order. This is especially true of misplaced modifiers. Split infinitives and prepositions at the ends of sentences are not really confusing, but they are often frowned on in media writing. (See Chapter 15.)

Put modifiers next to what they modify.

To avoid confusion, place modifiers as close as possible to what they modify. (See Pages 215–217.)

WRONG	*Standing on her head, he* watched the yoga teacher.
	[*Standing on her head* appears to modify *he*, the word that the phrase is next to, so it sounds as if he's standing on her head. This is an example of a *dangling participle* because the participial phrase *standing on her head* dangles at the start of the sentence instead of being next to the word it should modify.]
RIGHT	He watched the yoga *teacher standing on her head.*

Our Changing Language
Preposition Placement and Split Infinitives

The following two rules are enforced by many editors, but linguists have long disputed them. Linguists argue these rules are historically wrong with regard to common spoken and written usage, as they arose from 18th-century grammar books trying to apply Latin rules to English, a language structurally quite different. It's good to know these rules and to avoid breaking them if you take a writing test for an internship or job, or if your editor requires them. But in the digital age, we predict they will be followed less and less as people write more conversationally.

Move prepositions away from the end of a sentence.

Most editors prefer you not end a sentence with a preposition, unless it's impossible to rewrite the sentence to avoid doing this and still be conversational. (See Pages 209–211.)

WRONG	The president's economic policy is one thing he disagrees *with.*
RIGHT	The president's economic policy is one thing *with which* he disagrees.
RIGHT	He disagrees with the president's economic policy.

Keep the *to* next to the verb in an infinitive.

Most editors prefer that you not split the *to* from the verb in an infinitive. (See Pages 190–191.)

WRONG	*to boldly go* where no one has gone before
RIGHT	*to go boldly* where no one has gone before
	[unless you're quoting "Star Trek"]

---

4. Use the right form of the word.

Five of the eight parts of speech—nouns, pronouns, verbs, adjectives and adverbs—are shape-shifters. That is, they change their form depending on how they're used in a sentence and the number of items to which they refer.

Grammar Basics

Use the right noun form.

To use the right form of a noun, you have to determine whether it's singular or plural and then whether it's possessive. (See Page 151.)

WRONG	The *Finnegan's* live in Portland, Ore.
	[The meaning of the sentence calls for the plural and nonpossessive form of *Finnegan*, but *Finnegan's* is singular and possessive.]
RIGHT	The *Finnegans* live in Portland, Ore.

Use the right pronoun form.

Pronouns are like nouns in that to pick the right form, you have to determine whether they're singular or plural (*I* or *we*) and whether they're possessive (*your* or *you*). In addition, you have to determine whether they're used in the sentence as a subject or an object (*he* or *him*). (See Page 155.)

The following list includes words — some are pronouns, some not — and situations that often confuse writers when it comes to choosing the correct pronoun form.

as / like   *As* is a conjunction and should be used to introduce a clause that's either present in the sentence or implied by the structure of the sentence. If *as* is followed by a pronoun, it should be a *subject pronoun* (also known as a *nominative-case* pronoun).

Like is a preposition and should be used to introduce just a word or phrase with a noun or an *object pronoun* (also known as an *objective-case* pronoun).

WRONG	He did it the same as *her*.
RIGHT	He did it the same as *she* (*did it*).
	[*As* introduces an implied clause (*did it*), so the pronoun should be in the nominative case (*she*) as the subject of the implied clause.]
RIGHT	It was just like *him*.
	[*Like* introduces a single word, with no implied clause, so the pronoun should be in the objective case (*him*) as the object of the preposition *like*.]

as / than   When either of these words is followed by a pronoun at the end of a sentence, the pronoun should be in the *nominative case* because it is the subject of a clause in which the verb may be implied.

WRONG	She's faster than *him*.
RIGHT	She's faster than *he* [*is*].

pronouns   When nouns or pronouns appear together as compound subjects or compound objects, use the form of each pronoun that would be used in the sentence if it were the only pronoun. If one of the pronouns refers to you yourself, put it last.

WRONG	Give the report to the committee and *I*. [Give the report to *I*? No.]
RIGHT	Give the report to the committee and *me*. [Give it to *me*? Yes.]

myself Use only in a sentence in which *I* has been used earlier.

WRONG	You can give it *to myself or Christine*. [no *I* earlier in the sentence]
RIGHT	You can give it *to Christine or me*. [Notice, also, that for politeness, the *me* follows the other person.]
RIGHT	*I* hurt *myself*. [used to show *I* acted on *myself*]
RIGHT	*I, myself*, believe otherwise. [used for emphasis after *I*]

pronoun in front of a noun or gerund Only possessive pronouns can act as adjectives in front of a noun or *gerund*. Gerunds are *ing* forms of a verb used in place of a noun. If a pronoun directly precedes a noun or gerund, the pronoun should be possessive. (See Page 155.)

WRONG	They appreciated *us* staying to help.
RIGHT	They appreciated *our* staying to help.

that / which Use *that* to introduce *essential clauses* (also known as *restrictive clauses*) that are necessary for the meaning of the sentence and do not require commas. Use *which* to introduce *nonessential clauses* (also known as *nonrestrictive clauses*) that are not necessary for the sentence's meaning and do require commas.

We think it's clearer to use "parenthetical" for what AP calls "nonessential" and grammarians call "nonrestrictive," and "nonparenthetical" for "essential" and "restrictive." By "parenthetical" we mean anything that could be placed in parentheses as an afterthought or aside. Journalistic stylebooks tend to urge not using parentheses, so we suggest putting commas instead of parentheses around parenthetical elements in the middle of a sentence or just in front of them at the end of a sentence. You may notice we tend to use parentheses in this book because it's the more common practice in book publishing as opposed to journalistic media. (See Page 148.)

that / who Use *that* for inanimate objects and animals without names. Use *who* for people and animals with names.

who / whom, whoever / whomever *Who* and *whoever* are used as subjects of clauses. *Whom* and *whomever* are used as objects. A handy way to make sure you use each pair correctly is to begin reading a sentence after the choice between *who / whom* or *whoever / whomever*, adding either *he* or *him* to complete the thought. If *he* works better, use *who* or *whoever*. If *him* works better, use *whom* or *whomever*. (See Pages 148–149.)

Grammar Basics

Use the right verb form.

Verbs change form according to *tense* (time), *mood* (how the speaker feels about the truth of the statement) and *voice* (whether the verb shows the subject as being active or being passively acted on).

- **Verb tense:** The main problems with verb tense involve using the wrong *principal part* of irregular verbs (see Pages 177–179), the wrong verb in a changing time sequence (see Pages 179–183) or an incorrect verb tense in an unchanging time sequence (see Pages 179–183). Here are a couple of examples of verbs that pose common problems:

  lead / led   *Lead* is the main present-tense form of the verb *to lead*. It is also a noun that names an element that used to be put in paint and gasoline or the graphite in a pencil. The past tense of the verb *lead* is *led*.

  supposed to, used to   These verbs need to be in past tense when followed by *to*.

- **Passive voice:** In a passive-voice sentence, the subject is being passively acted on by someone or something—as the word *subject* is earlier in this sentence. Active voice is when the subject acts rather than is acted on. Technically, passive voice is not a grammatical error, but it can become a problem when writers use it for no apparent reason. Mainly, it's usually wordier and often more vague. (See Pages 166–169.)

PASSIVE	The complaints *were read by the manager*, and then action *was taken by him*. (Many people would leave out the "by him," and then we wouldn't be sure who took action.)
ACTIVE	*The manager read* the complaints and then *took action*.

- **Verb mood:** The main problem with verb mood is determining when to use the conditional- or the subjunctive-mood forms. Here are a couple of the most common problems. (See Page 184.)

  can / could, may / might, shall / should, will / would   The second word in each of these pairs is the *conditional-mood* form. With something that is not now true but could be true under the right conditions, use the conditional-mood form. This distinction comes up often in stories about government considering ordinances or bills. The two pairs most important to know are *can / could* and *will / would*.

WRONG	The bill *will* make gun owners register their automatic rifles.
RIGHT	The bill *would* make gun owners register their automatic rifles [*if passed into law*]. [*Could, might, should* and *would* are also used for past tense.]

  If I were (rich, you, etc.)...   This is probably the most common phrase in English requiring the *subjunctive mood*—the mood used to express wishes, doubts, prayers, conditions contrary to fact and with most verbs that are followed by the word *that*. (See Pages 187–188, 190). In this case, we use *I were* instead of the usual *I was*. Many people use the subjunctive correctly even though they don't know why they say it that way—it's just a phrasing they're used to hearing.

Use the right adjective or adverb form.

Adjectives and *adverbs* have three different forms apiece, depending on whether they're describing one thing, comparing two things or comparing more than two things. (See Pages 204–205.)

WRONG	He was the *oldest of two* brothers. [*Oldest* is for comparing three or more.]
WRONG	He was the *older of three* brothers. [*Older* is for comparing two.]

In addition to confusing which of the three forms to use, many people have trouble when the word *else* is required in a comparison.

WRONG	She threw the ball harder *than anyone* on the team. [This implies she was not on the team. If she was, this is not what you mean to say or write.]
RIGHT	She threw the ball harder *than anyone else* on the team. [This means she was on the team and threw the ball harder than any of the other players on it.]

People also commonly in conversation use an adjective form when an adverb is needed and so make this mistake in their writing. Remember, adjectives modify nouns or pronouns, and adverbs modify verbs, adjectives or other adverbs. (See Pages 206–207.)

WRONG	The vote *was taken quick* despite the shouts of dissenters. [*Quick* is an adjective, but an adverb is needed instead to modify the verb *was taken* and tell us the manner in which the action happened.]
RIGHT	The vote *was taken quickly* despite the shouts of dissenters.
WRONG	They felt *badly* for the candidate who lost by a few votes.
RIGHT	They felt *bad* for the candidate who lost by a few votes. [Many people use the adverb *badly* in a sentence like this since it follows a verb, but here *bad* is used to modify *they,* rather than the manner in which they *felt.*]

Also, some people have trouble deciding when to use the *articles* (a kind of adjective) *a* and *an*. Use *a* before a word that begins with a consonant sound and *an* before a word that begins with a vowel sound. If the word after *a* or *an* is an abbreviation, remember that the choice is determined by the initial *sound* of the following word, not by the letter itself.

an [not *a*] *FBI inquiry*
[because the initial sound is "eff"]

Many people also get confused by an *h* at the beginning of a word.

> *a* [not *an*] *historical event*
> [because the initial sound is "hih"]

5. Punctuate according to sentence grammar.

Punctuation rules are generally considered style matters. But punctuation can be most easily learned and consistently applied if you keep in mind that it's determined by grammar. For example, the placement of commas is not just determined by where you'd pause your voice when speaking, although that can be a useful rule of thumb.

A fragment is not a sentence.

A period, a question mark or an exclamation point at the end of a group of words suggests to the reader that's the end of a sentence. But to be a sentence, a group of words has to have a subject and predicate and express a complete thought. If it doesn't, it's a *fragment*, and to fix the problem, you need to add other words to complete the thought. (See Pages 137–138.)

WRONG	When the ice they were fishing from broke.
	[This is a fragment because it isn't a complete thought. What happened when the ice broke? This would be acceptable as a sentence, though, as an answer to the question "When did this happen?" because the question and answer form one complete unit.]
RIGHT	Thirty people on Lake Erie were rescued Thursday when the ice they were fishing from broke.

Use a comma and a coordinating conjunction between two or more complete thoughts.

When writers want to join two or more complete sentences, they should put a comma and a *coordinating conjunction* like *and* or *but* between them.

WRONG	The police funding was increased 5 percent for the year the Fire Department funding was increased 3 percent.
	[This is a *fused-sentence* error.]
WRONG	The police funding was increased 5 percent for the year, the Fire Department funding was increased 3 percent.
	[This is a *comma-splice* sentence error.]
RIGHT	The police funding was increased 5 percent for the year, and the Fire Department funding was increased 3 percent.

Put a comma after an introductory word, phrase or clause.

Put a comma after an introductory word, phrase or clause at the beginning of a sentence — that is, those that come before the clause with the main idea of the sentence. If two or more prepositional phrases come in a row at the beginning of a sentence, put a comma only after the final one.

(Although many books say the comma isn't needed after a "short" word or phrase at the beginning of a sentence, we think that vague and subjective and so we offer this guideline for consistency.)

WRONG	Because it was raining she took her umbrella.
RIGHT	Because it was raining, she took her umbrella.

Put a comma before a coordinating conjunction introducing a clause that could stand alone.

Put a comma before a conjunction such as *and* or *but* only if the conjunction and what follows could stand alone as a complete sentence.

WRONG	First, he'd make the phone calls, and then would write the story. [There's no subject after the *and*, so *and then would write the story* could not be a complete sentence.]
RIGHT	First, he'd make the phone calls and then would write the story.
RIGHT	First, he'd make the phone calls, and then he would write the story.

But if what follows the *and* is part of two or more things someone is being paraphrased as having said, leave out the comma so that it's clear the person said both things.

RIGHT	He said that first he'd make the phone calls and then he would write the story.

Put a comma before *and* in a series only if the *and* could be confusingly read as linking the last two items as one rather than leaving them separate.

WRONG	corn, squash, and beans (not confusing, so don't use the comma)
RIGHT	corn, and pork, and beans [Without the second comma, this would likely mean pork and beans as one selection.]

Change the commas in a series to semicolons if even one of the items in the series has a comma in it already.

WRONG	Plymouth, Mich., Paris, Tenn., and Chicago
RIGHT	Plymouth, Mich.; Paris, Tenn.; and Chicago

Use commas to separate parenthetical items.

Words, phrases or clauses that modify something they follow are set off by commas if they are an afterthought or an aside — something that could be placed in parentheses if journalism stylebooks allowed that. But if the words, phrases or clauses are essential to the meaning of the sentence, they are not set off by commas. As we noted earlier when explaining the use of *that* versus *which*, if a parenthetical element comes in the middle of the sentence, there should be commas on each side of it. But if it comes at the end of the sentence, there should just be a comma in front of it. (See below.)

WRONG	The actor playing an aging Sherlock Holmes in the movie "Mr. Holmes" Ian McKellen also played the wizard Gandalf in the Lord of the Rings and Hobbit movies and Magneto in the X-Men movies.
	[*Ian McKellen* should be set off by commas as a parenthetical afterthought because the sentence means the same without this detail.]
RIGHT	The actor playing an aging Sherlock Holmes in the movie "Mr. Holmes," Ian McKellen, also played the wizard Gandalf in the Lord of the Rings and Hobbit movies and Magneto in the X-Men movies.

Use dashes to set off parenthetical items containing a comma.

WRONG	One of the students, Heather Terry, a sophomore, won an award for feature writing.
RIGHT	One of the students—Heather Terry, a sophomore—won an award for feature writing.

Use apostrophes for contractions and possessives, not merely plurals.

Apostrophes should never be used to make possessive forms of any pronouns, except for pronouns that end with *one* or *body*.

WRONG	Who's book is this?
	[*Who's* is a contraction for *who is* (or *who has* when *has* is a helping verb as in *Who's been attending the meetings?*).]
RIGHT	Whose book is this?

Apostrophes should not be used to make nonpossessive plural forms of nouns. (See Pages 121–122.)

WRONG	The Fillmores' founded Unity in the late 19th century.
RIGHT	The Fillmores founded Unity in the late 19th century.

Know when to use a comma, a hyphen or nothing between multiple modifiers.

If two modifiers in a row can be reversed and the word *and* put between them, then normally you should use a comma to separate them—but there are exceptions. (See Page 231.)

WRONG	tall tan speaker
RIGHT	tall, tan speaker
	[Use a comma because you could say *tall and tan speaker* or *tan and tall speaker*.]

Grammar Basics

If two modifiers in a row fail the previous test for a comma, see whether the first modifies the second. If so, put a hyphen between them. Again, there are exceptions. (See Pages 232–233, 236.)

WRONG	well respected speaker
RIGHT	well-respected speaker

If two modifiers in a row fail both of the previous tests (or qualify as exceptions), put no punctuation between them.

WRONG	red, brick building
WRONG	red-brick building
RIGHT	red brick building

Capitalize after a colon only if what follows is a sentence.

Capitalize the first word after a colon if what follows is a complete sentence. Otherwise, the word after a colon is lowercased. (See Pages 234–235.)

Know how to punctuate quotations.

At the end of a quotation, periods and commas always go inside quotation marks; colons and semicolons always go outside; and question marks and exclamation points go inside if they're part of the quotation, outside if they're not. In front of a quotation, after a verb such as *said* attributing the quotation, use a colon to introduce a quotation of more than one sentence, a comma for a quotation of one sentence and no punctuation for a partial quotation (less than a sentence) or a paraphrase. (See Pages 229–231.)

Use semicolons between items in a series only when at least one of the items has a comma inside it.

The main use of semicolons in journalism is to connect items in a series that may not be complete sentences but have commas inside the items. In such a case, the word *and* at the end of the series should be preceded by a semicolon. (See Pages 234–235.) Journalists normally avoid using a semicolon in place of a comma and a conjunction to connect clauses that could stand alone as complete sentences.

Understanding in More Depth

The rest of this chapter consists of information that may seem less immediately practical but that will nonetheless give you a better understanding of grammar and why we have the rules we do.

Using Standard English

Grammar is the study of the form of words and their arrangement in speech or writing. But the way we use words in speech often differs from the accepted standards in writing. There are also different standards — ranging

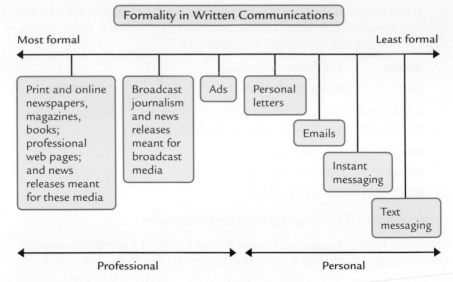

Figure 9.1 Formality in Written Communications chart.

from most formal to least formal—for writing for a newspaper, magazine, book, web page, or radio or television station as opposed to writing an email message, an online instant message or a phone text message (see Figure 9.1).

In this book, we mainly focus on the grammar and usage required for more formal media writing. For some situations—such as live broadcast reports, or reviews in a newspaper or magazine, blogs on the web, or quotations even in formal writing of sources speaking informally—a more relaxed standard is appropriate. But it's easier to lower your standards than it is to raise them, so by learning the highest standards, you'll be preparing yourself for all occasions.

Why Don't We Write How We Talk?

Most students easily understand on their own that writing for mass media is different from text messaging. But they often find it harder to understand why the informal English we use when speaking isn't appropriate for print, broadcast or online writing. Why can't we write how we talk? After all, isn't good writing conversational?

Conversation and written language—even written language meant to be read aloud—differ in many ways. What sounds right in conversation is often ineffective or inappropriate in writing.

According to a study by Albert Mehrabian, a professor emeritus of psychology at UCLA, we communicate up to 93 percent of our meaning in conversation in ways other than the words—tone of voice, pauses, stress, body language and gestures. That meaning can easily be lost when we record merely the words, as we do in writing.

But written language has its own advantages over conversation. One of the most important is that writing lets us reconsider and restate our thoughts and words. We normally speak much more loosely and informally than we would care to have recorded in writing. Although news sources often gripe about being misquoted by journalists, nobody insists that journalists print all the *uh*s, *er*s, stammers and false starts that a recording would reveal.

If your writing relies on how you talk rather than on what is considered correct in writing, you're using the wrong tool for the job. For example, the words you learned by ear may not be what you thought you heard. Did you really hear that *d* in *supposed to*? Or the people around you may not have used words in the precise way considered correct in writing.

In daily conversation, for example, most people use *lay* instead of *lie* to mean "rest." This would probably go unnoticed in daily conversation but could be considered incorrect if written. We do think, though, that broadcast and digital media are more accepting of conversational English and are influencing the older print media in that direction. That means that media are increasingly moving toward a standard of correctness based on how people talk and less on what experts prescribe as correct.

For example, AP now accepts *their* as a singular pronoun when it might otherwise be awkward to write *he or she* or *his or her*, as in "A person should honor their word." Of course, in that example, you could also easily change *A person* to *People* and be both grammatically correct and conversational, and AP prefers doing so when it's easy.

Conventional Wisdom

When you get down to it, the basic reason for knowing grammar is to communicate better. Knowing the precise meanings of words and the proper relationships between them—usage and grammar—make us better writers and better journalists. They help us communicate our ideas with correctness, clarity and conciseness.

An astute reader may notice, however, that some of the rules we present seem more like arbitrary conventions than natural, logical guides to better communication. But conventions represent agreement, and agreement, too, opens doors to communication.

Actually, a bigger problem is that not everyone subscribes to the same rules of style, spelling and grammar. Among journalists, the most widely accepted standards for style are set by *The Associated Press Stylebook and Briefing on Media Law* and the most widely accepted spellings in the latest edition of *Webster's New World College Dictionary*. We have tried to conform as much as possible to these while expanding on advice in and not in them and occasionally explaining where and why we might disagree.

Competing Grammars and Stylebooks

For grammar and usage not covered in *The AP Stylebook*, there is no single standard to consult next. We have gathered advice from many sources and have included here what we think are the most common, reasonable and useful standards.

A multitude of grammar and usage guides exist, and they take a variety of approaches. Two major approaches to grammar are the *traditional* that says, "This way is the right way" and the newer *descriptive* grammar taught in linguistic classes that says, "Anything is right if commonly said by native speakers."

In this book, our advice tends to follow the traditional approach stressed in the publishing world, while adopting descriptive ideas from linguists when we find them useful or compelling. The media prefer the consistency of traditional grammar's set prescriptive rules, and that is what journalists are expected to know when they take writing and editing tests for internships and jobs. But we can't overlook the fact that a century of scientific and historical research by linguists has disproved a number of the rules that have been passed on by teachers and editors.

When Is an Error Not an Error?

Sometimes, students ask: "How can that be an error when I hear people say that all the time?" Well, it wouldn't be a common error if people didn't commonly make that mistake. The real question is: At what point does a common error simply become acceptable as common usage?

Traditional rules have to be amended occasionally. Language is always changing, and to some extent what we now consider "errors" may be simply reflections of that change. Editors tend to resist such errors at least as long as they seem more an aberration than the norm. But when errors survive and become what people most commonly say, the rules need to change. As *1984* author George Orwell said in his famous essay "Politics and the English Language," break any of the rules to avoid saying something stupid.

Rules should change not only to reflect changes in the language but also to reflect research that proves traditional advice may have been inaccurate. The work of linguists is essential for making such calls on the best evidence available.

Our Changing Language
"Hopefully"

We've often been told by teachers, editors and usage manuals not to use the word *hopefully* as a *sentence adverb* (a word that modifies an entire sentence) — as in *Hopefully, the snow will miss our area* — because it doesn't say who's doing the hoping. But there aren't comparable rules against other sentence adverbs, such as *frankly* or *strictly speaking*, that likewise don't say who's being frank or speaking strictly.

Our advice for *hopefully* has been not to use it except in the accepted sense of "in a hopeful manner" — *She says she looks to the future hopefully* — not because it's illogical to use it as a sentence adverb but because the usage has been so universally condemned by convention. But AP decided several years ago to accept *hopefully* in either sense, and so the tide on that one has turned. When "errors" reach the point of standard usage, at some point we have to acknowledge that the language has changed and that the prescriptive standards should also adapt.

Why do the media often cling to outdated grammar rules? Sometimes, the rules hang on too long because media outlets don't want to lose credibility with members of their audience who know the old rules and expect the media to follow them. Deviations from standard grammar or usage by the media may sometimes cause the audience to become confused, maybe even to misinterpret what was said, which lowers trust.

A practical solution is for publications to create a stylebook, setting down standard rules to follow. This helps them avoid inconsistencies that draw readers' attention away from the content. When the audience discovers inconsistencies or misused words, credibility is undermined just as if a factual error had been made. In fact, when language is misused, factual errors often get created.

Besides, consistency saves time and money. Without consistency, a writer might add a comma only to see it taken out by an editor and then put back by a proofreader. If we agree on conventions, we can avoid wasting each other's time—and time, as the saying goes, is money.

Grammar and Confidence

Even professional writers often lack confidence in their grammar skills. Many people discover that studying practical grammar not only directly improves their ability to express themselves but also gives them greater confidence in their work, freeing them to concentrate on what's more important—the content and vision of their writing.

Communicating Well

Grammar is most useful, though, when it's not just helping you conform to conventions or feel confident that you know what you're doing—as important as those things are—but rather when it helps you get your message across better. Some sentences can be so ungrammatical and confusing, it's impossible to understand what the writer is trying to say.

Other times, the mistakes are unintentionally funny or totally misleading.

CONFUSING   As one of the worst examples of a convicted sexual harasser in many years, she said she was shocked at his behavior.

Who is the sexual harasser: the man or the woman who was shocked at his behavior? Here, we have not only confusion but also a possible lawsuit. If the writer had learned the rule to place modifiers next to what they describe, he or she could have avoided that problem.

> **RIGHT**   She said she was shocked at the behavior of the man, whom she called one of the worst examples of a convicted sexual harasser in many years.

Talking Shop

Grammar terms are part of the "shoptalk" of people who work with words. Just as sports have terms for what happens on the court or playing field, so speaking and writing have terms to describe what goes on in an utterance. Writers and editors often use these grammar terms to communicate with one another about writing.

But grammar terminology is confusing to many people. It's usually something studied too long ago to be remembered clearly. Most people, however, at least vaguely recall learning the eight *parts of speech*:

> *nouns* and *pronouns* (sometimes called *substantives*)
>
> *verbs*
>
> *adjectives*, *adverbs* and *interjections* (also called *modifiers*)
>
> *prepositions* and *conjunctions* (also called *connecting words*, *connectives* or *connectors*)

You might also have learned at least some of another set of terms called the *parts of a sentence*:

> appositives
> direct objects
> indirect objects
> nouns of direct address
> predicate complements *(predicate nominatives* and *predicate adjectives)*
> predicates
> prepositional phrases
> sentence adverbs
> subjects
> subjects of an infinitive

And so on. It's usually said that the parts of speech refer to what words *are*, the parts of a sentence to what words *do*—that is, how they are used in a sentence.

Then there are the *verbals* that don't fit well in either category: *infinitives*, *gerunds* and *participles*. And, of course, there are the terms for groups of words: *phrases*, *clauses* and *sentences*.

Separating grammatical terms into these categories helps, but don't feel bad if the groupings don't always make sense to you. For example, if you look closely at the definitions in this book, which are fairly standard ones, you'll see that some of the parts of speech are defined by what they *are* but others are defined by what they *do*—just as we define parts of a sentence.

Also, if you look in a dictionary, you'll find that many words can be more than one part of speech, depending on how they're used. For example, in the sentence *The mayor likes jogging*, the word *jogging* is a noun. But in the sentence *The mayor was jogging down the road*, the word *jogging* is a verb. And in the sentence *The jogging man crossed the park and headed north*, the word *jogging* is an adjective.

Confused? When English grammarians began in the 18th century to write books about the language, they based them on Latin and Greek grammar books. "Parts of speech" is really a mistranslation of "parts of a sentence." So, the two categories are not really logically separate. But sometimes, it seems more useful to speak of a word in a sentence as a noun and at other times as a subject or direct object, so you need to know both sets of terms.

Rather than define right now all the parts of speech, parts of a sentence, verbals and kinds of word groupings, we'll introduce the terms as they arise in the following chapters. That way, you will have to take in only as much terminology at a time as necessary. Meanwhile, as we said, consult the index at the back of the book if you need to track down a definition.

LaunchPad Solo | **Online Grammar Help**
macmillan learning | **Launchpadworks.com**

For practice with phrases, clauses and sentences, log on to *LaunchPad Solo for Journalism* and go to *Exercise Central for AP Style*.

CHAPTER 10

Phrases, Clauses and Sentences

A good sentence has a kind of rightness to it—a clear, exact way of saying something. And when a sentence works well, it has a certain lightness to it—a conciseness and charm that let it soar. As philosopher Eric Hoffer writes, "There are few things so subtle and beautiful as a good sentence."

This chapter looks at the groups of words that make up a sentence—phrases and clauses—and how they determine whether a sentence works well.

Let's begin with a few necessary definitions and examples. Then, we'll look at how to solve the most common problems involving phrases, clauses and sentences. Finally, we'll take a more in-depth look at these for those who want a more thorough understanding.

Phrases are groups of related words that lack either a *subject* (a doer) or a *verb* (an action or a state of being) or both.

> to the restaurant
>
> walking along the beach
>
> as long as his arm

Phrases serve many roles in a sentence, including replacing parts of sentences such as subjects and objects.

Clauses are groups of related words that have both a subject and a verb.

> he wants it all
>
> [An *independent* clause forms a complete thought independently. The test of an independent clause is that it could also work as a sentence by itself if a capital letter started it and a period or question mark followed it.]
>
> because he wants it all
>
> [A *dependent clause* is not a complete thought but depends on something else for it to make a statement.]

Sentences, like clauses, are groups of related words with a subject and verb, but, in addition, sentences *must* make a complete statement. Sentences have at least one independent clause and may have any number of dependent clauses.

He loves to watch television to relax. [one independent clause]

He loves to watch television to relax, but he sometimes regrets doing that. [two independent clauses joined by a comma plus *but*]

He loves to watch television to relax *even if he stays up later than he should.* [one independent clause and two dependent clauses. one starting with *even* and one with *than*. (italicized here)]

Solving Common Problems

Now that we've examined what phrases, clauses and sentences are, let's take a look at the two most common areas where they can cause problems:

1. Beware of common sentence errors.
2. Know the difference between *restrictive* versus *nonrestrictive* elements.

1. Beware of common sentence errors.

Common problems with sentences include fragments, fused sentences, comma-splice sentences and run-on sentences. Note that some books and instructors identify fused sentences as run-ons, or they classify fused sentences and comma-splice sentences together under the term *run-ons*.

Fragments

A *fragment* is a word or group of words that isn't a complete sentence. Either it lacks a subject or verb, or it's a dependent clause.

A tire for all seasons

Takes the guesswork out of the game

Because he was sick

Our Changing Language
Fragments

The use of fragments is becoming acceptable to more editors these days, but you shouldn't use fragments unless you have a specific reason. For example, fiction writers use them to capture the way people speak. Ad writers use them to stress a product name: *Joe's Shoes. For people who love their feet.*

> Also, many grammarians consider an answer to a question a sentence even though it may be incomplete by itself. They consider the other elements implied: *Why didn't he come? Because he was sick.* Many editors are also willing to accept a brief transition or a short question as a sentence:
>
> And now the news.
>
> Why?
>
> What more could I do? Sing? Dance?

Fused Sentences

A *fused sentence* unacceptably combines two or more independent clauses without putting punctuation between them.

WRONG	The mayor left town the auditor did, too.
RIGHT	The mayor left town, and the auditor did, too.
RIGHT	The mayor left town. The auditor did, too.
RIGHT	The mayor left town—the auditor did, too.

Comma-Splice Sentences

A *comma-splice sentence* unacceptably connects two or more independent clauses with only a comma.

WRONG	The officers were fired, the police chief was, too.
RIGHT	The officers were fired, and the police chief was, too.
RIGHT	The officers were fired. The police chief was, too.
RIGHT	The officers were fired—the police chief was, too.
RIGHT	The officers were fired; the police chief was, too.
	[Journalists would usually choose one of the previous correct versions rather than use a semicolon.]

> *Our Changing Language*
> ## When to Use Comma Splices
>
> Journalists should avoid comma-splice sentences, but some fiction writers use comma splices occasionally to imitate a rapid speaker. Also, many grammarians now say that a series of three or more short sentences may be connected with commas, as in Caesar's famous "I came, I saw, I conquered." These could also be written with semicolons or, as we'd suggest, periods.

Run-on Sentences

A *run-on sentence* may or may not be grammatical, but it usually doesn't work well because unrelated items, unimportant details or extra clauses are added as though the writer didn't know when to stop.

The novelist Ernest Hemingway, however, sometimes used this device to cover ground quickly and let the gaps imply details he didn't want to spell out. The following run-on sentence, although not from Hemingway, is either acceptable or not, depending on how effective you judge it to be:

> The blind man's Seeing Eye dog died, and it was a sad occasion, and all the man's friends went to the funeral, then went to the bar and drank to his health and said how unfair it was.

Such a sentence might work in fiction, but few magazine or newspaper editors are likely to approve it. The novels of William Faulkner notwithstanding, the best sentences rarely are longer than 2½ typed lines. Sentences containing much technical information shouldn't average more than about 20 words.

WRONG   Protesters arrived as early as 7 a.m. Friday at the Capitol, where they chanted for nearly 14 hours before police arrived to ensure the protesting remained peaceful, but many of the protesters grew more enraged by the police presence, and began throwing objects at the officers, so, in response, the governor called a state of emergency in the city late last night.

RIGHT   Protesters arrived as early as 7 a.m. Friday at the Capitol, where they chanted for nearly 14 hours before police arrived to ensure the protesting remained peaceful. Many of the protesters grew more enraged by the police presence and began throwing objects at the officers. In response, the governor called a state of emergency in the city late last night.
[There are numerous ways to rewrite a run-on sentence. This is only one.]

2. Know the difference between restrictive versus nonrestrictive elements.

Phrases and clauses (and even single words) can be classified as either *restrictive* or *nonrestrictive* (also called *essential* or *nonessential*). Knowing the difference helps you punctuate properly. Understanding about restrictiveness versus nonrestrictiveness can also help you know whether to use the word *that* or *which* in a sentence. (See Pages 147–148.)

A *restrictive* word, phrase or clause is essential to a sentence's meaning and is not set off by commas. A *nonrestrictive* word, phrase or clause is not essential to a sentence's meaning and is set off by commas, dashes or parentheses. Nonrestrictive items are always asides or afterthoughts, so we prefer the term *parenthetical* because it's easier to think of them as elements that could be set in parentheses.

To distinguish a restrictive from a nonrestrictive element, ask yourself whether the element could be set off by parentheses. If it could, it's nonrestrictive, so set it off with commas because journalism style tries to avoid parentheses.

Many books say the test is to remove the element from the sentence and ask yourself whether the sentence could still be understood. If it could, they say, the element is nonrestrictive and should be set off with commas. But we prefer to use the parentheses test because we have found some students misinterpreted AP's preferred term "nonessential" and were incorrectly placing commas around any word or phrase they thought could be edited out, as in this example:

> **WRONG** The senator said she was, very, excited by the response.
> [*Very* should not have commas around it because it's not nonrestrictive. True, the sentence can be understood without that word, and it should be edited out. But it clearly is not a parenthetical element.]

Here are some examples of words, phrases and clauses that are *parenthetical* (*nonrestrictive* or *nonessential*) and therefore should be set off by commas or dashes:

> "Yes, *Mena*, I'm over here."
> [*Mena* is a *noun of direct address* and is nonessential—the sentence carries the same meaning without it.]

> Kansas City's Dwight Frizzell, *an eclectic avant-garde composer*, released an album titled "Bullfrog Devildog President."
> [The phrase *an eclectic avant-garde composer* is acting as an *appositive* and is nonessential.]

> That actor—*who had never played professionally before*—won the part.
> [The relative clause *who had never played professionally before* works as an adjective modifying *actor* and is nonessential.]

Punctuating restrictive and nonrestrictive elements correctly clarifies what a sentence means. Look at this sentence, for example: *Their daughter Dawn arrived with her husband, Kirk.* The absence of commas around *Dawn* indicates that they have more than one daughter, so the name is essential to the meaning of the sentence. *Kirk*, however, is set off by a comma, which indicates that Dawn has only one husband, so his name is not essential to the meaning of the sentence.

> ### *Journalism Tip*
> ## Punctuating Nonrestrictive Phrases and Clauses
>
> Journalists usually avoid parentheses and set off nonrestrictive elements with commas. They use dashes instead of commas, though, when the parenthetical element has commas inside it or if they want a longer pause.

WRONG	Kei Kamara (**_the Sierra Leone forward_**) ran up the left side to receive the pass.
RIGHT	Kei Kamara, **_the Sierra Leone forward_**, ran up the left side to receive the pass.
WRONG	The whole package (**_two tickets, two soft drinks and two hot dogs_**) cost $60.
WRONG	The whole package, **_two tickets, two soft drinks and two hot dogs_**, cost $60.
RIGHT	The whole package — **_two tickets, two soft drinks and two hot dogs_** — cost $60.

Compare these nonrestrictive and restrictive versions of similar sentences:

When he was a child, he said, other boys made fun of him.
[The commas around _he said_ indicate that those words are not essential to the main thought and that a statement was made later in life about incidents that happened during childhood.]

When he was a child, he said other boys made fun of him.
[Here, a comma sets off only the introductory clause. The absence of a comma after _he said_ indicates that those two words are essential to the independent clause. In other words, he made the statement when he was a child rather than later in life.]

Understanding in More Depth

Phrases

Single words can be _subjects_ (people or things doing or being), _objects_ (people or things on the receiving end of actions), _verbs_ (actions or states of being), _modifiers_ (descriptions) or _connecting words_ (sentence glue). So can phrases. Using phrases in different ways can be especially effective in bringing variety to your sentences.

After each of the following examples, grammatical terms explain the italicized phrases. If you're unfamiliar with some of the vocabulary, don't worry. You can look up the terms in the index if you like, but feel free to skip them for now if you prefer.

Phrases as Subjects, Objects and Predicate Nominatives

Playing the mandolin is like _plucking a violin_.
[two _gerund phrases_, the first used as the subject of the sentence, the second as the object of the preposition _like_]

To try is *to succeed.*
[two *gerund phrases*, the first used as the subject of the sentence, the second as the predicate nominative]

Over there is where police found the body.
[*prepositional phrase* used as the subject of the sentence]

Phrases as Verbs

Wagner *had been going* to college for three years at the time.
[main verb *going* with two helping verbs]

You *shouldn't drink* the water.
[main verb *drink* with helping verb *should* and adverb *not*]

Phrases as Modifiers

Looking through the book, Chou decided to buy it.
[*participial phrase* used as an adjective modifying *Chou*]

Benitez had been visiting *with his sister* when the accident occurred.
[prepositional phrase used as an adverb modifying the verb *had been visiting*]

Phrases as Connecting Words

In spite of that, the commission turned down the request.
[*In spite of* is a phrase taking the place of a single preposition such as *despite*.]

The programs are *similar to* each other.
[phrase taking the place of a single preposition such as *like*]

Clauses

Clauses come in two principal kinds — independent and dependent — although the second can be further divided into two types. When we look at sentences, we'll see how these kinds of clauses are a useful way to vary your writing.

Independent Clauses

An *independent* (or *main*) *clause* is one that can stand alone as a complete sentence.

You could think of an independent clause as a sentence within a sentence with other clauses often attached to it to make a longer sentence. In a sentence with more than one independent clause, one of the clauses may start with a *coordinating conjunction* or a *conjunctive adverb*.

The City Council approved a budget for next year.
[A sentence made up of one independent clause]

The City Council approved a budget for next year, *but* it stuck to its promise of keeping increases to 4 percent.
[The second clause starts with the coordinating conjunction *but*.]

The City Council approved a budget for next year; *however,* it stuck to its promise of keeping increases to 4 percent.

[The second clause starts with the conjunctive adverb *however,* although both the semicolon and the word *however* are rare occurrences in journalism.]

Dependent Clauses

A *dependent clause* is one that cannot stand alone as a complete sentence — it works as a noun, an adjective or an adverb rather than as a complete statement — and must be joined to an independent clause.

The two kinds of dependent clauses are *subordinate clauses* and *relative clauses.*

Subordinate clauses begin with a *subordinating conjunction.*

The County Commission rejected the idea *because no one really pushed for it.*

[subordinate clause acting as an adverb modifying *rejected*]

(For more on subordinating conjunctions, see Page 211.)

Relative clauses begin with a *relative pronoun.*

Whoever made that rule no longer works there.

[relative clause acting in place of a noun as the subject]

He never did figure out *who had been at the door.*

[relative clause acting in place of a noun as the direct object]

The person *who had been there* was long gone.

[relative clause acting as an adjective modifying *person*]

(For more on relative clauses, see Page 147.)

Sentences

On the simplest level, a sentence consists of a subject and a verb — that is, someone or something doing or being: "Existence exists," said novelist Ayn Rand in a grammatically simple but philosophically complex sentence.

In some sentences, the subject is understood, as in a command: *Run!* Sometimes, the sentence contains a direct object and sometimes an indirect object: *Congress sent the president the bill* (indirect object: *the president;* direct object: *bill*).

Sometimes, the sentence contains a predicate complement: *"This looks like the big one," the general said* (predicate complement: *the big one*). Sentences also may contain modifiers and additional phrases and clauses.

Mastering the following forms of sentences gives your writing variety.

A *simple sentence* has one independent clause.

The team is in a slump.

Note that a sentence may have more than one subject and verb and still be a simple sentence because it has just one independent clause.

The team and the coach are hoping and praying.
[This sentence has a compound subject (*The team and the coach*) and compound predicate (*are hoping and praying*) but only one clause.]

A *compound sentence* has two or more independent clauses, each expressing a complete thought.

Compound sentences are used to show that thoughts are related and equal. They can be constructed in three ways.

- Independent clauses may be connected by a comma and a *coordinating conjunction* (*and, but, for, nor, or, so, yet*).

  The team is in a slump, *but* the coach is unconcerned.

- Independent clauses may be connected by a semicolon.

  The team is in a slump; the coach is unconcerned.
  [Grammatically correct, but journalists would avoid this.]

- Independent clauses may be connected by a *conjunctive adverb* with a semicolon in front of it and usually a comma following it.

  The team is in a slump; *however*, the coach is unconcerned.
  [This, also, is usually avoided in journalism.]

Conjunctive Adverbs

accordingly	besides	nevertheless	then
also	consequently	otherwise	therefore
anyhow	moreover	still	thus

A *complex sentence* contains one independent clause and one or more dependent clauses.

The team was in a slump already [independent clause] when its best pitcher broke his arm [dependent clause].

Dependent clauses are subordinated to the independent clause by *subordinating conjunctions* or *relative pronouns*. If you see a subordinating conjunction or relative pronoun, what follows is probably a dependent clause.

Subordinating Conjunctions

although	as though	if	till	when
as	because	since	unless	where
as if	before	that	until	whether

Relative Pronouns

that	what	which	who	whoever
		whichever	whom	whomever
		whose	whose	whosoever

A *compound-complex sentence* contains two or more independent clauses and one or more dependent clauses.

> The cat was on the mat [independent clause], and the dog was eyeing him [independent clause] when Mandeville came home [dependent clause].

Journalism Tip
Using Different Types of Sentences

Media writers should remember the following points about sentences.

Simple sentences are the easiest to understand and make a great way to stress a point clearly. But too many of them in a row sound choppy and distracting.

Compound sentences, complex sentences and *compound-complex sentences* should be used only when the writer wants to stress that two or more ideas are closely related. Otherwise, the writing can become illogical or confusing.

WEAK	Palmer, who also has a master's degree in philosophy, is socially adept when it comes to interacting with her patients.
	[What is the logical connection between her master's degree and her social skills? The sentence implies one, intentionally or not.]
BETTER	Palmer is socially adept when it comes to interacting with patients. But there's a more solitary, intellectual side of her, as well, as evidenced by her master's degree in philosophy.

With *complex sentences*, it's usually clearer not to separate the subject and verb of an independent clause with a dependent clause:

WEAK	The president, although the Cabinet advised against doing so, vetoed the measure.
BETTER	The president vetoed the measure, although the Cabinet advised against doing so.

Compound-complex sentences usually are too long to make good leads for articles, so if you've led with one, consider breaking it down.

CHAPTER 11

Subjects and Objects

The *subject* is the part of a sentence or clause that's doing something or being something, and *objects* are, among other things, receivers of the actions. Subjects and objects are sometimes called *substantives* and are the only words in a sentence that can name something that has substance — people, places and things. They also can name ideas or qualities. Those five things, in fact, define the function of a *noun*, the basic kind of substantive. *Pronouns* are the main kind of words that substitute for a noun by referring back to one.

We'll discuss in more depth at the end of this chapter what kinds of words can be subjects and objects and their various uses in sentences. But first, let's look at the most practical things to know about them when you're writing or editing.

Solving Common Problems

Probably, the most common mistakes with subjects and objects have to do with *subject-verb agreement*, *pronoun-antecedent agreement* and *unclear pronoun references*. But we'll discuss these in Chapter 13, Making the Parts Agree.

For now, the other common mistakes with subjects and objects boil down to seven main issues, most of which have to do with choosing the right word or the right form of a word:

1. Choose among *that* or *which*, or *who* or *whom*.
2. Understand how to use pronouns ending in *self* or *selves*.
3. Spell singulars, plurals and possessives correctly.
4. Choose the right pronoun case.
5. Make sure trademarks are capitalized.

6. Know when to capitalize names that are neither clearly proper names nor common nouns.

7. Make nouns and pronouns possessive before a gerund.

Let's begin.

1. Choose among *that* or *which*, or *who* or *whom*.

These words, as well as *whoever, whomever, whose* and sometimes *what*, are called *relative pronouns*. Relative pronouns relate back to an *antecedent*—a previous noun or pronoun—and at the same time serve as the subject or object of the clause in which they occur (except for *whose*, which is an adjective modifying a subject or object). The result is a kind of *dependent clause* called a *relative clause*.

When a relative pronoun appears in a sentence, run through the following three steps to make sure it's the right pronoun to use.

Step 1: Decide Between the That and Who Families

When the word refers to a *collective noun* (such as the name of an association, a business or a governing body), a thing (an inanimate object, abstraction and so on), or an animal without a proper name, the relative pronoun should be from the *that* family (*that* or *which*). When the word refers to a person or to an animal with a proper name, the correct relative pronoun should be from the *who* family (*who, whom, whoever, whomever, whose* or *who's*).

> Mobil is the oil company *that* (not *who*, despite the ads) wants to invite you to support public television.
> [The antecedent, *company*, refers to a business.]

> The dog *that* bit the child has not been found.
> [The antecedent, *dog*, refers to an animal without a name.]

> Who is this playwright David Henry Hwang *whom* everyone is discussing?
> [The antecedent, *David Henry Hwang*, refers to a person.]

> Their cat Fluffy, *who* just had kittens, wasn't straying far from the closet.
> [The antecedent, *Fluffy*, refers to an animal with a name.]

Step 2: Decide Between That and Which (or Possibly, What)

Choose *which* to set off something *nonrestrictive* (nonessential to the meaning of the sentence) — or, as we say, something *parenthetical*. Choose *that* to set off something *restrictive* (essential) — something you wouldn't put in parentheses.

NONRESTRICTIVE	The Nile, *which flows into the Mediterranean*, gives Egypt life.
RESTRICTIVE	The Nile is the river *that gives Egypt life*.

If you think of a nonessential clause as something parenthetical — an aside — you can remember that *which* introduces a clause that could be set off by parentheses, dashes or commas. *That* introduces a clause *not* set off by parentheses, dashes or commas.

RESTRICTIVE	The policy *that critics charged was flawed from the beginning* was amended. [The clause tells what policy of several.]
NONRESTRICTIVE	The policy, *which critics charged was flawed from the beginning*, was amended. [The clause merely adds a fact parenthetically about the policy under discussion.]
RESTRICTIVE	The house *that had a brick front* was theirs. [The clause tells what house.]
NONRESTRICTIVE	The corner house, *which had a brick front*, was theirs. [The clause merely adds a fact parenthetically about the house.]

Use *what* rather than *that* or *which* mainly in questions and also in place of the phrase *that which* or *those which*.

What book has Democrats seeing red these days?
[question]

Pundits say he stands a good chance to get *what* he wants.
[meaning *that which*]

Step 3: Decide Between Who *and* Whom, *or* Whoever *and* Whomever

The problem for a writer is that *whom* and *whomever* seem to be on the way out in spoken English, so you can't necessarily trust your ear when writing. For broadcast or more conversational writing, you might do what most people do in conversation and use *whom* or *whomever* only after a preposition. Even less formally, some people get rid of *whom* and *whomever* altogether.

But the distinction traditionally drawn, and that most editors still follow, especially in print and online, is this:

Use *who* or *whoever* when the clause calls for a subject pronoun and *whom* or *whomever* when the clause calls for an object pronoun. (See Page 123.)

Often, the hard part is determining what case to use, especially when the sentence has more than one clause, because the correct case must reflect the way the pronoun is used in its clause. Look at this sentence:

Word got out that disgruntled employees were giving free meals to *whoever* asked for one.

Here the preposition *to* can mislead many people into saying or writing *giving free meals to whomever*. Actually, though, the pronoun here is the subject of the clause *whoever asked for one*. This entire dependent clause takes the place of a single noun and acts as the object of the preposition *to*.

Here's another tricky one:

> The police officer asked the witness to point out *whomever* he saw at the scene of the crime.

This time, *whomever* is correct because it's the direct object of the verb *saw*, as in *he saw him*.

If determining the correct case in those last two examples left you scratching your head, help is on the way. It is possible to get *who* versus *whom* right every time without doing any extensive grammatical analysis. Here's how:

Begin reading the sentence immediately after the point at which you have a choice between *who* or *whom*, *whoever* or *whomever*. (If the sentence has more than one clause, this will ensure that you are looking at the correct one.) Then, insert *he* or *him*, *she* or *her*, or *they* or *them* wherever it makes sense. If *he*, *she* or *they* works better, use *who* or *whoever*. If *him*, *her* or *them* works best, use *whom* or *whomever*.

> *Who* did you say wrote the Miss Minimalist blog?
> [subject of clause, so use the *subject form*, more formally called the *nominative case*: *Did you say she wrote the Miss Minimalist blog?*]

> *Whoever* is going had better get ready.
> [subject of clause, so use the subject form: *He is going.*]

> To *whom* are you speaking?
> [object of preposition, so use the *object form*, more formally called the *objective case*: *Are you speaking to them?*]

> Talk with *whomever* you like, and you'll get the same answer.
> [object of preposition, so use the object form: *You like her.*]

To decide when *who* or *whom* needs *ever* at the end, remember that *whoever* is used in place of *anyone* or *anyone who* and *whomever* is used in place of *anyone whom*.

> *Whoever* [*Anyone who*] was interested could pick up a brochure at the fair.

> *Whomever* [*Anyone whom*] you want to invite may come.

> While we're at it, let's look at two more similarly confusing words.

Whose *Versus* Who's

Don't confuse the relative pronoun *whose* (the possessive form of *who*) with the contraction *who's*, meaning "who is" or "who has." Here, the test is, "Could I substitute *who is* or *who has*?" If yes, the correct word is *who's*. If no, the correct word is *whose*, which is acting as an adjective.

Who's
~~Whose~~ going to see the new Will Ferrell movie?

whose
She said she didn't care ~~who's~~ feelings were hurt.

2. Understand how to use pronouns ending in *self* or *selves*.

The "selfish" pronouns—*myself, yourself, himself, herself, itself, ourselves, yourselves, themselves*—should be used only when the pronouns or nouns to which they refer have been used earlier in a sentence. There are only two proper uses for the selfish pronouns: *reflexively* when something acts on itself (*I hurt myself*) or *intensively* when drawing attention to the noun or pronoun to which it refers by immediately renaming it (*I, myself, will do it*).

The first- and second-person forms of these pronouns come from the possessive case (*my, our, your*), but the third-person forms come from the objective case (*him, her, it, them*). Never say or write *hisself, theirselves* or *theyselves*—or for that matter, *ourself* rather than *ourselves*.

Don't confuse pronouns ending in *self* or *selves* with the properly required pronoun case in a sentence. *Myself* is the biggest offender, especially in a compound subject or object.

> From JeanAnn and ~~myself~~ *me*, good night.
> [objective-case pronoun needed for object of preposition]

> Bill and ~~myself~~ *I* are making a list of people who will attend.
> [nominative-case pronoun needed for subject]

Don't use a non-*selfish* pronoun intensively—that is, to draw attention to the noun or pronoun by immediately renaming it.

WRONG	"My teacher she said . . ."
RIGHT	"My teacher herself said . . ."

3. Spell singulars, plurals and possessives correctly.

Nouns in English change their spellings based on *number*—whether they are singular versus plural—and *case*—whether they are possessive.

Our Changing Language
Gendered Words

A few nouns also change their spellings for *gender*, but these are mostly disappearing. For example, a woman who writes poetry used to be called a *poetess*, but that is seen as a demeaning term today, and the preferred word is *poet* for both men and women. Some words have kept the distinction, but even *actress* and *hostess* are being replaced by *actor* and *host*. (See Page 242.)

Forming Singulars and Plurals of Nouns

The rule for making an English noun plural is, in most instances, to add *s* to the singular form if it does not end in *s*, or *es* if it does.

The plural of common nouns ending in *ch, s, sh, ss, tch, x*, and some ending in *z* or *zz* is usually formed by adding *es: churches, buses, washes, glasses, ditches, foxes, waltzes, buzzes*. But some nouns ending in *z* double the *z* before adding *es* to make the plural: *quizzes, whizzes*.

The plural of common nouns ending with a consonant followed by *y* is generally formed by changing the *y* to *i* and adding *es: try, tries*. The plural of proper nouns ending in a consonant followed by *y* is formed by adding *s: Holly, Hollys*.

If a noun ends with a vowel followed by *y*, generally the *y* stays the same and *s* is added: *day, days*.

The plural of a single letter is formed by adding *'s: A's*. The plural of a multiletter word or abbreviation or of a single-digit or multidigit number is formed without the apostrophe: *ABCs, 1s, 2010s*.

For a more comprehensive list of rules for spelling plurals, turn to the Understanding in More Depth section for this chapter, Page 157.

Forming Possessives of Nouns

Unlike in some languages, English nouns are spelled the same whether they're used in a sentence as a subject or as an object. (That is not true of pronouns, as we'll see later.) But the spelling of a noun does change if the noun owns something (*the girl's doll*) or has an attribute that's being discussed (*the computer's power*). When we add an apostrophe or *'s* to the end of a noun, we say that noun is in *possessive case*.

Journalism's rules for forming the possessive case of a noun may sometimes differ from what you learned in English class.

The most basic rule is add *'s* to the end of a noun not ending in *s* and just an apostrophe to the end of a noun ending in *s: a boy's goal, the boys' goals, Smith's house, the Smiths' house, Jones' car*, the *Joneses' car*.

But there are numerous exceptions, as the extended list of rules on Pages 161–162 shows.

Singulars and Plurals as Well as Person and Gender With Pronouns

Because pronouns have some different characteristics from nouns, in this section we'll look at forming the singulars and plurals of pronouns along

Subjects and Objects

A pronoun in the complete subject introduced by *as well as* is in the subject form, even though it does not influence the number of the verb.

> That photographer, as well as *we* two reporters, was in France to cover the summit.

A pronoun following *as* or *than* at the end of a sentence is usually in the subject form, although many people mistake a pronoun in such a position for the object of a preposition. But *as* and *than* are conjunctions, and a pronoun following a conjunction is typically the subject of a clause for which the predicate may be implied.

> He finished the test as quickly *as she* (did).

> The Rolling Stones were a more popular band in the '60s than *they* (were).

Object Form With Pronouns

If a pronoun is the direct object; indirect object; object of a preposition, participle, gerund or infinitive; or subject of an infinitive, it must be in the object form.

> Rescuers couldn't reach *them* in time.
> [*Them* is the direct object.]

> Graham Zusi kicked *him* the ball.
> [*Him* is the indirect object.]

> His brother borrowed the bike from *him*.
> [*Him* is the object of the preposition *from*.]

> Missing *him*, she sent a text.
> [*Him* is the object of the participle *missing*.]

> Cleaning *it* proved difficult.
> [*It* is the object of the gerund *cleaning*.]

> They took *him* to be *me*.
> [*Him* is the subject of the infinitive *to be*. The object of the infinitive is *me*.]

A pronoun used in a compound object should be in the object form.

WRONG	Between you and *myself* . . .
RIGHT	Between you and *me* . . .
	[The pronouns form a compound object of the preposition.] Substitute another preposition for *between*, and you wouldn't say, for example, "for *I*."
WRONG	They invited a friend and *he*.
RIGHT	They invited a friend and *him*.
	[*Friend* and *him* are compound direct objects. You wouldn't say, "They invited *he*."]

If you have a noun between a verb and the infinitive *to be*, use the object form after the infinitive. If not, use the subject form.

> Police took Talbot to be *her*.
> [*Talbot* is between the verb *took* and the infinitive *to be*.]

> Palmer was thought to be *she*.
> [There is no noun or pronoun between the verb *thought* and the infinitive *to be*.]

The second example above at first seems to be an exception to the rule that the *object of an infinitive*—like any other object—must be in the objective case. But actually, *was thought to be* is functioning here as a linking verb, making the following pronoun a *predicate nominative*, which is in subject form, although this is changing in less formal writing. (For more on predicate nominatives, see Page 158.)

ESL Tip

After verbs, pronouns are the most difficult grammatical element to master in most languages. Paying close attention to American conversation helps make the proper use of pronouns nearly automatic, but be aware that conversation often differs from what is considered correct in formal writing, as shown by examples in this chapter.

Possessive Form With Pronouns

Use the possessive form (possessive case) if the pronoun owns something or shows attribution.

> The president continued *his* address without missing a beat, even when the teleprompter failed.

Use the possessive form when the pronoun is followed by a gerund.

> A producer from Motown Records was there to hear *his* (not *him*) singing that night.

5. Capitalize *proper nouns* (nouns referring to actual names).

The basic rule is capitalize proper nouns (such as *Andrew*, *Colorado*) and lowercase common nouns (generic nouns, such as *truck* or *toothpaste*). A common mistake with ESL writers is to lowercase days of the week and months of the year (*Friday*, *January*) as done in many languages like Spanish, French and Italian. But the most serious violation of the capitalize-proper-names rule is when writers lowercase trademarks they may think are generic terms. This creates a possible legal problem that could result in a lawsuit for trademark infringement. See the list of trademarks and their generic equivalents on Pages 323–327.

Subjects and Objects

Kinds of Subjects

A *subject* is the noun or pronoun that is doing the acting or being in a sentence. To find the subject of a clause or sentence, ask "Who?" or "What?" before the verb.

> The Nebraska Cornhuskers won the game.
> [Who won the game? The Nebraska Cornhuskers.]

> The *fee* for graduate students is more this year.
> [What is more this year? The *fee*.]

Sometimes, the subject is also called the *simple subject* to distinguish it from the *complete subject*, which is the subject and its modifiers. In the preceding examples, *The Nebraska Cornhuskers* is the complete subject of the first sentence and *The fee for graduate students* is the complete subject of the second.

A *subject of an infinitive* is a noun (or its substitute) that comes between the verb and the infinitive. Oddly, if the subject of an infinitive is a pronoun, it takes the same form it would if it were an object of some kind.

> The police took *her* to be a modern Dillinger.
> [verb: *took*; infinitive: *to be*]

> He encouraged *them* to play sports.
> [verb: *encouraged*; infinitive: *to play*]

Our Changing Language

Predicate Nominative in Informal Writing

In formal speaking and writing, *predicate nominatives* — nouns or their substitutes that follow a *linking verb* (see Page 172) and restate the subject — take the same form as if they were the subject (nominative case).

WRONG	It's her.
RIGHT	It's she.

It's she probably sounds either odd or pretentious to you because in daily conversation, nominative-case pronouns are reserved mainly for subjects only, not for predicate nominatives. In the most formal writing, however, *It's she* is preferred over the more conversational *It's her*.

But the practice of using a nominative-case pronoun for a predicate nominative is seldom observed conversationally anymore, so in informal writing — such as for blogs, social media and broadcast — it will sound better to most of your audience to skip this. We are also seeing less of this even in formal writing because most people prefer the more conversational use of objective-case pronouns for predicate nominatives.

Subjects and Objects

Kinds of Objects

A *direct object* is the direct receiver of the action in a sentence. To find the direct object, ask "Whom?" or "What?" after the verb.

> The board thanked *him* for his 20 years of service.
> [Thanked whom? *Him*.]

> The company installed additional *servers* to handle the increased demands.
> [Installed what? *Servers*.] (The word *additional* is an adjective describing *servers*.)

A *predicate objective* (or *objective complement*) sometimes follows a direct object and restates it.

> The American public elected him *president*.
> [direct object: *him*]

> The proud parents named their new son *Taylor*.
> [direct object: *son*]

An *indirect object* is the person or thing *to whom* or *to which*, or *for whom* or *for which*, an action is done. To tell the difference between an indirect object and a direct object in front of a predicate objective, remember that you can put *to* or *for* in front of an indirect object.

> He gave the *Detroit Free Press* an exclusive.
> [He gave an exclusive to whom? The *Detroit Free Press*.]

> She gave *them* the report this morning.
> [She gave the report to whom? *Them*.]

An *object of a preposition* is a noun or its substitute following a preposition.

> In the *movie*, apes rule the planet.
> [preposition: *in*]

> The skid marks began near this *driveway*.
> [preposition: *near*]

If the object of the preposition is also acting as the indirect object of the sentence, its role as indirect object takes precedence by convention in labeling it. This is because usually a prepositional phrase acts as an adjective or adverb, not as a noun or pronoun, except when the object of the preposition is the indirect object.

> The editor gave the assignment to *her*.
> [*Her* is the object of the preposition *to* but should be called the indirect object of the sentence because the sentence could be rewritten as *The editor gave her the assignment*.]

An *object of a participle* is a noun or its substitute following a participle.

> The company will take an expected $200 million loss, including a probable *decline* in investments.
> [participle: *including*]

> A blond-haired man was spotted carrying a *gun*.
> [participle: *carrying*]

Subjects and Objects

An *object of a gerund* is a noun or its substitute following a gerund.

> Playing *poker* with them left him poorer.
> [gerund: *playing*]

> The witness said he didn't believe in naming *names*.
> [gerund: *naming*]

An *object of an infinitive* (or *infinitive complement*) answers "What?" "Whom?" or "Where?" after an infinitive.

> The police want him to answer some *questions*.
> [What do they want him to answer? *Questions*.]

> They thought Sumey to be *her*.
> [Whom did they think Sumey to be? *Her*.] (Notice that if the linking verb *was* replaced *to be*, the pronoun would change to the subject form of *she*. But as the sentence is written, *her* is in object form as the object of the infinitive.)

> They said they intend to return to *Oregon*.
> [Where do they intend to return? *Oregon*.]

Verbal Nouns: Gerunds and Infinitives

A *verbal noun* is a noun made from a verb. The two kinds are *gerunds* and *infinitives*.

We discuss gerunds here but will discuss infinitives in Chapter 12.

A *gerund* is a verb form ending in the present-participle form (*ing*) or some-times in the past-participle form (*ed*, *t* and so on) that is used in place of a noun.

> *Fishing* is a relaxing way to spend a morning.

> She was one of the *neglected*.

> He was a *drunk*.

More on Forming Singulars and Plurals of Nouns

Here are some additional rules to those listed earlier in the chapter.

The plural of nouns ending in *fe* or *lf* is often formed by changing the ending to *ve* and adding *s*: *knife, knives; self, selves; wife, wives; wolf, wolves*. The plural of some nouns ending in *f*, however, requires adding only *s*: *roof, roofs; proof, proofs*.

The plural of nouns ending in *o* is often formed simply by adding *s*: *duos, ghettos, pianos, radios, solos, trios, zeros*. The plural of many such nouns, however, requires *es*: *heroes, potatoes, tomatoes, tornadoes, volcanoes*.

The plural of most proper nouns ending in *es, s* or *z* is formed by adding *es*. The plural of most other proper nouns is formed by adding *s*: *Cortes, Corteses; Schwartz, Schwartzes; BlackBerry, BlackBerrys; Pacino, Pacinos*.

The plural of a few words is formed using *en*: *child, children; ox, oxen; woman, women*. This is a leftover from Old English (450 to 1066).

Some singular words from foreign languages maintain the foreign plural: *Bacterium* (singular) becomes *bacteria*, *criterion* (AP doesn't like *criterium*) becomes *criteria*, *datum* becomes *data*, *graffito* becomes *graffiti*, *medium* becomes *media*, *phenomenon* becomes *phenomena*, and *stratum* becomes *strata*. Notice that many people misuse the plural form of some of these for the singular. Two that don't follow this rule in AP are *cactus*, which becomes *cactuses*, and *memorandum*, which becomes *memorandums*. Note that similarly, *alumnus* (male singular) becomes *alumni* (male plural or the plural when both men and women are meant), and *alumna* (female singular) becomes *alumnae* (female plural for when only women are included). Also, AP now accepts media as either singular or plural depending on the meaning — usually plural but singular when referring to media as a monolithic group.

Some words have the same form in the plural as in the singular: *deer*, *sheep*.

To form the plural of compound words where the main sense is carried by the first word in the compound, add *s* to the end of the first word: *attorneys general*, *mothers-in-law*.

More on Forming Possessives of Nouns

Here are some additional rules to those listed earlier in the chapter.

Singular *common nouns* (generic names such as *witness, goodness, appearance*) that end in *s* or an *s* sound normally add *'s*: *a witness's testimony*. But if the next word starts with *s* or an *s* sound, the possessive common noun takes only an apostrophe: *witness' story, for goodness' sake, for appearance' sake*.

Compound words add the apostrophe or *'s* to the word nearest the object possessed: *attorney general's* (singular, possessive) *opinion, mothers-in-law's* (plural, possessive) *affection*.

In case of ownership by two people, either one or two possessives may be used, depending on the sense: *Mary and Bill's cars* (they own them together, so use just one *'s* for the two), but *Mary's and Bill's cars* (they own them separately, so each takes *'s*).

If you can turn the phrase around and insert *for* between the words, it's a descriptive phrase rather than truly possessive and does not need the apostrophe or *'s*: *citizens band radio* (radio band for citizens), *teachers college* (college for teachers, not one they own), *writers guide* (a guide for writers).

Sometimes, despite this rule, you have to use *'s* with descriptive phrases because the plural form doesn't end in *s*: *children's play, women's college*. Sometimes, too, a phrase can be turned around and *for* inserted, but *of* would work just as well: *teachers salaries*. Does this mean "salaries *for* teachers" or "salaries *of* teachers"? When it could go either way, the plural often substitutes for the possessive. In this example, however, you could drop the *s* and avoid the problem: *teacher salaries*.

Other exceptions include *baker's dozen, confectioners' sugar, nurse's aide* and *tinker's damn.* If the descriptive phrase is used in the name of an organization, use the apostrophe or not according to the organization's preference: *Actors' Equity, Ladies' Home Journal, Professional Golfers' Association of America.*

Some phrases that are merely descriptive rather than possessive are better hyphenated instead.

NOT TRULY POSSESSIVE	three weeks' vacation
BETTER	three-week vacation

Some editors insist that inanimate objects that could not really own something should not be made possessive. They would have you write *the power of the smartphone* rather than *the smartphone's power*, for example. But such a rule can cause problems with some idioms, such as *a week's pay.* Would anyone really write *the pay of a week*?

Double possessives, such as *a brother of Bill's,* occur only when two conditions are met: The word before *of* must involve only some of the possessions — in this case, one brother, not all of them — and the word after *of* cannot be an inanimate object. So, for example, write *a friend of the company*, not *a friend of the company's*, because a company is an inanimate object.

 **LaunchPad Solo** | **Online Grammar Help**
macmillan learning

Launchpadworks.com
For practice with subjects and objects, log on to *LaunchPad Solo for Journalism* and go to *Exercise Central for AP Style.*

CHAPTER 12

Verbs

Verbs give sentences life. They are the most important part of speech to master when learning to speak a language and also the most important to master for improving your writing.

A *verb* expresses action or state of being and tells what a noun or its substitute is doing or being: *runs, writes, is, seems*. It can sometimes stand alone as a complete sentence: *Go!*

Solving Common Problems

Although there's more to know about verbs than any other part of speech—which is why this chapter is longer—most problems with them are easy to master.

1. Know when there should or should not be an *s* at the end of a verb.
2. Don't confuse the verbs *can, may, shall* and *will* with *could, might, would* and *should*, or with each other.
3. Don't misuse helping verbs—the verbs added to a main verb.
4. Don't misuse irregular verbs—those that don't make their past forms by adding *ed*.
5. Normally, avoid passive voice.
6. Avoid using nouns as verbs that editors dislike.

1. Know when there should or should not be an *s* at the end of a verb.

If a verb follows *he, she, it, one* or a noun not ending in *s* and if it describes something in the present, it must end in *s*. If it follows *I, you, we* or *they* and if it refers to something in the present, it can't end in *s*.

RIGHT He is late.

RIGHT They are late.

163

Also, if the verb is *was* (describing something in the past), it can only follow *I*, *he*, *she*, *it*, *one* or a noun not ending in *s* — never *you*, *we*, *they* or a noun ending in *s*.

RIGHT	I was late, and she was late, too.
WRONG	We ~~was~~ late, and they ~~was~~ late, too.

(were) ... *(were)*

2. Don't confuse the verbs *can*, *may*, *shall* and *will* with *could*, *might*, *would* and *should*, or with each other.

When writing in the past tense, do not use *can*, *may*, *shall* or *will*. Instead, use *could*, *might*, *should* or *would*.

couldn't
He ~~*can't*~~ have gone far.

might
She said she ~~*may*~~ have done it differently.

Our Changing Language
Is It *Can* I or *May* I?

Although many still insist that *can* and *may* be distinguished — *can* for ability, *may* for permission — such a distinction is not made in French, Italian or Spanish, and even educated people often use *can* in place of *may* in a question like, "Can I help you with this?" Whether you edit the verb in such a sentence depends on how conversational you want the question to be. For more formal situations, you might want to change it. If the situation is less formal, you might not. And if the sentence is a quote, you shouldn't.

You may choose to use the past-tense forms — *could*, *might*, *should* and *would* — in the present, as well, for politeness.

RIGHT	Will you do this for me?
RIGHT	Would you do this for me?
	[sounds more polite]

3. Don't misuse helping verbs — the verbs added to a main verb. (If you're unsure what helping verbs or main verbs are, see Pages 170–171.)

Don't confuse the preposition *of* with the verb *have,* or its abbreviation *'ve* after a verb. Although these phrases may sometimes sound similar when spoken, using the preposition *of* does not make grammatical sense.

WRONG	RIGHT	WRONG	RIGHT
could of	could have, could've	should of	should have
might of	might have, might've	will of	will have
must of	must have, must've	would of	would have

Don't use a form of *have* in situations where it might imply something was intended that wasn't.

WRONG	He *had* his arm broken.
	[This implies the subject wanted his arm broken and hired someone to do it.]
RIGHT	He *broke* his arm.

Don't use *would have* with *could have*.

had

If he ~~would~~ not ~~have~~ had an operation the week before, he *could have* finished the race.

[Because having the operation happened before he finished the race, that verb must express an earlier time, not the same time.]

Don't use helping verbs such as *had* or *should* with *ought*.

The settlers ~~had~~ ought to leave.

Don't use *might* as a helping verb to *could*.

be able to

He said he might ~~could~~ help.

Our Changing Language
Should You Never Split Verb Phrases?

Some editors insist that the helping verb be kept next to the main verb. For example, some editors would rewrite *She would absolutely like to excel* to keep the adverb *absolutely* from interrupting the helping verb and main verb: *She absolutely would like to excel.* We discourage this as a standard practice for several reasons: It can make for sentences written in a nonconversational manner, the adverb *not* must be placed between the parts of the verb regardless, and changing the order may change the meaning of the sentence. (See Page 217.)

---

4. Don't misuse irregular verbs — those that don't make their past forms by adding *ed*.

Regular verbs distinguish the past from the present by adding *ed* or *t*: *edit, edited; leap, leaped* (or *leapt*). (Sometimes a final *y* becomes *i* before the ending: *rely, relied.*) But in English, as in all languages, many of the most commonly used verbs are irregular.

Irregular verbs in English distinguish the past from the present by changing the middle of the verb, by having a different form from the

Verbs

simple-past form for use with a helping verb, or by not changing forms at all from present to past to past with a helping verb:

sing, sang, sung [change in middle]

fall, fell, fallen [change in middle and different past participle]

broadcast, broadcast, broadcast [no change]

Probably, the most common mistake with irregular verbs — and the one that will most damage your credibility if you make it — is to confuse a past-tense form with the past-tense-with-helping-verb form (*past participle*). Because the simple past and past-participle forms are the same with regular verbs, mistaking the two forms is a problem only with irregular verbs, where the two may differ. The worst examples from the standpoint of your audience usually involve the verbs *to come*, *to do*, *to go* and *to see*.

Smith ~~come~~ *came* over to Lincoln often when he lived in Kearney.

She drove to town and got her hair ~~did~~ *done*.

He had already ~~went~~ *gone* home by the time the candidate arrived late.

The neighbors said they ~~seen~~ *saw* the flying saucer.

For a list of the *principal parts* (the most common verb forms) of common irregular and confusing verbs, take a look at the Understanding in More Depth section on Pages 177–179.

5. Normally, avoid passive voice.

All verbs are in either the active voice or the passive voice, but it may be easier to think of all *sentences* as being either active or passive.

Active-voice sentences stress the doer of an action by making the doer the subject.

ACTIVE VOICE, PRESENT TENSE	The printer *publishes* the magazine.
ACTIVE VOICE, PAST TENSE	The printer *published* the magazine.

Passive-voice sentences stress the receiver of an action by making the receiver the subject of the sentence and having the subject acted on.

PASSIVE VOICE, PRESENT TENSE	The magazine *is published* by the printer.
PASSIVE VOICE, PAST TENSE	The magazine *was published* by the printer.

Note that the passive voice always contains a form of the verb *to be* as a helping verb in addition to the past participle of the main verb (in these examples: *is published* and *was published*).

In the passive voice, there is also always a phrase starting with *by* or *for* either expressed or implied.

PASSIVE VOICE, EXPRESSED	The magazine was published *by the printer*.
PASSIVE VOICE, IMPLIED	The magazine was published. [Grammarian Richard Mitchell calls sentences like this, in which the doer has been left out, the "divine passive" because only God knows who did it. We'll use that term, also.]

Grammatically speaking, there's nothing wrong with writing sentences in a passive voice, but from a literary standpoint, a passive voice lacks the appeal of an active voice. Passive-voice sentences are wordier, more awkward sounding, less interesting, more stilted or formal and often more vague. Which of the following sounds best to you?

PASSIVE VOICE	A contract proposal *has been rejected* by area teachers.
(DIVINE) PASSIVE VOICE	A contract proposal *has been rejected*.
ACTIVE VOICE	Area teachers *have rejected* a contract proposal.

The active-voice sentence is shorter than the first and more specific than the second, while sounding less stilted and more to the point than the other two.

What we might call *extreme passive-voice sentences* (our term) can also turn powerful verbs into weak nouns.

ACTIVE VOICE	The military *interrogated* the prisoners.
PASSIVE VOICE	The prisoners *were interrogated* by the military.
(DIVINE) PASSIVE VOICE	The prisoners *were interrogated*.
(EXTREME) PASSIVE VOICE	Interrogations of prisoners *were made* by the military. [Here, the subject is *interrogations*, a thing, rather than *military*, a doer.]
(DIVINE AND EXTREME) PASSIVE VOICE COMBINED	Interrogations of prisoners *were made*.

In addition to those forms of passive voice, occasionally, but rarely, a sentence may imply the past participle of the main verb.

There will be no presentation by the candidate.

In that sentence, there's an implied past participle—*made*—*meaning there's an implied passive voice:*

IMPLIED PASSIVE   There will be no presentation *made* by the candidate.

Again, the sentence would be better rewritten:

ACTIVE   The candidate will make no presentation.

Our Changing Language
Always Avoid the Passive Voice?

Many students have been taught—incorrectly—always to avoid passive voice. The fact is, it should *usually* be avoided, but there are times when it's perfectly fine.

Journalists may choose the passive voice in the following instances:

- When the person being acted on is more important than the person doing the acting, such as is often the case in a crime or an accident story.

  The nation's prime minister *was shot* and *killed* by an assassin today. This also avoids convicting someone before a trial.

- When the person doing the acting is unknown.

  A one-armed man *is being sought* in connection with the death of a woman in Chicago.

- When reporters seek to preserve the confidentiality of their sources. It *is reported* that . . .

Some verbs should be used in passive voice. The verb *divorce* must always be in passive voice or transitive.

WRONG	They married then divorced. [transitive (followed by a direct object)]
RIGHT	They were divorced. [passive]
RIGHT	He divorced her. [transitive]

Don't shift between active and passive voice in the same sentence.

Learn how to spot passive voice using the following guidelines.

- The subject is acted on rather than doing or being anything itself.

ACTIVE VOICE   The City Council *voted* to censure the mayor.
[The City Council took action.]

PASSIVE VOICE   The mayor *was censured* by the City Council.
[The mayor was acted on by the City Council.]

- Passive voice uses some form of the verb *to be* as a helping verb.

  | **ACTIVE VOICE** | Police *arrested* a suspect this morning. |
  | **PASSIVE VOICE** | A suspect *was* [*to be* helping verb] *arrested* **this morning by police.** |

- Passive voice uses the past participle of the main verb, usually present but sometimes implied. (For regular verbs, this is the form ending in *ed*. For irregular verbs, see the list of principal parts on Pages 177–179 or in a dictionary.)

- In a passive-voice sentence, the word *by* or *for* is either present or implied. Passive voice is shorter than active voice only when a phrase introduced by *by* or *for* is missing, but that, of course, leads to a lack of clarity about who is doing the acting. Don't confuse passive voice with other sentences that might also use *to be* as a helping verb but don't have *by* present or implied:

  | **NOT PASSIVE** | The victim was walking home from a bar, he said. |
  | **NOT PASSIVE** | She says she is writing a second book now. |

- Only verbs that take a *direct object* (also called *transitive verbs*) (see Page 171) have a passive-voice form. The active-voice subject becomes the word after *by* or *for* in the passive-voice sentence.

6. Avoid using nouns as verbs that editors dislike.

Although many nouns are also used as verbs in English, editors often object to using the following as verbs.

NOUN	CHANGE TO
author	write
contact	call, write, visit, email
debut	have its debut
effort	try
gift	give
is headquartered	has headquarters in
host	hold
impact	affect
ink	sign
jet	fly
journal	write a journal
language	express, say, write
parent	rear
partner, partnership	to form a partnership with
pastor	lead a congregation

Verbs

NOUN	CHANGE TO
pen	write, sign
premiere	have its premiere
script	write
summer	to spend the summer
target	aim at

In addition, you should avoid using certain verbs as nouns.

VERB	CHANGE TO
disconnect	disconnection
win	victory

Our Changing Language

Verbs Used as Nouns

Obviously, that list is subjective, and you—even we—may see nothing wrong with some of these. But it's useful to know that some people will judge you for using these. We say check the dictionary or *The AP Stylebook* for recent changes in the language, especially from technology. For example, *friend* and *like* are OK as verbs in stories about Facebook, according to AP. But be aware that of all the words on that list, AP specifically objects only to *author* used as a verb, as of the 2018 stylebook.

Understanding in More Depth

What's the Difference Between a Verb and a Predicate?

A *predicate* is what a verb is called as a part of a sentence. Sometimes, it's called the *simple predicate* to distinguish it from the *complete predicate*, which is the verb and its associated words, such as modifiers, objects or complements.

> Two of the candidates *have dropped* from the race.
> [simple predicate: *have dropped*; complete predicate: *have dropped from the race*]

What Are Helping Verbs and Main Verbs?

> Verbs are either *main verbs* or *helping verbs*.

A *main verb* may stand alone, or it may have helping verbs accompanying it.

> The mayor *loves* her job.
> [*Loves* is the main verb.]

Verbs

She *has loved* working as mayor.
[*Loved* is the main verb, *has* the helping verb.]

Helping verbs are primarily used to make some verb forms, such as the *simple future tense, perfect tenses, progressive tenses* and *conditional mood.* These verbs will be discussed later in this section.

Common Helping Verbs

am	could	have	shall
are	did	is	should
be	do	may	was
been	does	might	were
being	had	must	will
can	has	ought	would

Helping verbs that show *mood* (see Page 164) are called *modal verbs* and include *can, could, may, might, shall, should, will, would* and *must.* Other words or phrases act like modals in some ways but like main verbs in others. They're called *semimodal verbs* and include *be able to, dare to, have to, have got to, like to, need to, ought to, used to* and *want to.*

Helping verbs are also sometimes used to help show emphasis. For example, we may use a form of the verb *to do* as a helping verb to show emphasis. Often, we underline or italicize the helping verb for emphasis. Less often, we change the helping verb *shall* to *will* or *will* to *shall* to show emphasis. (See Page 177.) Sometimes, we combine a couple of these techniques, although it's important to be consistent about using either an underline or italics for emphasis in one work (bold is not used for emphasis), nor all caps either, which are frowned on even in emails and social media.

TO DO	I do edit, he did edit
UNDERLINE OR ITALICS	I <u>have</u> edited, he *has* edited
REVERSAL OF *WILL* AND *SHALL*	I will edit, you shall edit

What Are Transitive Verbs and Intransitive Verbs?

All verbs are either *transitive* or *intransitive* in any given sentence. Some are transitive in one sentence but intransitive in another.

Transitive verbs have a *direct object* (a receiver of the action) that tells to what or to whom the action was done.

The legislature *passed* the bill.
[Passed what? Passed *the bill*, the direct object.]

Intransitive verbs do not take a direct object. The two kinds of intransitive verbs are *linking* (or *copulative*) *verbs* and *complete verbs.*

Verbs

Linking verbs take a *predicate complement* — either a *predicate nominative* (noun or pronoun following the linking verb) or a *predicate adjective* (adjective following the linking verb).

> That is *she*.
> [predicate nominative]

> He is *impressed*.
> [predicate adjective]

A linking verb can be thought of as an equals sign indicating an equation between the subject and the predicate complement.

A predicate adjective may be modified by an adverb:

> He said he *was excruciatingly* hungry. [*Was* is a linking verb, *hungry* a predicate adjective and *excruciatingly* an adverb modifying *hungry*.]

Linking Verbs

TO BE VERBS

am	was	have been	will be
is	were	had been	
are	has been	shall be	

VERBS USED FOR THE FIVE SENSES

appear	look	sound
feel	smell	taste

OTHER LINKING VERBS

act	grow	stay
become	remain	turn
continue	seem	wax

Knowing when a verb is a linking verb helps you deal with troublesome choices between adjectives and adverbs, such as whether a person feels *good* or feels *well*. (See Pages 206–207.)

Complete verbs take neither a direct object nor a predicate complement:

> The woman *hesitated*.

Transitiveness or intransitiveness can be a useful distinction to keep in mind when you are trying to decide among three of the most commonly confused pairs of verbs: *sit* versus *set*, *rise* versus *raise*, and *lie* versus *lay*. The first verb of each of those pairs — *sit*, *rise* and *lie* — is intransitive. You don't *sit something down*, *rise something up* or *lie something down*. The second of each pair — *set*, *raise* and *lay* — is transitive. You do *set something down*, *raise something up* or *lay something down*. For the *principal parts* (main forms) of these verbs, see the list on Pages 177–179.

But note these idiomatic exceptions: The sun, a hen or concrete *sets*, as could glue or a food dish, such as a pie.

Understanding Verb Tenses

Verb tense refers mainly to time — when the action or state of being that the verb represents takes place.

Grammar books disagree on the number of tenses in English, depending on how the term *verb tense* is defined. Essentially, although we speak in English of *three broad time frames* — past, present and future — we have a number of ways to express those time frames with different nuances in meaning.

We think it makes most sense to think of six basic verb tenses: *past perfect, past, present perfect, present, future perfect* and *future*, in that order from furthest in the past to furthest in the future, with six additional *progressive verb tenses* for the same time periods.

Using the Simple Tenses

Each of the three broad time frames has a form we'll call a *simple tense*. These are usually just called the past, present and future tenses. To demonstrate them, we'll show the *conjugations* (various forms) of a typical verb — *to edit* — for each of these tenses.

In the following list, the column on the left lists the various personal pronoun forms, with the first and fourth lines representing what are called the first person forms, the second and fifth lines the second person forms, and the third and sixth the third person forms, with the first through third being singular in number, the fourth through sixth plural. The other three columns show the corresponding verb form in each of the three simple tenses for the sample verb to edit.

Another way to think of the number and person of a verb is as the form the verb takes with different pronouns. All nouns, except *nouns of direct address*, are considered to be in third person — singular or plural, depending on the ending — and require a verb of the same person and number.

Simple Tenses

	PAST	PRESENT	FUTURE
I	edited	edit	will/shall edit
you (singular)	edited	edit	will edit
he/she/it/one	edited	edits	will edit
we	edited	edit	will/shall edit
you (plural)	edited	edit	will edit
they	edited	edit	will edit

Verbs

Use one of these simple tenses to identify a specific point of time. Some words that commonly suggest that a simple tense should be used include *ago*, *at*, *at that time*, *in* [*2019* or some other year], *last* [*week, month, year, century*], *on*, *then* and *when* (as a question).

> ### ESL Tip
>
> Notice that in English, a verb's present-tense forms are often the same as the infinitive minus the *to*. For example, the only exception for most verbs other than *to be* is that the third-person singular of almost all English verbs in the present tense ends with *s*. Verbs that don't end in *s* in the third-person singular are the modal verbs, such as *can, may, must, shall* and *will*.

Using the Perfect Tenses

In addition to the simple past, present and future, each of those time periods has a second form of expression called the *perfect tenses*, or *perfects*. They refer to completed (perfected) events taking place previous to other events in the same general block of time. In other words, they offer ways to form a verb indicating these possibilities:

- Something took place before another event in the past.

    She *had edited* that story before she edited the next one.
    [The verb "had edited" is used because this happened "before she edited the next one."]

- Something in the present started and finished before what's happening now.

    They *have edited* three stories and are editing another one apiece now.
    [The verb "have edited" is used because they started and finished in the past three stories before what they're editing now.]

- Something will already have happened when another event in the future takes place.

    You *will have edited* about 30 stories by the time your shift is over.
    [Before your shift will be over in the future, you will also in the future, but previous to your shift being over, have edited about 30 stories.]

Perfect Tenses

	PAST PERFECT	PRESENT PERFECT	FUTURE PERFECT
I	had edited	have edited	will/shall have edited
you (singular)	had edited	have edited	will have edited
he/she/it/one	had edited	has edited	will have edited
we	had edited	have edited	will/shall have edited
you (plural)	had edited	have edited	will have edited
they	had edited	have edited	will have edited

Often, simple past and present perfect are interchangeable in everyday use.

RIGHT	Koch *has spent* time in Paris living among the artists.
	[present perfect]
RIGHT	Koch *spent* time in Paris living among the artists.
	[simple past]

Either sentence is correct if Koch is still alive. But what if the sentence is about someone who has died?

WRONG	George Washington *has slept* here.
	[present perfect]
RIGHT	George Washington *slept* here.
	[simple past]

If you were writing a story about a modern-day inn in New Jersey with a historic past, you wouldn't write the first sentence because even though perfect tenses refer in some way to completed actions in the past, this sentence implies George Washington is still alive. Clearly, you'd write the second sentence in the simple past because there's no such implication in it.

A useful guideline for helping decide in many instances between using a simple tense and present perfect is to ask yourself whether the action in the statement continues beyond what happened in the past. Words that commonly suggest that an action is continuing and thus call for present perfect include *already, during, for, how long, not anymore, not yet, since, still, this* [*week, month, year, decade*], *today, until* and *up to now.*

PRESENT PERFECT	Lee has already published freelance articles.
	[This implies Lee published articles in the past and continues to do so.]
SIMPLE PAST	Lee published freelance articles.
	[There's no implication Lee might still publish articles.]
PAST PERFECT	Lee had published freelance articles before she started college.
	[Lee started college in the past but even before that, she had published articles. There's no implication as to whether she still does.]

ESL Tip

The use of the perfect tenses in English can be troublesome for speakers of English as a second language because the perfects force distinctions many students may not be used to making in their own languages. For example, the perfects are dying in many European languages, such as German and French.

Verbs

Using the Progressive Tenses

The third way of writing about the past, present or future uses the *progressive tenses*, or *progressive aspects*.

There are two progressive forms for each broad time frame — one corresponding to the simple tense and one to the perfect. The progressives are formed using some form of *to be* as a helping verb and the *progressive* (*ing*, or *present-participle*, form) of the main verb. We'll give examples of just the first- and third-person singular for each.

Progressive Tenses

PAST-PERFECT PROGRESSIVE	I had been editing he, she, it, one had been editing
PAST PROGRESSIVE	I was editing he, she, it, one was editing
PRESENT-PERFECT PROGRESSIVE	I have been editing he, she, it, one has been editing
PRESENT PROGRESSIVE	I am editing he, she, it, one is editing
FUTURE-PERFECT PROGRESSIVE	I will/shall have been editing he, she, it, one will have been editing
FUTURE PROGRESSIVE	I will/shall be editing he, she, it, one will be editing

Progressives stress the ongoing nature of an activity of limited duration. But they can be more complicated.

PRESENT	She *is sleeping*. [She started earlier and is still asleep now.]
SIMPLE PRESENT	She *sleeps*. [Possibly suggests this is something she does occasionally.]
PRESENT PROGRESSIVE	The town *is bordering* on the Mississippi River.

ESL Tip

Speakers of English as a second language should avoid the mistake of forgetting either the *to be* verb or the *ing* ending in progressives.

WRONG	We *learning* grammar. (But you sometimes hear this done in broadcast news as a kind of approximation of a headline, as in "Congress *going* home this weekend without a vote on the budget.")
WRONG	We *are learn* grammar.
RIGHT	We *are learning* grammar.

Our Changing Language
Shall Versus *Will*

You might have noted on the past few pages the choice between *will* and *shall* in first-person singular in the future tenses (simple future, future perfect, future progressive and future-perfect progressive). *Will* is by far the more common in conversation, but older, traditional grammars insisted on *shall* rather than *will* for first-person verbs. These days, though, *shall* sounds too pretentious and old-fashioned to most Americans, and we recommend against it, especially in broadcast. *Shall* is used more often in Britain than in the United States, but it's losing ground there, as well.

If you do decide to use *shall* in the first person, the same people who insist on *shall* usually teach that, for emphasis, you should use *shall* where you would normally use *will* and vice versa.

NORMAL	EMPHATIC
I *shall* sing.	I *will* sing!
You *will* leave tomorrow.	You *shall* leave tomorrow!

It seems to us, though, that *will* and *shall* can be equally emphatic in the same places. Gen. Douglas MacArthur, for example, said, when leaving the Philippines in World War II, "I *shall* return!" not "I *will* return!" Likewise, in the 1960s, the civil rights marchers sang "We *shall* overcome," not "We *will* overcome." In common usage, in fact, it seems more likely that *shall* will be used to show emphasis, and that's the main time you hear *shall* used.

Principal Parts of Common Irregular and Other Confusing Verbs

We've listed the *principal parts* (the most common verb forms) of each: the present, past, past-participle and present-participle forms. (See Pages 165–166 for a discussion of these terms.)

PRESENT	PAST	PAST PARTICIPLE	PRESENT PARTICIPLE
awake	awoke *or* awaked	awaked *or* awakened	awaking *or* awakening
bear	bore	borne	bearing
bid (*offer*)	bid	bid	bidding
bid (*command*)	bade	bidden (not *bidded*)	bidding
bring	brought	brought	bringing
broadcast	broadcast	broadcast	broadcasting
burst	burst	burst	bursting
come	came	come	coming

Verbs

PRESENT	PAST	PAST PARTICIPLE	PRESENT PARTICIPLE
dive	dived	dived (AP)	diving
do	did	done	doing
drink	drank	drunk	drinking
drive	drove	driven	driving
drown	drowned	drowned	drowning

(Don't say a victim *was drowned* unless an assailant held the person's head under the water.)

eat	ate	eaten	eating
fall	fell	fallen	falling
fly (*soar*)	flew	flown	flying
fly (*hit a baseball high*)	flied	flied	flying
forbid	forbade	forbidden	forbidding
forsake	forsook	forsaken	forsaking
get	got	got *or* gotten	getting
go	went	gone	going
hang (*suspend*)	hung	hung	hanging
hang (*execute*)	hanged	hanged	hanging
hide	hid	hidden	hiding
keep	kept	kept	keeping
kneel	knelt *or* kneeled	knelt *or* kneeled	kneeling
lay (*set down*)	laid	laid	laying
lead	led	led	leading
lie (*recline*)	lay	lain	lying
pay	paid	paid	paying
plead	pleaded (AP: not *pled*)	pleaded	pleading
prove	proved	proved (*proven* is an adjective)	proving
put	put	put	putting
raise	raised	raised	raising
ring	rang	rung	ringing
rise	rose	risen	rising
see	saw	seen	seeing
set	set	set	setting

(*place down*; also, *hens set, cement sets* and *the sun sets*)

PRESENT	PAST	PAST PARTICIPLE	PRESENT PARTICIPLE
shake	shook	shaken	shaking
shine	shone	shone	shining
show	showed	showed *or* shown	showing
shrink	shrank	shrunk	shrinking
sit (*seat oneself*)	sat	sat	sitting
slay	slew	slain	slaying
sleep	slept	slept	sleeping
spring	sprang	sprung	springing
steal	stole	stolen	stealing
strive	strove	striven	striving
swear	swore	sworn	swearing
swim	swam	swum	swimming
swing	swung	swung	swinging
tread	trod	trodden *or* trod	treading
wake	woke	waked	waking
weave	wove	woven	weaving
wring	wrung	wrung	wringing

Sequence of Tenses

To use the right verb for what you're trying to say, you need to understand two especially important things:

1. *The time order of the forms from furthest in the past to furthest in the future.* That order, called the *sequence of tenses*, is as follows: *past perfect, past, present perfect, present, future perfect, future.* Remember, for each tense, the perfect form precedes the simple form.

2. *Special rules regarding the use of each form.* Following are some of the most important guidelines for using English verbs in the three broad time frames.

Past Tenses

Past Perfect. Use past perfect for events that occurred before those described in the past tense and are now concluded. It's often used with *after, before, by, by the time, until* or *when* to show that one event occurred before another:

> *Until* he turned 50, he *had* never *tried* his hand at writing poetry.

Past-Perfect Progressive.   Use past-perfect progressive for actions continuing from one point in the past to another one closer to the present before concluding.

> The rioting *had been going* unchecked until police intervened.

Past.   Use past for events that occurred in the past and are now concluded. Use if the sentence answers the question "How long ago?" or, often, if you can use *in* or *on* to express a time element.

> He first *exhibited* the signs of Parkinson's disease in 2018.

Present for Past.   Journalists usually use the simple present to express the past in a headline.

> Governor *Signs* Death Penalty Into Law

In addition, in daily conversation, people often use the simple present to express the past.

> "So, then I *say* to him, 'What are you trying to pull?'"

Past Progressive.   Use past progressive for something that was happening in the past but has since ended.

> The band *was playing* to packed stadiums in 2018.

Present Tenses

Present Perfect.   Use present perfect for events that started in the past and have continued into the present or have some connection with the present. Usually, but not always, it's used when *already, ever, for, never, not yet* or *since* is used to express a time element.

> If you *have ever wondered* what makes fast-food French fries taste so good, the answer is a sugar coating.

Present-Perfect Progressive.   Use present-perfect progressive for actions that began in the past and are still continuing in the present. Use if the statement answers the question "How long has this been happening?" A sentence in the present-perfect progressive often uses the word *for* or *since*.

> The Seattle Sounders *have been playing* well *since* opening day.

Present.   Use present for something happening now.

> Her book *sits* prominently on the coffee table.

Present Progressive.   Use present progressive in place of the simple present for many situations in which something is happening right now, according to common usage.

> The president *is meeting* with his advisers at this moment.

Future Tenses

Present for Future. English often permits the use of the simple present with an adverb of time to convey future action.

> She *leaves tomorrow.*

Future Perfect. Use future perfect for events that will have been completed in the future before something else happens. Future perfect is usually used with *by, by the time* or *when.*

> *By the time* you read this column, the World Series *will have been decided.*

Future-Perfect Progressive. Use future-perfect progressive for actions continuing from now into the future when the focus is on what will have been happening to that point. Future-perfect progressive, then, projects into the future and looks back.

> This Monday, Tom Williams *will have been coaching* 30 years at Central.

Future. Use future for events that will definitely occur in the future.

> The statewide referendum *will decide* the issue this November.

Future Progressive. Use future progressive for events continuing in the future with no end in sight.

> A hundred years from now, parents *will* still *be shaking* their heads at their teenagers' taste in music.

Our Changing Language
Journalism and Sequence of Tenses

Many editors insist on using a special rule governing the sequence of tenses in *reported speech.* Under this rule, when one is paraphrasing (not directly quoting) what someone has said, simple present becomes simple past (for example, *edit* becomes *edited, can* becomes *could,* and *may* becomes *might*), simple past becomes past perfect (*edited* becomes *had edited*), and *shall* or *will* in the simple future or future perfect becomes *should* or *would* (although *should* is almost never used this way in conversation or in print, *would* being substituted):

QUOTE	"I am young, but I am wise."
REPORTED SPEECH	She said she was young but she was wise.

We are skeptical about using the rule at all, for these reasons:

1. It seems to be potentially confusing.

   She said she *was* in favor of the plan.
   (But is she still?)

   She said she *would* speak to the class.
   (But is that based on some condition?)

Verbs

Common usage here — *She said she is in favor of the plan* and *She said she will speak to the class* — is capable of more nuances of meaning.

2. Contrary to what its supporters — who often call this *the sequence-of-tense rule* — believe, it really is not a typical sequence-of-tense issue, and, even if it were, it would certainly not be the only issue.

   Sequence of tense involves making the verbs in a sentence clear as to the time relationship between the events they describe. But with the reported-speech rule, the verb tense is changed in relation to what was originally said, not in relation to the attribution verb *said*. If the latter were the case, then all the verbs in the sentence would have to be previous to the simple past of *said*. Instead, the rule specifies that something someone said in simple present should become simple past.

ORIGINAL STATEMENT	The issue *is* controversial.
REPORTED SPEECH	She said the issue *was* controversial.
	[But if this were a true sequence-of-tense issue, *was* would have to become *has been* or *had been*.]

3. The reported-speech rule is not as universally urged in style and grammar books as its supporters imply. Not only do the stylebooks mentioned have different versions of the rule, but also *The AP Stylebook* and the latest *UPI Stylebook and Guide to Newswriting*s, for example, don't have an entry for it at all. If your stylebook requires it, use it. If it doesn't, we suggest being flexible.

Keeping Verb Tenses Consistent

Once you've selected the proper verb tense, for the most part you'll want to keep the tense consistent.

For example, don't start out using *said* to attribute every quotation and then switch later to *says*. Pick one or the other (generally, use *says* for a feature story only) and stick to it.

You can, however, switch tenses for a reason — such as to go into a flashback or to mention an event that occurred at an earlier time or will occur in the future.

If switching tenses becomes necessary, it's important to follow the correct sequence of tenses, using an earlier tense for an event that occurred earlier, a later one for something later. For example, if you've been writing in present tense and now write about something that took place earlier, you would switch to the present perfect, past or past perfect.

Or, if you want to express that something was already taking place when another action occurred, use the past progressive in one clause and the simple past in another:

He *was speaking* [past progressive] when the alarm *rang* [past].

If we tried to use the past perfect with the past in that example, the meaning would be different:

He *had spoken* [past perfect] when the alarm *rang* [past].

This second sentence implies that he had already finished speaking before the alarm rang.

More on Active Voice Versus Passive Voice

Don't confuse passive voice with other verb forms.

The verb conjugations listed on Pages 177–179 in this chapter are all in the active voice. To help you recognize the difference between active and passive voice, here are sample sentences showing the passive voice beside the same sentence in active voice for the six basic verb tenses.

Passive and Active Forms for Simple and Perfect Tenses

	PASSIVE VOICE	ACTIVE VOICE
PAST PERFECT	It *had been edited* by me.	I *had edited* it.
PAST	It *was edited* by me.	I *edited* it.
PRESENT PERFECT	It *has been edited* by me.	I *have edited* it.
PRESENT	It *is edited* by me.	I *edit* it.
FUTURE PERFECT	It *will have been edited* by me.	I *will have edited* it.
FUTURE	It *will be edited* by me.	I *will edit* it.

Notice in the sentences in this list that only the passive-voice sentences use some form of the verb *to be* as a helping verb. A passive voice should not be confused with the progressive tenses, however, which also use *to be* as a helping verb.

Look at the differences between passive-voice forms and active-voice progressive forms in the following list. Notice the passive voice always uses the past participle of the main verb, the *ed* form, never only the present participle, the *ing* form, used by the active progressive tenses. (Following this list are examples of the use of the *ing* form of *to be* as a helping verb, not the main verb, in passive progressive constructions.) Also, active voice in the progressive does not have or imply *by* or *for,* and the subject always is doing something rather than being acted on.

	PASSIVE VOICE	ACTIVE VOICE
PAST PERFECT	It *had been edited* by me.	I *had been editing* it.
PAST	It *was edited* by me.	I *was editing* it.
PRESENT PERFECT	It *has been edited* by me.	I *have been editing* it.
PRESENT	It *is edited* by me.	I *am editing* it.
FUTURE PERFECT	It *will have been edited* by me.	I *will have been editing* it.
FUTURE	It *will be edited* by me.	I *will be editing* it.

Verbs

There are only two passive progressive tenses.

PASSIVE PRESENT PROGRESSIVE   It *is being edited* by me.

PASSIVE PAST PROGRESSIVE   It *was being edited* by me.

Another culprit that confuses some writers into needless changes is a sentence with a linking verb followed by an adjective or by a participle used as an adjective.

ACTIVE VOICE   The bagel was *burnt*.
[participle used as an adjective]

ACTIVE VOICE   The bills were long past *due*.
[adjective]

At first, these sentences might seem to be in passive voice. In the first one, you can even imagine an implied *by*. But in these examples, what might look like a past participle is an adjective, not a part of the verb, and so the sentences are in active voice. How can you tell?

If you can put the word *very* in front of what you think is the past participle, the word is an adjective, not a verb.

The bagel was *very* burnt.

The bills were *very* long past due.

Our Changing Language

Do You Graduate College or Graduate From It?

Many purists also insist that the verb *graduate* should be used in the passive voice, as in *She was graduated from the University of Arizona. The AP Stylebook*, however, says that the active voice, *She graduated from the University of Arizona*, is preferred although both are correct. Either way, don't forget the *from*.

What Is Verb Mood?

Verb mood is hard to define but has to do with how the speaker or writer regards the statement being made. There are four moods: *indicative*, *imperative*, *conditional* and *subjunctive*. It's easier to understand them when we see how each is used.

Indicative Mood

We would guess 90 percent of English sentences are in the *indicative mood*, meaning that the sentence in which the verb appears either states a fact or asks a question about a fact. All of the verb conjugations we've listed so far are in the indicative mood. Assume a verb is in the indicative mood unless the situation clearly calls for one of the other three moods.

Verbs

Imperative Mood

Some verbs are in the *imperative mood*, meaning that the sentence makes a command, issues instructions or entreats.

Add 1 cup of flour.

Please *be* careful as you pour in the boiling water.

Conjugating imperative-mood verbs is easy because there is only one verb tense (present) with only two conjugations:

Edit! [second-person singular or plural]

Let's [Let us] edit! [first-person plural]

Note that the imperative mood leaves out the subject of the clause, instead implying it.

Conditional Mood

Some sentences use the *conditional mood*, which, as the name implies, expresses a condition. The conditional mood in English is usually represented by one of four helping verbs, although it can use the other modal verb *must*, as well as the *semimodal verbs*. (See Page 170) In the conditional:

can becomes *could*

may becomes *might*

shall becomes *should*

will becomes *would*

The conditional mood has forms for many but not all of the indicative simple tenses, perfects and progressives, as these examples show.

Conditional Mood

PAST PERFECT	None
PAST-PERFECT PROGRESSIVE	None
PAST	I *could/might/should/would* edit.
PAST PROGRESSIVE	I *could/might/should/would* have been editing.
PRESENT PERFECT	I *could/might/should/would* have edited.
PRESENT-PERFECT PROGRESSIVE	I *could/might/should/would* have been editing. [same as past progressive]
PRESENT	I *could/might/should/would* edit. [same as past]
PRESENT PROGRESSIVE	I *could/might/should/would* be editing.
FUTURE PERFECT	I *could/might/should/would* have edited. [same as present perfect]

Verbs

Conditional Mood

FUTURE-PERFECT PROGRESSIVE	I *could/might/should/would* have been editing. [same as past progressive]
FUTURE	I *could/might/should/would* edit. [same as past]
FUTURE PROGRESSIVE	I *could/might/should/would* be editing. [same as present progressive]

Use *can* and *will* to express certainty, *could* and *would* when a condition is mentioned or implied.

I *can* go. [definite]

I *could* go if I finished work early. [conditional]

The law *will* close tax loopholes. [definite]

The bill *would* close tax loopholes.
[This sentence requires the conditional form because the bill is not yet a law—it would close tax loopholes if it were passed into law.]

The idea of the indicative form as being more certain than the conditional form is not as apparent with *may* and *might* and with *shall* and *should* because neither pair is used in everyday conversation the way traditional grammar asks us to use it in formal written language.

We suggest that when either *may* or *might* is needed, you use *may* in the present tense and *might* in the past and not bother with trying to figure out whether the situation is conditional because the meanings are too close to make much difference.

We suggest *would* as a more conversational alternative to the conditional *should*, especially in broadcast.

Because few people use the formal *shall* in conversation, instead using *will*, they're more likely to use *would* for the conditional form. In conversation, *should* is usually used only to mean "ought to." This is simply a case where the language has changed except in a few phrases that have persisted, such as *I should think not!*

Journalism Tip
Verb Moods

Journalists do most of their writing in the indicative mood, except for pieces that tell people how to do things, such as cooking or crafts articles. Such articles use the imperative mood in their instructions. But the conditional mood should be used whenever an article discusses what bills or other proposals would do if they were made into law. Editors should check for the subjunctive mood in sentences in which one of the clauses is in the conditional, as in the previous one.

Verbs

Subjunctive Mood

The *subjunctive mood* should be used to talk about any condition contrary to fact or to express a wish, doubt, prayer, desire, request, hypothetical situation or hope.

Consider the following sentence:

The bill would close tax loopholes if it *were* [not *was*] passed into law.

The *were* is in the subjunctive mood because it's proposing a hypothetical situation. In other words, although it may be a fact that I wish something, what I wish for has not yet come true, or I wouldn't be wishing for it.

By the way, the subjunctive is often used after *if* in sentences in which the verb in the main clause is in the conditional. But the subjunctive mood doesn't only have to follow *if*, nor does even have to follow every *if*.

Few people have trouble with the indicative and imperative moods or with half of the conditional forms (although *may* and *might*, *shall* and *should* can cause problems). The subjunctive, however, is not used nearly so often in English, and few people know how to use it correctly.

Here are some examples of the subjunctive:

If I *were* you [*but I'm not*], I'd quit.

I wish I *were* a cowboy [*but I'm not*].

The hijackers demanded that 17 terrorists *be* set free [*they have not yet been freed*].

The first two sentences may sound odd because many people use *I was*, the indicative-mood form, even when the subjunctive form is needed. You can tell that *was* is incorrect, however, because it's the normal past tense verb here, but the action of each sentence does not happen in the past.

As for the third example, most people would probably correctly use *be* because it sounds right, even though they would not even realize that they were using the subjunctive.

First, let's learn the conjugations in the subjunctive. Then, we'll look more closely at how this mood is used.

The most distinctive subjunctive forms occur for the verb *to be*.

Subjunctive Forms of To Be

	PRESENT TENSE	PAST TENSE		PRESENT TENSE	PAST TENSE
I	be	were	we	be	were
you	be	were	you	be	were
he/she/it/one	be	were	they	be	were

It's important to remember the past-tense forms because some of the most common mistakes using (or not using) the subjunctive involve the

Verbs

verb *to be*. Notice that in the indicative mood, the first- and third-person singular forms use *was* but the subjunctive calls for *were*: *if I were you; if she were taller.*

For all verbs other than *to be*, the *present tense of the subjunctive mood* is the infinitive minus the *to*. This form differs from the present tense of the indicative mood only in the third-person singular: *He asked that the editor edit* [not *edits*] *his story carefully for potential libel.*

PRESENT TENSE OF THE SUBJUNCTIVE MOOD

I edit	we edit
you edit	you edit
he, she, it, one edit	they edit

The *past tense of the subjunctive mood* for all verbs other than *to be* is the same as the past tense of the indicative mood (*I edited*, etc.).

Because all the other tenses are the same in the subjunctive as in the indicative, we often use the subjunctive without realizing it.

Following are some specific situations in which to use the subjunctive.

Use the subjunctive in most dependent clauses beginning with *if*.

If usually introduces a condition contrary to fact, so the subjunctive is needed. Occasionally, the condition is not contrary to fact: If the condition is either true or noncommittal (as in this sentence), the indicative is required. Recognizing the difference can sometimes be tricky.

Here are some sentences that use the subjunctive because they contain an *if* that introduces a condition contrary to fact:

If she *were* rich [*but she's not*], she would quit her job.

If compassion *be* a crime, then judge me guilty.
[The speaker does not really believe compassion should be considered a crime.]

By contrast, here are some sentences that use the indicative because they contain an *if* that introduces a condition that is true or about which the speaker is noncommittal as to truth or falsity:

If this experiment *works*, I will be famous.
[It may or may not work—it's not clearly false.]

He must have found a ride home if he *is* not in his office.
[He probably found a ride home if he's not in his office.]

If the verb in the independent clause is in the indicative mood, the verb in the dependent clause is also usually in the indicative. But if the verb in the independent clause is in the conditional mood, the verb in the dependent clause is usually in the subjunctive.

I *can* do it if I *have* the proper tools. [*Can* and *have* are both indicative.]

I *could* do it were I *given* the proper tools.
[*Could* is conditional; *were given* is a passive-voice form of the subjunctive.]

Note, however, that although linguists consider *must* and the semi-modal verbs as conditional, those verbs—unlike *could, might, should* and *would*—do not take the subjunctive mood in an accompanying clause. Rather, they take the indicative.

The president must take action quickly if he *wants* [not *want*] to avert a disaster.

Likewise, when *should* is used in its normal conversational meaning of "ought to," it doesn't take the subjunctive in another clause.

The president should take action quickly if he *wants* [not *want*] to avert a disaster.

Use the subjunctive in dependent clauses after verbs requiring *that* when the suggestion following is contrary to fact at present: *advise that, anxious that, ask that, demand that, doubt that, eager that, forbid that, hope that, insist that, move that, pray that, prefer that, propose that, recommend that, request that, require that, rule that, suggest that* and *urge that*.

The terrorists *demand that* $1 million *be* paid for the hostages' release.

They *insist that* the police negotiator *come* unarmed.

The contract requires that new hires *be* enrolled in the existing pension fund. [Although correct as written, many editors would probably prefer *The contract requires new hires to be enrolled.* . . .]

Verbs requiring *that* but not implying a condition contrary to present reality do not need the subjunctive: *believe that, conclude that, guess that, imply that, infer that, know that, notice that, say that, suppose that, think that* and *wonder that*.

I *believe that* this *is* true.

I *suppose that* he *is* tired.

Use the subjunctive after *as if*.

He sings *as if* he *were* a professional.

Use the subjunctive in these idioms: *be it said, be that as it may* (but note the indicative *may* instead of the conditional in this expression even though used with the subjunctive), *come Monday, come what may, far be it* (for, from) *me, God be with you, God bless, God forbid, lest we forget, long live the king, so be it, suffice it to say* and *would that I were*.

Suffice it to say she was mad.

God bless America!

People sometimes use the subjunctive with some constructions that do not really require it.

If there ~~be~~ are . . .

. . . whether you ~~be~~ are . . .

> *Our Changing Language*
> ## Subjunctive Mood
>
> Learning the differences between the subjunctive and indicative moods is much more important in other languages like French, Italian and Spanish than in English. That's because the forms of the two moods have evolved to vary only a little in modern English conversation. Most people tend to use a subjunctive form that differs from the conditional only in certain phrases, like "If I were you," without knowing why. So, you can get by most of the time without many people noticing if you get it wrong.

What Are Verbals?

Sometimes, a form of a verb is used as a part of speech other than a verb. A verb form used as something other than a verb is called a *verbal*, and the three kinds are *gerunds*, *participles* and *infinitives*.

Gerunds

A *gerund* is the present- or past-participle form of a verb used as a noun. (See Page 123.)

Participles

A *participle* is the present- or past-participle form of a verb used as an adjective. (See Page 212.)

Infinitives

An *infinitive* is the form of a verb that normally has *to* in front of it, although sometimes *to* can be omitted.

    May I help *cook*?

To is usually considered a preposition, but it isn't when the word is part of an infinitive. When *to* is followed by a verb, the construction is an infinitive, not a prepositional phrase.

Don't confuse the conjunction *and* with the word *to* in an infinitive in American English.

Many people substitute *and* for *to* in an infinitive preceded by *try* or *come*. For example, they might write, *I'll try and do it* or *He'll come and work*. Although the English poet John Milton used the idiom *try and* in the 17th century, most editors incorrectly think the phrase a modern illiteracy and insist you write *try to*. *Try and* is the way it's said still today in England, but you should avoid it in American media writing.

Infinitives may be used as nouns (<u>*To eat*</u> *is* <u>*to live*</u>), adjectives (*The issue <u>to be*</u> <u>*argued*</u> *is a complex one*) or adverbs (*He went* <u>*to visit*</u> *his mother*).

Although an infinitive is never used in a sentence as a verb by itself, it can be part of a verb phrase, with or without the *to*: *He was supposed to leave today. I may leave, also.*

When the infinitive *to be* is part of a linking verb, as in *believed to be* or *thought to be*, a pronoun following it should be in the subject form (nominative case), although this construction is rare in conversation, or in broadcast or informal writing, so we won't insist.

The benefactor *was believed to be* she.

Our Changing Language
To Split or Not to Split an Infinitive

It's often considered bad grammar to split an infinitive — to put another word between the *to* and the verb. But this is a rule linguists have long opposed. It turns out it never really described how English has been spoken by most people or written by even some of the best writers.

But because many people are unaware that the rule itself has long been considered wrong by linguists, they worry that a split infinitive will lower the credibility of their work. We suggest even then, though, you should consider going ahead and splitting an infinitive when not doing so would sound too awkward. (See Page 121.) And there is certainly no problem with a helping verb between the *to* and the main verb of the past-tense infinitive, as in:

to *have* read

to *have* loved

 LaunchPad Solo
macmillan learning

Online Grammar Help
launchpadworks.com

For practice verbs, log on to *LaunchPad Solo for Journalism* and go to *Exercise Central for AP Style.*

Verbs

CHAPTER 13

Making the Parts Agree

For sentences to be grammatical and clear, it's important the words agree with each other. These are the three main ways they must do this:

Each subject and its verb must agree in *number* (singular or plural).

Each pronoun must agree with its *antecedent* — the noun it replaces — in number, gender (male, female or neuter) and person (first, second or third).

Each word, phrase or clause in a series must be stated in *parallel* — similar — wording.

Solving Common Problems

1. Make sure each subject and its verb agree in number.

Subject-verb agreement (more consistently but less commonly called *subject-predicate agreement*) problems are some of the most common ways sentences go wrong. A singular subject needs a singular verb, and a plural subject needs a plural verb. Although that sounds easy enough, some situations can be tricky. Here are some likely sources of trouble.

Conjunctions

A *conjunction* connects words, phrases or clauses. We will discuss conjunctions in greater detail in Chapter 14.

And connecting two or more items in a subject usually makes the verb plural. The exception is when the words connected by *and* are part of a single thing.

> Larson and O'Connor *oppose* the bill.
> [plural subject (*Larson and O'Connor*), plural verb]

> Pork and beans *is* not exactly the chef's favorite dish.
> [The subject *Pork and beans* refers to a single dish, so the verb is singular.]

Or used alone to connect two or more items in a subject makes the verb singular unless one of the items is plural. Then, the verb agrees with the nearest noun or pronoun.

> Mary Teagate or *Phil Anderson is* answering calls today.

> Mary Teagate or *her colleagues are* answering calls today.

The number of the subject is not affected by parenthetical words, phrases or clauses that are set off by commas — such as those starting with *along with, as well as, in addition to, including, such as* or *together with.*

> Blaylock, as well as they, *is* voting in favor of annexation.

We discuss subject-verb agreement with conjunctions in more detail in the Understanding in More Depth section (see Pages 199–202).

Collective and Uncountable Nouns

Collective nouns are singular in form but plural in meaning. When it comes to verb agreement, form trumps meaning, and collective nouns generally take singular verbs in American English.

Collective nouns include *army, assembly, audience, board, breed, cast, choir, class, club, commission, committee, community, company, corporation, council, couple, covey, crew, crowd, department, faculty, family, firm, flock, furniture, gang, group, herd, jury, mob, orchestra, panel, press, public, remainder, staff, team, union* and *U.S.* The names of associations, boards, companies and so on are also considered collective nouns.

Use a singular verb when the collective noun is being used in the sense of a single group operating together in agreement. Use a plural verb if the noun is used to name a group operating as individuals or in disagreement.

> The jury *was* seated.
> [acting as a unit]

> The jury *were* split.
> [Sounds odd, but you can't always trust your ear when it comes to traditional grammar. To avoid the obvious ugliness — to American ears, at least — of this sentence, add the word *members* after *jury*, or, better yet, substitute the word *jurors*. But don't add *members* or change *jury* to *jurors* if they're acting in agreement.]

The word *couple*, in particular, is often plural rather than singular.

Couple is singular when it refers to a unit and plural when it refers to two individual people, as in the rule for other collective nouns.

SINGULAR	A married couple still sometimes *pays* more under U.S. tax law than two people living together but filing separately, but not so many as before 2018. [The *couple* here is two people acting as a unit, filing jointly.]
PLURAL	A couple *were* holding hands in the park. [Again, this may sound odd. The *couple* here refers to two people acting as individuals, holding each other's hands.]

But be careful when deciding whether the two are acting as a unit or separately. As that great copy-editing teacher John Bremner used to point out, if you write that *a couple was married*, then for pronoun consistency, you'd also have to write that *it went on a honeymoon but had a falling out, and it later divorced*. It would have been better originally to treat the couple getting married as two separate people rather than as a unit acting together.

Uncountable (also called *noncountable*) *nouns* are nouns that have no plural, although many of them look plural already. They are not so consistent as collective nouns in that some take a singular verb, some a plural. (See Page 200 for a list of which ones are which.)

Journalism Tip
Groups of People in the News

Many news stories focus on meetings of and actions by groups of people—boards, commissions, committees, councils and juries, for example. Remember, although each of these collective nouns names a number of people, the noun itself is considered singular for both verb and pronoun agreement.

WRONG	The City Council *are* holding *their* next meeting at a working retreat.
RIGHT	The City Council *is* holding *its* next meeting at a working retreat.

Names of Teams and Musical Groups

We think names of teams and musical groups should logically be treated as singular if the name is singular, plural if the name is plural.

The Seattle Mariners *are* playing the Detroit Tigers on Friday.

Manchester United *is* playing Barcelona for the cup.

The Beatles *were* his biggest influence.

ZZ Top *was* his favorite Southern rock band.

But *The AP Stylebook* in its 2018 edition's entry under collective nouns is less easy to follow consistently. It seems to contradict itself. First, it says names of teams or musical groups that are singular in form and have no plural should be treated as plural (as in "the Orlando Magic are"). Then, it says singular names of each are usually singular ("Coldplay is," despite the fact there is no plural of Coldplay). We think our advice is clearer and more consistent. "If your publication has its own rule for musical groups or teams, follow that." (For example, note that *Rolling Stone* magazine uses plural verbs with singular band names: "The Clash *were* very much dependent on the band chemistry. . . ." [italics added].)

Other Confusing Nouns

Don't mistake plural nouns ending in *a* with their singular forms ending in *on* or *um*. *Criteria, data* and *media* are plural, not singular (although AP now also accepts media [italics] as singular when it refers to the media as a monolithic group). (For examples, see Pages 160–161.)

Units of measurement, such as distance, money, time and weight, take a singular verb even though they are plural in form when referring to a single amount rather than the units of measurement individually.

> Five dollars *is* not too much to ask of a friend.

Fractions and percentages can be singular or plural, depending on the noun or pronoun following them.

> One-third of the *book is* a flashback.

> One-third of the *customers are* regulars.

You might think that this is an exception to the rule that a verb must agree in number with its subject rather than with something that comes between them like a prepositional phrase (see Pages 200–202), but it is not. Instead, fractions and percentages can be either singular or plural depending on the sense of the sentence. Unlike most sentences, in which the number of an object of a preposition is not a reliable indicator whether the verb should be singular or plural, the number of the object of a preposition after a fraction or percentage is.

> The author of the *books is* Suzanne Collins.
> [The object of the preposition—*books*—is a plural noun and is not a reliable indicator of the correct verb number, which is singular because we're referring to one author.]

Indefinite Pronouns

Both, few, many, others and *several* are plural.

> Many *were* inspired by the candidacy of Barack Obama.

Another, anybody, anyone, anything, each one, either, everybody, everyone, everything, little, many a, more than one, much, neither, nobody, no one, nothing, other, somebody, someone and *something* are singular, even though some of those words refer to more than one person or thing.

> Everyone in Kansas City, Mo., seems excited by the Royals' World Series victory.

All, any, each, more, most, none, plenty, some and *such* can be either singular or plural depending on the context.

> Some *are* coming.

> Some *is* left.

Make *none* singular if it means "no one" or "not one" (which it means most of the time), plural if the sense is "no two" or "no amount."

> None of the people invited *has* arrived.
> [not one]

None of the experts *agree*.
[no two]

This is the rule *The AP Stylebook* follows, despite common usage of most Americans to make *none* always plural and despite the pleas of many authorities—including Theodore Bernstein, Bergen Evans, and William and Mary Morris—that *none* is more often plural than singular.

The UPI Stylebook, though, says that *none* can be either singular or plural provided any related pronoun agrees, as in these two examples it cites:

RIGHT	"None *are* so blind as *those* who will not see."
RIGHT	"None *is* so blind as *he* who will not see."

Each is singular.

Each is going by car.

Either and *neither* used by themselves are singular pronouns.

Neither of them *has* ~~have~~ been found.

Either of the two *offers* ~~offer~~ law-enforcement experience.

In the constructions *either . . . or* and *neither . . . nor*, the words are used as conjunctions, not pronouns. The verb following them is singular or plural, depending on whether the noun or pronoun following the *or* or *nor* is singular or plural.

Neither his parents nor *John is* sure what happened next.

Neither John nor his *parents are* sure what happened next.

Intervening Nouns and Pronouns

If a noun or pronoun comes between the subject and the verb, the verb still agrees with the subject, not with the intervening noun or pronoun.

Wednesday's *newspaper*, along with its supplements, *is* our biggest edition ever.
[The subject is the singular noun *newspaper*. The phrase *along with its supplements* is a parenthetical modifier, so the plural noun *supplements* does not influence the number of the verb.]

Prepositional Phrases

If a subject contains a prepositional phrase, the noun or pronoun following the preposition is almost never the actual subject, so the verb instead agrees with the noun or pronoun before the preposition.

Three *trees* in the garden *were* blown over.

For more on prepositional phrases, see Pages 200–202.

Subject and Predicate Nominative in Disagreement

When the subject is plural and the predicate nominative is singular, or vice versa, many people are unsure what the number of the verb should be.

The number of the verb should always agree with the number of the subject. Both of the following sentences, therefore, are correct.

> The committee *is* Ernie Havens, Ruth Brent and Bree Oliver.

> Ernie Havens, Ruth Brent and Bree Oliver *are* the committee.

Inverted Order

Although the subject precedes the verb in most sentences, the subject in some sentences follows the verb. This inverted order occurs most often in questions and causes little confusion. But here are a couple of other situations in which subject-verb agreement problems arise as a result of subjects following verbs.

In a sentence beginning with *here*, *there* or *where*, the verb agrees with the number of the subject, which follows the verb.

> Here *are* is the *answers* to Sunday's crossword.

> There *are* is no two *ways* about it.

Don't write stilted sentences with inverted word order. They sound awkward and can sometimes result in confusion about subject-verb agreement.

WRONG	From the mouths of fools sometimes *come* wisdom.
STILTED	From the mouths of fools sometimes *comes* wisdom.
BETTER	Wisdom sometimes *comes* from the mouths of fools.

2. Make sure each pronoun agrees with its antecedent in number, gender and person.

Just as verbs have to agree with their subject, pronouns have to agree with the noun to which they refer—their *antecedent*—in number, gender and person.

Some of the same issues that cause difficulty in knowing whether a subject is singular or plural can occur when you are choosing the right number for a pronoun: Collective nouns, uncountable nouns and indefinite pronouns are often the culprits. So, to make pronouns and antecedents agree, it's important to master subject-verb agreement, as well.

Here are a few of the most common problems with pronoun-antecedent agreement:

Don't refer to a collective noun that represents a business, a government, an association or other group as *they, their* or *theirs* but rather as *it* or *its*.

> The City Council gave *its* their approval.

They, their, theirs or *them* are normally plural, but the *AP Stylebook* as of 2018 also now accepts the common usage of all of them as singular to refer to a singular antecedent that could be either male or female. You can often avoid the issue entirely, though, by making the whole sentence plural:

TRADITIONALLY WRONG	*A reporter* should check *their* facts.
RIGHT BUT SEXIST	*A reporter* should check *his* facts.
RIGHT BUT WORDY	*A reporter* should check *his or her* [or worse, *his/her*] facts.
RIGHT	*Reporters* should check *their* facts. [Make the whole thing plural.]

For more on gender bias in language, see Chapter 7.

Our Changing Language
Are *They, Their, Theirs* and *Them* Never Singular?

AP changed the traditional rule about not using these normally plural pronouns as singulars because the spoken language had long ago changed, and even well-educated speakers were using them in conversation as singulars when they could refer to either a male or female person. AP's rule also reflects the trend to more gender neutrality of language in many situations, although oddly English composition classes are often lagging on this and may still follow the traditional rule. We see AP's change, though, as a positive step to bring formal writing more in step with informal common usage on this matter. It certainly sounds better in broadcast, which should be even more conversational than the printed word, and in other informal uses such as in social media.

Clear Pronoun Reference

Make sure it's clear to which noun a pronoun refers. Try repeating the antecedent or otherwise rewriting the sentence.

CONFUSING	The man spoke loudly because he was hard of hearing — which practically drove his wife crazy. [What drove the woman crazy? Her husband's loud speaking or his hearing problem? The antecedent of *which* is unclear.]
CLEAR	The man spoke loudly because he was hard of hearing, but the noise practically drove his wife crazy.

It's usually better not to use a pronoun before you introduce the noun to which it refers. This is especially important in broadcast.

POSSIBLY CONFUSING	If he loses the race, Paul Bennett says, he won't return to his district.
BETTER	Paul Bennett says that if he loses the race, he won't return to his district.

3. Make sure each sentence's words, phrases and clauses have parallel structure.

When parallel ideas are not expressed in a parallel manner, the rhythm of a sentence is thrown off, and the logical relationships are muddied.

Make Items in a Series Parallel

To make ideas parallel, similar items should be written in similar ways. For example, the items in a series should be alike, whether all nouns, all gerunds, all infinitives, all phrases or all clauses. A series of verbs should all be in the same tense, voice and mood, except in instances such as flashbacks or flash-forwards, in which a change in time is clearly intended.

WRONG	He admires Kathy for her intelligence, energy and because she is a good leader.
	[The nouns *intelligence* and *energy* are out of balance with the clause *because she is a good leader*.]
RIGHT	He admires Kathy for her intelligence, energy and leadership.
WRONG	The fishing equipment cost as much or more than a bicycle.
	[The conjunctions are not balanced because part of one is missing.]
RIGHT	The fishing equipment cost as much *as* or more than a bicycle.

Make Verbs Parallel

Verbs in a sentence or longer piece of writing should agree with each other in tense unless you have a reason to shift to a different time period.

WRONG	First, he walked in, then he smiled, and then he *says*, "Hello."
	[Past and present tenses of the verbs are mixed.]
RIGHT	First, he walked in, then he smiled, and then he *said*, "Hello."
RIGHT	I work in Boston now, but last year I worked in Chicago.
	[The verb tenses change because they describe different times.]

For more rules about making verbs parallel, see Page 202.

Understanding in More Depth

More on Subject-Verb Agreement With Conjunctions

When the correlative conjunctions *not only . . . but also* are used, the following verb should agree with the nearer subject, and there should not be a comma before the *but also*.

Not only Mark but also his sister *has* won a scholarship.
[There is only one clause here, so there's no comma before *but also* and the verb is singular.]

But if *not only . . . but also* connect a dependent and an independent clause, the verb following *but also* should agree with the subject of the independent clause.

> Not only has Mark won a scholarship, but also so *has* his sister.
> [There are two clauses here, a dependent one introduced by *Not only* and an independent one introduced by *but also*. So, there is a comma before *but also*, and the verb following it agrees with the singular subject of the independent clause, *sister*.]

More on Subject-Verb Agreement With Uncountable Nouns

These uncountable nouns take a singular verb: *advice, apparatus, athletics, civics, courage, economics, fun, health, information, jazz, kudos, linguistics, mathematics, measles, mumps, news, shambles, summons* and *whereabouts*.

These uncountable nouns take a plural verb: *assets, barracks, earnings, goods, odds, pants, pliers, proceeds, remains, riches, scissors, shears, tactics, thanks, tongs* and *wages*.

These uncountable nouns may take a singular or plural verb depending on the context: *ethics, gross, headquarters, mechanics, politics, savings, series, species* and *statistics*. Often, why one of these words is singular in one place, plural in another cannot be easily explained other than as idiomatic use.

> Politics *is* her favorite subject.

> Her politics *are* socialistic.

More on Subject-Verb Agreement With Other Confusing Nouns

In American usage, *number* and *total* are usually singular if preceded by *the*, plural if preceded by *a*.

> *The number* of people expected *is* small.

> *A total* of 50 people *are* expected to attend.

According to the entry for *majority* in *The AP Stylebook, majority* and *plurality* are singular by themselves but may be either singular or plural when followed by *of*, depending on the sense of the sentence.

> **SINGULAR**   A majority of two votes is not adequate to control the committee.

> **PLURAL**   The majority of the houses on the block were destroyed.

We would suggest the same rule should apply for nouns like *abundance, array, cornucopia, myriad* and *variety*, which are normally not considered collective nouns but which are also singular in form, although they describe a plural number.

> **SINGULAR**   A variety *is* available.

> **PLURAL**   A variety of choices *are* not possible under these conditions.

More on Prepositional Phrases

When there's a phrase beginning with *one of the, one of these* or *one of those* followed by a relative pronoun like *who, which* or *that*, the verb after that pronoun will agree with the object of the preposition right before it. That's because the actual antecedent of the clause introduced by a relative pronoun is the object of the preposition *of* in such a construction, not the subject of the previous clause.

WRONG	One of those *solutions* that *is* cheap looks good.
RIGHT	One of those *solutions* that *are* cheap looks good.
	[Because *solutions* is the plural antecedent of *that*, the verb must also be plural: Of those solutions that are cheap, one looks good.]

If the *one* in such a construction is preceded by *only, one* is usually the antecedent, and the construction becomes singular again.

WRONG	She is the *only one* of those people who *are* always on time.
RIGHT	She is the *only one* of those people who *is* always on time.
	[She's the only one who is on time.]

But be careful — there is an exception to this rule:

WRONG	*Only one* of those solutions that *is* cheap *looks* good.
RIGHT	*Only one* of those solutions that *are* cheap *looks* good.
	[*One* is the subject here of *looks*, so *one . . . looks good*. But the antecedent of the relative pronoun *that* is *solutions*, so *solutions that are cheap*.]

More on Pronoun-Antecedent Agreement

When *one* is the antecedent, the pronoun following should be *one* again, not *he* or *you* unless both are changed to agree.

    one has
One does what ~~you have~~ to do.

 You
~~One~~ should be prepared because *you* never know who might call.

[person of subjects not balanced]

After *neither . . . nor*, the pronoun must agree with the number — and we would suggest also the gender in order to be logical and nonsexist — of the noun that follows *nor*.

  Neither Frank nor Jennifer would do *her* part.

But better yet, rewrite the sentence to avoid this awkward-sounding construction.

  Frank wouldn't do his part, and neither would Jennifer.

More on Making Verbs Parallel

Verbs should agree with each other in voice and not needlessly shift from active to passive.

WRONG	She *was presented* [passive voice] the award and then *left* [active voice].
RIGHT	She accepted the award and then left.

The mood of the verbs should be as consistent as possible.

> **WRONG**   Read the book, and then you should complete the exercises.
> [The first clause is in the imperative mood, the second in the conditional.]

> **RIGHT**   Read the book, then complete the exercises.

> **RIGHT**   You should read the book, and then you should complete the exercises.

Of course, it's normal for the conditional to accompany the subjunctive in multiclause sentences. (See Pages 189–190.)

 **LaunchPad Solo**
macmillan learning

Online Grammar Help
Launchpadworks.com

For practice with subject-verb agreement, pronoun-antecedent agreement and parallel structure, log on to *LaunchPad Solo for Journalism* and go to *Exercise Central for AP Style*.

CHAPTER 14

Modifiers and Connecting Words

Five of the eight traditional parts of speech fall into two categories: modifiers and connecting words. And yet, thankfully, there's not nearly so much to learn about these as about nouns, pronouns and verbs. Adjectives, adverbs and inter-jections are *modifiers*, and prepositions and conjunctions are *connecting words*.

Modifiers are words that describe or limit subjects, objects or verbs. They provide details.

Connecting words join together parts of a sentence.

Each of these categories has its own set of rules and common problems that writers face with them. So we'll discuss each separately, beginning with modifiers.

Solving Common Problems With Modifiers

Adjectives and adverbs — the most common kinds of modifiers — pose the most common problems. Interjections are also common but pose fewer problems.

An *adjective* modifies a noun or its substitute by telling how many, what kind, which or whose.

> *red* balloon, *short* dog, *superior* medicine, *good* job

An *adverb* typically modifies a verb, an adjective or another adverb, generally by telling how, when, where, to what degree or extent, or how much.

> turning *slowly*, *extremely* stupid, *rarely* seen

In addition to these main uses, an adverb may sometimes modify a verbal (participle, infinitive), preposition, conjunction or clause:

completely drunken sailor [modifying participle *drunken*]

boldly go [modifying infinitive *go*]

Frankly, I don't care. [modifying the clause]

An *interjection* expresses an emotional outburst. Many books don't consider it a modifier but in a category of its own. We call it a modifier because it may stand alone, modifying an implied sentence, or it may appear at the beginning of a sentence it modifies. The interjection is punctuated with an exclamation point when it stands alone or may be followed with a comma when joined to the sentence it modifies.

Ouch!

Ouch! That hurts!

Ouch, that hurts!

In addition to adjectives, adverbs and interjections, there are other words that can be used as modifiers, which we'll discuss in the Understanding in More Depth section on Page 212.

Here are guidelines to follow to avoid the seven main mistakes writers make with modifiers:

1. Use the correct forms of adjectives and adverbs.
2. Don't confuse adjectives with adverbs.
3. Know the difference between coordinate adjectives and compound modifiers.
4. Know how to use articles correctly.
5. Set off sentence adverbs with commas from the rest of the sentence.
6. Don't use double negatives.
7. Punctuate interjections correctly.

Let's take a look at each of these mistakes and how to fix them.

1. Use the correct forms of adjectives and adverbs.

Most adjectives and adverbs have three forms that show comparison: the *positive*, the basic form of an adjective or adverb that implies no comparison; the *comparative*, the form used in comparisons of two items or groups; and the *superlative*, the form used in comparisons involving more than two items or groups. Some adjectives and adverbs have only the positive form.

For most short adjectives, to make the comparative form, add *er* to the end of the positive form or *less* as a separate word in front of the positive form. To make the superlative form, add *est* to the end of the positive form or *least* as a separate word in front of the positive form.

tall [positive]

taller *or* less tall [comparative]

tallest *or* least tall [superlative]

Two main exceptions are *good*, *better* and *best*; and *bad*, *worse* and *worst*.

For most longer adjectives, add the word *more* or *less* in front of the positive form to make the comparative and *most* or *least* in front of the positive to make the superlative.

beautiful [positive]

more beautiful *or* less beautiful [comparative]

most beautiful *or* least beautiful [superlative]

To form most adverbs, add *ly* to the end of the positive form of an adjective. This *ly* form is then the positive form of the adverb. Form the comparative by putting the word *more* or *less* in front of the positive form, and the superlative by putting the word *most* or *least* in front of the positive form.

quick [positive form of the adjective]

quickly [positive form of the adverb]

more quickly *or* less quickly [comparative form of the adverb]

most quickly *or* least quickly [superlative form of the adverb]

Don't confuse the comparative and superlative forms.

Don't say someone is "the *oldest* of the two brothers." If there are only two, he's the *older*.

Also, sometimes writers list several items and then refer to *the latter one*. But *latter*, like *former*, should be used only when two items have been listed. That's because they are comparative, not superlative, forms. In such cases, *last*, and *first* or *second* are called for instead.

Don't include more items than intended in a comparison by leaving out the word *else* when it's needed.

The new forward is *faster than anyone* ^else^ *on the team*.
[Assuming the new forward is also on the team, he or she cannot be "faster than anyone on the team" because the team includes this forward.]

Don't use comparative or superlative forms with modifiers referring to something absolute.

Something cannot be *more unique* than something else because *unique* means "one of a kind." Something is either one of a kind or it isn't. Likewise, something cannot be *most unique*, *rather unique*, *somewhat unique* or *very unique*. Another word that should not be used with comparatives is *perfect*, contrary to the famous phrase in the Preamble to the Constitution "in Order to form a more perfect Union." Others include *complete*, *limitless*, *perpendicular* and *square*.

2. Don't confuse adjectives with adverbs.

Use adjectives to modify nouns or pronouns. Use adverbs to modify verbs, adjectives or other adverbs.

Don't mistakenly use an adjective when an adverb is required to describe the manner in which something happens.

The microbrew is noted for going down ~~smooth~~ *smoothly*.

The sports car brakes ~~quicker~~ *more quickly* than the sedan.

Don't confuse a predicate adjective (see Page 212) with an adverb. *Linking verbs* — such as *appear, be, become, feel, grow, look, seem, smell, sound, taste* and *wax* — take a predicate adjective rather than an adverb as a modifier. The *predicate adjective* follows the linking verb and refers back to the subject.

He waxed ~~poetically~~ *poetic*.

They feel ~~badly~~ *bad* for the losing team.

The chef's meal tasted ~~superbly~~ *superb*.

> ### *ESL Tip*
>
> Speakers of English as a second language should note that English modifiers other than predicate adjectives and appositives (see Pages 212–213) usually come *before* the word modified, contrary to the usage in a number of other languages. There are also English sentences in which the modifier follows what it describes, but when in doubt, try putting the modifier before the word modified.

Some intransitive verbs in some uses may be *linking verbs* and take a predicate adjective. But in other uses, they may be *complete verbs* or *transitive verbs* (see Pages 171–173) that are followed by an adverb.

He says it feels *good* to be alive.
[*Feels* is a linking verb here and is followed by the predicate adjective *good*, which modifies the subject *it*. The word *good* is an adjective, so you use it after a linking verb.]

The sculptor said her hands cannot feel the clay *well* with heavy gloves on.
[*Well* is an adverb modifying the transitive verb *feel*. If you want to describe the action of touching rather than the sculptor, you should use the adverb *well*.]

The patient feels *well* enough to be discharged.
[*Feels* here is a linking verb, and the predicate adjective *well* modifies the subject *patient*. When *well* describes someone's health, it's an adjective.]

Consider this sentence: *The thunder sounded [loud or loudly]*. To choose between an adjective and an adverb, decide whether the subject is acting. If the sentence means the thunder *clapped* (acted), then it sounded *loudly* (adverb). If it means the thunder *was* (being) loud, then it sounded *loud* (adjective).

So, a flower smells *sweet*, not *sweetly*, because the flower is not acting, just being—it has no nose with which to smell. Likewise, you wax (linking verb) *poetic*, but you wax (transitive verb) *carefully* your car.

Our Changing Language
Do You Feel *Well* or *Good*?

You usually don't need to worry because in most instances either is correct. There *can* be different meanings, as noted above. But generally speaking, contrary to some, you can say or write either "I feel *well* (healthy)" or "I feel *good* (*good* being the adjective describing *I*)." But if you mean how something is done, you need the adverb *well*, not the adjective *good*.

WRONG	Feighery does it *good*.
RIGHT	Feighery does it *well*.

Modifiers and Connecting Words

3. Know the difference between *coordinate adjectives* and *compound modifiers*.

Many times, a pair of modifiers precedes a noun or pronoun. Such modifiers usually work either as *coordinate adjectives* or as *compound modifiers*.

Coordinate adjectives are adjectives equal in importance. You can recognize them by this test: If you reverse their order, they still sound right.

The *long*, *narrow* passage was hard to navigate.
[*Long* and *narrow* are coordinate adjectives because you could write them as *narrow, long* to reverse the order.]

Notice that coordinate adjectives are punctuated with a comma unless there is an *and* between them.

Compound modifiers are pairs of words in which the first word, no matter what part of speech it normally is, modifies the second word. Together, the two then modify the noun or pronoun that follows, and there's a hyphen between them.

well-intentioned friend

oil-depletion allowance

Occasionally, it's unclear which kind they are, and in those cases, no punctuation is put between them. (See Page 276.)

4. Know how to use articles correctly.

Articles are the adjectives *the*, *a* and *an*. *The* is called the *definite article* and indicates a particular, unique item. *A* and *an* are called *indefinite articles* and indicate a particular item from a number of similar items. The articles do not have comparative and superlative forms, and, for that reason, some grammarians treat them as a separate part of speech rather than as adjectives.

A is used before a word that begins with a consonant sound. *An* is used before a word that begins with a vowel sound.

> *a* history book
>
> ~~an~~ *a* historical event
>
> *an* owl
>
> *an* hour

If an indefinite article precedes an abbreviation, remember to choose between *a* and *an* by the first sound of the abbreviation, not the letter itself: *a UFO*, not *an UFO*, because the first sound is of a consonant: *yoo-eff-oh*.

Don't put *the* in front of a singular possessive name (one with an apostrophe before the *s*) unless there is only one person with that name referred to.

WRONG	The Moore's [as on a sign in front of a house, owned by a family with the last name Moore]
RIGHT	The Moores [if the intent is to say the Moores live here]
RIGHT	The Moores' [if the intent is to say the Moores own this house]

5. Set off sentence adverbs with commas from the rest of the sentence.

Sentence adverbs (*frankly, hopefully, personally, regrettably, sincerely, strictly speaking, to be honest*) modify the whole sentence of which they're a part rather than a particular word and are set off by a comma after at the beginning of a sentence, before at the end of a sentence, or two around in the middle of a sentence.

6. Don't use double negatives.

Avoid double negatives such as *not never, not no, not none* and *not nothing*.

The adverbs *hardly, rarely* and *scarcely* are also considered negative and do not take a *not*.

> He ~~can't~~ *can* hardly write.

The word *but*, which is normally a conjunction, is sometimes used as an adverb, and it, too, is considered negative and doesn't take a *not*.

> She ~~doesn't have~~ *has* but one friend, she said.

The prefixes *im, in, ir, non* and *un* make adjectives negative. Negative adjectives may be used with negative adverbs, but it's often clearer to rewrite them more positively.

ACCEPTABLE	It is *not improbable* that Margaret Thatcher will go down in history as one of the greatest British prime ministers.
CLEARER	Margaret Thatcher may go down in history as one of the greatest British prime ministers.

7. Punctuate interjections correctly.

An *interjection* is an exclamation expressing strong emotion: *Ah! Ouch!* Interjections can stand alone or be used to modify entire sentences: *Ouch, that hurts!*

In general, the interjection is the part of speech that gives us the least trouble. But a couple of rules are worth noting.

Interjections that stand alone should normally be followed with an exclamation point unless the writer means the use ironically, in which case a period is used. Interjections modifying a sentence that follows can take a comma after the interjection, with the exclamation point at the end of the sentence.

Never use more than one exclamation point with an interjection (or anywhere else for that matter).

Avoid interjections that use profanity or off-color slang in "family publications" such as newspapers, unless, as *The AP Stylebook* says, the words "are part of direct quotations and there is a compelling reason for them."

Solving Common Problems With Connecting Words

Prepositions, *conjunctions* and *conjunctive adverbs* are the glue that holds sentences together and makes transitions between ideas possible. There are guidelines to follow to avoid common problems with connecting words:

1. Pay attention to how you use prepositions and whether the preposition is necessary.

A *prepositional phrase* consists of a preposition and the noun or noun substitute that follows it (*the object of the preposition*).

> *to* school, *after* the fall, *toward* the future, *in spite of* it all

The preposition itself is a connecting word that shows the relationship between its object and something else in the sentence. But the prepositional phrase of which it's a part usually acts as either an adjective or adverb.

> The computer *with a Blu-ray burner* is more expensive.
> [acts as an adjective modifying *computer*]

> The suspect was seen running *from the scene* of the crime.
> [acts as an adverb modifying *running*]

Prepositions usually indicate direction (*to, toward, over, under, from*) or location (*on, at, beside, near*). To spot most of these types of prepositions, imagine a bird and some trees. Prepositions are those words that describe the relationship the bird could have with the trees as it flies. It could fly *between* the trees, *toward* the trees, *in* the trees, *at* the trees, *from* the trees, *under* the trees, *over* the trees and so on.

But other prepositions show time (*in, at, during, until*), indicate possession (*of, with*), show responsibility (*for*) or agency (*by*), exclude (*except, without*), or show similarity (*like*).

In form, prepositions may be single words (*at, to, from*), compound words (*into, upon*) or phrases (*according to, because of, in accordance with, in spite of, on top of*). Sometimes, participles are also used as conjunctions or prepositions (*excepting, regarding*). (See Page 213.)

Repeat the preposition in parallel prepositional phrases if that helps avoid confusion.

Some editors insist that parallel prepositional phrases should always be used to repeat the preposition; for example: *The protesters said they were concerned about pollution and about road congestion.* We, however, wouldn't insist on the second *about* in this example because the sentence is clear without it.

Sometimes, though, parallel prepositions help avoid confusion. Notice the lack of parallel prepositions in this sentence: *Obscurantism means opposition to progress or enlightenment.* Does this mean *obscurantism* is enlightenment or opposition to it? If the former, reverse the sentence order: *Obscurantism means enlightenment or opposition to progress.* If it's the latter, add *to* before *enlightenment*: *Obscurantism means opposition to progress or to enlightenment.* (By the way, it's the latter.)

Here's another example:

> *The presidential candidates had different opinions on boosting the economy and climate change.*

Does this mean the presidential candidates had different opinions on the effects of boosting the economy on climate change or that they had different opinions from each other on both issues? In either case, rewriting is necessary to make it clear:

> *The presidential candidates had different opinions on how boosting the economy would affect climate change.*

> *The presidential candidates had different opinions on boosting the economy and on climate change.* [Repeating the preposition *on* makes this meaning clear.]

Some readers might have noticed a third possible reading that one or both candidates actually wanted to boost climate change as well as the economy. That's the least likely meaning, but the text itself is more ambiguous than it should be.

Use prepositions to separate items that might otherwise run together confusingly.

Usually, this involves proper nouns appearing next to each other.

> *Ted Winston Sunday said . . .*

In such cases, either put *on* between *Winston* and *Sunday* or rewrite.

> *Ted Winston said Sunday . . .*

Try not to end a sentence with a preposition because many editors still object to the practice. But if rewriting the sentence in accordance with the rule would make it sound awkward or overly formal, we'd say it's better to go ahead and leave the preposition at the end.

Avoid using *up* as a verb by itself or with a verb when it is not needed for the meaning of the verb itself.

The candidate said she would ~~up~~ *increase* the spending on social services.

The EPA spokesman said workers would hurry ~~up~~ the project.

Don't forget to look up any words you're not sure how to spell.
[Here, the *up* is necessary because *to look* is to see but *to look up* means to check in a reference.]

2. Make sure that you use the correct conjunction to connect equal or unequal parts of a sentence.

A *conjunction* connects words, phrases or clauses.

this *and* that

Either the city cleans the lake *or* the state will intervene.

It's been two years *since* the war in the region ended.

That was then. *But* today, he had a different story.

Coordinating Conjunctions

Coordinating conjunctions — such as *but, or, yet, for, and, nor,* and *so* — are used when the words, phrases or clauses they connect are of equal rank. (A convenient mnemonic device for remembering these conjunctions is the acronym BOY FANS.)

How do we know when the words, phrases and clauses are of equal rank? The rule is that a word equals another word (*wine and roses*); a phrase equals another phrase (*to be or not to be*); an independent clause equals another independent clause (*I'm going, and I'm not coming back*); and a dependent clause equals another dependent clause (*He said gun-free schools would follow if the court ruled in gun-control advocates' favor or if Democrats won enough seats in the election*).

Subordinating Conjunctions

Subordinating conjunctions — such as *although, as, because, if, since, until, whether* and *while* — connect two unequal parts of a sentence.

Most often, these unequal parts are independent and dependent clauses. Subordinate conjunctions typically introduce dependent clauses that modify the independent clause by explaining cause, contrast, reason or time. (See Page 220.)

Modifiers and Connecting Words

Understanding in More Depth

More About Other Kinds of Modifiers

A *participle* is a form of a verb, usually ending in *ing*, *ed*, *t* or *en*, that is used as an adjective.

Add one *beaten* egg. [adjective modifying *egg*]

Finishing a doctoral degree, she found she had little time for her personal life. [participial phrase acting as an adjective modifying *she*]

Participles also are used in making verb tenses and progressive forms of the verb. In this case, they function as part of the verb itself.

The president *is considering* a veto of the bill.

The only problem with participles is what is called a *dangling participle*—when the participial phrase is not placed next to the noun or pronoun it modifies. Dangling participles should be corrected by rewriting the sentence so that the participial phrase is next to what it modifies.

WRONG   Starting the meeting early, the bill was placed first on the agenda by the commissioners.

[*Starting the meeting early* is a dangling participle because it's placed next to *the bill*, not who started the meeting early: the *commissioners*.]

RIGHT   The commissioners started the meeting early and placed the bill first on the agenda.

An *infinitive* is a form of a verb preceded by *to*. It may be used in place of a noun, an adjective or an adverb.

To win would be a long shot. [infinitive acting as a noun]

It was a good day *to run*. [adjective modifying the noun *day*]

That's unlikely *to happen*, she said. [adverb modifying adjective *unlikely*]

Although many editors insist you not split an infinitive by placing a modifier between the *to* and the rest of the verb, we suggest this may be a rule to retire. (See Page 191.)

A *predicate adjective* is an adjective that follows a linking verb and describes the subject.

The bridge seems *unsafe*. [linking verb: *seems*]

He felt *small*, he said, in the presence of the basketball stars. [linking verb: *felt*]

A *noun of direct address* modifies the sentence by naming the person to whom a statement is addressed. Nouns of direct address are set off by a comma or commas.

Tom, can you hear me?

Here it is, *Shirley*.

An *appositive* is a word or phrase that follows a noun or one of its substitutes and modifies it by renaming it. Appositives are set off by commas or dashes. Although appositives act as adjectives, an appositive could replace the noun it modifies.

> The runner, *Gustav*, sat on the ground doing yoga stretches to warm up.
>
> His house—*the one without a roof*—is for sale.

More About Participles

We've already seen how *participles* (a verb form usually ending in *ing*, *ed*, *t* or *en*) are used in making verb tenses and progressive forms. (See Page 212.)

The other major use for participles is as adjectives.

> *Talking*, they reached an agreement. [*Talking* describes *they*.]
>
> The *frightened* victim was *hurt*. [*Frightened* and *hurt* describe *victim*.]
>
> Lawyers gathered *written* statements from the witnesses. [*Written* describes *statements*.]

Participles are also used occasionally as prepositions or conjunctions, as in the case of *excepting*, *including* and *regarding*.

> All were right, *excepting* the last one. [as conjunction]
>
> *Regarding* that, we'll have to wait. [as preposition]

More About Interjections

As we said earlier, not all grammarians consider interjections to be modifiers. In fact, many books say interjections don't have a grammatical connection to other words in a sentence. We disagree.

Although often used alone or set off from the rest of the sentence it modifies by an exclamation point, an interjection also may be connected to the beginning of the sentence by a comma. Written this way—which is common because journalists don't like to use exclamation points—interjections work like sentence adverbs, modifying the entire sentence.

We consider interjections to act as adverbs because although interjections don't have the comparative forms of other adverbs, neither do the adverbs *no* or *yes*.

Note that other parts of speech, such as the verb *Damn!* or phrases like *For heaven's sake!* or even whole sentences such as *Damn it all!* can be used as interjections.

More About Correlative Conjunctions

Correlative conjunctions are similar to coordinating conjunctions in that they connect words, phrases or clauses of equal rank. The difference is that correlative conjunctions are used in pairs.

Modifiers and Connecting Words

Correlative Conjunctions

as . . . as	not only . . . but also
both . . . and	not so . . . as
either . . . or	since . . . therefore
if . . . then	whether . . . or
neither . . . nor	

Most writers know that *either* and *or* go together, as do *neither* and *nor*. Not many media writers, however, seem to know the following:

The negative form of *as . . . as* is *not so . . . as*.

It is *as* long *as* it is wide.

It is *not so* long *as* it is wide.

Not only must be followed by *but also*.

Not only liberals *but also* some conservatives took issue with parts of the bill.

 **LaunchPad Solo**
macmillan learning

Online Grammar Help
Launchpadworks.com
For practice with modifiers and connecting words, log on to *LaunchPad Solo for Journalism* and go to *Exercise Central for AP Style.*

CHAPTER 15

Getting Words in the Right Order and Punctuation

The order of your words and the way you punctuate them are two important clues for readers in understanding clearly what you mean.

Getting Words in the Right Order

Confused words become must may be, readers in or the order correct.

No, that's not a misprint. We just wanted to illustrate our point:

Words must be in the correct order, or readers may become confused.

Of course, no one would intentionally jumble sentences and hope to be understood, but we sometimes unintentionally jumble parts of them. Even if readers can figure out what we mean, why should they have to work at it? Shouldn't our writing be straightforward and clear?

Sometimes, we jumble our word order because that's the way we hear them said in conversation. But as we noted in Chapter 9, the rules of written English sometimes differ from those of conversational English. In such cases, we should usually adjust the word order to the rules of written English.

Solving Common Problems

1. Place modifiers as close as possible to the word they modify.

The jumbled word order that causes the biggest confusion for readers is a result of misplaced modifiers.

Modifiers should be placed as close as possible to the word they modify. When this doesn't happen, we call the often confusing and sometimes comical result a *misplaced modifier.*

Sometimes, misplaced modifiers merely require a momentary pause to sort them out. For example, television talk-show hosts often say something like this to a guest: *As a musician, our viewers are probably wondering why you became interested in this issue.* As we said, it may take only a moment—if that—to realize the speaker didn't mean that the viewers are musicians. But why shouldn't the speaker say what she or he means?

But misplaced modifiers don't just result in momentary pauses to grasp the meaning or laughs at a writer's expense. Readers might genuinely be confused by the following sentence: *Facing an indictment on a tax-evasion charge, the mayor fired the public works director.* Who was facing an indictment? The mayor or the director?

> *The mayor, who was facing an indictment on tax-evasion charges,* fired the public works director. [if it was the mayor]

> The mayor fired *the public works director, who was facing an indictment on tax-evasion charges.* [if it was the public works director]

The *dangling participle* is a kind of misplaced modifier that's so common it has its own name.

Generally speaking, avoid *nominative absolutes*. A *nominative absolute* is a noun or its substitute followed by a participial phrase. It looks similar to a dangling participle, but a nominative absolute modifies the whole sentence rather than a noun or its substitute, so it acts as a *sentence adverb.*

> *The computer having gone down,* the paper was late.
> [*Computer* is a noun, *having* a participle.]

> The Tigers lost, *poor hitting being to blame.*
> [*Hitting* is a gerund, *being* a participle.]

Unlike dangling participles, nominative absolutes are considered grammatical, but sentences with them might still be better rewritten in a more conversational tone.

> The paper was late because the computer went down.

> The Tigers lost because of poor hitting.

Avoid *dangling infinitives*—infinitive phrases not placed next to the words they modify.

WRONG	*To get ahead in this business, the audience* must be kept in mind.
	[The phrase *to get ahead in this business* modifies *the audience*, but no doubt the writer meant it to modify *you*, a word that never appears in the sentence. A reader may be able to figure this out, but a dangling infinitive makes it tougher.]

RIGHT   *To get ahead in this business, you* must keep the audience in mind.

Avoid *squinting modifiers* — modifiers placed between two separate things they reasonably could be read as modifying, such that the reader can't be sure what's meant.

The word *only* poses a particular problem with placement, not only because it's often misplaced but also because writers are seldom aware of how confusing the result can be. Look at this sentence, for example: *Ostroushko only has one of the handmade instruments.* Does that mean he has *only one* or that *only Ostroushko* has one? The sentence should be rewritten for clarity. If he has only one, then *only* belongs in front of one. If only he has *one*, then it belongs in front of *Ostroushko*.

2. Adverbs require extra attention to placement in verb phrases because different orders are preferable here depending on the meaning.

It's OK to put an adverb in the middle of a verb phrase.

Some writers and editors believe that an adverb should never be placed in the middle of the parts of a compound-tense verb. For example, they would rewrite *The watch was consistently gaining time* as *The watch consistently was gaining time* or *The watch was gaining time consistently.* But several commentators, including Wilson Follett, whose *Modern American Usage* is one of the most quoted usage guides, say the placement of the adverb in such sentences should normally be between the two parts of the verb. Follett offers this advice on alternative placement of adverbs:

For emphasis, put the adverb at the start of the sentence.

   Really, I don't want any.

If the adverb is not needed for emphasis, put it in front of a single-word verb, between the helping verb and the main verb, or after the first helping verb if there is more than one.

   I *really want* some.

   I *don't really want* any.

   I *had really been wanting* some.

If the adverb modifies the main verb alone, put it after the helping verbs.

   Smoking *has been positively linked* to higher rates of cancer.

If the adverb is a phrase, put it after the whole verb.

   We *have heard again and again* the same thing from the city.

Understanding in More Depth

The problems in this section are jumbled word orders that are common but less confusing. We think you need to know that many editors insist you never end a sentence with a preposition or split an infinitive, but we also think these are rules to consider retiring in part or in whole. We've rewritten them here to reflect how we suggest handling them for the time being.

Understanding Preposition Placement

The best-known rule about prepositions is not to end a sentence with one. The rule goes back to 18th-century English grammar books that based their rules on Latin grammar rather than on how the English language actually works. Because Latin words have different endings depending on the role they play in a sentence, words in Latin sentences can be moved around without the meaning of the sentence being changed. An exception is that a Latin sentence cannot end with a preposition.

Our Changing Language
Ending Sentences With Prepositions

As famous as the rule not to end a sentence with a preposition is Winston Churchill's rejoinder: "That is the type of arrant pedantry up with which I will not put." The fact is, English speakers have ended sentences with prepositions for hundreds of years, and some sentences, such as Churchill's, sound awkward when they don't end with a preposition. For example: *What are you waiting for?* sounds better to most of us than *For what are you waiting?*

Although many disagree with this rule, it's a good idea to avoid the likely objection of your editor and try to rewrite a sentence that ends with a preposition whenever you can do so in a way that still sounds conversational. This is usually easy, although some sentences require more effort. For example, *They're fun to add your own touches to* may be a puzzler at first, but some thought might yield, *It's fun to add your own touches to them*.

The colloquial expression "Do you want to come with?" sounds odd to people from regions where people more commonly ask, "Do you want to come with me (us)?" Many English speakers end sentences with pronouns rather than prepositions.

Understanding Split Infinitives

Because Latin infinitives are one word, the grammarians who wrote the first English grammars in the 18th century decided that English infinitives should not be split. Many journalists today still follow the rule not to split infinitives.

SPLIT INFINITIVE	She would like *to quickly make* her mark.
NONSPLIT INFINITIVE	She would like *to make* her mark *quickly*.
	[Note that moving an adverb from the middle of an infinitive often means placing it after an object following an infinitive so that it is actually no longer next to the word it modifies.]

Our Changing Language
When to Split Infinitives

Sometimes, it's nearly impossible to say what we want without splitting an infinitive. Humorist James Thurber was adamant on this point: "When I split an infinitive, it's going *to damn well stay* split." Many grammarians now agree and allow latitude when the writer can't find an acceptable alternative, wants *to strongly stress* a point or is imitating conversation.

In most instances, a conversational alternative can be found to keep the traditionalists happy. But if not, it's better to break this rule than to create an awkward sentence. AP agrees in its entry under verbs.

Punctuating for Clarity

Punctuation guides the reader in how to understand the way the words should be read and understood—when to pause and for how long (commas as opposed to periods, for example), when to raise your voice mentally or aloud to indicate a question (question mark), when a noun is possessive and whether it refers to one or more people (apostrophe), whether two modifiers in a row are to be understood as one or two words (comma or a hyphen or nothing), even whether two clauses were said by the same person (comma or not), and so on.

But look in different grammar books and stylebooks, and you'll see punctuation rules differ from one another. Most American journalists, though, accept *The AP Stylebook* as an arbiter of punctuation. But there are situations the stylebook doesn't cover.

We've found that a knowledge of phrases, clauses and sentence structure is key to punctuating correctly and consistently, which is why we say punctuation is to a great extent a function of grammar. Knowing grammar helps you remember and understand the rules and figure out solutions when the stylebook rules don't go far enough.

Three issues pose by far most of the common problems with punctuation:

1. How to use commas.
2. How to punctuate quotations.
3. How to punctuate pairs of modifiers.

Getting Words in the Right
Order and Punctuation

The third issue is a much smaller concern than the first two, but like them requires enough explanation that we've devoted a separate "Common Problems" section to each.

Solving Common Problems With Commas

1. Know when always to use a comma.

The following rules describe circumstances in which you should *always* use a comma.

Use a comma after said when introducing a direct quotation that is one sentence long.

> Henry David Thoreau said, "The question is not what you look at, but what you see."

Use a comma before and after the abbreviation for a state following a city, and before and after a year following a month and date.

> Roberto and Carmen met in Pulaski, Tenn., at the Butter Bowl.

> On May 2, 2018, it happened again.

Use a comma after words in a series but not before the conjunction unless the meaning would be unclear. (This rule may be contrary to what you learned in English class for academic writing, but it's the way journalists do it.)

> The new budget proposals would cut spending for student loans, building repairs, road improvements and farm subsidies.

What would be an example of a series that might be unclear without a comma before the conjunction? One in which the same conjunction appears in the series as part of an item could make someone have to pause to figure out the meaning:

> He went to town to buy a can of corn, a can of peas and carrots, and a can of beans.

Use a comma before the abbreviation etc. at the end of a series.

> Send us what you've got: the documents, the recordings, etc.

Use a comma after introductory clauses, phrases or words. If there are two in a row, put it only after the last one.

What do we mean by introductory clauses, phrases or words? Something in the sentence before the main idea is expressed. Here are some examples:

> Because clouds covered the sky, it was difficult to see the comet last night.
> [The comma follows an introductory dependent clause. The words *although, because, if* or *since* at the start of a sentence arc examples of subordinate conjunctions that introduce dependent clauses.]

Listening to the band, he decided to audition.
[The comma follows an introductory participial phrase.]

In July, Taylor was born.
[The comma follows an introductory prepositional phrase.]

Often, she was without shelter.
[The comma follows an introductory adverb.]

Gee, the rain smells good.
[The comma follows an introductory interjection. For added emphasis, you could use an exclamation point either after the interjection or after *good*. If you put an exclamation point after the interjection, you would capitalize *the*.]

Through the door into the building, the SWAT team charged.
[If there is more than one prepositional phrase at the beginning of a sentence, put a comma after the last one only.]

We know that many writers and editors are inconsistent about the use of commas after introductory clauses, phrases or words, sometimes putting the comma in and sometimes not. Their justifications always amount to either they wouldn't pause there when speaking the sentence or the introductory clause, phrase or word is "short enough" not to do so.

But such a subjective approach wastes time and money because different people would speak the sentence different ways, so a writer might put in a comma that an editor would take out and a proofreader would put back. And as for how short the introductory part is, you couldn't have a shorter introductory word than *No*, yet it would be followed by a comma: No, he disagreed.

So, we suggest always putting a comma after introductory words, phrases or clauses, even when they're only one word long. Then everyone on a publication's staff will be using the same playbook.

If a gerund (a verb used as a noun) or gerund phrase, or an infinitive (verb preceded by *to*) or infinitive phrase is the subject of the sentence, it is not considered an introductory word, phrase or clause, so it should not be followed by a comma.

Jogging is fun. [*Jogging* is a gerund used as the subject.]

Jogging five miles is something she did every morning. [*Jogging five miles* is a gerund phrase used as the subject.]

To live is to be. [*To live* is an infinitive used as the subject.]

To live well is to live a good life. [*To live well* is an infinitive phrase used as the subject.]

Compare the previous examples to the following sentences with introductory phrases that would take commas:

Jogging five miles, she tired.
[*Jogging five miles* is a participial phrase, not a gerund phrase. Participial phrases can never be the subject of a sentence and must always be followed by a comma at the start of a sentence.]

To live well, one must eat well.

[*To live well* is an infinitive phrase modifying the subject of the sentence, *one*. *To live well* here is not the subject of the sentence but an introductory phrase requiring a comma.]

If the introductory clause or phrase is attribution using a word like *said* or *says*, always put a comma at the end when introducing a direct quotation that is one sentence long. If what follows is more than a one-sentence quote or less than one, such as a partial quote or paraphrase, do not put a comma there, according to the following examples. (See Pages 128–129, 138.)

Cooper said, "To leave out premarital testing from this bill is like taking a Missouri census and leaving out Kansas City."

[A comma is used to introduce a one-sentence quote.]

Cooper said: "To leave out premarital testing from this bill is like taking a Missouri census and leaving out Kansas City. I wouldn't do it."

[A colon is used to introduce a quote of more than one sentence.]

Cooper said that leaving out premarital testing from the bill was "like taking a Missouri census and leaving out Kansas City."

[No comma or colon is used to introduce a paraphrase or partial quote.]

Use a comma between two independent clauses joined by a conjunction to form a single sentence. No comma is needed when what follows the conjunction is not an independent clause.

A dentist and her assistant discussed tooth care with the students, and they used Mr. Gross Mouth to illustrate their points.

[A comma is needed before the conjunction at the start of the second independent clause.]

A dentist and her assistant discussed tooth care with the students and used Mr. Gross Mouth to illustrate their points.

[No comma is used before *and* here because *and used Mr. Gross Mouth to illustrate their points* could not stand alone as a complete sentence—it's the second half of the compound predicate *discussed . . . and used* and is not a clause by itself.]

Use a comma between two imperative clauses linked by a conjunction, such as those often used in recipes.

Braise the meat for 10 minutes, and then remove it from the pan.

[These are independent clauses because the subject is implied in the imperative.]

Use commas to set off a conjunctive adverb (*however, likewise, at the same time, therefore*) wherever it may occur in a clause or sentence, as in these examples. (See Pages 140, 142–143.)

Nitish, however, was early.

However, Nitish was early. [In journalism, we'd change this *however* to *but* and drop the comma.]

Nitish was early, however.

John was late; however, Nitish was early. [Here, a semicolon separates the two clauses, although journalists would make them two sentences. Nitish is set off with a comma still from the rest of its clause.]

Use commas to set off a noun of direct address wherever it might appear in a sentence, according to the following examples.

John, could you come help me?

Could you, John, come help me?

Could you help me, John?

Use commas around parenthetical elements — nonrestrictive (nonessential) words, phrases or clauses. (See Pages 139–141.)

The yellow car, which was in the driveway, belongs to Carey.

Use a comma between coordinate adjectives — that is, if you can reverse the adjectives and put *and* between them. (See Page 207.)

The sleek, spotted cat pounced on the mouse.

Use a comma before the adverbs *also, as well, too* or *yet* at the end of a sentence.

Roberto Dumas came to the event, too.

Use a comma before *not* when showing contrast.

She said she thought independent voters preferred Stevens, not Malkowitz.

Use a comma in a headline in place of the word *and*.

City Council rejects tax increase, approves spending cuts

But beware of possible unintentional double meanings that might be created.

Louisiana Governor defends his wife, gift from korean

2. Know when never to use a comma.

The following rules describe circumstances in which you should *never* use a comma.

Never use a comma before a dependent clause unless the sentence could be misread without it, such as when it follows a negative statement.

The game was called because it was raining.

[*Because it was raining* is a dependent clause at the end of a sentence and can't be misread, so there is no comma in front of it.]

But look at this next sentence punctuated two ways:

He's not doing that, because he wants to.

He's not doing that because he wants to.

[This sentence means two different things depending on whether the comma is used. With the comma, the dependent clause is saying the reason he's not doing it is because he doesn't want to do it. Without the comma, the sentence is saying the reason he's not doing that is not because he wants to but for some other reason.]

Never use a comma between clauses that form part of a compound direct object.

> Bridges said *none of the workers required medical treatment* and *the leak did not pose a danger to public safety.*
> [Think of this construction as *He said this and that.* The clauses here are really part of a compound direct object joined by *and*. Putting a comma between them (before *and*) would change the meaning. The sentence would no longer state that Bridges was saying the leak did not pose a danger. Rather, it would imply that the reporter was editorializing about the leak.]

Never use a comma before a paraphrase or partial quotation.

> Feldman said "old-age blues" set in when he turned 30. [No comma after *said* because the quotation is not a complete sentence.]

Never use a comma after a period, an exclamation point or a question mark in a quotation when the sentence continues past it.

> **WRONG**   "Swim!," her father yelled.
>
> **RIGHT**   "Swim!" her father yelled.

Never use a comma after a quotation mark. The comma, if needed, goes before the quotation mark.

> "The beverage-container ordinance will probably be supported by the voters," MacDonald said.

Never use a comma before the conjunction at the end of a series unless the meaning would be confusing without one. (See Page 220.)

Never use a comma between compound adjectives — that is, two words that team up as one adjective, with one word describing the main adjective. Use a hyphen instead.

> The sun beat brightly through a *cloud-free* sky the morning of the accident.

Never use a comma between adjectives when you can't reverse them.

> a new stone wall [*New* and *stone* are not coordinate adjectives here—you cannot reverse them.]

Never use a comma around the abbreviation Jr. or Sr. after a name. (This may be contrary to what you learned in English class, but it is the way journalists do it.)

> Martin Luther King Jr. was a 20th-century civil rights leader.

Never use a comma around the abbreviation *Inc.* in a company name. (This is another exception to your training in English class.)

> Merck & Company Inc. is a pharmaceuticals company.

3. Know when you might want to use a comma.

You may use a comma to separate a series of three or more short independent clauses.

> "I came, I saw, I conquered."

You may use a comma to separate the same word used two times consecutively.

> Whatever is, is.

Solving Common Problems With Quotations

The handling of quotations is the second most common source of punctuation problems. Because journalists live and die by the quote, this is an especially important matter for them to master. So, the discussion here includes both punctuation and related issues that arise concerning quotations.

1. Know what and how to quote.

Quote someone's words to add color, detail or authenticity to a news or feature story.

If the words aren't colorful, don't provide important details, or don't help authenticate or back up a point being made, then don't quote them. Consider leaving them out, using a partial quote or paraphrasing them instead.

> **USELESS QUOTE** She said, "I'm happy to be here."
> [This quote provides neither color nor an important detail.]
>
> **BETTER** She said she was happy to be here.
> [Even though four of these words are an exact quote, they're so common that you need not call attention to them by using quotation marks.]
>
> **GOOD, COLORFUL QUOTE** Silber said, "It's been so dry around here that the cows are giving powdered milk."
>
> **GOOD QUOTE PROVIDING IMPORTANT DETAIL** Christiansen said, "Posicorp is looking to expand into a new market next year with a product line aimed at kids."
>
> **GOOD QUOTE BACKING UP A POINT** The grocery's owner charges that the Eversons' lawsuit threatens to drive him out of business. "Since this whole mess began, I've dropped about $150,000 in attorney fees," Mohr said, "and my business has declined 7 percent since all the bad publicity began."

Put quotation marks only around the exact words a speaker or writer uses, not around paraphrases.

> The president said the new military aircraft would be built next year.
> [Don't insert quotation marks here. The word *said* can be properly used with either quotes or paraphrases, so an editor should not assume that the words are a quote. Inserting quotation marks would probably create a misquotation because the writer gave no indication that the words were quoted.]

Quotation marks should be a contract with the reader that these are the exact words the source used. Journalists shouldn't normally rewrite a quote and leave it in quotation marks, but public relations writers might be expected to do that.

If the quote is wordy or grammatically incorrect, consider not using it, paraphrasing it or using a partial quote. If it contains profanity, possibly use hyphens in place of some of the letters of the offending word.

RIGHT	"I don't give a s---- what the president thinks," Stauffer said.
WRONG	"I don't care what the president thinks," Stauffer said. [These are not Stauffer's exact words, so they should not be presented as a quote.]
RIGHT	Stauffer said she didn't care what the president thought. [The statement is paraphrased, so there are no quotation marks.]

Single-word quotations generally don't need quotation marks. At that point, aren't you really paraphrasing? Sometimes, however, a single word may be so colorful that it's worth quoting by itself.

He said he felt fine. [No quotation marks needed around *fine*.]

He said he felt "wondrous." [The word is unusual enough that it could be quoted.]

Don't draw attention to clichés by putting quotation marks around them.

WRONG	An Iowa City, Iowa, student is "sadder but wiser" after a con artist took him for $400 he had saved. [Not only is it unnecessary to quote a cliché, but also, in this case, a reader might mistakenly think the student is being quoted. It's better to avoid using clichés altogether.]

Don't put quotation marks around the names of musical groups, dance companies or theater troupes.

WRONG	"The Beatles"
RIGHT	The Beatles

Don't use a quotation mark in place of the word *inches* or *seconds*. Likewise, don't use an apostrophe in place of the word *feet*.

WRONG	12"
RIGHT	12 inches; 12 seconds

Newspapers typically use quotation marks around all titles except those of magazines, newspapers, the Bible and other sacred books, reference books and descriptive titles of musical works (such as Symphony No. 1 or Opus 23). Actual titles of musical works, such as "Symphonie Fantastique" or "Visage," are set in quotation marks.

This differs from what you learned in English class, where titles of books, films and magazines, for example, are underlined or italicized.

2. Know how to attribute quotations and paraphrases.

Quotations

Include attribution (who said it) every time a different source is quoted and thereafter only when necessary to remind the reader.

> Fire Chief Lawrence Wong estimated damage to the warehouse at "maybe $200,000," but the owner said it could go even higher.
>
> Bill Pendergast, who bought the building last May, said, "I probably lost $200,000 worth of stored equipment alone, not to mention the damage to the warehouse itself."
>
> [The speaker changes, so attribution is required. Had the first paragraph been followed instead by another quote from Wong, no new attribution would be needed.]

The first time a quotation is used from a particular person, that person's full name and qualifications are usually cited.

> "We condemn all violence," said Muhammad Rashad, leader of an Islamic prayer group.

On second reference, the person's last name only is cited.

> "Our group supports only peaceful protest," Rashad said.

If the person has a title that was used on first reference, such as the Rev., Dr., Professor or Gov., that title is dropped on all following references, although sometimes the title — written out and without capital letters — can be used in place of the name on some of the later references.

> The governor said . . .

Stick to one tense in attributions — either *said* or *says* — throughout. Use *said* for hard-news stories, *says* for feature stories.

> "I'm not happy with the verdict," Teresa Caruso said. She ~~says~~ *said* the jury didn't take into account all the evidence.

Don't strain for synonyms for *said* or *says*. Journalists prefer *said* and *says* to other attributions because these words are brief and neutral.

- *Stated* is longer.
- *Claimed* and *according to* can imply doubt. Some editors prefer *according to* when a document is being quoted. *According to* is also correct when you mean "in accordance with rules."
- *Admitted* implies guilt.
- *Refuted* means "successfully answered."
- *Added* means the statement was an afterthought.
- Nobody ever *grinned*, *smiled* or *laughed* a statement. Somebody *said it with a grin*.
- To say someone *believes*, *desires*, *feels*, *hopes*, *thinks* or *wants* something or similar words is mind reading unless the person used these words.

If *said* or *says* is followed by a time element and a paraphrase, follow the time element with the word *that*.

> The president said Friday *that* he would send the proposal to Congress.
> [Omitting *that* would create confusion about whether the president gave the speech on Friday or intended to send the proposal to Congress on Friday.]

Although some editors prefer that attribution generally be placed after the first sentence of a quote, it can properly appear before or in the middle of the first sentence of a quote, instead.

> The senator said, "I won't comment on unfounded accusations."

> "The worst thing about the situation," Rep. Maggie Feldman said, "is that we can't find reliable information."

In fact, a more conversational approach, especially useful in broadcast, is to put the attribution before the quote. Also, attribution should not follow a multiple-sentence quote but either precede it, with the attribution followed by a colon, or follow a comma at the end of the first quoted sentence.

The order of source and attribution verb should usually be *source said*, not *said source*.

> "I can't believe I hit the jackpot," Mary Koch said.

The *source said* order is more conversational because usually the subject precedes the verb in English. But you may want to use the *said source* order if the source and the *said* would otherwise be separated by a long description, such as a title. "This is outrageous," said Marisa Peters, president of a local citizens rights group.

Put a comma, not a period, between a quotation and its attribution — unless the period is there for an abbreviation. In that case, add a comma.

> **WRONG**   "We exceeded our fundraising goal by $10,000." She said.

> **RIGHT**   "We exceeded our fundraising goal by $10,000," she said.

If the attribution precedes a quote, the punctuation at the end of the attribution should be as follows: nothing in front of a partial quote or paraphrase, a comma in front of a one-sentence quote, a colon in front of a quotation of two sentences or more.

> The airline analyst said airfares from smaller airports stack up well against those from Detroit. [no punctuation in front of a paraphrase]

> The airline analyst said airfares from smaller airports "compare well with those from Detroit." [no punctuation in front of a partial quote]

> The airline analyst said, "Airfares from Toledo, Lansing and Flint compare well with those from Detroit." [a comma in front of a one-sentence quote]

> The airline analyst said: "Airfares from Toledo, Lansing and Flint compare well with those from Detroit. It just depends on your destination."
> [a colon in front of a multiple-sentence quote]

If the attribution follows a one-sentence quote, partial quote or paraphrase, use a comma at the end of the quote or paraphrase.

"Airfares from Toledo, Lansing and Flint compare well with those from Detroit," the airline analyst said. [comma following a one-sentence quote]

Airfares from smaller airports "compare well with those from Detroit," the airline analyst said. [comma following a partial quote]

Airfares from smaller airports stack up well against those from Detroit, the airline analyst said. [comma following a paraphrase]

Although AP often uses a comma after a multiple-sentence quote, it is better to move the attribution after the first sentence, following a comma, or in front of the first sentence, followed by a colon.

AVOID "Airfares from Toledo, Lansing and Flint compare well with those from Detroit. It just depends on your destination," the airline analyst said.

BETTER "Airfares from Toledo, Lansing and Flint compare well with those from Detroit," the airline analyst said. "It just depends on your destination."

BETTER The airline analyst said: "Airfares from Toledo, Lansing and Flint compare well with those from Detroit. It just depends on your destination."

Paraphrases

Attribute every paraphrase, or readers are likely to think *you* are making the statement.

People shouldn't rush to a judgment before the investigation is complete. *, the attorney said.*

If a person is paraphrased as saying two clauses in one sentence, don't separate the clauses with a comma.

Chung said that *the road was icy* and *the other car was speeding*.

If a person is paraphrased after the word *said*, many editors insist that the clause following it must drop back a tense in time from the original statement tense to maintain the proper sequence of tenses. But there is disagreement about this. (See Page 46.)

He said he was [not *is*] going.

3. Know how to carry quotations across paragraphs.

Don't put a quotation mark at the end of a full-sentence quote if the quote is continued at the start of the next paragraph.

Peters said: "I'm upset by the whole situation.
"I didn't know what I was getting into when I came here."

Don't go from a partial quote to a full-sentence quote within the same quotation marks. Instead, add quotation marks at the end of the partial quote and the beginning of the full sentence, starting a new paragraph between them.

WRONG	Jones said he was "happy to be alive. I can't believe it happened."
RIGHT	Jones said he was "happy to be alive." "I can't believe it happened," he said.

4. Know how to handle these special issues with quotes.

Place periods and commas inside closing quotation marks.

"Prohibitions against doctors' advertising are unfortunate," Rhysburg said, "because we end up with uneducated patients."

Place semicolons — if you use them — or colons outside closing quotation marks.

Nixon said, "I am not a crook"; others weren't so sure.

Fredericks spoke with pride of his "future farmers": his sons, Chris and Sam, and his daughter, Jane.

The AP makes an exception if the semicolon or colon is part of the quoted material, but in practice this exception rarely, if ever, occurs. Also, journalists tend to avoid *compound sentences* (sentences with two or more clauses that could stand alone as complete sentences) joined by a semicolon.

Place question marks and exclamation points inside closing quotation marks if they are part of the quotation, outside if they are not.

Have you read Ezra Pound's "Cantos"?

"Darn it!" she yelled.

Although AP permits ellipses (. . .), journalists generally don't use them to indicate words left out of quotations. Instead, we suggest you use paraphrases or partial quotes.

ORIGINAL He said, "Abraham Lincoln was ahead of his time in opposing slavery, but nonetheless, Lincoln said he thought that after the slaves were freed, they should be shipped off to Africa."

PREFERRED He said Abraham Lincoln wanted to free the slaves then ship them to Africa. [paraphrase]

PREFERRED He said Abraham Lincoln was "ahead of his time in opposing slavery," but that he wanted to free the slaves then have them "shipped off to Africa." [partial quotes]

NOT PREFERRED He said, "Abraham Lincoln . . . thought that after the slaves were freed, they should be shipped off to Africa." (Avoid ellipses.)

Capitalize the first word of a quotation only when it is a complete sentence directly quoted.

Thomas said the conditions were "appalling."
Thomas said, "The conditions are appalling."

Use single quotation marks around quotes within a quote or for quotes in headlines. Most publications also use them for quotations in captions or blurbs.

> Houston said, "According to Abraham Lincoln, 'You can't fool all of the people all of the time,' but I disagree."

> Mayor: 'I Won't Resign' (headline)

Solving Common Problems With Punctuating Pairs of Modifiers

1. Use the correct *conjunction* (connecting word) to connect equal or unequal parts of a sentence — a coordinating one for equal parts, a subordinating one for unequal parts — and punctuate them correctly.

When a *coordinating conjunction* — such as *and, but, for, nor, or, so* and *yet* — connects two independent clauses, put a comma before the conjunction but not after it (a common mistake).

RIGHT	The judge said he would open the hearing to the press, but he didn't.
WRONG	The judge said he would open the hearing to the press but, he didn't.

Generally speaking, don't put a comma before a *subordinating conjunction* such as *although, as, because, if, since, until, whether* and *while*.

The main dispute is over *because*. Some books insist that a clause introduced by *because* is always preceded by a comma, but media writers put a comma before a conjunction only in the following cases:

- If it introduces an *independent clause* (one that could stand alone as a complete sentence). (See Page 222.)
- When the meaning could be confusing without it, as when the conjunction follows a negative statement.

  He said he didn't agree, because he was a libertarian.
  [The reason he didn't agree was that he was a libertarian, so put a comma.]

  He said he didn't agree because he was a libertarian.
  [If he did agree, but not because he was a libertarian, leave the comma out.]

2. Set off conjunctive adverbs by placing a comma after them.

Conjunctive adverbs (adverbs used as connecting words) are good transition words because they show a strong logical relationship between the sentences they connect. Unlike conjunctions, they're followed by a comma.

Common Conjunctive Adverbs

accordingly	however	on the contrary
also	in addition	on the other hand
anyhow	indeed	otherwise
at the same time	instead	so
besides	in the first place	still
consequently	likewise	then
first, second, etc.	meanwhile	therefore
for example	moreover	thus
for this reason	most important	
furthermore	nevertheless	

Unlike conjunctions, which always come at the beginning of the clauses they introduce, conjunctive adverbs can be placed at the beginning, in the middle or at the end of a clause. Another way conjunctive adverbs differ from conjunctions is that, unlike conjunctions, conjunctive adverbs may be used in a compound sentence after a semicolon and introducing an independent clause.

The battle was over; however, all was not still.

Again, though, media writers generally avoid this construction because they prefer to avoid semicolons.

3. Know the difference between punctuating *coordinate adjectives* (two equal modifiers next to each other) and *compound modifiers* (two modifiers next to each other, but the first modifies the second).

Coordinate Adjectives

We suggest following a rule first advocated by Dr. Don Ranly, professor emeritus at the Missouri School of Journalism, that you systematically not put a comma between adjectives when one or more of them refers to number, color, age, material, ethnicity, nationality or race.

These exceptions are based on three problems:

- In the case of number, reversing the two adjectives won't work grammatically:

    three pink flamingos (number and color)

- In the cases of ethnicity, nationality and race, common professional usage follows the practice of positioning these adjectives right before the noun:

    tall Hispanic male (ethnicity)

    healthy Italian man (nationality)

    optimistic African-American woman (race)

- In the cases of color, age and material, we suggest these exceptions because people tend to disagree about the results of the coordinate adjective reversal test when one of these is in the phrase.

old silk dress (age and material)

Also, note that although these categories are exceptions to putting a comma between modifiers, they do not necessarily imply that no hyphen might be required:

light-blue sky

Polish-American hero

Compound Modifiers

Use a hyphen between *compound modifiers* that precede the word they modify.

She was a *part-time* worker. [*Part-time* precedes the word it modifies, the noun *worker*.]

She worked *part time*. [*Part time* follows the word it modifies, the verb *worked*.]

The hyphen is usually retained, however, in a compound adjective that follows a linking verb — in other words, if the compound is a predicate adjective.

The work was *part-time*.

The object floating in the sky appeared *saucer-shaped*.

Sometimes, however, the hyphen will be dropped, especially if the sentence continues past the predicate adjective.

The *better-qualified* candidate was Sally. [The compound adjective needs the hyphen.]

Sally was *better-qualified*. [Some would drop the hyphen here, but we suggest retaining it to minimize possible confusion, as in implying she was better off when qualified.]

Sally was *better qualified* than the other applicant. [This sentence is clear without the hyphen.]

Do not use a hyphen after *less, least, many, most, very* or an adverb ending in *ly*.

This is an *easily remembered* rule.

Use a hyphen in a compound modifier after any word ending in ly other than an adverb, such as the adjectives *friendly, likely, seemly, surly, timely* and *ugly* or the noun *family*.

He described it as a *"friendly-service"* company.

Doctorian's is a *family-owned* business.

Ages are not hyphenated in a predicate adjective.

He is 4 *years old*. [*The AP Stylebook* does not hyphenate an age when it's a predicate adjective despite the fact that other compound predicate adjectives normally *are* hyphenated.]

AP has various rules and exceptions for when hyphens are used in the spelling of words. (See Pages 276–279.)

Understanding Punctuation in More Depth

Punctuation other than commas and quotation marks pose few problems.

Semicolons

Use a semicolon between items in a series that has commas within the items. Remember to put a semicolon before the final conjunction.

> The American flag is red, white and blue; the Canadian flag is red and white; and the German flag is red, gold and black.

A semicolon may be used between independent clauses when a conjunction is absent, but journalists would typically avoid this and instead use something else — a comma followed by a conjunction, or a dash without a conjunction, if the thoughts are closely related. If they're not, a journalist would make them two separate sentences.

> **RIGHT, BUT NOT COMMON IN JOURNALISM**   The Padres are weak this year; they have the worst record in the league.

> **BETTER**   The Padres are weak this year — they have the worst record in the league.

> **BETTER**   The Padres are weak this year. They have the worst record in the league.

Use a semicolon in a headline to join two sentences, but make sure the two sentences don't seem absurd joined into one thought.

> 5½-Foot Boa caught in toilet; woman relieved

> Coach suspended in sexual probe; players honored

A semicolon can be used before a conjunctive adverb connecting two independent clauses, but journalists would usually rewrite the clauses as two sentences.

> **RIGHT, BUT NOT COMMON IN JOURNALISM**   Frome's lawyer contended he was mentally incompetent; however, the jury decided the evidence was not so clear.

> **BETTER**   Frome's lawyer contended he was mentally incompetent. The jury, however, decided the evidence was not so clear.

Colons

Use a colon to introduce a quotation of more than one sentence.

> Jimenez said: "As of now, there can't be a merger. We need more cooperation first between the city and county fire departments. We have to work together more."

Use a colon to introduce a list of items that begin with bullets or dashes.

> In other action, the commission:
> —Approved Belle Kaufman's request that she be allowed to build a guesthouse in back of her home.
> — Rejected the request by Ralph Kawaski that a parcel of land he owns on Route 1 be rezoned to allow him to build for a dog-race track.

Use a colon after an independent clause to introduce a single-item summary or an explanation with a dramatic pause. Here, the colon is used to stress what follows by pointing to it.

> He said you could summarize Jesus' message in three words: Love your neighbor.

If what follows the colon could stand alone as a complete sentence, as in the preceding example, capitalize it. Otherwise, do not.

Use a colon to take the place of *says* in a headline.

> Levin: 'I Want to Be Your Mayor'

Use a colon to introduce a subtitle.

> Theodore Bernstein wrote *The Careful Writer: A Modern Guide to English Usage.*

Use a colon to show time if it's not an even hour.

> 7:30 p.m.

Use a colon to separate chapter and verse in a Bible or Quran citation.

> James 1:5   Quran 2:256

Dashes

Use dashes to set off a list or parenthetical material containing commas in the middle of a sentence.

> The Jayhawks' defense — the linemen, the linebackers and the defensive backs — was exhausted after being pounded by the Sooners' offense.

Use a dash for emphasis when a pause longer than that for a comma is needed or when there's a sharp turn of thought. (Some broadcasters prefer an ellipsis instead for this. See Page 50.)

> He said he would do it — later.

Use a dash after a dateline or the wire-service credit in a newspaper story.

> LONDON —
> NEW BEDFORD, Mass. (AP) —

Use a dash in front of the attribution in a blurb or pull quote (material pulled from the text and highlighted in larger type for typographic purposes).

> 'Let's face it: Hearst started the Spanish-American War.'
> —Mayor Jonathan Richardson

Note the use of single quotation marks in such cases. (See Page 231.)

A dash is used in many publications as a bullet introducing items in a list.

> In other business, the City Council:
> —Approved a $525,000 contract with James Bros. Construction Co. to reroof City Hall.
> —Refused to rezone a half-acre tract at 202 Trenton Place for construction of a neighborhood market.
> —Approved the rezoning of 10 acres at Hinton and Market streets from single-family residential use to multiple-family apartments.

Put a space on each side of a dash unless it is used as a bullet item.

This is a wire-service rule, and it also keeps spell-checker programs from flagging words on each side of a dash as one unrecognized word. If your keyboard or software doesn't offer a dash, use two hyphens with no space between them.

Parentheses

Although journalists usually avoid parentheses, you may use parentheses to set off an aside, such as nonessential information or words inserted to clarify a quotation. If the aside contains at least one complete sentence, put the period at the end inside the parentheses. If not, put it outside.

> She said her favorite movie was "Das Boot" ("The Boat").

> Her dress was inappropriate for the funeral. (It was bright red.)

Hyphens

Use a hyphen between compound modifiers that precede the word they modify, but do not use a hyphen after very or an adverb ending in ly. (See Pages 255–271.)

> high-profile case

> very high-profile case

> highly publicized case

Use a hyphen after some prefixes, especially when, without one, a vowel would be doubled. (See the section on hyphenation in spelling, beginning on Pages 276–279.)

> pre-empt   re-elect

Use hyphens in *suspensive* cases involving a modifier that applies to several words.

> She most enjoyed the 3- and 4-year-old children.

Use hyphens in place of to in odds, ratios, scores and some vote tabulations.

The odds were 3-2.   The Senate voted 48-2 in favor of the amendment.

Use hyphens when fractions or numbers from 21 to 99 are written out , such as at the start of a sentence.

two-thirds   Eighty-seven

Apostrophes

Remember, the bottom of the apostrophe always points to the left. If it points to the right, it's not an apostrophe but a single open quotation mark.

Use an apostrophe to show possession with nouns.

the dog's breath   the building's grandeur

Use an apostrophe to show that something has been left out in contractions.

don't [do not]   I'll [I will]

decade of the '90s [decade of the 1990s]   rock 'n' roll [rock and roll]

Use an apostrophe to make the plural of a single letter but not of a single numeral.

A's   3s

Use an apostrophe with a pronoun to form a contraction.

it's [it is]   who's [who is]

Do not use an apostrophe to form the possessive of any pronoun except those ending in one or body.

one's   anybody's   theirs

Do not use an apostrophe in place of the words *feet* and *minutes*.

WRONG   10'
RIGHT   10 feet; 10 minutes

Slashes

Use a slash to form a fraction or mixed number if your keyboard does not have a single key for the fraction.

1/10   2 1/2

Do not use such expressions as *and/or, c/o, either/or* or *his/hers* except in quoted material.

Periods, Exclamation Points and Question Marks

If only all punctuation were as easy as using these three symbols! Periods, exclamation points and question marks don't give writers much trouble, so we won't go into all their uses. Instead, we'll just note a few frequent problems.

Don't shoehorn too many ideas into one sentence.

Editor Kenn Finkel has said that the main problem journalists have with periods is not getting to them soon enough.

Know when to use periods in abbreviations. (See Page 404.)

Journalists typically confine the use of exclamation points to quotations in which people express strong emotion or to strong opinions expressed in editorials or personal columns.

In other uses, exclamation points risk making an article sound biased, sensational or gushy. Still, they have their place, as in the first sentence of this section.

In the case of an ironic, fake exclamation, the writer may choose not to put an exclamation mark as a clue to the reader:

"How cute." (No exclamation mark because the writer is showing there's no real emotion.)

Never use two exclamation points next to each other or an exclamation point next to a question mark.

Exclamation points and question marks signal a full stop. Only one is needed or correct.

Journalists should avoid putting a question mark in parentheses to suggest dubiousness.

> **WRONG**   The music (?) consisted of squawks and static.

Such a practice has no place in a news story that readers expect to be free from personal opinion.

 **LaunchPad Solo**
macmillan learning

Online Grammar Help
Launchpadworks.com

For practice with getting words in the right order and punctuation, log on to *LaunchPad Solo for Journalism* and go to *Exercise Central for AP Style.*

PART THREE

Reference Lists

Bias-Related Terms *241*

One Word, Two Words, or Hyphenated? *255*

Spelling *272*
Spelling Rules 272
JOURNALISM TIP: Spelling and Your Career 274
Hyphenation as a Spelling Problem 276
Words Often Misspelled 280

Tightening *287*
What to Tighten, A-Z 287

Trademarks and Generics *323*
Former Trademarks Now Also Considered Generic 326
Not Trademarks 327
Trademarks that Pose Other Spelling Issues 327

Usage *328*
Usage Differences 328
Misused and Confused Words and Phrases 329

Bias-Related Terms

The following list of terms — some preferred and some to be avoided — is controversial. As soon as it is published, some of the entries may be out-of-date. Each time we publish the list, we add and delete terms. The first core set of examples was provided by permission of the Multicultural Management Program at the University of Missouri School of Journalism, which constructed a Dictionary of Offensive Terms with the help of multicultural journalists from across the nation. Other examples are drawn from observation of language in today's media, as well as from a number of resources listed at the end of the book (See Pages 411–415). This is a list of slurs, insulted and derogatory labels used against those who are marginalized: women, people of color, the disabled, LGBTQ, and the bullied, and can help you decode shifts in your audience.

Speech matters. As minorities and women bring their voices to the national conversation, new perspectives will emerge about what is fair language. See below for a list on biased terms. *Watch your language.*

Sexism, racism and other "isms" – insults categorizing humans based on their existence at birth, that is, gender, skin color, religion, when they were born, physical condition, and so forth.

Racism – a belief that race is the primary determinant of human traits and capacities; prejudice or discrimination that racial differences produce an inherent superiority of a particular race.

Sexism – a belief that sex is the primary determinant of human traits and capacities; prejudice or discrimination that sexual differences produce an inherent superiority of a particular sex. Generally, the word describes discrimination against women, yet sexism may describe discrimination against all genders.

Ageism – a belief that age is the primary determinant of human traits and capacities; prejudice or discrimination that age differences produce an inherent superiority of a particular age range.

Hate speech – speech expressing hatred of a particular group of people based on their nation of origin, ethnicity, skin color, religion, gender, gender identity, sexual orientation or disability.

A

actor   Not *actress*. Use *actor* unless *actress* is part of a title, such as the Oscar categories "Best Actress" and "Best Supporting Actress." When the Me Too Movement against sexual harassment and sexual assault began in October 2017, women in movie and television work mobilized. They demanded changes in pay, safety and increased high-level work. Only 10 percent of U.S. movies have gender balance. Women account for half of moviegoers, a quarter of protagonists. Similarly, women in broadcast network television, cable and streaming programs are 25 percent of professionals shaping the content.

African   Of or pertaining to Africa or its people or languages. Not a synonym for *black* or *African-American*.

African-American   Not interchangeable with *black*. Ask members of the group in your audience for their preference. Don't use the terms *articulate*, *intelligent* and *qualified* as modifiers for *African-American*; you would not use those terms to describe white people in the same context.

AIDS victim   Do not use; *person with AIDS* is preferred.

alien   Do not use; *undocumented immigrant* is preferred (not *an illegal*). Those terms are wrong when the person is a *refugee*.

all people are created equal   Use instead of *all men are created equal* unless you need to quote the Declaration of Independence verbatim.

alumnae and alumni   Not *alumni* for a group of men and women who have attended a school. *Alumna* (plural *alumnae*) is correct for a woman (women); *alumnus* (plural *alumni*) for a man (men). *The AP Stylebook* tells you that *alumni* is the correct term for a group of men and women. But just as *man* does not stand for men and women, *alumni* does not stand for both sexes.

American   Applies to people from both North, South, and Central America. AP style says it may be used to refer to citizens of the U.S.; instead, use *U.S. citizen* or *U.S. resident*.

American Indian   Interchangeable with *Native American*; ask source to determine preference; use correct tribal name if possible. *Wampum, Tonto, Injun, Hiawatha, Indian giver, heathen, wild Indian, circle the wagons, warpath, warrior, powwow, scalping, tepee, brave, squaw, savage* and other similar terms offend.

anchor   Use *anchor* for all people anchoring the news.

Anglo   Always capitalized. Used interchangeably with *white* primarily in parts of the Southwest regions of the U.S. to denote a white inhabitant of non-Hispanic descent.

Arab   A native of Arabia or any of a Semitic people native to Arabia but now dispersed throughout surrounding lands. Not interchangeable with *Arab-American* or persons from Middle Eastern countries. There are 3 million Arab Americans in the U.S.

"the Arab world"   Although 22 countries are in the League of Arab States, this phrase misleads. Some 413 million people inhabit a variety of lands—from

North and Northeast Africa to Southwest Asia. Generalizations cannot cover their experiences, religions or politics. Again, name the country instead of making a sweeping generalization that is less specific.

articulate Offensive when referring to a minority group member and his or her ability to handle the English language; usage suggests that "those people" are not considered well-educated or well-spoken. Usually, drop adjectives as they are judgments.

artisan Preferred to *craftsman*.

Asian Refers specifically to things or people of or from Asia; not interchangeable with *Asian-American*. Do not use *Oriental* or *Asiatic* when referring to people.

Asian-American Preferred generic term for U.S. citizens of Asian descent. Be specific when referring to individuals or particular groups: *Filipino-Americans*, *Japanese-Americans*, *Chinese-Americans* and so on. *Serene*, *quiet*, *shy*, *reserved* and *smiling* are disparaging stereotypes of Asian-Americans, as are *buck-toothed*, *delicate*, *obedient*, *passive*, *stoic*, *mystical*, *China doll* and *dragon lady*. Avoid *nip*, *chink*, *chink in the armor*, *coolies*, *Chinaman*, *geisha*, *inscrutable*, *Jap*, and references to the *Asian invasion*, describing Asian immigration. By 2055 Asians are projected to become the largest immigrant group in the U.S.

assembly member Use for all elected to an assembly (also *assemblywoman*, *assemblyman*).

B

banana Do not use; offensive term for an Asian-American who allegedly has abandoned his or her culture. Just as objectionable are *coconut* for a Mexican-American and *oreo* for an African-American.

bandito Do not use; often applied derisively.

basket case Do not use; term began as British army slang for a quadruple amputee who had to be carried in a basket.

bastard Do not use; also do not use *illegitimate*.

beauty Avoid descriptive terms of beauty when not necessary. For instance, use *blond* and *blue-eyed* for a woman only if you would use the same phrasing for a man.

beefcake Do not use; offensive term referring to male physical attractiveness. Do not use *cheesecake* to refer to female physical attractiveness.

bellhop Not *bellman*.

bi Term derived from *bisexual*, which is preferred. See *bisexual*.

Bible-beater, -thumper, -whacker, Holy roller Do not use; unacceptable terms for evangelical Christians.

Bible Belt Do not use for sections of the U.S., especially in the South and Midwest.

birth name or given name Not *maiden name.*

bisexual Term for a person sexually attracted to members of both sexes; use carefully and only when absolutely relevant, if at all.

black Ask your source for clarification. Although *African-American* may be preferred by your audience, both terms are considered acceptable usage in *The AP Stylebook.* Your audience will tell you what is preferred. Do not use *coon,* nor refer to black cuisine as *fried chicken, watermelon.* Do not use the archaic *colored* or *negro* unless the name is used in a title, such as the National Association for the Advancement of Colored People or the United Negro College Fund.

blind Use *visually impaired* or *person with low vision*; do not use *the blind.*

blond Use *blond* for men and women.

boy Insulting when applied to an adult male, especially a man of color.

boy next door Do not use; as domestic terrorists are primarily white, this term implies surprise that the criminal is not a minority.

broad Do not use; offensive term for a woman.

brotherly and sisterly love Not *brotherly love.*

brunette Use one spelling, *brunette*, for men and women.

business professional Use for all those in business (also *businessman* or *business-woman*).

buxom Do not use; offensive reference to a woman's chest size.

C

camera operator Use for all people operating cameras, not *cameraman* or *camerawoman.*

Canuck Do not use; derisive term for a Canadian.

career woman Do not use; out-of-date. Simply report her business title.

Caucasian Always capitalized. Usually, but not always, interchangeable with *white. White non-Hispanic* is the preferred term, used for decades by the U.S. Census.

chairperson, convener, presider, coordinator, chair Use for all chaired meetings (also *chairwoman* or *chairman*).

Charlie, gook Do not use; derisive terms popularized in the Vietnam War referring to a Vietnamese person.

Chicano/Chicana Popular terms in the 1960s and 1970s to refer to Mexican-Americans could be offensive to older Mexican-Americans; check with source.

chick Do not use; offensive term referring to a woman. Avoid *chick flick* or *chick lit*, terms that denote movies and literature that feature women, often in a derogatory manner.

Chico First name inappropriately applied to a Mexican or Mexican-American; do not use generically. Avoid *José, Pancho* and *Julio.*

chief   Offensive when used generically to describe a Native American; use only when title is one given by a tribe.

Chinatown   Refers to some Asian-American neighborhoods; avoid as a blanket term for all Asian-American communities.

coconut   Do not use; offensive term for a Mexican-American who seemingly has abandoned his or her culture. Just as objectionable are *banana* for an Asian-American and *oreo* for a black person.

codger   Do not use; offensive reference to an older person. Do not use *well-preserved, Pop, matronly, golden years, old-timer, coot, geezer*. Use age only.

coed   Do not use; outdated from the days when men were the dominant gender in college. Today, women outnumber men in college (women 56 percent/ men 44 percent and as graduates (women 32.6 percent/ men 31.3 percent). Use *student*.

cojones   Do not use; vulgar Spanish word for *testicles*, often used to indicate machismo.

colored   In most societies, the word is derogatory. Use only when part of an official title, as in *National Association for the Advancement of Colored People*. In some African countries, *colored* denotes individuals of mixed racial ancestry. If the word is used, place it in quotation marks and provide an explanation of its meaning.

common person, average person   Not *common man, average man, average Joe, John Doe*. The U.S. common person is female, as women are 51 percent of the population.

community   Do not use; implies a monolithic culture in which people act, think and vote in the same way, as in *Asian-American, Hispanic, African-American* or *gay community*. Be more specific: *Hispanic residents in a north-side neighborhood*. You are not the judge of whether a group is a community.

congressional representative, member of Congress   Use for a member of Congress (also *congressman* or *congresswoman*).

conjoined twins   Not *Siamese twins*.

coon   Do not use; objectionable reference to an African-American.

coot   Do not use; offensive reference to an older person.

cougar   Do not use; focuses on women's sexuality and your judgment, not newsworthy.

councilor   Use for a member of a council (also *councilwoman* or *councilman*).

cracker, hillbilly, Okie, redneck   Do not use, even when people refer to themselves this way.

craftsman   Do not use; *artisan* is preferred.

crip, cripple, crippled   Do not use; derogatory terms for disabled people.

cybergeek   Do not use; derogatory reference to an inventor, a programmer or a technical expert. Avoid *nerd* and *techie*. Use the person's title.

D

dago   Do not use; derogatory reference to an Italian or Italian-American.

deaf, hearing impaired and speech impaired   Not *deaf and dumb*, *deaf and mute*. Deaf people are not dumb.

dear   Usage such as *he was a dear man* or *she is a dear* are personal judgments, not newsworthy.

deliverer, delivery person   Not *deliveryman*.

disabled   A disabling condition may or may not be handicapping. Use *disabled* and *disability* rather than *handicapped* or *handicap*. Don't use *disabled* as a noun. Do not use *crippled*, *crip* or *invalid*. Use *person* (*people*) *with a disability* (*disabilities*) or check with the individual. Reminder: 11 percent of the U.S. population is disabled; 89 percent are perhaps *temporarily abled*.

divorced   Not *divorcé* or *divorcée*. A person's marital status seldom is pertinent to a story. Especially be careful when you start to state a woman's marital status. Women continue to be tagged with marital identifiers more than men. Fewer than half (48 percent) of U.S. adults are married.

door attendant   Not *doorman*.

drafter   Not *draftsman*.

Dutch treat   Do not use; implies that Dutch people are cheap. Use *separate checks*.

dwarf   Do not use; *little people* is preferred. Do not use *midget*.

E

English, French, Irish   Not *Englishmen*, *Frenchman*, *Irishman*.

Eskimo   Many people referred to as *Eskimo* prefer *Inuit*, *Native Alaskan*, *native person*; ask source for preference.

every person for himself or herself   Not *every man for himself*.

F

factory worker   Not *factory man*.

fag, faggot   Do not use; offensive term for a gay man or lesbian. Do not use even if members of the group refer to themselves by the term.

fairy   Do not use; offensive term for gays.

female   Do not use in place of *woman* (the noun). Do not use *woman* or *female* as an adjective. Do not identify by gender unless it is pertinent to the story.

fiancé   Language is moving toward one spelling, *fiancé*, for all instances. As with the issue of *divorcé*, do not overemphasize a woman's marital status.

firefighter   Use instead of *fireman* or *firewoman*.

fisher   Not *fisherman*.

flip   Do not use; derogatory term for a Filipino or Filipino-American.

foreman, forewoman   Not *foreman* for both sexes.

full-figured   Do not use. Descriptions of a woman's physical appearance are rarely relevant. If you would not describe a man's physical appearance in a story, do not describe a woman's appearance. Physical descriptions are relevant only in a few fields—sports, health, fashion. Do not use *Amazon, statuesque, stunning, barracuda, gold-digger, airhead, feminine wiles, foxy, fragile, frigid, little woman, petite.*

G

gabacho   Do not use; derogatory Spanish word applied to whites.

gaijin   Do not use; exclusionary Japanese term referring to foreigners.

gang member   Use only when verified. See *wannabe.*

gay   Preferred; homosexual is offensive. Identify a person's sexual orientation *only* when pertinent to the story. Sexual orientation is rarely relevant. See *homosexual.*

gender enders   Avoid these terms: *actress, comedienne, executrix, heroine, poetess* and *starlet.* Instead, use gender-neutral terms such as *actor, comedian, executor, hero, poet* and *star.*

ghetto   Avoid; stereotype for a poor minority community, name the city district.

girl   Use only when the person is under 18 years of age; insulting when used to refer to a woman. (See *boy.*)

golden years   Avoid; characterizes people's later years as uniformly idyllic. Census data show the disparity of older citizens' poverty.

gorgeous   Avoid giving your judgments of the physical attributes of women and men.

gringo   Do not use; derogatory Spanish term applied to whites.

Guido   An Italian first name; offensive when used to denote membership in the Mafia or as a description of street punks.

gyp   Do not use; offensive term meaning "to cheat"; derived from *gypsy.*

H

handmade, synthetic   Preferred to *man-made.* Use *manufactured, constructed, fabricated* or *created.*

harebrained   Do not use to characterize people; offensive.

harelip   Avoid; offensive term for *cleft lip.*

harem   Do not use to describe a gathering of women; derisive.

Hebrew   A language. Do not use for *Jew.* Citizens of Israel are Israelis; not all Israelis are Jews.

hero   Use for both men and women; do not use *heroine* for women.

high yellow   Do not use; avoid any description of skin color or degrees of color Avoid *mulatto* and *half-breed*.

Hillbilly, okie, redneck   Do not use; terms applied to people generally from rural areas.

Hinduism   A religion in India; adherents are Hindus. Do not confuse *Hindu* with *Hindi*, one of many languages spoken in India.

Hispanic   Term referring generically to those with Latin American or Spanish heritage; not necessarily interchangeable with *Chicano, Latino, Mexican-American* or other specific Hispanic groups. Ask source which term is preferred. Use ethnic background *only* when pertinent to the story. Many Hispanics are second-, third-, fourth- and fifth-generation U.S. citizens, so do not assume a Hispanic is a recent immigrant. Do not use *hot-blooded, Latin lover*.

homemaker   Not *housewife*. Currently, 2 million men and 10 million women are "stay-at-home" parents.

homosexual   Do not use as noun or adverb; a person's sexual orientation is rarely relevant to a story. *Homosexual* connotes a clinical illness and evokes the pejorative "homo." Preferred terms are *gay* for a homosexual man and *lesbian* for a homosexual woman. *Dyke, fruit, fairy* and *queer* are objectionable. Do not use those terms, even if members of the group refer to themselves by any of these terms. Use *sexual orientation* rather than *sexual preference*.

honorifics   Usually not useful. Women and men are identified on first reference with full name and on second reference by last name. Use the courtesy title *Mrs.* only if the person prefers it or confusion would result. Otherwise, *Ms.* is the courtesy title preferred for a woman if *Mr.* is used for a man; *Ms.* does not focus on marital status just as *Mr.* does not. Use evenhanded treatment for women and men.

hours of work   Not *man-hours*.

houseworker   Not *maid*.

humanity, humankind, people   Not *mankind*.

hymie   Short for Hyman, a man's first name. Do not use for a person of the Jewish faith. Do not use *kike* or *Heeb*.

I

illegal immigrant, undocumented immigrant   Not *illegal alien* or *undocumented worker*. Not all undocumented immigrants are from Mexico or Latin America. Immigration from Latin America is declining.

impotent   Clinical term referring to male sexual dysfunction; not appropriate when used to stereotype or characterize males.

Indochina   Formerly *French Indochina*, now divided into Cambodia, Laos and Vietnam.

insurance agent   Not *insurance man*.

Islamic   Refers to Islam, the religion. Adherents are Muslims. An *Islamist*, or *Islamic fundamentalist*, believes the Quran should be the basis for religious, political and personal life.

J

JAP   Acronym for *Jewish American princess*; do not use; a stereotype of a young Jewish woman.

Jew   A Jewish person. Always use as a noun, never as a verb or an adjective.

Jew down   Do not use; highly offensive.

jive   Do not use; derisively applied to black slang or speech.

john   Do not use; inappropriate term for a man who uses female or male prostitutes. Use sex buyer. In a national push in the U.S., men who buy sex are being prosecuted following years of a strategy used in Europe to stop violence against women and children.

L

lamebrain   Do not use; offensive.

Latino/Latina/Latinx/Latinxs   Refers specifically to those of Spanish-American ancestry. Use ethnic identifiers for everyone in your story or no one.

layperson   Member of the congregation as distinguished from the clergy (or *layman* or *laywoman*).

lazy   Avoid labels; show what a person does rather than use value judgments. Especially avoid when describing nonwhites who are commonly and unfairly stereotyped more often than whites.

leader   Use with caution; implies the person has the approval of an entire group of people. Be more specific: *black politician*.

lesbian   Preferred term for a homosexual woman; *gay* may also be used. Rarely is a person's sexual orientation relevant to your story.

letter carrier, postal worker   Not *mailman*. Use for a man or woman who works for the U.S. Postal Service.

LGBTQ/LBGTQIA   Self-designated initialism since the 1990s that stands for *lesbian, gay, bisexual, transgender, queer or questioning, intersex,* and *asexual* used to refer to non-heterosexuals. Spell out first occurrence, then abbreviate. Do not use *gay community*.

lily-white   Any characterization of skin color should be avoided. Avoid *paleface* and *redskin*.

line repairer   Preferred to *lineman*.

M

Mafia, Mafiosi   Secret society of criminals and its members; do not use as a synonym for *organized crime* or the *underworld*.

maiden name   Avoid. Use *birth name* or *given name*.

man   Do not use to denote both sexes. Use *humanity, a person* or *an individual*. Avoid *man and wife*. Use either *wife and husband* or *husband and wife*; *woman and man* or *man and woman*.

"Man, The"   A reference to the white establishment; offensive.

manhole cover   A more neutral term is *utility cover*.

man-made   Better to use *handmade, manufactured* or *synthetic*.

maricón   Do not use; derisive Spanish term for a gay person.

meter reader   Preferred to *meter man* or *meter maid*.

Mexican   From or of Mexico; not a substitute for *Mexican-American*.

Mexican-American   Preferred term for U.S. residents of Mexican origin.

minority/minorities   On its way to becoming out-of-date; use *racial, ethnic* and *immigrant group(s)* instead. Better yet, drop racial labeling.

"Myth, The" or "the male myth"   Avoid any word, description or phrase contributing to the stereotype of black males as strictly athletic, well-proportioned or having a high sexual drive and exaggerated sex organs. Avoid *stallion, stud, hunk, womanizer* and *lady killer*.

N

Native American   Preferred to *American Indian*; check with source; use correct tribal name if at all possible.

Negro   Do not use except when used in a title such as United Negro College Fund. Use *African-American* or *black*, depending on the source's preference. Check local stylebook for preferred local usage.

news carrier   Not *newsboy*.

N Word   The term this stands for is so offensive, even when it has been voiced as an example of offensive language, the person uttering the word may be fired for using it. The original term was included in the first through the ninth edition of this text as the list was generated by people of color. Language changes. Do not use the original term even when people refer to themselves with it. Highly offensive term for a black person.

nurse   Not *male nurse*.

O

old maid   Do not use; archaic term referring to an unmarried woman. Don't refer to a woman's marital status unless you would for a man in the same story. Again, fewer than half the adults in the U.S. are married.

old wives' tale   Do not use. Use *superstition* or *tale of wisdom*.

operate   Use *operate a machine* rather than *man a machine*. Use *work, staff* or *serve*.

operational space flight   Not *manned space flight*.

oreo   Do not use; offensive term for a black person who allegedly has abandoned his or her culture; derisively used to mean "black on the outside and white on the inside."

Oriental   Do not use; use *Asian-American, Asian* or a specific term. Sometimes acceptable to describe things, not people, such as *Oriental rug*.

P

peon   A Spanish-American peasant; avoid; sometimes derisively applied to entire groups of Hispanics or others.

people at work   Not *men at work*.

personnel   Not *manpower*. Use *staff*, *workforce* or *workers*.

person-on-the-street interview   Not *man-on-the-street interview*.

pickaninny   Do not use; offensive term for a black child.

pimp   Use only to refer to someone who profits from selling sex of others; highly objectionable stereotype of African-American or other men.

Polack   Do not use; derogatory term for a Polish person.

police officer   Not *policeman*.

postal worker   Not *postman*. Use *letter carrier* or *mail carrier*.

PR   Do not use; offensive acronym for *Puerto Rican*.

project   Do not use, as in *public housing project*; has come to be a racial code word, as in *people in the projects*. Use *public housing* or *subsidized housing*.

proper names   Do not make slurs on people's given names; see *Chico*, *Hiawatha*, *Ivan* and *Leroy*.

prosthesis, artificial limb   Not *peg leg*. Avoid *hook*.

Q

qualified minorities   Do not use; unnecessary description that implies members of racial, ethnic and immigrant groups are generally unqualified.

queer   Do not use to describe a gay or lesbian even if members of the group describe themselves with the term. LBGTQ is growing in use and one day may become the preferred term.

R

redskin   Do not use; objectionable description of a Native American. Avoid any reference to skin color.

refugee   Use to describe immigrants fleeing from oppression or persecution while they have refugee status. Do not use for people who are settled in the U.S. and no longer have refugee status. A person who flees a hurricane-devastated area is an *evacuee*, not a refugee.

retarded   Do not use; refer to a specific medical condition. Avoid *stupid* and *ignorant*.

rubbing noses   Do not use; stereotypically an "Eskimo kiss." Eskimos (many of whom prefer *Inuit* or *Native Alaskan*) do not rub noses, and many object to the characterization.

Russian   Use only to refer to people who are from Russia or of Russian descent and to the language spoken in the region. If a label is necessary, refer to country of origin.

S

sales representative   Preferred to *salesman*.

samurai   As a term or caricature, it can be offensively stereotypical; avoid unless referring specifically to the historical Japanese warrior class.

sanitation worker, trash collector   Preferred to *garbage man*.

savages   Do not use; offensive when applied to Native Americans or other native cultures. Do not use *heathen* or *primitive*.

senile   Do not use to refer to older people; offensive. *Dementia* is the correct term for the mental or physical deterioration of old age.

senior citizen   Avoid. In general, give ages only when relevant. Do not describe people as *senile*, *matronly* or *well preserved*. Do not use *dirty old man*, *codger*, *coot*, *geezer*, *silver fox*, *old-timer*, *Pop*, *old buzzard* or *blue-haired*. Do not identify people as grandparents unless it is relevant to the story. Many people object to the term *senior citizens* as "an unsavory euphemism"; alternatives are *the aged*, *the old* and *the retired*. Life expectancy was 19 years one thousand years ago, 37 years in 1800. Today, U.S. male life expectancy is 73.4 years, and 80.1 years for women.

shiftless   Do not use; highly objectionable as a description of the poor.

shine   Do not use; objectionable reference to a black person.

shrew/shrill   Do not use; derogatory characterization of a woman who competes in the workplace or whose behavior is seen as nagging.

siesta   A Latin tradition of a midday nap; use advisedly. Do not use to denote laziness.

silver fox   Do not use; objectionable term referring to an older person.

skirt   Do not use; dated and offensive term referring to a woman or girl.

"Some of my best friends are . . ."   Old phrase usually used by someone accused of racial bias or wanting to appear unbiased, as in *Some of my best friends are Hispanic*.

soulful   Objectionable adjective when applied strictly to blacks.

spade   Garden tool or card suit. Do not use in reference to an African-American; highly insulting. Do not use old phrase, "call a spade a spade."

Spanish   The language or a person from Spain; not interchangeable with *Mexican*, *Latino/Latina* or *Hispanic*.

spastic   Do not use to describe those with muscular dysfunctions, tics or jerky physical movements. Do not use *spaz*. Use the correct medical condition identified by the source or medical attendants: *has cerebral palsy*.

sped, spec ed   Do not use; offensive reference to a child in a special education class.

spokesperson   Not *spokesman*.

suffers from   Do not use. A person has a disease, such as *has leukemia* or *a person with AIDS*.

swarthy   Do not use; objectionable reference to skin color. Other objectionable terms are *paleface*, *redskin* and *lily-white*.

T

taco   Do not use; objectionable reference to a Mexican.

telephone worker   Not *telephone man*.

those people   Do not use; objectionable phrase used by one group to refer to another group. Avoid *you people*.

token   Do not use; refers to someone hired solely because of race, ethnicity or gender; implies the person was not qualified for the job.

trades worker   Not *tradesman*. Be specific if possible: *construction worker*.

transgender   General term for individuals, groups and behaviors that vary from conventional gender roles. Self-identification as woman, man, neither or both. Not a noun. Do not use *transvestite*, *transgendered* or *tranny*. Ask the subject what personal pronoun (*he, she or they*) is to be used. The Williams Institute shows 698,000 LBGT adults have received transition therapy.

U

Uncle Tom   Do not use; derogatory term used to refer to a black person who has abandoned his or her culture by becoming subservient to whites; no person or group can claim exclusive power to define what it is to be black in the U.S.

V

vegetable   Do not use to describe someone in a comatose state or a person incapable of caring for himself or herself. *Persistent vegetative state* is the medical terminology, if applicable.

W

wannabe   Refers to someone who mimics a style or behavior of another group or wants to be a member of another group; use advisedly. For instance, a person dressed in red or blue isn't necessarily a *wannabe Blood or Crip gang member*; nor is the person necessarily a gang member. Use the term *gang member* advisedly for the same reasons.

WASP   Acronym for *white Anglo-Saxon Protestant*; offensive to some.

welch, welsh   Do not use; offensive term meaning to break an agreement.

wetback   Do not use; derisive term for an illegal immigrant, specifically a Mexican who has crossed the Rio Grande.

wheelchair   Do not use *wheelchair-bound* or *confined to a wheelchair*. Preferred expression is *uses a wheelchair*.

white-bread Do not use; term denoting blandness; can have a racial connotation.

white trash Do not use; derogatory term for poor whites. Implies that it's unusual for a white person to be "trash" but normal for someone who is not white.

whore/"ho" Do not use; derogatory. A man's sexual status has no commensurate descriptor. Avoid *trollop, tart, cunt, whore, bitch, loose woman* and *hussy*. A person paid for sex is a *sex worker*, whether male or female.

without rhythm Do not use; a stereotype of whites; implies that other races have rhythm.

woman Preferred term for a female adult; *girl* is appropriate only for those under age 18. Do not use *gal* or *lady*. Avoid derogatory terms for women, such as *babe, ball and chain, bimbo, broad, chick, doll, honey, little woman, skirt* and *sweetie*. Do not use adjectives describing female physical attributes or mannerisms. Older terms such as *buxom, cougar, feminine, foxy, fragile, full-figured, gorgeous, pert, petite, statuesque* and *stunning* are all sexist. One of the markers of social media is the disproportionate online abuse of women and expressions of misogyny (ingrained prejudice against women).

wop Do not use; derogatory reference to an Italian.

worker Preferred to *workingman* or *workman*.

workers' compensation Not *workmen's compensation*. Close to half of the workforce is female.

X

Xmas Do not use; offensive to many Christians.

Y

yanqui Do not use; derogatory Spanish term for a North American white. Avoid *gringo*.

yellow Do not use; offensive term referring to skin color; a derogatory term meaning "coward."

One Word, Two Words or Hyphenated?

Experienced editors know that a good spelling ability isn't enough—beyond it are compound words to trip you. Compounds tend to start as two words, go through a hyphenation stage as they become more common, then end as one word. But it's hard to predict where any given compound stands according to AP or the dictionaries—first *Webster's New World College Dictionary* then *Webster's Third International*—that you're supposed to consult if AP doesn't have it. (If it's not in any of them, you're supposed to make it two words as a noun or verb, or hyphenated as an adjective.) You'll also notice as you browse this list that there are many inconsistencies among words you'd think would be treated the same.

We haven't tried to include every compound word in *The AP Stylebook*, rather we mainly put this list together to save time with those words we've had to look up. And don't be surprised if some have changed by the time you read this book. If you spot any that have changed or if you have words we didn't list that you've had to look up, please email Melanie McFadyen at melanie.mcfadyen@macmillan.com to update this for future editions. But these are among the most common we've found, and most of these won't have changed, so this list should still be useful for saving time on a deadline.

One Word, Two Words or Hyphenated?

A

able-bodied

about-face

aboveboard

absent-minded

accident-prone

ad hominem, ad-lib (n., v., adj.), ad nauseam

A-frame

African-American (adj., n.)

aftereffect, after-hours, afterthought

air bag, air base, air-condition (v.), air-conditioned, air conditioner, air conditioning, aircraft, airfare, air force base, airhead, airline, airlines (but check individual name), air lock, airmail, airport, air show, airstrike, airstrip, airtight, airtime, air traffic controller, airwaves, airways

a la carte, a la king, a la mode

A-list

all-around (AP says not *all-round*), all-clear, all-out, all-purpose, all ready (everyone is ready), all right, allspice, all-star, all time (n.), all-time (adj.), already (by now)

alma mater

a lot

also-ran (n.)

ambassador-at-large

anchorman, anchorwoman (AP now accepts also the nonsexist forms of *anchor* and *co-anchor,* which we prefer—see Chapter 7.)

angel food cake, angel hair pasta

animal welfare activist

antebellum

anteroom

anti-abortion, anti-aircraft, anti-bias, antibiotic, antibody, anticlimax, antidepressant, antidote, antifreeze, antigen, antihistamine, anti-inflation, anti-intellectual, antiknock, anti-labor, antimatter, antipasto, antiperspirant, antiseptic, antiserum, anti-social, antithesis, antitoxin, antitrust, anti-war

any body (any one person), anybody (any person at all)

any more (something additional: *I don't have any more*), anymore (adv.)

any one (any one person or thing), anyone (any person at all)

any way (in any manner), anyway (in any event)

applesauce

apron strings

archbishop, archdiocese, archenemy, archrival

arm-wrestling

arrowhead

art film, art form, artifact, artwork

ashcan, ashtray

attorney general, attorneys general

autoerotism, automaker, auto racing, autoworker

awe-struck

a while (noun as object of preposition or in phrases such as *a while ago* or *a while back*), awhile (adv.)

B

baby boomer, baby-sat, baby-sit, baby sitter, baby-sitting

backboard, backcountry, backcourt, backcourtman, back door (n.), backdoor (adj.), backfield, backfire, backhanded, back porch (n.), back-porch (adj.), backrest, back road, backroom, back-scratching, back seat (n.), back-seat (adj.), backspace, backstabbing, backstop, back street (n.), back-street (adj.), backstretch, back-to-back, backtrack, back up (v.), backup (adj., n.), backwater, backwoods, backyard (adj., n.)

badman

bail out (v.), bailout (n.)

baldfaced

ball carrier, ballclub, ballgame, ballhandler, ballpark, ballplayer, (there don't appear to be commonly used gender-neutral terms for ball boy/ball girl, baseman, defenseman, lineman and linesman in sports), ballpoint pen, ballroom

bandleader, band saw, band shell, bandwagon, bandwidth

bank robber

bare-bones (adj.), barefaced, barehanded, bareheaded

barhop, barkeeper, barmaid (although not recommended as sexist), barroom, barstool

bar mitzvah, bas mitzvah, bat mitzvah

barrel-chested, barrelhouse

baseboard heating, baseline

batboy, batgirl

bathtub

battle-ax, battlefield, battleground, battleship, battle station

beanbag chair

bedbug, bedclothes, bedpan, bedpost, bedrail, bed rest, bedrock, bedsheet

beekeeper, beeswax

bell-bottom, bellboy (although not recommended as sexist), bellhop, bellwether

belly button, belly dance (n.), belly-dance (v.), belly dancer, belly-flop

best-seller, best-selling

biannual (twice a year), biennial (every two years), bifocal, bilingual, bimonthly, bipartisan, biweekly

big band (n.), big-band (adj.), big-bang theory, big house, Big Three automakers, big-ticket, big time (n.), big-time (adj.), bigwig

bikeway

biodegradable, biodiversity, bioterrorism

bird dog (n.), bird-dog (v.), birdhouse, birdseed, bird's-eye, bird-watching (adj., n.)

birthmark, birth mother, birthparent, birthplace, birthrate

blackboard, black-eyed peas, blackout

blast off (v.), blastoff (adj., n.)

blind side (n.), blindside (v.)

blockbuster

bloodbath, bloodhound, bloodstain (n., v.), bloodstained (adj.)

blow-dryer, blow up (v.), blowup (n.)

blue blood (n.), blue-blooded (adj.), blue chip stock, blue collar (n.), blue-collar (adj.), blue line, blue-sky (adj.)

boardinghouse, boarding school

boardroom

bobsledding

bodybuilder, body check (n., v.), body count, bodyguard, body mass index, bodysuit

boilerplate

boldface

boll weevil

bombproof

bona fide

bonbon

bondholder

boo-boo

bookcase, bookdealer, bookend, bookmobile, bookshelf, bookshop, bookstore, bookworm

boombox, boomtown

Boston cream pie

bottom line (n.), bottom-line (adj.)

bowlegged

bowl game

boxcar, box kite, box office (n.), box-office (adj.), box score

boyfriend

brain wave

brand name (n.), brand-name (adj.), brand-new (adj.)

bread-and-butter pickles, breadbox, breadwinner

break dancing (n.), break-dancing (adj.), break down (v.), breakdown (n.), break in (v.), break-in (adj., n.), breakthrough, break up (v.), breakup (adj., n.)

breast-fed, breast-feed, breast-feeding

bricklayer

bridegroom, bridesmaid

broad-minded, broadside

b-roll

broodmare

brother-in-law, brothers-in-law

brown-nose (v.), brown-noser (n.), brownout

brush fire

buckshot

bug boy

build up (v.), buildup (adj., n.)

bulldozer

bullet hole, bulletproof

bullfight, bullfighter, bullfighting, bullpen, bull's-eye

Bundt cake

bushelbasket

businesslike, businessman, businesswoman

bus line, busload

buttercream, butterfat

button-down

buy out (v.), buyout (n.)

by-election, bygone, bylaw, byline, bypass, byproduct, bystreet

C

cabdriver

cabinetmaker

cakewalk

call up (v.), call-up (adj., n.)

camera-ready (adj.)

candleholder, candlelit, candlemaker, candymaker

cannot

carefree, caretaker

carmaker, car pool (n.), carpool (v., adj.), carport

carry on (v), carry-on (adj., n.), carry over (v.), carry-over (adj., n.)

car seat, carsick, carwash

caseload

cashbox, cash cow, cash flow

cast iron (n.), cast-iron (adj.), cast member

catch all (v.), catchall (adj., n.)

cave in (v.), cave-in (adj., n.)

CD-ROM

cease fire (v.), cease-fire (adj., n.)

cellphone

center field (adj., n.), center fielder, centerfold

cha-cha

chain saw

chairman, chairperson, chairwoman

change over (v.), changeover (n.), change up (v.), change-up (adj., n.)

check-in (adj., n.), check in (v.), check out (v.), checkout (adj., n.), check up (v.), checkup (n.)

cheesecloth, cheesemaker

chicken-fried steak, chickenpox

child care (adj., n.)

chipmaker (n.), chipmaking (adj.)

chock-full

chowhound

Christmastime, Christmas tree

churchgoer, church member

citizens band

city editor, city hall, citywide

claptrap

clean-cut, clean up (v.), cleanup (adj., n.)

clear-cut

clearinghouse

click-thrus

cloak-and-dagger

clockwise

closed shop

close-knit, close up (v.), close-up (adj., n.)

clubhouse

coal mine, coal miners

coastline

coatdress, coattails

co-author, co-chairman, co-defendant, coed (but avoid as sexist), coeducation (but avoid as sexist), coequal, coexist, coexistence, co-host, co-op (short form of *cooperative*), cooperate, cooperative, coordinate, coordination, co-owner, co-partner, co-pilot, co-respondent (in a divorce proceeding), co-signer, co-star, co-worker

coconut

coffeecake, coffee grinder, coffee maker, coffeepot, coffee table (n.), coffee-table (adj.), t,

coleslaw

colorblind

commander in chief

concertgoer

congressman, congresswoman

con man

consumer price index (generic), Consumer Price Index (U.S.)

continentwide, cop out (v.), cop-out (n.)

copy desk, copy edit, copy editor, copyright (n., v., adv.)

cornbread, corn dog, corn flour, cornstarch

cost-effective, cost of living (n.), cost-of-living (adj.), cost-plus

count down (v.), countdown (n.), counteract, countercharge, counterintelligence, counterproposal, counterspy, countertop

countryside, countrywide

countywide

courthouse, court-martial (n., v.), courtroom

cover up (v.), cover-up (adj., n.)

crabcake, crabmeat

crack up (v.), crackup (adj., n.)

crawfish (not crayfish, says AP)

crawl space

cream puff

crew member

crisscross

cropland

cross-country (now hyphenated in all uses), cross-examination, cross-examine, cross-eyed (adj., adv.), crossfire, cross over

(v.), crossover (adj., n.), cross rate, cross section (n.), cross-section (v.), crosstown

crowdsourcing

cure-all

curtain raiser

custom-made

cut back (v.), cutback (adj., n.), cut off (v.), cutoff (adj., n.), cutoffs, cut out (v.), cutout (n.)

cyberattack, cyberspace

D

damn it

dark horse

dashcam

databank, database, data processing (adj., n.)

date line (the international one), dateline (on a news story)

daughter-in-law, daughters-in-law

daylight-saving time, daylong, daytime, day to day (adv.), day-to-day (adj.)

D-Day

dead center, dead end (n.), dead-end (adj.)

deaf-mute (but avoid as offensive)

deathbed

decade-long

decision maker, decision making (n.), decision-making (adj.)

deep freeze (postpone), deep freezer, deep-sea

(adj.), deep water (n.), deep-water (adj.)

degree-day

derring-do

desktop (adj., n.)

dial-up

die-hard (adj., n.)

dinner table

disk operating system

ditchdigger

docudrama

dogcatcher, doghouse, dog walker

dollhouse

door to door (n.), door-to-door (adj.)

dot-com

double-barreled shotgun, double bind, double-breasted, double-check, double-click, double-faced, doubleheader, double-parked (v., adj.), double play, double take, double talk, double-team, double-think, double time

downdraft, downgrade, down-home (adj.), downside, downstage, downstate, down-to-earth, downtown

dressing room

drive-by (adj.), drive in (v.), drive-in (adj., n.), drive-thru (adj., n.), driveway

drop-down (adj.), drop out (v.), dropout (n.)

drugmaker, drugstore

dry-roasted

dump truck

dust storm

Dutch oven

dyed-in-the-wool
(adj.)

E

earmark (v.)

earthquake

easygoing

e-book, e-business,
e-commerce, email,
e-reader

editor in chief, editors
in chief

electrocardiogram

empty-handed

end line, end user (n),
end-user (adj.), end zone

en route

esports

euro, eurodollar,
eurozone

evenhanded,
even-steven

every day (adv.),
everyday (adj.)

every one (each
individual item),
everyone (all people)

ex-convict, ex-governor,
ex-president

extra-base hit, extra-
dry (adj.), extra-large
(adj.), extralegal,
extramarital, extra-
mild (adj.),
extraterrestrial,
extraterritorial,
extra-virgin olive oil

eyesore, eyestrain, eye
to eye (adv.), eye-to-eye
(adj.), eyewitness

F

facedown (adj., n.), face-
lift, face off (v.), faceoff
(adj., n.), face to face
(adv.), face-to-face (adj.)

fact-finding (adj., n.)

fade out (v.),
fade-out (n.)

fair ball, fair catch,
fairway

fall out (v.), fallout (n.)

faraway (adj.) (as in
faraway land; but not:
a land far away), far-
fetched, far-flung, far-
off (adj.), far-ranging,
farsighted

farmhouse, farmland,
farmstead, farm-to-
table, farmworker

farmers market

fashion-forward label

fastball, fast break

father-in-law,
fathers-in-law

feather bedding
(mattress),
featherbedding (union
practice)

fender bender

Ferris wheel

ferryboat

fiberglass (generic, not
the trademark)

field goal, field house,
field trip, fieldwork

figure skater, figure
skating

filmgoer, filmmaker,
filmmaking (adj., n.),
film ratings

fingertip

firearm, fire breather,
fire chief, firefight,
firefighter, fireman,
fireproof, firetruck, fire
wagon, firewall

first aid (n.), first-aid
(adj.), first baseman,
first-class (adj) (as in a
first-class hotel; but note:
The hotel was first class.),
first-degree (adj.),
firsthand

fistfight

flagpole, flagship

flameout

flare up (v.), flare-up
(n.)

flash flood (adj., n.),
flash flood watch

flatbread, flat iron
steak

flea market

flimflam, flimflammed

flip-flop

floodwaters

floor leader,
floor-length

floppy disk

flower girl

flu-like

flyswatter

folk singer, folk song

follow-through, follow up
(v.), follow-up (adj., n.)

foodborne

foolproof

foot-and-mouth disease

forebrain, forecast,
forefather, foregoing,
foreman, fore-
topgallant, fore-topmast,
fore-topsail, forewoman

fortnight

fortuneteller, fortunetelling

forty-niner *or* '49er

foul ball line, foul line, foul shot, foul tip, foul up (v.), foul-up (n.)

four-flush, Four-H Club (4-H Club is preferred), 4-H'er

fraidy-cat

frame up (v.), frame-up (n.)

free-for-all, freelance (v., adj.), freelancer (n.), free on board, free-range, freestanding, free throw, free-throw line, freewheeling, freewill offering (but redundant)

freeze-dried, freeze-dry, freeze-drying

frontcourt, front line (n.), front-line (adj.), front page (n.), front-page (adj.), front-runner

fruitcake, fruit grower

fullback, full-court press, full-dress, full faith and credit bond, full-fledged, full house, full-length, full page (n.), full-page (adj.), full-scale, full-size (adj.), full time (n.), full-time (adj.)

fundraiser, fundraising

G

game plan

general obligation bond

geotagging

get away (v.), getaway (n.), get together (v.), get-together (n.)

gift wrap (n.), gift-wrap (v.)

gingerbread, gingersnap

girlfriend

give away (v.), giveaway (n.)

globe-trotting

go ahead (v.), go-ahead (n.), go between (v.), go-between (n.), go-go

goal line, goal-line stand, goal post, goaltender, goaltending

gobbledygook

godchild, goddaughter, godson

goodbye, good-looking, good night, goodwill (adj., n.)

goose bumps

grand cru wine, granddad, granddaughter, grandfather, grandmother, grandson

grant-in-aid

graphical user interface

greenmail

gross domestic product, gross national product

groundbreaking, groundhog, ground-rule double, ground rules, groundskeeper, groundswell, groundwork, ground zero

grown-up (adj., n.)

G-string

guesthouse

gunbattle, gunboat, gunfight, gunfire, gunpoint, gunpowder

gung-ho

H

hair dryer, hairsbreadth, hairstyle, hairstyling, hairstylist

half-and-half, halfback, half-baked, half-blood, half brother, half-cocked, half-court press, half dollar, halfhearted, half-hour (adj., n.), half-life, half-mast, half-mile pole, half-moon, half note, half sister, half size (n.), half-size (adj.), half-staff, half tide, halftime, halftone, halftrack, half-truth

handball, hand-carved, handcrafted, handheld (n.), hand-held (adj.), handhold, handmade, handoff, hand-painted, hand-picked, hand-set (v.), handset (n.), hand-sewn, hand-stitched

hands-free, hands off (v.), hands-off (adj.), hands on (v), hands-on (adj.), hand to hand (n.), hand-to-hand (adj.), hand to mouth (n.), hand-to-mouth (adj.), hand warmer, handwashing, handwrought

hangover, hang up (v.), hang-up (n.)

hanky-panky

hardback, hard-bound, hard copy, hardcover,

hard drive, hard headed, hard line (n.), hard-line (adj.), hard-liner (adj.), hard pressed (pred. adj.) hard-pressed (adj. before a noun), hardworking

harebrained, harelip

has been (v.), has-been (n.)

hash browns, hashtag

H-bomb

headache, headlong, head-on, headscarf

health care (adj., n.), health club

hearsay

heartbeat, heartfelt, heartrending, heartwarming

heatproof

helter-skelter

heyday

hideaway, hide out (v.), hideout (n.)

hi-fi

higher-up (n.)

high-five (n., v.), high jinks, high point, high-rise (adj., n.), high-step (v.), high-stepper, high-tech

hillbilly (but avoid as offensive except when referring to the subgenre of country music), hillside, hilltop

hip-hop

hit and run (v.), hit-and-run (adj., n.)

hitchhike, hitchhiker

hit man

hocus-pocus

hodgepodge

ho-hum

hold over (v.), holdover (n.), hold up (v.), holdup (adj., n.)

home-baked, home builder, homebuyer, home field (n.), home-field (adj.), homefront, homegrown, homemade, homemaker, homeowner, homepage, home plate, homeroom, home run, home school (v.), home-schooled (adj.), home-schooling (n.), hometown

hoof-and-mouth disease

hook shot, hook up (v.), hookup (n.)

horsepower, horse race, horse racing, horse rider, horse-trader

hotbed, hot dog, hotheaded, hotline, hot plate, hot sauce, hot seat, hot spot, hot tub

houndstooth

hourlong

house call, housecleaning, household, househusband, houseplant

hurly-burly

hush-hush

hydroelectric, hydrophobia

hyperactive, hypercritical, hyperlink, hypertension, hypertext

I

ice age (adj., n.), ice storm, ice storm warning

improvised explosive device

inasmuch, inbound, in-depth, indoor (adj.), indoors (adv.), infield, infighting, in-group, in-house, in-law, inpatient (adj., n.), input (n.), insofar, in spite of

Indochina

infrared, infrastructure

interracial, interstate

intramural, intranet, intrastate

J

jack-o'-lantern

jai alai

Jaycees

jellyroll

jerry-built

jetliner, jet plane

job hunting (n.), job-hunting (adj.)

johnnycake

jukebox

jumbo jet

jump ball, jump shot

jury-rigged

K

keynote, keywords

kick off (v.), kickoff (adj., n.)

kilowatt-hour

kindergarten

kindhearted

knickknack

knock off (v.), knock-off (n.), knock out (v.), knock-out (adj., n.)

know-how

kowtow

L

ladyfinger

lamebrain, lame duck (n.), lame-duck (adj.)

landline

last-ditch effort

latecomer

lawsuit

layup

left guard, left hand (n.), left-handed (adj.), left-hander, left wing (n.), left-wing (adj.), left-winger

lengthwise

let up (v.), letup (adj., n.)

life jacket, lifelike, lifelong, lifesaver (generic, not the candy trademark), life-size, life span, lifestyle, lifetime, life vest

lift off (v.), liftoff (adj., n.)

lightbulb, lighthearted, light-year

like-minded, like-natured, likewise

linebacker, line drive, lineman, line up (v.), lineup (n.)

live-blog, live shot, livestream, livestreaming

lockout

long distance (n.), long-distance (adj., or in reference to phone calls), long-lasting, long-lived, long-range, long run (n.), long-run (adj.), long shot (n.), long-shot (adj.), long-standing, long term (n.), long-term (adj.), long time (n.), longtime (adj.)

look-alike

loveless, lovelorn, lovemaking, love match, love nest, love seat, lovesick, lovey-dovey, loving cup

lowball, lowbred, low-class, low-cut, lowdown

lowercase

lumberyard

lunchbox, lunch cart, lunchroom, lunchtime

M

machine gun (n.), machine-gun (adj., v.), machine-gunner, machine-made

mad cow disease

mailman (but instead use the nonsexist *mail carrier*)

major league (adj., n.), major leaguer

makeshift, make up (v.), makeup (adj., n.)

man-to-man

mapmaker

mark to market

marketbasket, marketplace

mash up (v.), mashup (n.)

meatball, meatcutter, meatloaf

medevac

medium-rare

melon balls

melt down (v.), meltdown (n.)

ménage à trois

menswear

merry-go-round

metalwork

mid-America, mid-Atlantic, midcourt, midfield

middle class (n.), middle-class (adj.), middleman

midnight, midsemester, midshipman, midterm, midwinter

milkshake

milquetoast

mindset

mine shaft

minibus, minicamp, miniseries, miniskirt, minivan

minor league (adj., n.)

mix up (v.), mix-up (adj., n.)

mock-up (n.)

moneymaker, money-saving

monthlong

moped

mop up (v.), mop-up (adj., n.)

moral obligation bond

mother-in-law, mothers-in-law

motorboat, motor home

mountain man

mousehole

moviegoer, movie house, moviemaker, moviemaking

MP3

mudslide, mudslinging

multicolored, multilateral, multimillion, multimillionaire

muscle ache

mutual field

N

nail clippers

name tag

narrow gauge (n.), narrow-gauge (adj.), narrow-minded

nationwide

near shore (prep. phrase), nearshore (adj.), nearsighted

neoconservative,

nerve-racking

net asset value

newfangled, new wave (n.), new-wave (adj.)

newsmagazine, newsroom, newsstand, news writer, news writing

nickname

nightclub, night shift, nightspot, nighttime

nitpicking

nitty-gritty

no man's land

nonaligned, nonchalance, nonconference, nondescript, nonentity, nonpartisan, nonprofit, nonrestrictive, nonsense, nonsensical, nonviolent

no one

O

OB-GYN

oceangoing

odd-looking, odd-numbered, oddsmaker

off-Broadway, off-color, off-duty,

offhand, offline, off-off-Broadway, off-peak, off-road, offseason, offset, offshore, offside, off-site, offstage, off-white

officeholder

oilman

old-fashioned, Old Florida, old-time, old-timer, old times, Old West, Old World

one-fourth, one-half, one-sided, one-third, one time (n.), one-time (adj.)

ongoing, online

open-faced sandwich, open-minded

outact, outargue, outbluff, outbrag, outclimb, outdated, outdistance, outdrink,

outeat, outfield, outfielder, outfight, outfox, outhit, outleap, outmatch, out of bounds (adv.), out-of-bounds (adj.), out of court (adv.), out-of-court (adj.), outpatient (adj., n.), outperform, outpitch, outpointed, outpost, outproduce, output, outquote, outrace, outscore, outshout, outsource, outstrip, outswim, outtalk, outwalk

ovenproof

overall, overbuy, overexert, overrate, override, oversize, over the counter (adv.), over-the-counter (adj.), overtime, overview

P

pacemaker, pacesetter

paddy wagon

painkiller

pantsuit

pantyhose

Pap (test, smear)

paper bag, paper clip, paper towel, paperwork

pari-mutuel

parkerhouse roll

parkland

part time (adv.), part-time (adj.)

partygoer

passed ball

passer-by, passers-by

pat down (v.), pat-down (adj., n.)

patrolman, patrolwoman

paycheck, payday, payload

peacekeeper, peacekeeping, peacemaker, peacemaking, peace offering, peacetime

pell-mell

penalty box

penny-wise

pen pal

percent

pet store

petty officer

pick up (v.), pickup (adj., n.)

pigeonhole (n., v.)

pile up (v.), pileup (adj., n.)

pillowcase

pinch hit (v.), pinch-hit (adj., n.), pinch hitter

pingpong (generic, not the trademark)

pin up (v.), pinup (n.)

pipeline

pitchout (n.)

pitmaster

pivotman

place kick, place-kicker, place mat

play off (v.), playoff (adj., n.)

plus-size clothing

pocketbook, pocket watch

point-blank

policyholder, policymaker, policymaking (adj., n.)

pom-pom (weapon), pompom (cheerleader paraphernalia)

pooh-pooh

porterhouse steak

postcard, postdate, postdoctoral, postelection, postgame, postgraduate, post-mortem, post office, postoperative, postscript, postseason, postwar

pothole, potluck, potshot, pot sticker

pound cake, pound-foolish

powder keg

power line, power play, power-play goal

prearrange, precognition, precondition, pre-convention, precook, precut, predate, pre-dawn, predispose, pre-election, pre-eminent, pre-empt, pre-establish, pre-exist, prefix, preflight, pregame, preheat (but AP says to avoid—just say *heat the oven*), prehistoric, preignition, prejudge, premarital, premenstrual, prenatal, preregister, preschool, preseason, preset, pretax, pretest, pretrial, prewar, prewash

pret-a-porter

price-earnings ratio, price tag

prima-facie (adj.)

prime rate, prime time (n.), prime-time (adj.)

print out (v.), printout (n.), printshop

prizewinner, prizewinning

pro-business, pro-labor, pro-life, pro-peace, pro-war

problem-solving

producer price index

profit-sharing (adj., n.), profit-taking (adj., n.)

profit role

pull back (v.), pullback (n.), pull out (v.), pullout (n.), pull up (v.), pullup (n.)

punch line

purebred

push-button (adj., n.), push up (v.), push-up (adj., n.)

put out (v.), putout (n.)

Q

Q&A format

quarterback

question mark

quick-witted

R

racetrack

racquetball

set up (v.), setup (adj., n.)

sewer line

sexually transmitted disease

shake up (v.), shake-up (adj., n.)

shape up (v.), shape-up (adj., n.)

shirtdress, shirt sleeve (n.), shirt-sleeve (adj.)

shoeshine, shoestring

shoot out (v.), shootout (n.)

shopworn

shortchange, shortcut, short-handed, short-lived, short sale, shortstop

shotgun

showcase, show off (v.), showoff (n.), showroom, showstopper

shut down (v.), shutdown (n.), shut in (v.), shut-in (n.), shut off (v.), shut-off (n.), shut out (v.), shutout (adj., n.)

side by side (adv.), side-by-side (adj.), side dish, side effect, sidestep, side street (n.), sidetrack, side trip

sightseeing, sightseer

sign up (v.), sign-up (adj., n.)

single-handed

sister-in-law, sisters-in-law

sit down (v.), sit-down (adj., n.), sit in (v.),

sit-in (adj., n.), situp (n.), sit up (v.)

skyrocketing, skywriting

slantwise

slap down, slap shot

sledgehammer

sleight of hand (n.), sleight-of-hand (adj.)

slideshow

sloppy Joe

slow down (v.), slowdown (n.)

slumlord

slush fund

small-arms fire, small-business man/woman

smartphone, smartwatch

smash up (v.), smashup (adj., n.)

smoke bomb, smoke screen, smokejumper

snow avalanche bulletin, snowdrift, snowfall, snowflake, snowman, snowplow, snowshoe, snowstorm, snowsuit

so called (adv.), so-called (adj.) (but AP says to use sparingly and without quotation marks)

softcover, soft pedal (n.), soft-pedal (v.), soft-spoken, software

songwriter

son-in-law, sons-in-law

sound barrier, sound bite, sound effects,

soundstage, soundtrack (adj., n.)

source code

spacecraft, spaceship, space shuttle, spacewalk

spareribs

speechmaker, speechmaking, speechwriter, speech writing

speedboat, speed bump, speed-reading, speed up (v.), speedup (adj., n.)

spell check, spell checker (n.)

spin off (v.), spinoff (adj., n.)

split end

spokesman, spokesperson, spokeswoman

spongecake

sport utility vehicle

sports editor, sportswear, sports writer

spot-check, spotlight

springtime

squeeze play

staff writer

stage fright

stained glass (n.), stained-glass (adj.)

stakeout

stalemate

stand-alone (adj.), stand in (v.), stand-in (adj., n.), stand mixer, stand off (v.), standoff (adj., n.), stand out (v.), standout (adj., n.), stand up (v.), standup (n.), stand-up (adj.)

standard-bearer

standing room only

starboard

start up (v.), startup (adj., n.)

statehouse, statewide

states' rights

station wagon

steady-state theory

stepbrother, stepchild, stepdaughter, stepfamily, stepfather, stepmother, stepparent, stepsister, stepson

steppingstone

stir-fry (n., v.)

stockbroker, stock index futures, stockman, stock market prices, stockpot

stone carver

stool pigeon

stopgap, stop off (v.), stop-off (n.), stop over (v.), stopover (n.)

storm tide, stormwater

storyline, storyteller

stove top (n.), stove-top (adj.)

straight-laced (strict or severe)

strait-laced (pertaining to confinement, as a corset), straitjacket

street dance, street gang, streetlamp, streetlight, street people, street-smart (adj.), street smarts (n.), street sweeper, streetwalker, streetwise

strikebreaker, strike zone

strong-arm (v., adj.), strong-willed

stylebook

subbasement, subcommittee, subculture, subdivision, submachine gun, suborbital, subprime, subtotal, subzero

sugarplums

summertime

sunbathe, sunbather, sunbathing, sundress, sun-dried tomatoes, sun porch

superagency, supercarrier, supercharge, super collider, superconducting, superhighway, superhuman, supermodel, superpower, supersonic, super-skinny, supertanker

supragovernmental, supranational

surface-to-air missile

sweatpants, sweatshirt, sweatsuit

sweet-and-sour sauce

T

tablecloth, tablespoon, table talk, table tennis

tag end

tailback, taillight, tailpipe, tailspin, tail wind

tailor-made

take charge (v.), take-charge (adj.), take down (v.), takedown

(adj., n.), take-home pay, take off (v.), takeoff (adj., n.), take out (v.), takeout (adj., n.), take over (v.), takeover (adj., n.), take up (v.), takeup (adj., n.)

talebearer

talk show (n.), talk-show (adj.)

tap dance (n.), tap-dance (v.), tap dancer

tape-record (v.), tape recording (n.)

task force

tattletale

tax-deductible

T-bone steak

teachers college

teakettle

teammate, team teaching

tear gas (AP says this is two words, perhaps implying it's an exception to the rule of making a noun two words but hyphenated as an adjective.)

teaspoon

teenage (adj.), teenager

teeny-weeny

telecommute, teleconference, telecourse, telemarketing, teleprompter (the generic form—AP no longer lists the former trademark form)

telltale

temperature-humidity index

tenderhearted

tenfold

term paper

terror-stricken

terry cloth

Texas leaguer

Tex-Mex

Thai red curry paste

thank you (v.), thank-you (adj., n.)

theatergoer

thermonuclear

Third World

3-D, three R's, threesome

throw away (v.), throwaway (adj., n.)

thruway

thumbscrew, thumbs-down, thumbs-up, thumbtack

thunderbolt, thundershower, thunderstorm, thunderstruck

tick-tack-toe, ticktock

tidal wave

tidbit

tiebreaker, tie-dye, tie in (v.), tie-in (adj., n.), tie up (v.), tie-up (adj., n.)

tight end

Tiki bar (inexplicably, the first word is capitalized in AP)

time-lapse, timeout, timesaver, timesaving, time share (n.), time-shared (adj.), time sharing (n.),

time-sharing (adj.), timetable, time zone

tip off (v.), tipoff (adj., n.), tiptoe, tiptop

titleholder

tollbooth, tollhouse

tongue-lashing, tongue-tied

tonic water

top-notch

torch singer, torch song

touchback (n.), touchdown (n.), touch screen (n.), touch-screen (adj.), touch up (v.), touch-up (adj., n.)

town house, townspeople

toy maker

track and field, track lighting

tractor-trailer

trade in (v.), trade-in (adj., n.), trademark, trade off (v.), trade-off (adj., n.), trade route, trade show

trans-Atlantic, transcontinental, transoceanic, trans-Pacific, transsexual

trapshooting

trash can

trenchcoat

trendsetter

trigger-happy

triple play

truck driver, truck stop

trustbuster

try out (v.), tryout (n.)

T-shirt

tune up (v.), tuneup (adj., n.)

turbocharged, turboprop

turnkey (adj., n.), turn off (v.), turnoff (n.), turnpike

tutti-frutti

24/7

two-by-four, twofold, two-on-one break

U

U-boat

ultrahigh frequency, ultraleftist, ultramodern, ultrarightist, ultrasonic, ultraviolet

un-American, unarmed, unshaven

underclass (adj., n.), underdog, underfoot (adj., adv.), undergarment, underground, underhand, underscore, undersheriff, undersold, understudy, underway (now one word in all uses, nautical or not, according to the 2015 *AP Stylebook*)

unidentified flying object

union shop

upbeat, upgrade, uplink, upstage, upstate, upstream, up-tempo

uppercase, upper hand

upside down (adv.),
upside-down (adj.)

U-turn

V

vacationland

variable interest rate,
variable rate

v-chip mortgage

V-E Day, V-8 engine, V-J
Day, V-neck

vice admiral, vice
chancellor, vice consul,
vice president, vice
principal, vice regent,
vice secretary, vice versa

videocassette (adj., n.),
videodisc, video game,
videophone, videotape
(n., v.), videotext

Vietnam

voicemail, voice-over,
voiceprint, voice track

voir dire

volleyball

voodoo

vote-getter

W

wagonmaker, wagon
master

waistline

walkie-talkie

walk in (v.), walk-in
(adj., n.), walk on (v.),
walk-on (adj., n.), walk
out (v.), walkout (n.),
walk up (v.), walk-up
(adj., n.)

wallboard, wallcovering,
walleye, wall hanging,
wallpaper, wall-to-wall

war chest, war crime,
warhead, war horse
(horse), warhorse
(veteran), warlike,
warlord, wartime

warmhearted, warm up
(v.), warm-up (adj., n.)

washcloth, wash out
(v.), washout (n.),
washstand

washed up (v.),
washed-up (adj.)

wastebasket, wasteland,
wastepaper, wastewater

watchband

water bed, watercolor,
waterline, waterlogged,
watermark, water polo,
waterproof, watershed,
water ski (n.), water-ski
(v.), water-skier, water
skiing, waterspout,
water tank, watertight,
water wings

wavelength

wax paper

weak-kneed,
weakside

weather-beaten,
weather forecaster,
weatherproof,
weatherstripping,
weather vane

web browser, webfeed,
webpage, website

weedkiller

weekend, weeklong,
weeknight

weightlifting

well-being, wellhead,
wellspring, well-to-do,
well-wisher

westernmost

wet bar

wheelbarrow,
wheelchair

wheeler-dealer

whereabouts

wherever

whirlwind

whistleblower,
whistle-stop

white collar (n.),
white-collar (adj.),
whiteout (weather
condition), white paper,
whitewash (n., v., adj.),
white water (n.),
white-water (adj.)

wholehearted,
wholesale price index,
whole wheat (n.),
whole-wheat (adj.)

wide-angle, wide-awake,
wide-brimmed, wide-
eyed, wide-open, wide
receiver, wide-screen,
widespread

wife beater

wild card (n.), wild-
card (adj.), wildfire,
wildlife, wild pitch

willpower

windbreaker (AP
no longer lists as a
trademark), wind chill
factor, wind gauge,
windmill, wind power,
wind shear, wind-swept

window-dress (v.),
window dressing (n.),
windowpane, window
seat, window-shop (v.),
window-shopping

wind up (v.), windup
(adj., n.)

wineglass, winemaker,
winemaking, wine taster

wingspan

winter storm warning, winter storm watch, wintertime

wire-rim, wire-rimmed, wiretap

wood-burning (as in wood-burning stove), woodburning (as in woodburning kit), woodcarver, woodcarving, woodcutter, wood heat, woodlot, woodpile, woodsmoke, woodstove (our rule), woodwork

word-of-mouth (adj., n.), word processing (adj., n.)

workday, workforce, workhorse, workmanlike, work out (v.), workout (adj., n.),

workplace, workstation, workweek

working class (n.), working-class (adj.), workingman, workingwoman

world-weary, worldwide

worn-out

worrywart

worthwhile

wrap around (v.), wraparound (adj.)

wristwatch

write down (v.), write-down (n.), write in (v.), write-in (adj., n.)

wrongdoing

X

X-ray

Y

yard line, yard sale, yardstick, yardwork

year-end (adj.), yearling, yearlong, year-round

yellow-bellied, yellow-belly

yesteryear

yo-yo

Z

zero-base budgeting

zigzag

zip-close bag

Spelling

Spelling Rules

President Andrew Jackson once said, "It's a damn poor mind that can think of only one way to spell a word!" Good minds or not, professional writers and editors are expected to be able to spell words correctly. And that spell-checker in your word processor makes correct spelling even more important because people assume that you now have no excuse for misspellings.

There are problems, though, with relying too heavily on spell-checkers. Sure, they can be great for helping you catch most typos. But they won't catch *it's* when you mean *its* or *there* when you mean *their*. Publications and the best websites require a consistent spelling of words according to their official stylebooks and dictionaries, but no spell-checker will have all the same spellings. *The AP Stylebook*, for example, occasionally demands exceptions to the suggested spellings of its preferred dictionary, *Webster's New World College Dictionary*. Because many newspapers, magazines, broadcast stations and websites base style rules on those of the Associated Press and its recommended dictionaries, we follow that protocol in this book.

We begin with a few spelling rules that will save you time by eliminating the need to look up many spellings. A list of often-misspelled words follows. Learn as many of these as possible to reduce the time you spend with a dictionary, or simply use this list as a quick reference. In addition to these, we have put together a separate list of compound words to find whether something should be one word, two words or hyphenated on Pages 255–271.

Prefixes

A *prefix* is a syllable, a group of syllables or a word united with or joined to the beginning of a word to alter its meaning or create a new word.

Prefixes usually have no effect on the spelling of the root word.

legal, illegal
[*Il* is a prefix meaning "not." You don't change the spelling of the root *legal* to add the prefix.]

If a word has the prefix *dis* or *mis*, there should be two *s*'s only if the root starts with an *s*.

disappear, disappoint, disservice, misspell

Suffixes

A *suffix* is a sound, syllable or group of syllables added to the end of a word to change its meaning, give it grammatical function or form a new word. For example, *ish* added to *small* creates *smallish*; *ed* added to *walk* creates *walked*. There are some instances where suffixes change the spelling of words. Here are a few basic rules:

Change *y* to *i* before the suffixes *er* and *est*.

happy, happier, happiest

Change a final *y* to *i* before adding a suffix that begins with any vowel other than *i*.

likelihood, sickliest; but drying, lying, sixtyish

The words *mimic, panic, picnic* and *traffic* add a *k* before the suffixes *ed, er* and *ing*.

mimicked, mimicker, mimicking

Words ending in *al* or *ful* form adverbs by adding *ly*.

minimally, carefully

Words ending in *ic* generally form adverbs by adding *ally*.

basically

An exception to this rule is *publicly*.

Vowels (the letters *a*, *e*, *i*, *o*, *u* and sometimes *y*) and consonants (the other letters of the alphabet) also may affect spelling, depending on where they fall in the word.

Double a final consonant before adding a suffix if (1) the suffix starts with a vowel, (2) the root word ends with a consonant, (3) a single vowel precedes the final consonant, and (4) either the root word is one syllable or the root word's final syllable is stressed.

DOUBLED CONSONANT   admitted, beginning, committed, deferred, dropped, forgettable, occurred, preferred, regrettable

SINGLE CONSONANT   benefited, canceled, galloped, happening, traveled, sadness, shipment

Don't double the final consonant for words with two vowels before the final consonant (*eaten, woolen*) or words ending in *x* (*fixing, taxed*). Note also these exceptions: *bused, handicapped, kidnapped, programmed* and *transferred*.

To decide whether a word should end in the suffix *able* or *ible*, remember that words ending in *able* generally can stand alone without the suffix and words ending in *ible* generally cannot stand alone without the suffix. Also, if a consonant is doubled immediately before the suffix, then the word is usually spelled with *ible*.

> acceptable, adaptable, workable
>
> credible, divisible, tangible
>
> horrible, infallible, permissible, terrible
> [doubled consonant before *ible*]

If a word ends in a single *e*, drop the *e* before adding *able*.

> likable, lovable, movable, salable

If a word ends in two *e's*, keep both when adding *able*.

> agreeable

Add *ible* if the root ends in a soft *c* sound, but first drop the final *e*.

> forcible

Exceptions to these rules include *accessible, capable, collectible, durable, flexible, indispensable, repressible* and *responsible*.

Words ending in *maker* are not hyphenated.

> drugmaker
>
> filmmaker

Words ending in *wide* are not hyphenated.

> citywide
>
> statewide
>
> worldwide

Journalism Tip
Spelling and Your Career

If it's not enough to persuade you that a knowledge of spelling is useful because it saves you time and embarrassment, you should know that one of the most common types of tests given to prospective interns and job applicants in the professional writing and editing business is a spelling test. So, even if you're one of those people who think there's no need to learn spelling when there are spell-checkers — even though you need to learn math despite being able to use calculators — it's time to accept the fact that, like it or not, knowing how to spell may be important in getting that job you want.

The Silent *e*

A silent *e* on the end of a word usually is kept if the suffix starts with a consonant.

> hopeful

A silent *e* is usually dropped if the suffix starts with a vowel.

> hoping

Exceptions to this rule are *European* and *dyeing* (meaning "to color").

If the silent *e* follows a *c* or a *g*, the *e* is usually dropped before a suffix that starts with a consonant (*acknowledgment*, *judgment*) but kept before a suffix that starts with a vowel (*advantageous*, *enforceable*, *knowledgeable*, *manageable*, *noticeable*, *outrageous*).

An exception to this rule is *arrangement*.

Other Spelling Rules

Form plurals and possessives as described on Pages 160–162.

Use *i* before *e* except after *c*. But there are some notable exceptions.

> ancient, aweigh, beige, caffeine, counterfeit, financier, foreign, forfeit, heifer, height, inveigle, leisure, neighbor, neither, protein, science, seize, seizure, sleigh, sleight, sufficient, their, weigh, weight, weird

To decide between *ede* and *eed*, remember that one-syllable words typically are spelled with a double *e* but only four words of two syllables are. Other words take *ede*.

> **SINGLE-SYLLABLE WORDS WITH *eed***   bleed, deed, feed, need, peed, seed
>
> **DOUBLE-SYLLABLE WORDS WITH *eed***   exceed, indeed, proceed, succeed
>
> **WORDS WITH *ede***   concede, intercede, precede, recede

Supersede is the only word ending in *sede*.

To decide whether a word should be spelled with a *c* or an *s*, remember that nouns usually have a *c*, verbs an *s*.

NOUN	VERB
prophecy	prophesy
advice	advise

Exceptions are *license* and *practice*, which have the same spelling for both noun and verb.

Don't subtract letters when words are joined together.

> overrule
>
> withhold

Spelling

To decide between *ary* and *ery*, remember that only seven common words end in *ery*: *cemetery, confectionery, distillery, millinery, monastery, periphery* and *stationery* (paper). For words other than these, use *ary*.

To decide between *efy* and *ify*, remember that only four common words end in *efy*: *liquefy, putrefy, rarefy* and *stupefy*. For words other than these, use *ify*.

AP drops the *s* from words that could end in *ward* or *wards*.

> backward, forward, toward

AP spells most words that could end in *og* with *ogue*, except for *catalog*.

> demagogue
>
> dialogue
>
> monologue (according to *Webster's New World College Dictionary*)

Hyphenation as a Spelling Problem

Rules for Hyphenation

Writers and editors often are confused about whether a word is written as one word, as two words or with a hyphen. Here are some rules that may help. The rules are followed by a useful reference list.

Compound modifiers are generally hyphenated. (See Pages 232–234, 236.)

But note that AP makes a number of inexplicable exceptions such as these:

> angel food cake
> angel hair pasta
> animal welfare activist
> body mass index
> child care (in all cases, AP says)
> health care (only listed without a hyphen)
> mad cow disease
> sexually transmitted disease
> wind chill index
> winter storm (warning, watch)

Not mentioned in AP, but examples of other compound modifiers that copy editors seldom hyphenate:

> gasoline tax increase
> high school (cheerleader)

Suffixes are not usually hyphenated unless adding one would result in three *l*'s in a row.

catlike

shell-less

There is generally no hyphen or space before the suffixes *goer, long, maker, wear* or *wide*.

churchgoer, concertgoer, filmgoer, moviegoer, partygoer, playgoer, theatergoer

monthlong, weeklong, yearlong

candlemaker, cheesemaker, chipmaker, coffee maker (one exception, based on *Webster's New World*), drugmaker, filmmaker, moviemaker, wagonmaker

activewear, daywear, eveningwear, eyewear, headwear, menswear, outerwear, shapewear, sportswear, swimwear, womenswear

citywide, countrywide, countywide, industrywide, nationwide, statewide, worldwide

There's normally no hyphen in words ending in *wise* except for *penny-wise* and *street-wise*, in which *wise* means smart rather than regarding or in the direction of.

clockwise

lengthwise

otherwise

Many compounds that use a preposition such as *down, in, off, out, over* or *up* are hyphenated, but many other compound words with prepositions at the end have dropped the hyphen.

break-in, carry-over, close-up, fade-out

breakup, fallout, holdover, takeoff

Some prefixes are generally not hyphenated.

a (not, out)

ante (before)

anti (against)

bi (two)

by (near) — exception: *by-election*

dis (opposite)

full (complete)

hydro (water)

hyper (above, excessive)

infra (below)

inter (among, between)

intra (within)

mid (middle)

mini (small)

multi (many)

non (not)

pan (all)

post (after)—exceptions: *post-bellum, post-mortem, post-obit*

pre (before)

re (again)—exceptions: When two different words would otherwise be spelled the same, hyphenate the one that means "again": *re-cover* (cover again), *re-creation* (a new creation).

semi (partly)

sub (under)

trans (across)

ultra (beyond)

un (not)

under (beneath)

up (above)

Some prefixes generally are hyphenated.

after (following)—exception: no hyphen if used to form a noun

all (every)

co (with)—exceptions: AP says to retain the hyphen when forming words that "indicate occupation or status" (*co-author, co-pilot, co-star*) but not to hyphenate other combinations (*coed, coeducation, coequal, coexist, coexistence, cooperate, cooperative, coordinate, coordination*).

ex (former)—exceptions: words that mean "out of," such as *excommunicate, expropriate*

like (similar)—exceptions: *likelihood, likeness, likewise*

odd (unusual)—exception: *oddball*

off (away)—exceptions: *offbeat, offcast, offhand, offload, offprint, offset, offshoot, offshore, offside, offspring, offstage*

one (single)

pro (for)—exceptions: words that do not connote support for something, such as *produce, profile, pronoun*

self—exceptions: *selfish, selfless, selfsame*

well (very)

wide (completely)—exception: *widespread*

Words beginning with the prefixes *half* and *pre* are sometimes hyphenated, sometimes not. You'll just have to look them up. If they do not appear in AP or *Webster's New World College Dictionary*, hyphenate them.

The prefix *vice* remains a separate word.

vice president

When a prefix is added to a number or to a word that starts with a capital letter, use a hyphen after the prefix.

anti-American, mid-20s, pre-Columbian, trans-Atlantic and trans-Pacific (these last two being AP exceptions to *Webster's New World*)

When a prefix is added to a word that starts with the same letter, use a hyphen after the prefix.

pre-election, pre-eminent, pre-empt, pre-exist, semi-invisible

Exceptions are *cooperate* and *coordinate*.

Looking Up Words for Hyphenation

Compound nouns pose spelling problems because they are so inconsistent. Some are written as two words, some are one word, and some are hyphenated. A compound noun generally starts as two words. Then, as the phrase becomes more common, the two words get lumped together as one, perhaps going through a preliminary hyphenated stage. If you look through the "One Word, Two Words or Hyphenated?" list on Pages 255–271, you'll see how unpredictable and inconsistent compound nouns can be.

To decide whether a word is one word, two words or hyphenated, here's the procedure for looking it up, according to *The AP Stylebook*:

1. Check *The AP Stylebook*.
2. If it's not there, check *Webster's New World College Dictionary*.
3. If it's not in the *New World*, check *Webster's Third New International Dictionary*.
4. If it's not in the *Third*, we suggest you make the word two words if it's a noun or verb, or hyphenate it if it's an adjective.

Follow these steps in order and do not stop until you either find the word or reach the fourth step. Otherwise, there's a good chance you won't be spelling the word right. For example, it would be possible for AP to have a certain compound as two words, for *Webster's New World* to hyphenate it and for *Webster's Third* to have it as one word. So, if you thought you'd save time by skipping to *Webster's New World* or *Webster's Third*, you'd be spelling the word incorrectly, according to AP.

Following these rules, we've put together the previously mentioned reference list on Pages 255–271. You might want to check that list before going through the four-step procedure because if we have the word there, it could save you some time.

Spelling

Words Often Misspelled

A

aberration

abet

abhorrence

abridgment

abscess

acceptable

accessible

accessory

accidentally

accommodate

accumulate

achievement

acknowledge

acknowledgment

acoustics

acquaintance

acquit

acquitted

across

adherent

admissible

adviser

affidavit

aficionado

afterward

aggressor

alleged

allotted

all ready (all were
ready)

all right
(not *alright*)

a lot (meaning much
or many, but avoid
except in a quote)

already (previously, by
now)

Alzheimer's disease

analysis

annihilate

anoint

antiquated

appalled

apparent

appearance

appellate

Arctic

argument

arrangement

ascend

asinine

assassin

assistant

athlete

attendance

auxiliary

B

baccalaureate

bachelor

backward

baker's dozen

baker's yeast

ballistic

bankruptcy

barbecue

barbiturate

barrenness

battalion

beggar

beginning

bellwether

benefited

benefiting

berserk

bicycle

bona fide

bookkeeper

broccoli

Brussels sprouts

burqa

business

C

caffeine

calendar

caliber

campaign

canceled

cancellation

cantaloupe

carburetor

caress

Caribbean

catalog

categorically

caterpillar

cemetery

census

centennial

chaise longue (not *lounge*)

changeable

chauffeur

chief

children's play

chimichurri

chitterlings

Cincinnati

circuit

citizens band

coconut

coed

collectible

collector's item

colossal

commemorate

commitment

committal

committee

compact disc

comparable

compatible

competent

conceit

conceive

condemn

confectioners' sugar

confident

confit

congratulations

connoisseur

conquer

conscience

conscientious

conscious

consensus

consistent

controversy

convenient

coolly

corroborate

counterfeit

coup d'etat

courageous

criterion (not *criterium* in AP)

criticism

criticize

cruelly

D

deceit

deductible

defendant

defensible

definitely

deity

demagogue

dependent

derring-do

descendant

descent

description

desiccate

desirable

desperately

deteriorate

deterrent

development

dialogue

diaphragm

diarrhea

dietitian

difference

dilapidated

dilemma

dilettante

diphtheria

dirigible

disappear

disappoint

disastrous

discernible

discipline

disc jockey

disillusioned

dissension

disservice

dissociate

divisive

do's and don'ts

doughnut

Down syndrome

drought

drowned

drunkenness

duffel bag

duly

dumbbell

dumbfounded

dumpster

durable

E

ebb

ecstasy (capitalize when the drug is meant)

eerie

Spelling

eighth
elegant
eligible
embarrass
emphysema
employee
endeavor
environment
equipped
erroneous
especially
espresso
exaggerate
exceed
excitable
excusable
exhibition
exhilarating
existence
exorbitant
experience
explanation
extension
extraordinary
exuberant
eyeing

F

facetious
Fahrenheit
familiar
feasible
February
fierce
fiery
financier
firefighter

fluorescent
fluoride
forcible
foreign
forfeit
fortunately
forty
forward
fourth
fraudulent
frittata
fuchsia
fulfill

G

gaiety
galloped
garish
garrulous
gaudy
gauge
genealogy
glamorous
glamour
goodbye
gorilla
government
grammar
grievance
guarantee
guard
guerrilla

H

handkerchief
harass
height

heir
hemorrhage
hemorrhoid
heroes
hierarchy
hitchhiker
homicide
hygiene
hypocrisy
hysterical

I

ifs and buts
illegibly
illegitimate
immediately
impostor
inadmissible
inadvertent
inaugurate
incidentally
inconvenience
incredible
independent
indispensable
inevitable
inflammation
inherent
innocence
innocuous
innuendo
inoculate
inseparable
insistence
insulation
intercede
Internet

interrupt
irascible
iridescent
irrelevant
irreligious
irresistible
irreverent

J

jeopardy
jewelry
judgment
judicious

K

keenness
ketchup
khaki
kidnapped
kimchi
kimono
kindergarten
knowledgeable

L

laboratory
laid
lambaste
laser disc
legerdemain
legionnaire
legitimate
leisure
liability
liaison
license

lieutenant
lightning
likable
likelihood
liquefy
loathsome
loneliness
luscious

M

mahjong
maintenance
malarkey
manageable
maneuver
marijuana
marriage
marshal
massacre
mayonnaise
meander
medicine
medieval
Mediterranean
memento
menswear
merited
metallic
mic (short for
microphone)
millennium, millennia
millionaire
mimicked
miniature
minuscule
miscellaneous
mischievous

mishap
missile
misspell
mollify
monastery
murmured
mustache
mystifying

N

naive
naphtha
necessary
neighbor
newsstand
nickel
niece
ninth
noticeable
nowadays
nuisance

O

oblige
observer
occasion
occurred
occurrence
offense
offered
OK'd
omission
omitted
opossum
opportunity
oppressive

optimistic

ordinarily

original

oscillate

overrule

Oyez

P

paid

papier-mâché

paraffin

parallel

paralyzed

paraphernalia

paraplegic

parishioner

parliamentary

particularly

pastime

pavilion

peaceable

peculiarly

penicillin

percent

peremptory

permanent

permissible

perseverance

persistent

Philippines

physician

picnicking

pierce

pigeon

plaque

plausible

playwright

pneumonia

poinsettia

Portuguese

possession

potatoes

practically

precede

predecessor

preferred

preparation

prerogative

presence

presumptuous

pretense

prevalence

preventive

primitive

privilege

procedure

proceed

prodigy

professor

profited

propeller

prosecutor

protester

prurient

publicly

purify

pursue

Q

quadriplegic

quandary

quantity

quantum

quarreling

querulous

query

questionnaire

queue

quotient

R

rarefy

rarity

readable

receipt

receive

recommend

reconnaissance

reconnoiter

recur

referee

reference

referred

rehearsal

relevant

religious

reminiscence

renovation

renowned

repetitious

repressible

reservoir

resistance

responsibility

restaurateur

resurrection

retinue

Reye's syndrome

rheumatism

rhyme

rhythm

ridiculous

rock 'n' roll

S

sacrilegious

salable

sanitarium

schedule

scissors

secession

seize

seizure

separate

sergeant

sheriff

short-lived

siege

sieve

signaled

silhouette

similar

sincerely

sizable

skier

skiing

skillful

skulduggery

soldier

solicitor

soliloquy

soluble

soothe

sophomore

sovereign

spiraled

strictly

stupefy

subpoena

subtlety

subtly

succeed

successful

superintendent

supersede

surfeit

surprise

surveillance

susceptible

symmetry

synonymous

T

tariff

teachers college

teenage

tempcramcntal

tendency

tentacles

tepee

theater

thoroughly

till

tinker's damn

tiramisu

tobacco

toboggan

tomatoes

tornadoes

tournament

toward

tranquillity

transferal

transmitter

traveler

travelogue

truly

Tucson

tumultuous

twelfth

tying

typing

tyrannous

U

ukulele

uncontrollable

undoubtedly

upward

usable

V

vacancy

vacillate

vacuum

vengeance

verifiable

veterinary

vicious

victuals

videodisc

vilify

villain

virtually

volcanoes

volume

voyageur

voyeur

W

Wednesday

weird

wherever
wholly
wield
wiener
willful
wiry
withhold

witticism
women's college
wondrous
woolen

X

X-ray

Y

yield

Z

zany
zucchini

Tightening

What to Tighten, A–Z

Here's a list of words and phrases editors typically cut or rewrite. Use the following guidelines to interpret the list:

When a word or phrase can easily be left out without changing the meaning of a sentence, we have indicated to *cut*.

When a word or phrase should be rewritten in a simpler, more straightforward way, we have indicated one or more possible changes.

When a phrase is a cliché, we have labeled it as such, leaving a fresher approach to your own creativity.

We have put parentheses around some words in the list. This indicates different phrases built on the same wording. For example, *absolute* (*guarantee, perfection*) indicates both the phrases *absolute guarantee* and *absolute perfection*.

The advice in this list should work for most of your writing or editing, but use your own judgment. For example, you shouldn't use any of this advice to rewrite quotations unless you remove the quotation marks to indicate a paraphrase. Also, the suggestions may not work in a particular sentence where the sense of the word or phrase is something other than what we assumed here.

Finally, some of the words we suggest you cut, such as *case* and *character*, are obviously useful in some contexts, but they can usually be cut and the sentence rewritten more directly without them.

A

a distance of	*cut*
a great deal of	much, many
a lot	many, much

a period of	*cut*
abandon	leave
abbreviate	shorten
absolute (guarantee, perfection)	*cut* absolute
absolutely (certain, complete, essential, sure)	*cut* absolutely
accelerate	speed
accidentally stumbled	stumbled
accompany	go with
accomplish	do
achieve	do
acid test	*cliché*
acquire	get
acted as (chairman, chairwoman)	presided
activity	*cut*
actual (experience, fact)	*cut* actual
acute crisis	crisis
add insult to injury	*cliché*
adequate enough	enough
adult in the room	*cliché*
advance (planning, reservations)	*cut* advance
advent	arrival
adverse weather conditions	bad weather
affluent	rich, wealthy
aforementioned	this, that, these, those
after all is said and done	*cliché*
aggregate	total
agree to disagree	*cliché*
aired their differences	*cliché*
all in a day's work	*cliché*
all of	all
all of a sudden	suddenly
all things considered	*cliché*
all things to all people	*cliché*
all throughout	throughout
all-time record	record
all too soon	*cliché*
all walks of life	*cliché*

almighty dollar	*cliché*
amidst	amid
amorphous	formless
analogous	similar
and/or	*rewrite the sentence*
announce the names of	announce, identify
another additional	another
anticipate in advance	anticipate
any and all	any, all
any questions you may have about	questions about
appeared on the scene	appeared
appears	seems
appoint to the post of	appoint
appreciate in value	appreciate
apprehend	arrest
approximately	about
the Arab street	*cliché*
ardent admirers	*cliché*
area	*cut*
area of	*cut*
arguably	*cut*
arise	get up
armed gunman	gunman
armed to the teeth	*cliché*
arrive at a decision	decide
as a consequence of	because
as a matter of fact	*cut*
as a result of	because
as already stated	*cut*
as far as the eye could see	*cliché*
as of this date	*cut*
ascertain	find out
aspect	*cut*
assemble together	assemble
assess a fine	fine
assist	help, aid
assuming that	if
at a tender (young) age	*cliché*

at an earlier date	previously
at first blush	*cliché*
at long last	*cliché*
at present	now
at the conclusion of	after
at the end of the day	eventually
at the present time	now
at the time when	when
at this point in time	now
at which time	when
attach together	attach
attempt	try
autopsy to determine the cause of death	autopsy
awkward predicament	predicament

B

back in the saddle	*cliché*
badly decomposed body	body (if long dead)
balanced approach	*cliché*
balancing the budget on the backs of the poor	*cliché*
ball is in (her, his, their) court	*cliché*
ballpark guess	*cliché*
(bare, basic) essentials	essentials
basic fundamentals	fundamentals
be acquainted with	know
be associated with	work with
be aware of	know
be cognizant of	know, notice
beat a (dead horse, hasty retreat)	*cliché*
bed of roses	*cliché*
beginning of the end	*cliché*
begs the question	*cliché*
best left unsaid	*cliché*
better late than never	*cliché*
between a rock and a hard place	*cliché*
beverage	drink
bewildering array	*cliché*

big in size	big
big oil	*cliché*
biggest ever	biggest
biography of (her, his) life	(her, his) biography
bite the bullet	*cliché*
bitter (end, dispute)	*cliché*
black helicopter crowd	*cliché*
blame it on	blame
blanket of snow	*cliché*
blazing inferno	*cliché*; inferno, blaze
bleeding-heart liberal	*cliché*
blessing in disguise	*cliché*
blissfully ignorant	*cliché*
bloodcurdling (scream, sight)	*cliché*
blood-red	*cliché*
bloody riot	*cliché*
boggles the mind	*cliché*
bolt from the blue	*cliché*
bombshell [announcement]	*cliché*
bond together	bond
bonds of matrimony	*cliché*
bone-chilling temperatures	*cliché*
bone of contention	*cliché*
boots on the ground	*cliché*
bored to tears	*cliché*
both	*cut except for emphasis*
both alike	alike
bouquet of flowers	bouquet
breakneck speed	*cliché*
breathless anticipation	*cliché*
brief in duration	brief
bring to a conclusion	conclude, end, finish
bring (to a head, up to date)	*cliché*
broad daylight	daylight
brutal (assault, beating, murder, rape, slaying)	*cut* brutal
brute force	*cliché*
budding genius	*cliché*

built-in safeguards	*cliché*
burn the midnight oil	*cliché*
burning (desire, issue, question)	*cliché*
busy as a (beaver, bee)	*cliché*
but one thing is certain	*cliché*
by leaps and bounds	*cliché*
by the name of	named
by the same token	likewise

C

call an audible (in a non-football context)	change plans
calm before the storm	*cliché*
calm down	calm
came to a stop	stopped
can of worms	*cliché*
cancel (each other, out)	cancel
can't see the forest for the trees	*cliché*
case	*cut*
case of	*cut*
champing at the bit	*cliché*
character	*cut*
charmed life	*cliché*
check (into, on, up on)	check
checkered (career, past)	*cliché*
cherished belief	*cliché*
chief protagonist	protagonist
(children, kids) of all ages	*cliché*
chip off the old block	*cliché*
circle around	circle
city of	*cut*
clean slate	*cliché*
clear as a bell	*cliché*
close down	close
close (proximity, scrutiny)	near, scrutiny
closed-door (hearing, meeting)	*cliché*
closed fist	*cliché*
close-up look	*cliché*

coarsening of the culture	*cliché*
coequal	equal
cognizant	aware
cold (as ice, comfort, shoulder)	*cliché*
collaborate together	collaborate
collect together	collect
colorful (display, scene)	*cliché*
combine together	combine
combined total	total
come full circle	*cliché*
come to a head	*cliché*
come to an end	end
come-to-Jesus moment	*cliché*
comfortable in (her, his, your, my) own skin	*cliché*
coming future	future
commence	begin, start
commented to the effect that	said
common accord	accord
communication	letter, memo
commute back and forth between	commute between
competency	competence, ability
competent	able
complete	fill out, finish
complete (chaos, monopoly, overhaul)	*cut* complete
completely (demolished, destroyed, done, eliminated, empty, finished, full, naked, surrounded, true, untrue)	*cut* completely
comply with	follow, obey
component	part
concept	idea
concept of	*cut*
conceptualize	think of
concerning	about
concerted effort	*cliché*
concrete proposals	proposals
condition	*cut*
conduct a poll	poll

conjecture	guess
connect the dots	*cliché*
consensus of opinion	consensus
consequent result	result
consideration	problem
considered opinion	*cliché*
conspicuous by (his, her, its, their) absence	*cliché*
constructive	helpful
consult	ask
consume	eat
consummate	finish
contemplate	think
contingent upon	depends on
continue on	continue
continue to remain	*cliché*
contribute	give
controversial (issue, person)	*cliché*
contusion	bruise
cool as a cucumber	*cliché*
cooperate together	cooperate
costs the sum of	costs
count up	count
countenance	face
crack of dawn	*cliché*
crony capitalism	cronyism (cronyism doesn't affect only capitalism)
cross to bear	*cliché*
crying (need, shame)	*cliché*
crystal clear	*cliché*
curate	*cliché* if not referring to managing a collection
current (temperature, trend)	*cut* current
currently	now
customary	usual
cut and run	*cliché*
cutting edge	*cliché*

D

dangerous weapon	weapon
daring daylight robbery	*cliché*
dark horse	*cliché*
dashed the hopes	*cliché*
dastardly deed	*cliché*
date with destiny	*cliché*
days are numbered	*cliché*
dead as a (doornail, skunk)	*cliché*
dead body	body
deadly earnest	*cliché*
deadly poison	poison
debate about	debate
deceased	dead
decide (about, on)	decide, select
deciding factor	*cliché*
deem	think, believe, judge
deficit	shortage
definite decision	decision
definition of insanity	*cliché*
demonstrate	show
depart	leave
depreciate in value	depreciate
depths of despair	*cliché*
descend down	descend
described as	called
desirable benefits	benefits
desire	wish, want
despite the fact that	despite
determine	find out
devoured by flames	*cliché*; burned
dialogue	talk, talks, negotiations, discussion
dyed-in-the-wool conservative	*cliché*
died of an apparent heart attack	apparently died of a heart attack
died suddenly	died
different	*cut*

dig in (her, his, their) heels	*cliché*
disclose	show
discontinue	stop, quit
disingenuous	*cliché*; insincere
divide up	divide
do it for the children	*cliché*
do your own thing	*cliché*
dog-tired	*cliché*
dotted the landscape	*cliché*
double-check twice	double-check
double down	*cliché*
downright lie	lie
down-to-earth	*cliché*
drastic action	*cliché*
draw a blank	*cliché*
draw first blood	*cliché*
draws to a close	ends
dried up	dried
drink (down, up)	drink
dropped down	dropped
drowned to death	drowned
ducks in a row	*cliché*
due to the fact that	because
duly noted	noted
duplicate	copy
during the course of	during
during the time that	while
dwell	live

E

each and every	every
earlier on	earlier
early (beginnings, pioneer)	*cut* early
easier said than done	*cliché*
Easter Sunday	Easter
eat up	eat
edifice	building
educationist, educator	teacher

effectuate	cause
egg on (his, her, their) face(s)	*cliché*
electrocuted to death	electrocuted
eliminate altogether	eliminate, cut
eloquent silence	*cliché*
eminently successful	*cliché*
emotional roller coaster	*cliché*
employment	job
empty out	empty
enable to	let, allow to
enclosed (herein, herewith, within)	here's, enclosed
encounter	meet
end (product, result)	*cut*
endeavor	try
enhance	add to, improve
ensuing	following
enter a bid of	bid
enter (in, into)	enter
entirely (complete, new, original, spontaneous)	*cut* entirely
entwined together	entwined
epic (response, slap down, struggle, etc.)	*cliché*
errand of mercy	*cliché*
essentially	*cut*
estimates about	about, estimates, guesses
ever since	since
every fiber of his being	*cliché*
exact (counterpart, duplicate, facsimile, replica, same)	*cut* exact
exactly identical	identical
exceeding the speed limit	speeding
exchanged wedding vows	married
execute	do, sign
exercise in futility	*cliché*
exhibit	show
expedite	speed
experience (n.)	*cut*

experience (v.)	cut (Instead of *He said he was experiencing pain*, try *He said he was in pain*.)
experienced veteran	veteran
extensively	greatly
extinguish	put out
eyeball to eyeball	*cliché*
eyesight	sight
eyewitness	witness

F

fabled	*cliché*
fabrication	lie, making, manufacture, product, production
face up to	face
facilitate	ease, help
facilities	buildings, space
factor	*cut*
factor of	*cut*
facts and figures	*cliché*
faded dream	*cliché*
failed policies of the past	*cliché*
failed to	did not
fairly	*cut*
false pretense	pretense
falsely fabricated	fabricated, made up
famed, famous	*cut*
far and wide	*cliché*
far cry	*cliché*
fat chance	*cliché*
fatal (killing, murder, slaying)	*cut*
fate worse than death	*cliché*
favored to win	favored
feasible	possible
feeding frenzy	*cliché*
feel-good movie	*cliché*
fell down	fell
fell on (bad, hard) times	*cliché*

fell on deaf ears	*cliché*
fell through the cracks	*cliché*
festive occasion	*cliché*
few and far between	*cliché*
few in number	few
field	*cut*
field of	*cut*
fiery rebuttal	*cliché*
file a lawsuit against	sue
filled to capacity	filled
final analysis	*cliché*
final (completion, conclusion, ending, outcome, result)	*cut* final
final word	*cliché*
finalize	finish, complete, end
finish up	finish
finishing touch	*cliché*
fire swept through	*cliché*
first (annual, began, commenced, initiated, priority, started)	*cut* first
first time ever	first time
firstly	first
flat as a board	*cliché*
flatly rejected	rejected
float a loan	lend
fly in the ointment	*cliché*
focus like a laser	*cliché*
fold up	fold
follow after	follow
follow in the footsteps of	*cliché*
food for thought	*cliché*
fools rush in	*cliché*
foot the bill	*cliché*
for all intents and purposes	*cliché*
for free	free
for openers	*cliché*
for the purpose of	to
for the reason that	because

foregone conclusion	*cliché*
foreseeable future	future
forthwith	*cut*
forward	send
foul play	*cliché*
frame of reference	*cut*
freak accident	*cliché*
free and open to the public	free
free (gift, pass)	*cut* free
free of charge	free
free up	free
freewill offering	offering
frequently	often
fresh (beginning, start)	*cut* fresh
from time immemorial	*cliché*
front headlight	headlight
(frown, smile) on (his, her) face	frown, smile
full and complete	complete
fully clothed	clothed
function	act, work
funeral services	services (in obituary; otherwise, *funeral*)
furnish	send, provide
furrowed brow	*cliché*
fused together	fused
future (plans, potential, prospects)	*cut* future

G

gainfully employed	employed, working
gala (event, occasion)	*cliché*
game changer	*cliché*
game plan	*cliché*
gather (together, up)	gather
general (public, rule)	public, rule
generally agreed	agreed
generous to a fault	*cliché*
get this show on the road	*cliché*

getting into full swing	*cliché*
gin up (the base, the voters)	*cliché*
girl power	*cliché*
give (a green light, consideration, encouragement, instruction, rise) to	approve, consider, encourage, instruct, cause
give (a, the) nod	approve
give back	*cliché*
given the green light	*cliché*
glass ceiling	*cliché*
glass, half (empty, full)	*cliché*
go	walk, run, jump, skip, hop, gallop
go for broke	*cliché*
go for it	*cliché*
go to the mat	*cliché*
goals and objectives	goals
goes without saying	*cliché*
going nowhere fast	*cliché*
good (as gold, spced)	*cliché*
good success	success
good to go	*cliché*
gory details	*cliché*
gradually (waning, wean)	*cut*
grand total	total
grateful thanks	thanks
grave (concern, crisis)	*cliché*
gravitas	*cliché*; serious dignity
great lengths	*cliché*
great majority of	majority of
great minds think alike	*cliché*
great open spaces	*cliché*
greatly	*cut*
green light/green-light (v.)	*cliché*; give the go-ahead, approve, OK
green with envy	*cliché*
ground rules	rules
ground to a halt	*cliché*

H

had ought	ought
hail of bullets	*cliché*
hale and hearty	*cliché*
half a hundred	50
hammer out	*cliché*
hang up	hang
hanging in there	*cliché*
happy camper	*cliché*
hardest hit are (minorities, women)	*cliché*
hardy souls	*cliché*
has got to	has to, must
has the (ability, capability, skill, talent) to	can
hastily summoned	*cliché*
have a (need, preference) for	need, prefer
have an (effect, impact) on	affect
have got	have
have got to	have to, must
have the belief that	believe
head over heels	*cliché*
head up	head
heart (of gold, of the matter)	*cliché*
heartfelt thanks	*cliché*
heart's (content, desire)	*cliché*
hearty meal	*cliché*
heat up	heat
heated argument	*cliché*
heave a sigh of relief	*cliché*
(He'd, She'd) like to have that one back	*sports cliché*
helicopter parents	*cliché*
Herculean effort	*cliché*
hereby	*cut*
herein	*cut*
hereto	*cut*
herewith	*cut*
high as a kite	*cliché*

high (noon, technology)	*cut* high
hit a home run	*cliché in nonbaseball stories*
hit the nail on the head	*cliché*
hobbled by injury	*cliché*
hockey mom	*cliché*
hoist up	hoist
honest truth	truth
hook, line and sinker	*cliché*
hope for the future	*cliché*
hopes and fears	*cliché*
hostile environment	*cliché*
hot (potato, pursuit)	*cliché*
hot-water heater	water heater
hour of noon	noon, noon hour
hunker down	*cliché*
hurry up	hurry

I

I gotta tell you	*cliché*
idea of	*cut*
if and when	if, when
if (when) push comes to shove	*cliché*
ignorance is bliss	*cliché*
illuminated	lighted
imbibe	drink
implement	do, start, begin
important essentials	essentials
in a similar fashion	similarly
in a very real sense	*cut*
in fact	*can often cut*
in (full swing, high gear, our midst)	*cliché*
in lieu of	instead of
in light of	because of, considering
in my opinion	*cut*
in no uncertain terms	*cliché*
in order to	to
in question	*cut*

railroad

rainstorm

ranch house, ranchland

rangeland

rank and file (n.), rank-and-file (adj.)

rawhide

razor strop

razzle-dazzle

razzmatazz

ready-made, ready-to-wear

rearview mirror

recover (regain), re-cover (cover again), re-elect, re-election, re-emerge, re-employ, re-enact, re-engage, re-enlist, re-enter, re-entry, re-equip, re-establish, re-examine, reform (improve), re-form (form again), resign (quit), re-sign (sign again), retweet

reddit

red-haired, red-handed (adj., adv.), redhead, redheaded, red-hot, red line, redlining, redneck (derogatory term)

rendezvous

rib-eye steak

ride-sharing

riffraff

right guard, right hand (n.), right-handed (adj.), right-hander (n.), right of way, right-to-work (adj.), right wing

(n.), right-wing (adj.), right-winger

ring bearer

rip off (v.), rip-off (adj., n.)

riverboat

roadside

rock 'n' roll

rocky road ice cream

role model

roll call (n.), roll-call (adj.), roll over (v.), rollover (n.)

roller coaster, roller skate (n.), roller-skate (v.), roller skater (n.)

roly-poly

rough cut

round table (n.), round-table (adj.), round trip (n.), round-trip (adj.), round up (v.), roundup (n.)

rubber band, rubber stamp (n.), rubber-stamp (v., adj.)

ruby red grapefruit

runback (n.), run down (v.), rundown (n.), run-down (adj.)

runner-up, runners-up

running back, running mate

rush hour (n.), rush-hour (adj.)

S

safe-deposit box

sales pitch

sandbag, sandstorm

saucepan

savings and loan association

school age (n.), school-age (adj.), school board, schoolbook, schoolboy, school bus, schoolchild, school day, schoolgirl, schoolhouse, schoolteacher

scot-free

screen saver

seat belt

search engine optimization

seawater

second guess (n.), second-guess (v.), second-guesser, second hand (n.), secondhand (adj., adv.),

second-rate

secretary-general, secretary of state, secretary-treasurer

seesaw

self-assured, self-defense, self-esteem, self-governing, self-government

sell out (v.), sellout (adj., n.)

semiannual, semi-automatic, semicolon, semifinal, semi-invalid, semiofficial, semitrailer, semitropical, semiweekly

send off (v.), send-off (n.)

sergeant-at-arms

service mark, serviceman, service member, servicewoman

in spite of the fact that	although
in terms of	*cut*
in the (aftermath, final analysis, last analysis, nick of time, same boat, wake of)	*cliché*
in the event that	if
in the not-too-distant future	soon
in the shape of	*cut*
in this (day and age, time frame)	*cliché*
in view of the fact that	because
inaugurate	begin, start
include among them	include
inconvenience	trouble
incumbent (governor, president, representative, senator)	*cut*
incursion	invasion
indeed	*cut*
indicate	show
indication	sign
indignant	upset
individual	person, man or woman
inevitable	sure, certain
inextricably (linked, tied)	*cliché*
infinite capacity	*cliché*
inform	tell
informed by	*cliché for* influenced by
infringe (on, upon)	infringe
initial	first
initiate	begin, start
innocent bystander	*cliché*
input	opinion, suggestion
inquire	ask
institute	start
insufficient	not enough
interface	connect, talk, meet
interim period between	interim
interrogate	question
inundate	flood

iron out (difficulties, disagreements, troubles)	*cliché*
irons in the fire	*cliché*
irregardless	regardless (*Irregardless is not a word.*)
is (code, a dog whistle) for	*cliché*
is going to	will
is hopeful that	(he/she hopes; they hope)
is productive of	produces
is reflective of	reflects
is representative of	represents
… isn't just for. … anymore	*cliché*
issue in question	issue
it appears (seems) that	*cut*
it goes without saying	*cliché*
it is (her, his, their) contention	(she, he, contends; they contend)
it is (her, his, their) intention	(she, he says; they say; she, he intends)
it takes a village	*cliché*
it would appear that	*cut*
(I've got to, I gotta) tell you	*cut*

J

Jewish rabbi	rabbi
Joe Sixpack	*cliché*
join (in, together)	join
joint (cooperation, partnership)	*cut*

K

keeled over	*cliché*
keeping (his, her, their) options open	*cut*
kick the hornet's nest	*cliché*
kind of	*cut*
knee-jerk liberal	*cliché*
knit together	combined, figured out
know about	know

L

labor of love	*cliché*
laceration	cut, gash
lag behind	lag
laid to rest	*cliché*
largest ever	largest
lashed out	*cliché*
last (analysis, but not least, word)	*cliché*
last-ditch effort	*cliché*
later on	later
laundry list (of desired programs, for example)	*cliché*
leaps and bounds	*cliché*
learning experience	experience, something to learn from, educational
leave no stone unturned	*cliché*
leaves much to be desired	*cliché*
left up in the air	*cliché*
legal hairsplitting	*cliché*
lend a helping hand	*cliché*
level	cut (Instead of *She teaches on the college level*, try *She teaches college courses*.)
level playing field	*cliché*
like a bolt from the blue	*cliché*
lingered on	lingered
lion's share	*cliché*
local residents	residents, locals
locate	find
lock horns	*cliché*
lonely (isolation, solitude)	cut
long (arm of the law, years)	*cliché*
lose out	lose
low ebb	ebb
low-hanging fruit	*cliché*
lucky few	*cliché*

M

made a motion	moved
made a pretty picture	*cliché*
made a ruling	ruled
made a (speech, statement, talk)	spoke
made an escape	escaped
made an inquiry regarding	asked about
made contact with	met, saw
made mention of	mentioned
made the acquaintance of	met
made (up, out) of	made of
main essentials	essentials
maintenance	upkeep
maintenance engineer	janitor, custodian
major breakthrough	breakthrough
make a killing	*cliché*
make a list of	list
make adjustments	adjust
make an approximation	estimate
makes one's home	lives
man up	*cliché*
mantle of snow	*cliché*
manufacture	make
many and various	*cliché*
many in number	many
marked (contrast, improvement)	*cliché*
married (her husband, his wife)	married
mass exodus	*cliché*
massive	big, large
matinee (performance, show)	matinee
matter of	*cut*
matter of life and death	*cliché*
maximization	best, improvement
maximize	increase as much as possible
maximum possible	maximum
meaningful	big, important

meaningful dialogue	*cliché*
meet head-on	*cliché*
meets the eye	*cliché*
merchandise	goods
merchandize	sell
merge together	merge
mesh together	mesh
met (his, her) Maker	died
method in (his, her, their) madness	*cliché*
might possibly	might
minimize	lessen as much as possible
miraculous escape	*cliché*
mix together	mix
mixed blessing(s)	*cliché*
modicum of	some
moment of truth	*cliché*
momentous (decision, occasion)	*cliché*
monkey (on, off) (his, her, their) back(s)	*cliché*
more preferable	preferable
more than meets the eye	*cliché*
most all	most
most unique	unique
mother of all	*cliché*
motley crew	*cliché*
mourn the loss	*cliché*
move	walk, run, jump, skip, hop, gallop
mutual cooperation	cooperation
mutually beneficial	*cliché*

N

name of the game	*cliché*
nanny state	*cliché*
narrow down	narrow, reduce
narrow escape	*cliché*
nature	cut (Instead of *He has a serious nature*, try *He is serious.*)
necessary (requirement, requisite)	cut

necessitates	calls for
needless to say	*cut*
never a dull moment	*cliché*
never at any time	never
new (addition, baby, beginning, bride, construction, creation, initiative, innovation, normal, record, recruit)	*cut* new
newly created	new
nick of time	*cliché*
night of terror	*cliché*
nipped in the bud	*cliché*
no brainer	*cliché*
no easy answer	*cliché*
no place like home	*cliché*
no sooner said than done	*cliché*
none the worse (for the experience, for wear)	*cliché*
not to be outdone	*cliché*
nothing burger	*cliché*
now comes the hard part	*cliché*
numerous	many

O

objective	goal
obscene profits	*cliché*
obtain	get
of course	*can often cut*
off of	off
official (capacity, protest)	*cliché*
oftentimes	often
old (adage, cliché, habit, legend, maxim, proverb, tradition, veteran)	*cut* old
old (boy, boys') network	*cliché*
old school	*cliché*
on a few occasions	occasionally
on a roll	*cliché*
on account of	because
on any given day	on any day

on more than one occasion	*cliché*
on the face of it	*cliché*
on the fly	*cliché*
on the grounds that	since, because, as
on the occasion of	when
one and the same	identical
one day at a time	*cliché*
one fell swoop	*cliché*
one of life's little ironies	*cliché*
one of the last remaining	*cut* remaining
ongoing	*cut*
only time will tell	*cliché*
open secret	*cliché*
operative (adj.)	*cut*
opt for	*cliché*; choose
opt out	decline
optics	*cliché* when used to mean *appearance* or *perception*
optimistic	hopeful
optimization	best, improvement
optimum	best
order out of chaos	*cliché*
orient	adjust
orientate	adjust
original source	source
output	production
outside the box	*cliché*
over a period of years	for years
over and above	*cliché*
overview	review, survey
overwhelming (majority, odds)	*cliché*
own home	home
own worst enemy	*cliché*

P

paid the penalty	*cliché*
painted a grim picture	*cliché*
(pair of, two) twins	twins

pale as a ghost	*cliché*
Pandora's box	*cliché*
par for the course	*cliché*
parameters	limits, boundaries, variables
paramount issue	*cliché*
part and parcel	*cliché*
participate	take part
participate in the decision-making process	have a say
party	person
passed (away, on)	died
passing phase	phase
past (experience, history)	*cut* past
pay (off, out)	pay
paying the piper	*cliché*
peace dividend	*cliché*
penetrate into	penetrate
per	a, according to
perceive	see
perfect storm	*cliché*
perfectly clear	clear
perform a task	do
perhaps	*can often cut*
permanent importance	*cliché*
personal (experience, friend)	*cut* personal
personalize	make more personal
personally (involved, reviewed)	*cut* personally
peruse	read, examine
phase	*cut*
phone is ringing off the hook	*cliché*
physical size	size
physician	doctor
picture of health	*cliché*
picture perfect	*cliché*
pie in the sky	*cliché*
pitched battle	*cliché*
pizza pie	pizza
place	put

plan (ahead, for the future, in advance)	plan
play hardball	*cliché*
play it by ear	*cliché*
play the race card	*cliché*
pocketbook	purse
point with pride	*cliché*
polemics	arguments
polish up	polish
political correctness run amok	*cliché*
ponder	consider
populace	people, population
position	job
possess	own, have
poster child	*cliché*
postpone until later	postpone
powder keg (used as a metaphor)	*cliché*
power (lunch, tie, user)	*cliché*
powers that be	*cliché*
preceded in death	died earlier
pre-owned	used
present a report	report
present incumbent	incumbent
presently	soon
pretty as a picture	*cliché*
primary	first, main
prior history	history
prior to	before
prioritize	rank
problem	*cut*
proceed	go, move ahead
process	*cut*
process of	*cut*
prohibit	forbid
promoted to the rank of	promoted to
proposition	*cut*
protrude out	protrude
provide	give

provided	if
purchase	buy
purloin	steal
pursuant to	following, in accordance with
pursue	chase
pushing the envelope	*cliché*
put a lid on it	*cliché*
put emphasis on	stress
put into effect	start

Q

qualified expert	expert
quality time	*cliché*
question of	*cut*
quite	*cut*

R

radical transformation	transformation
rain (couldn't, didn't) dampen the (spirits, enthusiasm)	*cliché*
raise up	raise
rapprochement	reconciliation
rarely ever	rarely
rat race	*cliché*
rationalization	excuse, reason, explanation
raze to the ground	raze
really	*cut*
really unique	unique
rear taillight	taillight
reason is because	because
reason why	reason, why
(recall, recede, refer, remand, retreat, revert) back	*cut* back
receive	get
(recur, repeat, resume, restate) again	*cut* again
red-hot	*cliché*
red-letter day	*cliché*
reduce down	reduce

refer back to	refer to
referred to as	called
register (a complaint, an objection)	*cut* register
register approval	approve
register stamp of approval to	approve
regret	are sorry
regular (monthly, weekly) meeting	*cut* regular
reign of terror	*cliché*
reigns supreme	*cliché*
reins of government	*cliché*
reinvent the wheel	*cliché*
reliable sources	sources
relocate	move
remainder	rest
remains to be seen	*cliché*
remark	say
remedy the situation	*cliché*
remunerate	pay
renowned	*cut*
repeated again	repeated
requires	asks for, calls for, needs
reside	live
residence	house, home
resigned her position as	resigned as
resource center	library
respond	answer
rest up	rest
resultant effect	effect
results achieved	results
reveal	show
reverted back	reverted
revise downward	lower
right stuff	*cliché*
ripe old age	*cliché*
rise up	rise
road to recovery	*cliché*
rode roughshod over	*cliché*
root cause	cause

rose to (new, the) heights	*cliché*
rose to the (cause, defense) of	supported, defended
round of applause	*cliché*
roundly attacked	attacked
rushed to the hospital	*cliché*

S

sadder but wiser	*cliché*
safe haven	*cliché*
salt of the earth	*cliché*
scored a gain	gained
sea of (upturned) faces	*cliché*
seal off	seal
seasoned (journalists, observers, reporters, etc.)	*cliché*
seat of the pants	*cliché*
second to none	*cliché*
secondly	second
seldom ever	seldom
select few	*cliché*
self-confessed	confessed
senseless murder	*cliché*
serious (crisis, danger)	*cut* serious
seriously (consider, inclined)	*cut* seriously
settle up	settle
shared sacrifice	*cliché*
sharp as a tack	*cliché*
shattering effect	*cliché*
shift into high gear	*cliché*
shopping list (of desired programs, for example)	*cliché*
short (minutes, years)	*cut* short
shot in the arm	*cliché*
shovel-ready	*cliché*
shrouded in mystery	*cliché*
sigh of relief	*cliché*
silhouetted against the sky	*cliché*
simple life	*cliché*

Tightening

sing "Kumbaya"	*cliché*
single unit	unit
sink down	sink
situated (in, at)	in, at
situation (as in classroom situation, crisis situation)	*cut*
($64, $64,000) question	*cliché*
skin in the game	*cliché*
skirt around	skirt
sky-high	*cliché*
slowly but surely	*cliché*
small in size	small
smartest guy in the room	*cliché*
smoking gun	*cliché*
smooth as silk	*cliché*
snatched victory from the jaws of defeat	*cliché*
snug as a bug in a rug	*cliché*
so that	so
soccer mom	*cliché*
social amenities	*cliché*
societal	social
soft on crime	*cliché*
soiree	party
sort of	*cut*
speak truth to power	*cliché*
speak volumes	*cliché*
spearheading the campaign	*cliché*
spell out	explain
spirited debate	*cliché*
spliced together	spliced
split apart	split
spotlight the need	*cliché*
spouse	husband, wife
sprung a surprise	surprised
square peg in a round hole	*cliché*
staff of life	*cliché*
stand up	stand
staple together	staple

star-studded	*cliché*
start up	start
started off with	started with
states	says
states the point that	says
staunch supporter	supporter
steaming jungle	*cliché*
stern warning	*cliché*
stick to your guns	*cliché*
sticks out like a sore thumb	*cliché*
still (continues, persists, remains)	*cut* still
stinging rebuke	*cliché*
stolen loot	loot
storm(s) of protest	*cliché*
storm-tossed	*cliché*
straight-and-narrow path	*cliché*
straight as an arrow	*cliché*
straight (losses, games, wins) in a row	*cut* in a row
strangled to death	strangled
straw that broke the camel's back	*cliché*
stress the point that	stress that
stretches the truth	*cliché*
strife-torn	*cliché*
strong, silent type	*cliché*
stubborn as a mule	*cliché*
submit	send, give
subsequent	later
substantial	big, great, large
substantially	largely
succeed in doing	accomplish, do
such is life	*cliché*
sum and substance	*cliché*
sum total	total
summer (months, season)	summer
summoned to the scene	summoned
superhuman effort	*cliché*
supportive	helpful
supreme sacrifice	*cliché*
surrounding circumstances	circumstances

sustain	suffer
sweat of his brow	*cliché*
sweeping changes	*cliché*
swing into high gear	*cliché*
sworn affidavits	affidavits
synergize	*cliché*

T

take a deep breath	*cliché*
take into consideration	consider
take place	happen
take them one at a time	*cliché*
talking points	*cliché*
tangled together	tangled
tarnished image	*cliché*
tax-and-spend liberal	*cliché*
teachable moment	*cliché*
team player	*cliché*
telling effect	*cliché*
temblor	earthquake
temporary reprieve	reprieve
temporary respite	respite
tender mercies	*cliché*
tendered her resignation	resigned
terminate	stop, end
textbook example	*cliché*
that	*can often cut*
that dog won't hunt	*cliché*
that (being) said …	*cliché*
That's not who we are.	*cliché*
the above	*cut; repeat the antecedent*
the area of	*cut*
the fact (is, that)	*cut*
the field of	*cut*
the limelight	*cliché*
the month of	*cut*
the reality is	*cut*
the truth is	*cut*
therein, thereof, thereon	*cut*

there's the rub	*cliché*
thick as pea soup	*cliché*
think about it	*cliché*
thirdly	third
this day and age	*cliché*
thorn in the side	*cliché*
thorough investigation	*cliché*
threw caution to the wind	*cliché*
through their paces	*cliché*
throughput	*cut*
throw a monkey wrench into	*cliché*
throw in the towel	*cliché*
throw [someone] under the bus	*cliché*
throw support behind	support
thunderous applause	*cliché*
tied together	tied
time (immemorial, of one's life)	*cliché*
tip of the iceberg	*cliché*
to be sure	*cut*
to script	to write
to summarize	*cut*
to the tune of	*cliché*
today's society	*cliché*
ton of bricks	*cliché*
tongue (firmly planted) in cheek	*cliché*
too numerous to mention	*cliché*
took to task	*cliché*
torrent of abuse	*cliché*
total (abstinence, extinction, operating costs)	*cut* total
total strangers	strangers
totally (demolished, destroyed)	*cut* totally
touch base	*cliché*
tower of strength	*cliché*
transport	carry
trapped like rats	*cliché*
trials and tribulations	*cliché*
triggered	*cliché*; prompted
true colors	*cliché*

true fact	fact
tumultuous applause	*cliché*
tuna fish	tuna
turn thumbs down	*cliché*
12 (midnight, noon)	*cut* 12
two alternatives	alternatives, choices
two-way street	*cliché*

U

ultimate	final, last
ultimate (conclusion, end, outcome)	*cut* ultimate
uncharted sea	*cliché*
underground subway	subway
underlying purpose	purpose
undertake a study	study
uneasy (calm, truce)	*cliché*
unexpected surprise	surprise
uniformly consistent	consistent
universal panacea	panacea
unpaid debt	debt
unprecedented situation	*cliché*
untimely end	*cliché*
untiring efforts	*cliché*
up (in arms, the air)	*cliché*
upcoming	coming, impending
updated	current
upset the apple cart	*cliché*
uptight	*cliché*
usual custom	custom
utilization	use
utilize	use
utterly indestructible	indestructible

V

vanish into thin air	*cliché*
various and sundry	*cliché*
vast expanse	*cliché*
vehicle	car, truck

very	*cut*
viable	workable
viable (alternative, option, solution)	*cut* viable
view with alarm	*cliché*
violence erupted	*cliché*
violent (assault, attack, killing, murder, rape, slaying)	*cut* violent
vitally necessary	necessary
voiced (approval, objections)	*cliché*; approved, objected

W

wait-and-see attitude	*cliché*
walk(s) of life	*cliché*
warm and fuzzy	*cliché*
war-torn	*cliché*
was employed	worked
was in possession of	had
watchful eye	*cliché*
watershed	*cut*
watery grave	*cliché*
We can walk and chew gum.	*cliché*
wealth of information	*cliché*
weaponized	*cliché* in political circles, such as weaponized the IRS or "deep state"
wear and tear	*cliché*
wear many hats	*cliché*
wee, small hours	*cliché*
weighty (matter, reason, tome)	*cliché*
well-known	*cut*
wellness	health, prevention
went up in flames	burned
were scheduled to	would
what makes (her, him, them) tick	*cliché*
what went down	*slang cliché for* what happened
where there's smoke, there's fire	*cliché*
whether or not	whether
which are	*can often cut*
which is	*can often cut*

while at the same time	while
whirlwind (courtship, romance, tour)	*cliché*
white (as snow, stuff)	*cliché*
white (male) privilege	*cliché*
who are	*can often cut*
who is	*can often cut*
who said	said
whole nine yards	*cliché*
wide-open space	*cliché*
widow, widower	*cut* of the late
will be a participant in	will participate in
will hold a meeting	will meet
win out	win
winds of change	*cliché*
wipe the slate clean	*cliché*
with bated breath	*cliché*
witness	see
word to the wise	*cliché*
words (can't, fail to) express	*cliché*
world-class	*cliché*
worse for wear	*cliché*
worst ever	worst
wrapped in mystery	*cliché*
write down	write
writing on the wall	*cliché*

Y

(80, 90, etc.) years young	*cliché*
you be the judge	*cliché*
you can't make this stuff up	*cliché*
You go, girl!	*cliché*
you know	*cut*
(You've got, You have) to wonder	*cliché*
young juvenile	juvenile

Z

zoo animals	animals (*if context is clear*)

Trademarks and Generics

It's often unclear to writers and speakers whether a name for something is generic and should be lowercase or a trademark that should be capitalized. First, here's a list of trademark names that are often used when the generic term is intended. Following that is a list of former trademarks that are now generic and a third list of non-trademarks that might cause wonder as to whether they are. Finally, we've added a small fourth list of trademarks that pose spelling problems.

BRAND NAME	GENERIC
Adrenalin	adrenaline or epinephrine
Alexa	smart speaker (actually just the name of the voice on Amazon smart speakers)
Aqua-Lung	underwater breathing apparatus
AstroTurf	artificial surface
Bake-off	baking contest
Band-Aid	adhesive bandage
Bubble Wrap	inflated packaging material
ChapStick	lip balm
Clorox	bleach
Coke	cola
Cool Whip	whipped cream topping
Crayola	crayons
Crisco	vegetable shortening
Crock-Pot	slow cooker
Cuisinart	food processor
DayGlo	fluorescent colors
DayQuil	cold medicine

Deepfreeze	freezer
DisposAll	garbage disposer
FaceTime	video chat
Fiberglas	fiberglass
Fig Newtons	fig cookies
Formica	plastic or wood laminate
Freon	refrigerant
Frisbee	toy flying disk
Fudgsicle	fudge ice-cream bar
Google	a web search or to search the web
Hacky Sack	foot bag
Hallmark card	greeting card
Hi-Liter	highlighting marker
Hula Hoop	toy hoop
iPad	tablet computer
iPhone	smartphone
iPod	digital music player *or* MP3 player
Jacuzzi	whirlpool bath
Jaws of Life	vehicle extraction tool
Jeep	*jeep* for military vehicle; otherwise, four-wheel-drive vehicle
Jell-O	gelatin
Jockey shorts	underwear
JumboTron	large-screen TV
Kitty Litter	cat-box filler
Kleenex	tissue
Kool-Aid	soft-drink mix
Krazy Glue	super adhesive
Land Rover	all-terrain vehicle
Lava Lamp	liquid-motion lamp
La-Z-Boy	reclining chair (although the company makes other furniture, as well)
LEGO blocks	plastic toy construction blocks
Levi's	jeans
Little League Baseball	youth baseball
Lucite	acrylic plastic
Mace (short for *Chemical Mace*)	tear-gas spray

Magic Marker	felt-tip marking pen
Memory Stick	flash memory
Moon Pie	marshmallow sandwich
Muzak	background music, canned music or elevator music
Nerf	foam toy
Novocain	procaine hydrochloride
NyQuil	cold medicine
Onesies	infant bodysuit
Oreo	cookie
Ouija	fortunetelling board game
Pablum	baby food
Photoshop	photo editing software
Photostat	photocopy
Ping-Pong	table tennis, or pingpong
Play-Doh	modeling clay
Plexiglas	plexiglass or acrylic glass
Popsicle	flavored ice on a stick
Post-it	self-stick note
PowerPoint	slide presentation
Prozac	antidepressant
Pyrex	oven glassware
Q-tips	cotton swabs
Quaalude	methaqualone
Ray-Ban	sunglasses
Realtor	real estate agent
Rollerblade	in-line skate
Rolodex	address-card file
Saran Wrap	clear plastic wrap
Scotch tape	transparent tape
Seeing Eye dog	guide dog
Sharpie	permanent marker
Sheetrock	gypsum wallboard
Skype	video call
Slim-Fast	diet shake
SPAM or Spam	canned luncheon meat (may be used in all lowercase to mean unsolicited commercial email)

Stetson	cowboy hat
Styrofoam	plastic foam
Tabasco	hot-pepper sauce
Tater Tots	hash-brown potatoes in small cylinders
TiVo	digital TV recorder
Tupperware	plastic storage container
Tylenol	acetaminophen
Valium	diazepam anxiety drug
Vaseline	petroleum jelly
Velcro	fabric fastener
Viagra	erectile-dysfunction drug
Walkman	portable audio device
Weed Eater	weed and grass trimmer
Weedwacker	weed and grass trimmer
Windex	glass cleaner
Xerox	photocopy
Zantac	ulcer drug
Ziploc	zippered plastic bag

Former Trademarks Now Also Considered Generic:

aspirin

cellophane

davenport (a large couch in America or a small writing desk with a lid in Britain)

dry ice

dumpster

escalator

flip phone

heroin

hovercraft

kerosene

laundromat

linoleum

mimeograph

teleprompter

thermos (now a generic term for a vacuum bottle but one manufacturer uses it as a brand name)

touch-tone

trampoline

videotape

Webster's dictionary

windbreaker

yo-yo

zipper

Not Trademarks:

diazinon—a particular chemical insecticide

lanolin—substance from sheep wool used in cosmetics and ointments

Lazy Susan—generic term for a turntable shelf but capitalized anyway, according to *Webster's New World*

lindane—a form of benzene hexachloride used in insecticides

linoleum—a kind of washable flooring

latex—used in paint and elastic

malathion—an organic phosphate used in insecticides

methoxychlor—a chemical used in some insecticides

napalm—a flammable jellylike chemical used in flame throwers and bombs

terry cloth—cloth used in towels

tommy gun—nickname for Thompson submachine gun

Trademarks That Pose Other Spelling Issues:

Coca-Cola

Dr Pepper

Kmart

Life Saver (candy)

7-Eleven

7UP or Seven-Up

Time Warner Inc.

Walmart

Usage

Usage Differences

That so many people don't make the distinctions listed here is evidence the language is changing. As a result, many of these entries could be candidates for Our Changing Language boxes. Although there are too many to label individually, we think some distinctions are important and worth fighting for, and others are at least those that media writers should be aware are issues for some people.

Some items in the list are single entries of words and phrases that many people misunderstand or muddle. Some items consist of multiple-entry listings, primarily pairs of words and phrases but sometimes three or more, that either sound alike or seem enough alike in meaning that people confuse them. The multiple-entry items are listed in groups — the words in each group are listed alphabetically, and each group is listed alphabetically by the first word in the group.

When we've listed words or phrases in pairs or more, we've suggested usages we think are the most distinctive and clearest for each word. That doesn't necessarily mean any other use is wrong. To illustrate: Many speakers and writers commonly make no distinction between *that* and *which*, but those who do make the distinction we list here. Even more commonly, *though* and *while* are each often used in speech and writing in place of *although*. But each of these three words has a unique nuance, and our suggestion is to try to use the one that matches the intended meaning listed here.

And finally, for additional word-choice advice, check out the list of biased terms on Pages 241–254, the list of words and phrases to tighten on Pages 287–322 and the list of trademarks on Pages 323–327.

Misused and Confused Words and Phrases

A

a while   Use as the object of a preposition: *It's been going on for quite a while.* Also used in expressions *a while ago* and *a while back.*

awhile   the general adverb form: *It's been going on awhile.*

abjure   to renounce

adjure   to entreat earnestly

above   Some editors insist this preposition not be used as an adjective, although *The AP Stylebook* seems to use it that way sometimes. For example, "The plane flew *above* the clouds," not "The *above* statement should appear as a warning."

abrogate   to annul

arrogate   to claim unduly

abstruse   hard to understand

obtuse   slow at understanding

accede   to agree reluctantly

exceed   to surpass

accept   to receive

except   prep., but for; to exclude

access   to enter

assess   to evaluate

excess   surplus

accident   To be an accident, an occurrence, such as a car wreck, must be unforeseen, unexpected and unintended. In a legal sense, it must also be the result of no one's fault or negligence. AP warns to be careful when "negligence is claimed or proven."

collision   when two moving objects hit

crash   when a moving object hits something else that is mobile or stationary

acetic   sour; acidic

aesthetic   artistic

ascetic   austere

Usage

acquiesce (in, to)   to accept, comply or submit tacitly or passively

act   a single thing that's done
action   something done that's made up of more than one act

acute   critical; intense; crucial
chronic   persistent; recurring; prolonged

ad   advertisement
add   to derive a sum

adapt   to adjust
adopt, approve   to accept. You *adopt* or *approve* a resolution.
enact   You enact a law.
pass   to enact. You *pass* an ordinance.

addition   something added on; the arithmetic process of making sums
edition   version of a published work

adherence   support for
adherents   supporters

adhesion   when things stick together by virtue of a medium such as glue
cohesion   when things stick together because of their common property

adventuresome   willing to take risks
adventurous   fond of adventure

adverse   unfavorable. Things are *adverse*.
averse   opposed. People are *averse* to things.

advice   noun
advise   verb

affect   to influence or produce a change in. Avoid as a noun, except in psychology to describe an emotion.
effect   n., result; v., to cause or accomplish

affinity   This noun may be followed by the prepositions *between*, *of* and *with* but not *for*. But *penchant for* is correct.

affluence   abundance

effluence   the process of flowing out

effluents   things that have flowed out, especially sewage

after   following. Don't write, "The driver was killed after his car hit a truck," as it implies that something or someone else killed him following the accident.

aggravate   to make worse. Only existing conditions are aggravated.

annoy   to bother

irritate   to make the skin itch

aggregate   collection. If you take things in the aggregate, you look at them collectively as a whole, although you recognize them not to be a single item.

total   sum. When separate items are added together into one sum, you have their total.

agree to   You *agree to* something.

agree with   You *agree with* someone.

agreement   not *agreeance*

aid   help

aide   an assistant

ail   to be sick; to make sick

ale   malt beverage

ain't   Change to *isn't*, *aren't* or *am not*.

air   gas, atmosphere

e'er   ever (poetic)

ere   before (poetic)

err   to make a mistake

heir   an inheritor

aisle   row

I'll   contraction for *I will* or *I shall*

isle   island

alibi   legal defense that one was somewhere else when a crime was committed

excuse   reason put forward to request forgiveness. Except in a legal sense, this is generally the word you want.

all   Don't use this redundantly, as in the example "Fife, Griffith, and Smith were *all* released." The *all* does not tell us anything new in this example.

all-around   not *all-round*

allegedly   This word itself offers little or no legal protection and may actually get you into trouble. Instead, give the charge and identify the person making it.

all-important   An overblown and overused phrase. Whether it's correct depends on the word being modified, but few things, if any, are worthy of it.

all intents and purposes   not *all intensive purposes*

allowed   permitted
aloud   audibly

all ready   everyone prepared
already   by now

all together   everyone grouped
altogether   thoroughly

allude   not mention directly
elude   evade

allusion   an indirect reference
delusion   mistaken belief, especially one caused by a mental disorder
elusion   an escape
illusion   erroneous perception or belief
reference   specific mention

all ways   all methods
always   constantly

almost   nearly, as in *almost all*
most   greatest amount, degree or size, as in *most dangerous game* or *most people*

altar   sacred platform in a house of worship

alter   to change

alternate   v., take turns; n., proxy

alternative   n., choice; adj., substitute. Note that this is the only form to use as an adjective.

although   the preferred form at the start of a sentence or clause; the one to use as a subordinating conjunction

though   the only correct form at the end of a sentence; the one to use as a simple adverb with commas on each side of it in the middle of a sentence. Many writers, though, also use it in place of *although*.

alumna   woman who has attended a school. (At some schools, graduation is implied.)

alumnae   women who have attended a school

alumni   men, or men and women, who have attended a school

alumnus   man who has attended a school

amateur   nonprofessional

novice   beginner

amend   to make a formal change

emend   to correct

amid   in the middle of something larger: *amid all that confusion*

among   surrounded by three or more separate things: *among the hungry of the world*

between   relationship involving only two or a number of things compared two at a time

amoral   outside of morality

immoral   in opposition to a moral code

amount   how much (weight or money)

number   how many (individual items)

ancestors, forebears   those from whom you are descended

descendants   those descended from you

anchors aweigh   not *anchors away*

and   Many books tell you not to begin a sentence with *and* or *but*. But technically, either can begin a sentence because both are coordinating conjunctions, which by definition can start a sentence or an independent clause. Journalists often begin sentences with *but* and seldom with *and*, although we would accept either.

anecdote   short, amusing story

antidote   cure for a poison

angel   heavenly being

angle   degree measurement between two lines or planes; a slant

anima   female identification in men

animus   male identification in women

ant   a kind of insect

aunt   sister of mother or father

anticipate   to foresee with the possibility of forestalling

expect   to foresee without necessarily being able to forestall

antiseptic   something that prevents bacteria from growing

disinfectant   something that destroys or neutralizes bacteria

anxious   experiencing desire mixed with dread. One is *anxious about* or *for*.

eager   marked by enthusiasm and impatience. One is *eager to*.

any   used with a choice among more than two

either   used with a choice between two

any more   something additional: *I don't have any more.*

anymore   adv., now, nowadays

any one   any single person or thing

anyone   any person at all

any way   in any manner

anyway   in any event. Note there is no *s* at the end except in colloquial speech.

apparent   appears to be real

evident   evidence makes clear

obvious   unquestionable

appose   to put side by side

oppose   to set against

appraise   to evaluate

apprise   to inform

apt   implies possibility

liable   implies an unpleasant probability; responsible

libel   written slander

likely   implies probability

arbitrate   to judge

mediate   to serve as a person who conciliates or reconciles

arc   a curve; something in that shape

ark   something offering protection

are   v., form of *to be*

hour   n., 60 minutes

our   pron., possessive form of *we*

aren't I?   Change to *am I not?*

aroma   pleasant smell

stench   foul smell

arouse   to excite or stimulate

rouse   to stir or waken

arrant   notorious

errant   straying

as   conj., introduces clauses

like   prep., introduces words or phrases; noninclusive

such as   prep., conj.; introduces inclusive words, phrases or clauses. *A book like this* means not this one but another; *a book such as this* means this one or one like it.

as compared with   see *compare to*

ascent climb

assent agreement

aside n., digression; adv., to one side, out of the way, apart from

beside prep., alongside

besides in addition to

as if not *as though* (although some authorities, including AP, now accept either). *As if* is generally preferred when introducing a subjunctive-mood verb.

as to not *as for*. *About* or *on* is often preferable to *as to*.

assert to state as true

claim n., legal right; justified demand; v., to assert, particularly without proof (suggests the person using this word to describe what someone else said doubts it's true); to assert ownership

assignation appointment

assignment allotted task

assistance help

assistants helpers

assume to hold a hypothesis without proof. You also *assume* a role.

decide on You *decide on* a course.

presume to believe without proof

assure to remove worry or uncertainty. People are *assured*.

ensure to make an outcome inevitable. Events are *ensured*.

insure to provide insurance. Objects or lives are *insured*.

astride prep., with a leg on each side

bestride v., to straddle. When you *bestride* a motorcycle, you are sitting *astride* it.

as yet Change to *yet*.

attendance number attending; act of attending

attendants people who attend

attorney   someone who transacts business for you, legal or not; not a profession. A person can have "power of attorney" without being a lawyer.

lawyer   professional attorney in legal matters (member of the bar)

auditions   technically, auditions are heard, and this is the common word when actors try out for a role

trials or tryouts   technically trials or tryouts are watched, and this is the common word for sports, as when trying out for a team

auger   tool for boring

augur   to be an omen

aught   n., zero; adv., at all

ought   v., should

aural   pertains to the ear

oral   pertains to the mouth; spoken

verbal   pertains to language, spoken or written

autarchy   totalitarian government

autarky   policy of economic nationalism

automatic   an automatic weapon continuously fires as long as the trigger is held down-payment

semiautomatic   a semiautomatic weapon fires once for each trigger pull

avenge   v., to right a wrong

revenge   n., retaliation for satisfaction, not justice; to gain vengeance

vengeance   n., retribution or the desire for it

average, mean   the sum divided by the number of parts: $4 + 9 + 2 = 15$; $15/3 = 5$ (average)

median   the number with as many scores above as below. In the sequence 2, 7, 13, 16, 21, the median is 13.

range   the highest minus the lowest

avert   to turn yourself away from

avoid   to keep away from

evade   to avoid by cleverness

prevent   to forestall, anticipate or keep from occurring

avocation   hobby

vocation   job; profession

awesome   something evoking awe, an emotion of mingled reverence, wonder and dread. It is often used as slang for lesser feelings, such as approval.

awful   an adjective. Don't use in place of adverbs such as *very*, *really* and *extremely*.

B

bail   money forfeited to a court if an accused person fails to appear at the trial

bale   bundle, as of hay

bond   bail as posted by a bondsman. To be specific, say someone *posted bail* or *bail was set at* instead of referring to bond.

baited   A hook, witness or bear is *baited*.

bated   Breath is *bated*, meaning "abated."

balance   in accounting, the credits minus the debits

remainder   part left over

ball   sphere

bawl   to cry

baloney   nonsense

bologna   a kind of lunch meat usually pronounced the same as *baloney*

band   musical group; something that encircles and constricts

banned   barred

bankrupt   should not be used to describe a company reorganizing under bankruptcy laws. A person or company is *bankrupt* only if declared to be by a court.

barbell   has adjustable weight

dumbbell   has fixed weight

bare   adj., nude

bear   n., the animal; v., to carry

baron   nobleman

barren   infertile

base   n., foundation, military headquarters, bag in baseball; adj., lacking quality

bass   adj., low-voiced; n., a type of fish; a voice or musical instrument with a low register. The voice or instrument is pronounced the same as *base*; the fish is pronounced like *mass* with a *b* instead of an *m*.

bases   plural of *base* and *basis*. As the plural of the former, pronounced *base-iss*; the plural of the latter, pronounced *bay-sees*.

basis   main support. Pronounced *base-iss*.

bazaar   marketplace

bizarre   odd

beach   n., sandy area; v., to run aground

beech   a kind of nut tree

beat   n., rhythm; v., to strike

beet   a kind of vegetable

because   preferred word for direct causal relationship

due to   Avoid using to mean *because*. If you do use it, the phrase should follow a form of *to be* and must modify a noun: Instead of *He resigned due to ill health*, write *His resignation was due to ill health*.

since   a temporal relationship

begs the question   This classically refers to circular reasoning rather than meaning "requires asking." But it's becoming more and more commonly used to mean "raises the question," especially in the media, and few people these days seem to know the traditional meaning.

belittle   Use to mean disparage, not merely ridicule.

bellow   to shout

billow   to surge in waves

bemused   adj., engrossed in thought, preoccupied, befuddled or confused; doesn't mean amused or slightly confused

confused   muddled or stupefying

berry   small fruit
bury   to put under something

berth   place of rest
birth   the emergence of something, especially living

beside   at the side of
besides   in addition to

best   for comparisons of three or more
better   for comparisons of two
bettor   one who gambles

be sure to   not *be sure and*

bi   prefix normally meaning every two. *Biweekly* means every two weeks.
semi   prefix meaning every half. *Semiweekly* means twice a week.

biannual   twice a year
biennial   once in two years

bide   to stay or wait. You ask someone to *bide* their tongue, not *bite* it.

bigger portion   not *bigger half*

bight   inward curve in a coast; slack part of a rope loop
bite   v., action involving the teeth; n., wound made by teeth, mouthful
byte   computer term for one group of binary digits

bimonthly   every two months
semimonthly   twice a month; every two weeks

blatant   conspicuous
flagrant   too obvious to ignore

bloc   coalition with a joint purpose or goal
block   cube; obstruction

blond   adjective for either sex; noun for male

blonde   noun for female, although some, male or female, would object to being reduced to a hair color

blow   A *blow* is dealt, not administered.

boar   male hog

boor   insensitive person

bore   n., someone who causes boredom; v., to drill

board   v., to get on a ship; n., plank or committee

bored   v., made a hole in; adj., experiencing ennui (boredom)

boarder   lodger who takes meals

border   boundary

boat   small, open vessel; exception: U-boat, submarine

ship   seagoing vessel larger than a boat

bold   fearless

bowled   past tense of *bowl*

bolder   more bold than

boulder   big rock

bomb   It's not a *bomb* if it doesn't have an explosive charge. A tear-gas canister is, therefore, not a *bomb*.

born   to have been given birth

borne   to have given birth to; to have put up with; to have carried

borough   a municipal area with at least some self-governing rights; formerly, meant a walled town

borrow   to be lent something

burro   ass; donkey

burrow   n., hole in the ground; v., to dig. Our favorite stylebook rule, from an old *UPI Stylebook*, said that a burro is an ass, a burrow is a hole in the ground, and a journalist should know the difference.

bosom   The word is singular in regard to one person: For example, a woman has a *bosom*, not *bosoms*. But it also applies to both sexes: *He clasped the child to his bosom.*

bough   a branch

bow   n., forward part of a boat, a loop, an archer's weapon; v., to bend
in respect

bouillon   broth
bullion   gold or silver ingots

boy   young male
buoy   n., floating marker; v., to lift up

Brahman   Hindu caste; cattle breed
Brahmin   aristocrat

brake   v., to stop; n., stopping mechanism
break   v., to shatter; n., interval

bravery   what someone has within
courage   what someone shows when tested

breach   violation, opening or tear
breech   bottom, rear or back

breath   n., air taken into the lungs
breathe   v., to take air into the lungs

briar   pipe
brier   thorned plant; root used for making pipes

bridal   pertains to a bride or marriage ceremony
bridle   what you put on a horse's head to restrain it; rigging on a kite

bring   to carry toward
take   to carry away

Britain   country
Briton   inhabitant

broach   to make a hole; to start a discussion
brooch   ornament

brunet   adjective for male or female; noun for male

brunette   noun for female, although many, male or female, would object to being reduced to a hair color

bunch   a number of inanimate objects

crowd   a number of people

burger   hamburger

burgher   person who lives in a town

burglary   involves entering a building with the intent of committing a crime

larceny   taking of property that equals or exceeds an amount set by law

robbery   stealing involving violence or the threat of violence

theft   stealing without violence or threat of violence

bus   n., vehicle; v., to move by means of a bus (present participle: *busing*)

buss   to kiss (present participle: *bussing*)

buy   v., to purchase

by   prep.

bye   n., something secondary; goodbye

C

cache   n., storage place

cash   n., money; v., to pay or get money for a check

calendar   chart that records dates

calender   machine for pressing cloth or paper

colander   strainer

calk   cleat

caulk   to make watertight

callous   adj., hardened emotionally

callus   n., hardened skin

Calvary   where Jesus was crucified (near Jerusalem); often part of church names

cavalry   soldiers on horseback

Usage

can, could   is able. *Could* is the past and conditional form of *can*.

may, might   has permission; will possibly. *Might* is the past and conditional form of *may*. Some say *may* implies that uncertainty still persists, while *might* refers to a possibility in the past, but others say *might* is less definite than *may*.

canapé   appetizer

canopy   awning

cannon   gun

canon   church law; body of literature; a type of musical composition

cannot help, can only   not *cannot help but*

canvas   cloth used for tents

canvass   to go through a district to seek support or opinions

cape   a sleeveless garment over the back and shoulders; land projecting into the water

cloak   usually, a sleeveless garment worn from the shoulders to the knees or below and not necessarily just over the back and shoulders; something that hides or conceals; v., to hide with a cloak

capital   city

Capitol   building (note capital letter in all cases)

carat   unit of weight; used with diamonds and other gems

caret   editing mark for inserting something

carrot   vegetable

karat   measure for the purity of gold (24 being pure)

karate   martial art

careen   to sway (especially a boat or ship)

career   v., to move quickly, especially at full speed; n., course or profession

carom   to rebound after striking

carousal   drunken revel

carousel   merry-go-round

cast   n., group of actors; v., to throw

caste   social class

caster   little wheel under furniture
castor   ingredient in perfume; name of a laxative oil: *castor oil*

casual   not formal
causal   pertaining to a cause

celebrant   participant or presiding official in a religious service
celebrator   participant in a nonreligious celebration

celibate   unmarried; abstaining from sexual intercourse
chaste   morally pure; abstaining from sexual intercourse

cell   a small unit of biology or of a group
sell   to offer for others to buy

cellar   a basement; an underground room
seller   one who sells

cement   the powder in concrete
concrete   the rocklike substance of which roads, sidewalks and walls are made

censer   incense burner
censor   n., one who previews things to prevent others from seeing material deemed harmful; v., to preview things to prevent others from seeing potentially harmful material
censure   official reprimand

centers around   Use *centers on* or *revolves around* because the center is the middle of a circle—the point around which things circle.

cereal   grain used for food; food made from grain
serial   arranged in a series or sequence

ceremonial   formal
ceremonious   overly concerned with formalities

cession   an act of granting, surrendering or transferring something
session   the term of a meeting

Usage

chafe   to rub; to wear away by rubbing

chaff   husks

champagne   bubbly wine made only in the Champagne province in France. An imitation of that wine made elsewhere is *sparkling wine*.

Champaign   city in Illinois

champing at the bit   not *chomping at the bit*

channel   the number of a station on a TV or satellite radio

station   a media outlet on radio, internet or TV when referred to by its name rather than number or frequency

character   what a person is

reputation   what others think a person is

cheap   inexpensive

cheep   to chirp

childish   immature; pejorative term

childlike   maintaining the positive qualities of childhood

choose   present-tense form of *to choose*

chose   past-tense form of *to choose*

choral   adj., written for a choir or chorus

chorale   n., choral composition or choir

coral   n., substance built by sea creatures that forms a reef; adj., reddish pink

corral   n., fenced-off area for horses

chord   harmonizing musical notes

cord   string or rope; unit of wood; part of the body: spinal cord, vocal cord

cite   to quote in support

sight   something seen; the sense

site   n., a place; v., to locate

citizen   one who shares in the political rights of a nation. A person is a *citizen* only of a nation, not of a city, county, region or state.

resident   a person who lives in an area

city   An area isn't a *city* unless it's incorporated.

civic   pertains to a city

civil   pertains to polite society, laws other than military or criminal, or an internal war

classic   n., something of the highest rank; adj., recognized for many years as a model

classical   adj., pertaining to a certain historical period, especially ancient Greece and Rome, or pertaining to serious music

client   person who uses the services of a professional

customer   person who buys something

patient   person who's treated by a health or medical provider

climactic   refers to a climax

climatic   refers to the weather

close   to shut; to end

clothes   garments

cloths   fabrics

coarse   rough or crude

course   class; series; division of a meal; field for a sport

collaborate   to work together

collude   to cooperate secretly to deceive; although the term is often used and even defined in dictionaries as conspiring, colluding is not a federal crime in the U.S. except in antitrust law

connive   to provide secret help or indulgence

conspire   to plot together in secrecy an unlawful act; conspiracy is a crime

comic   n., funny person

comical   adj., funny

commandeer   to seize something for use by the government, especially the military. Using it merely to mean to take something by force is colloquial. Using it to mean to take charge of is incorrect.

commensurate   corresponding to

commiserate   to feel sympathy for

Usage

common   shared; belonging to jointly

mutual   reciprocal; having the same relationship

compare to   to point out similarities

compare with   to point out similarities and differences

contrast   to point out differences and, perhaps, similarities, as well

complacent   satisfied

complaisant   obliging

complement   v., to complete by supplementing; n., that which supplements and completes

compliment   v., to praise; n., praise

complementary   supplying what's missing in another

complimentary   free; praising

comply with   not *comply to*

compose   to create or put together: *The whole is composed of the parts.* Some editors insist that *compose* be used only in passive voice, but others permit it to be used actively to mean constitute. AP accepts its use in both voices.

comprise   to contain: *The whole comprises the parts.*

constitute   to form or make up: *The parts constitute the whole.*

comprehensible   understandable

comprehensive   complete

compulsive   obsessive

impulsive   spontaneous; based on whim rather than thought

concerned about   preoccupied

concerned with   engaged in

concert   requires two or more performers

recital   given by one performer

condone   Use to mean excuse, forgive, pardon or overlook. Do not use to mean accept, approve, certify, endorse or sanction.

connotation   implied meaning or emotional flavor of a word or phrase

denotation   actual or literal meaning of a word or phrase

conscience   n., a moral sense

conscious   adj., awake

consciousness   n., awareness

consecutive   one after another without a break

successive   one after another

consequent   following as a natural result; used when the events are related

subsequent   following; used when the events are not related

consul   diplomat

council   deliberative body; assembly of advisers

counsel   n., legal adviser or advice; v., to advise

contact   n., a connection point or someone with whom one communicates. It's best avoided as a verb; use instead words like *call, visit* or *write*.

contagious   transmitted by contact

infectious   transmitted by water, air and the like

contemptible   deserving of scorn

contemptuous   showing or feeling scorn

contiguous to   not *contiguous with*

continual   repeated

continuous   uninterrupted

contrast to   not *contrast with*

controversial   Avoid this buzzword. Instead, show why the person or thing is controversial rather than merely labeling it so.

convince   AP says you *convince that* or *of*; some editors say you convince yourself; *The Washington Post Deskbook* says *convince* is "to win over by argument."

persuade   The AP says you *persuade to*; some editors say you persuade others; *The Washington Post Deskbook* says *persuade* is "to win over by appeal to reason or emotion."

copyright   adj., n. , v. AP says, for example, write "a copyright story."

copyrighted   v., past tense of copyright; e.g., "She copyrighted her work."

core   center

corps   group of people

corpse   dead body

co-respondent   a person in a divorce suit charged by the complainant with committing adultery with the person from whom the complainant is seeking a divorce

correspondent   one who writes; that which matches with something else

couldn't care less   Do not use *could care less*.

couldn't help   Don't use *couldn't help but*.

council   see *consul*

councilor   member of a council

counselor   adviser; lawyer; aide at an embassy

country   a geographical territory

nation   a political entity

courage   see *bravery*

courteous   kind beyond politeness

polite   having good manners

creak   to squeak

creek   a stream

credible   believable; trustworthy (not merely persuasive)

creditable   worthy of approval, credit or praise

credulity, credulousness   synonyms meaning a tendency to believe too readily

credulous   gullible

crescendo   Because a crescendo is a gradual rise in sound volume or intensity, it is redundant to write "rose to a crescendo."

criteria   plural
criterion   singular

crochet   a kind of knitting
crotchet   an odd fancy

cue   signal; billiard stick
queue   lineup

currant   n., a kind of berry
current   n., flow; adj., present

customary   set by custom
habitual   set by habit
usual   ordinary

cymbal   percussive musical instrument
symbol   something that stands for something else

cypress   tree
Cyprus   country

D

dais, podium   a platform to stand on while speaking
lectern   the reading desk behind which a speaker stands

damage   harm done to something
damages   compensation a court awards someone for a loss or an injury

damaged   means partially harmed. Don't say *partially damaged* or *completely damaged*.
destroyed   means completely harmed. Don't say *partially destroyed* or *completely destroyed*.

data   usually takes a plural verb: *The data have been gathered* (many separate items); occasionally takes a singular verb: *The data is sound* (viewed as a unit)
datum   singular

but   a first appearance. Do not use as a verb.

decease to die; to go away
disease illness

decide whether not *decide if*

decimate The word, originally meaning to kill every tenth person, has come to mean destroy, and most authorities now find that meaning acceptable.

defective faulty
deficient lacking

definite certain, clear or fixed
definitive thorough; authoritative

defuse to stop
diffuse v., to scatter; adj., scattered

déjà vu Use to refer only to the *illusion* that something has been experienced before. If it actually was experienced, the feeling isn't *déjà vu*.

democracy rule by the people directly
republic rule by representatives of the people. In the strictest sense, the U.S. is a republic rather than a democracy.

demur v., to raise objections; n., an objection raised
demure adj., quiet and serious

deny to say something is false
dispute v., to argue; n., an argument
rebuff v., to snub; n., a snub
rebuke v., to condemn for an offense; n., a reproof
rebut to argue to the contrary
refute to prove something is false

depart *Depart* should be followed by *from* except in the phrase *depart this life*.

depositary person you entrust with keeping something safe
depository place where things are kept safe

deprecate   to disapprove of

depreciate   to belittle or devalue

desert   n., barren region, also used in phrase *just deserts*; v., to abandon

dessert   n., sweet course in a meal. Remember the two *s*'s by this hint, "If it's dessert, I'll take two!"

desert island   not *deserted island*. *Desert* as an adjective means barren and uninhabited.

detract   to lessen; to take from

distract   to divert attention

devalued   not *devaluated*

device   noun

devise   verb

diagnose   Doctors diagnose a patient's *condition*, not the patient.

dialogue   According to language columnist William Safire (1929–2009), although many insist that the word be used only as a noun to mean a conversation between two people, it may also be used as a verb and as a noun to mean a conversation among more than two people. The word is derived from the Greek *dia*, meaning "across," not from *di*, meaning "two," Safire points out. The use of the word as a verb is not a recent invention but dates back to 1597.

die   to lose life or to cut with a die; forms: *died, has died, is dying* (losing life), *is dieing* (cutting a die)

dye   to change color with a chemical; forms: *dyed, has dyed, is dyeing*

different from   *The AP Stylebook* says never to write *different than*. But *The Washington Post Deskbook* probably is correct in stating that either is correct, but *different from* is preferred. Patricia O'Connor adds helpfully in her book *Woe Is I* that "*different than* is almost always wrong" but that both are acceptable just before a clause, such as something was different from how or than it was years ago. In Britain, the common phrasing is *different to*.

differs from   is different

differs with   disagrees

dilemma   Often misused to mean merely an unpleasant situation or a quandary, the word means a choice between two (and only two) bad alternatives, although it can also mean (but rarely does) a hard choice between two good alternatives. It shouldn't be used to mean a choice between a good alternative and a bad one. Also note that there is no *n* in *dilemma*.

disapprove   to express disfavor
disprove   to show something to be false

disassemble   to take apart
dissemble   to conceal true feelings

disburse   to pay money
dispense   to deal out
disperse   to scatter or vanish

disc   as in *compact disc*, *disc jockey*, *Blu-ray Disc*; part of a plow
disk   any round, flat object; computer disk; anatomical structure

discover   to find something that was not seen before
invent   to create something

discredit   to destroy confidence in
disparage   to belittle

discreet   prudent
discrete   separate

disinterested   impartial (may be interested but neutral)
uninterested   indifferent (lacking interest)

dissent from   not *dissent with*

distinct   unmistakable
distinctive   unique
distinguished   excellent

divers   adj., several; n., people who dive in the water. The adjective is pronounced like the word *diverse*, the noun like the word *diver* with a *z* on the end.
diverse   different

dock large excavated basin used for receiving ships between voyages

pier platform extending from shore over water

wharf platform parallel to shore

done past participle of *do*

dun v., to annoy, as for payment of a debt; adj., grayish brown

dose amount of medicine

doze to nap

doubt if Change to *doubt that* or *doubt whether*, depending on meaning.

doubt that used in negative statements and questions; *I don't doubt that*

doubt whether used in positive statements indicating uncertainty as to options; *I doubt whether*

draft adj., drawn from a keg, such as draft beer, or used for pulling loads, as a draft horse; n. conscription; v., to conscript

draught chiefly the British spelling of draft; AP says use draft beer, not draught beer

dribble to bounce a ball

drivel nonsense

drier less moist

dryer device for drying things

drunk adj., used after the verb *to be*

drunken adj., used before nouns

dual composed of two

duel fight between two people

due to see *because*

E

each other involving two

one another involving more than two

eclectic   drawing on a variety of sources

electric   operated by electricity: *electric can opener*

electrical   pertains to electricity but not necessarily operated by it: *electrical engineer*

electronic   produced by a flow of electrons in vacuum tubes, transistors or microchips

ecology   the science of the relationship between organisms and environment

environment   surroundings

economic   pertains to finances, especially their management

economical   thrifty

economics   the social science dealing with economic matters such as the production and consumption of wealth

eek   an exclamation

eke   to get with difficulty

effective   having an effect

effectual   true to its purpose

efficacious   produces the desired effect

efficient   competent; productive

egoistic   self-centered

egotistic   boastful

either of the three   Change to *any of the three.*

elder, eldest   used with people

older, oldest   used with things or people

electric   see *eclectic*

elegy   sad song or poem, often written of someone who has died

eulogy   funeral oration

elicit   to draw out

illicit   prohibited

eligible   qualified to be chosen

illegible   indecipherable

elongated   increased in space

extended   increased in range

prolonged   beyond normal limits

protracted   extended needlessly to the point of boredom

emanate   to emit

eminent   prominent

immanent   inherent in; present throughout the universe

imminent   about to happen

emerge   to come into view

immerge   to plunge into

immerse   to put completely into liquid

emigrant   one who leaves a country, or *emigrates.*

immigrant   one who enters a country, or *immigrates.*

endemic   native

epidemic   rapidly spread

engine   Large vehicles (ships, airplanes, rockets) have engines.

motor   Small vehicles (including boats) and appliances have motors. A car
    may be said to have either an engine or a motor.

enormity   great wickedness

enormousness   vastness

entitled   deserving (of); gave a title to (active voice)

entitlement   benefit

titled   designated by a title (passive voice); gave a title to (active voice)

right   just claim; protection from government overreaching, as opposed to an
    entitlement

entomology   study of insects

etymology   study of word origins

envelop   to surround; to cover (accent on *vel*)

envelope   container for a letter (accent on *en*)

Usage

envisage   to imagine; to visualize

envision   to foresee; to visualize

epigram   concise, clever statement or poem

epigraph   an inscription on a monument or building, or a quotation at the beginning of a piece of writing

epitaph   statement or inscription in memory of someone dead

epithet   term characterizing someone or something

equable   steady

equitable   fair

equally (as) good as   Change to *as good as*.

equivalent   of equal value

erasable   capable of being erased

irascible   quick-tempered

errant   misbehaving; traveling to seek adventure (see also *arrant*)

erring   sinning; making mistakes

error   a deviation from the truth

lie   an intentional untruth told to deceive; see also *lay*

mistake   an inaccuracy resulting from a misunderstanding or carelessness

erstwhile   means former, not *earnest*

eruption   sudden, violent outbreak

irruption   forcible entry; sudden increase in animal population

eschatology   branch of theology dealing with death and judgment

scatology   obsession with excrement

especially   particularly; notably

specially   for a special purpose or occasion

estimate   Because an estimate is an approximation, it is redundant to follow it with *about*. So, instead of writing "The crowd was *estimated at about 500*," write "The crowd was *estimated at 500*."

ever so often   frequently

every so often   occasionally

every body   each single person
everybody   all of the people; everyone; all the people

every day   adv.: *editing every day*
everyday   adj.: *everyday editing*

every once in a while   not *every once and a while*

every one   each single one
everyone   everybody; all the people

evoke   to call up or inspire emotions, memories or responses
invoke   to call for the help of, as in prayer

exalt   to raise in rank; to praise
exult   to rejoice

exceedingly   extremely
excessively   too much

exceptionable   objectionable
exceptional   unusual

excite   to arouse emotionally
incite   to stir to action

exercise   to work out physically
exorcise   to drive out (as in *driving out demons*)

expatiate   to elaborate
expiate   to atone for

expatriate   someone who has left a country to live elsewhere
ex-patriot   former patriot

exploded   Avoid the hyperbolic expression that someone "exploded" when
what you mean is that he or she became angry.

extant   still existing
extent   range

extended illness   Change to *long illness*.

extra bases   A double is only an *extra-base* hit.

F

face   v., to confront immediately, so should not be used for something someone will confront in the future, such as a jail term before being sentenced.

facetious   merely amusing
factious   creating dissent
factitious   not genuine
fictitious   imaginary
fractious   unruly, irritable

faint   adj., weak; v., to swoon
feign   to pretend
feint   fake attack

fair   n., periodical exhibition; adj., just
fare   n., price to travel, passenger or food provided; v., to progress

faker   someone who engages in fraud
fakir   holy man, especially a Muslim or Hindu who performs magic feats

famed   The English writers William Shakespeare and John Dryden used *famed* in place of *famous*, but most editors reject that usage because they consider it journalese.

famous   well-known
infamous   notorious

farther   used for literal distance
further   used for figurative distance

fatal   resulting in death
fateful   deciding the fate of

faze   to disturb
phase   stage of development

feat   deed

feet   plural of foot, whether referring to multiples of 12 inches or to the human appendages on which shoes are worn

fete   lavish party

feel   should be reserved for physical or emotional sensations

think   the proper term to use for mental activity

fewer   smaller in number; used for plural items; opposite of many

less   smaller in amount; used for singular items; opposite of much

under   Some editors prefer this be used for spatial comparisons only, such as *under the bridge*, rather than to indicate a smaller amount, such as *under $100*.

figuratively   in a metaphorical sense

literally   actually; often confused with *figuratively* by exaggerating something to hyperbolic terms (e.g., *I have literally never been hungrier.*)

figurine   representation, up to 2 feet tall, of a person or an animal

sculptor   artist who creates three-dimensional art

sculpture   any three-dimensional work of art

statue   big representation of a person or an animal

statuette   representation, from 1 to 2 feet tall, of a person or an animal

statute   law

filet   net or lace with a pattern of squares; *filet mignon* (other boneless strips of meat may be spelled either as *filet* or *fillet*)

fillet   a narrow strip (as of ribbon or meat); to cut meat or fish so as to create a fillet

find   to discover

fined   penalized

fine   penalty of money

sentence   penalty of time. A convict is *sentenced to five years and fined $5,000*, not *sentenced to five years and a $5,000 fine.*

fir   a kind of evergreen tree

for   preposition

fur   the hair of an animal; garment made from the hair of an animal

Usage

fired   A legally dangerous word too often used loosely, *fired* shouldn't be used to describe someone who was laid off from or who quit a job.

first annual   Change to *first*. Something isn't annual until the second time.

fiscal   financial
physical   pertaining to the body

fitful   restless or spasmodic, not something that's fitting. A fitful sleep, for example, would be one of tossing and turning.

flack   pejorative term for a press agent
flak   antiaircraft shells; strong criticism

flair   talent
flare   n., light; v., to start suddenly

flammable   preferred over *inflammable* by The Washington Post. But many editors consider *flammable* an illiteracy.
inflammable   Use this rather than *flammable* when speaking of temperaments.

inflammation   medical condition
inflammatory   arouses emotions

flaunt   to show off
flout   to defy; to disdain

flea   a kind of insect
flee   to leave

flew   past tense of *fly*

flier   formerly AP's preferred term for handbill or someone who flies in an aircraft, but now only preferred in the phrase "take a flier," meaning take a risk
flyer   since 2017, this is AP's preferred spelling for a handbill or someone who flies in a plane
Flyer   used in the proper names of some trains and buses

floe   layer, expanse; ice floe
flow   v., to move as a liquid does; to move gently; n., a current

flotsam   wreckage of a ship or its cargo floating at sea

jetsam   things jettisoned from a ship to lighten its load

lagan (ligan)   jetsam attached to a buoy to make recovery easier

flounder   v., to struggle helplessly; n., a fish

founder   to sink or become disabled. *First you flounder, then you founder.*

flour   ground grain

flower   blossom

flowed   past tense of *flow*

flown   past participle of *fly*; sometimes mistakenly used for *flowed*

flu   influenza

flue   smoke duct in a chimney

following   Avoid using as a preposition. Change to *after*.

forbear   to cease; to refrain from

forebear   ancestor

forbid   you *forbid to*

prohibit   you *prohibit from*

forbidding   difficult

foreboding   n., prediction or portent; adj., ominous

forced   compulsory; strained

forceful   effective; full of force

forcible   involves use of brute force

forego   to precede

foregoing   preceding

forgo   to go without; to relinquish

forgoing   giving up; abstaining from

foreword   introduction

forward   onward

formally   in a formal manner

formerly   previously

fort   enclosure for defense
forte   n., strength; adj., loud (Italian)

forth   onward
fourth   place after third

forthcoming   about to take place; willing to give information
forthright   frank

fortuitous   accidental; by chance
fortunate   lucky

foul   adj., rotten
fowl   n., bird

freeze   to form ice
frieze   decorative band

fullness   abundance
fulsome   disgusting; insincerely excessive; do not use to mean full, as in a *fulsome figure*

furl   to roll up
furrow   n., wrinkle, rut in the soil; v., to wrinkle

G

gaff   hook
gaffe   blunder

gait   a way of walking
gate   entrance

gamble   to wager
gambol   to frolic

gantlet   flogging, as in *running a gantlet*; sometimes, also used as a variant of the preferable *gauntlet* when referring to a glove
gauntlet   glove, as in *throwing down a gauntlet*

gender   grammatical term for whether a word is masculine, feminine or neuter; sex-based role assigned by society (used when distinction is sociological rather than biological)

sex   describes whether a being is male or female (used when distinction is biological rather than sociological)

genius   Avoid this overused, loosely used word.

genteel   affectedly elegant

gentile   to Jews, anyone not Jewish; to Mormons, anyone not Mormon

gentle   not rough

gibe   to taunt

jibe   to conform; to change course

jive   to kid; to talk in a lingo

gild   to cover with gold

guild   workers' union

glutinous   like glue

gluttonous   pertaining to overeating

gorilla   ape

guerrilla   fighter

gothic   gloomy or fantastic, as in *gothic novel*

Gothic   all other uses, such as medieval or pertaining to the Goths

gourmand   big eater

gourmet   connoisseur of food

grate   grill for holding wood in a fireplace

great   larger than normal

grill   n., metal bars for cooking meat or fish; v., to broil meat or fish, to question harshly

grille   screen or grating, such as on the front of a car

grisly   gruesome

gristly   having cartilage

grizzled   gray-streaked

grizzly   n., brown bear; adj., gray

guarantee   n., pledge to replace a product or refund the purchase price if the product doesn't work; v., to make such a pledge

guaranty   n., warranty; pledge to assume someone else's responsibility; a financial security

H

hail   v., to greet, to acclaim after the fact; n., ice from the sky

hale   v., to take into court, to drag; adj., healthy

half   see *(in, into) halves*

half a   not *a half*

half brothers, half sisters   children with only one parent in common

stepbrothers, stepsisters   children related by the marriage of parents

half-mast   Flags are lowered (not raised) to half-mast on ships and at naval stations only.

half-staff   Flags are lowered (not raised) to half-staff everywhere else.

hall   large room

haul   v., to drag forcibly, to carry; n., booty, distance to be traveled

hangar   aircraft shelter

hanger   someone or something that suspends something else: *paper hanger*, *coat hanger*

hanged   executed

hung   put up

hapless   unfortunate

hopeless   lacking hope

hardy   bold, rugged. A plant that can survive under unfavorable conditions is *hardy*.

hearty   jovial; nourishing

heal   to recover from injury

heel   back of the foot; bottom of the shoe; end piece of bread

healthful giving health. Foods are *healthful*.

healthy having health. Living things are *healthy*.

hear to listen

here at this place

heartrending not *heart-rendering*

helix three-dimensional design

spiral two-dimensional design; exception: *spiral staircase*

hero someone who does something that's brave, not merely someone who dies

heroin drug

heroine female hero, although some consider this term a diminutive sexist one and prefer *hero* for either males or females

hew to chop

hue color

hike now OK in AP for increase as well as noun and verb for a walk

hippie a 1960s term for a flower child, or New Age type

hippy having big hips

hire to employ; to gain use of

lease to grant or gain by contract, especially property

let to grant by contract, especially property

historic having importance in history

historical concerned with history. A *historic* book made history, but a *historical* book is about it.

hoard n., storehouse; v., to store

horde n., swarm

Hobson's choice This is not a dilemma; it means no choice at all.

holey full of holes

holly a kind of plant popular at Christmas

holy sacred

wholly entirely

holocaust   A bad fire or accident is not a holocaust unless many people are killed or there is great destruction. Have enough respect for the Holocaust (the mass killing of civilians, especially the genocide of 6 million Jews, by the Nazis) in World War II not to use this word lightly.

home   place where a person or family lives. A *home* cannot be sold.

house   building occupied by a person or family. A *house* can be sold.

homicide   slaying or killing

manslaughter   homicide without premeditation or malice

murder   malicious, premeditated homicide (or, in some states, a homicide done while committing another felony). Do not call a killing a *murder* until someone has been convicted.

homogeneous   having similar structure: *Mayan and Egyptian pyramids are homogeneous.*

homogenize   to make homogeneous

homogenous   having similar structure because of common descent: *Mayan and Egyptian pyramids are not thought to be homogenous in that they seem to have developed independently.*

however   May be used grammatically to show a contrast at the beginning, middle or end of a sentence, provided it is placed next to, or as close as possible to, what it modifies. It generally works best in the middle of a sentence because at the end it tends to come well after the contrast to which it draws attention and at the beginning could be replaced with the more concise *but*.

hurdle   to jump

hurtle   to throw

hypercritical   too severe

hypocritical   pretending to be something you're not

I

I hope   not *I would hope*

ideal   model or goal

idle   not busy

idol   worshipped image

idyll   scene, poem or event of rural simplicity; romantic interlude

identical with   not *identical to*. Compare to *compare to* versus *compare with*.

if   introduces a conditional clause: *if a, then b*

whether   introduces a noun clause involving two choices (the *or not* is redundant). Although most authorities say *if* and *whether* may be used interchangeably, many editors still insist on the distinction.

weather   atmospheric conditions

whither   where

wither   to dry up

imaginary   existing only in the imagination

imaginative   showing a high degree of imagination

imbecilic   The word is *imbecile* as either an adjective or a noun, although now its use is considered offensive.

immigrate   see *emigrate*

impassable   not capable of being passed

impassible   incapable of suffering or showing emotion

impeach   to accuse, not to convict

imperial   pertaining to an empire or emperor

imperious   domineering or proud

imply   to hint. Writers or speakers *imply*.

infer   to deduce. Readers or listeners *infer*.

imposter   one who levies a tax

impostor   one who pretends to be someone else

impracticable   said of a plan that's unworkable or a person who's unmanageable

impractical   said of an unwise plan or a person who can't handle practical matters

impugn   to challenge

impute   to attribute

impulsive   see *compulsive*

in behalf of   in formal support of

on behalf of   in formal representation of

(in, into) halves   not *in half*

in to   in and toward; preposition followed by an infinitive: *She went in to vote.*

into   in and within; preposition only: *She went into the building.*

into **[something]**   informal. Change to *interested in*.

inapt   inappropriate

inept   incompetent

inasmuch as   in view of the fact that

insofar as   to the degree that

incidence   rate at which something occurs

incidents   things that occur

incite   to arouse; see also *excite*

insight   clear understanding

including   Should only be used when what follows is part of the whole, not a complete list of the whole. In the latter case, *comprising* is better.

incredible   unbelievable

incredulous   skeptical

inculcate (in, into)   not *inculcate with*

independent of   not *independent from*

indeterminable   can't be determined

indeterminate   not fixed

indict   to charge with a crime

indite   to put into writing, although we would not recommend using this less-than-common word. Mainly, we note this appears sometimes as a misspelling of *indict*.

indoor   adjective

indoors   adverb

industrial   pertaining to industry
industrious   hardworking

inequity   unfairness
iniquity   wickedness

infinite   going on forever; large
infinitesimal   small

infectious   see *contagious*

inflammable   see *flammable*

ingenious   inventive
ingenuous   honest; forthright, perhaps to the point of naïveté

injuries   They're *suffered* or *sustained*, not *received*.

insistent   demanding
persistent   continuing firmly

insoluble   can't be dissolved
insolvable   can't be solved
insolvent   can't pay debts

instill into   not *instill with*

instinct   nonthinking, automatic response of animals
intuition   knowledge gained without conscious reasoning

integrate with   not *integrate into*

interment   burial
internment   detention

interstate   between states

intrastate   within a state
investigation of   not *investigation into*

Usage

ironically   adverb used to indicate something means the opposite of what it says or, more loosely, that there is a reversal in a turn of events. Should not be used to mean merely *coincidentally*.

it's   contraction for *it is* or *it has*.

its   possessive form of *it*

J

jail   where suspects and people convicted of misdemeanors are kept. Cities and counties have *jails*.

prison   where felons are kept. States and the federal government have *prisons*.

jam   made from the whole fruit (usually not citrus fruit)

jamb   side of a doorway or window frame

marmalade   made from the pulp and rinds of citrus fruit

preserves   fruit preserved by cooking with sugar

jerry-built   built poorly of cheap materials

jury-rigged   rigged for temporary use

judicial   pertaining to a judge or court

judicious   sound in judgment

juridical   pertaining to the administration of justice

juggler   person who juggles

jugular   neck vein

just deserts   not *just desserts*. Here, *deserts* means deserves, not after-dinner treats.

K

killed in a wreck   not *after* (or *following*) *a wreck*

(a) kind of   not *kind of a*

knave   rogue

nave   part of the interior of a church

knead   to mold

kneed   past tense of *knee*

need   to require

L

lam   an escape, as in *on the lam*. Because this is slang, journalists should avoid using it except in a quotation from a source, in which case they need to know how to spell it.

lamb   baby sheep

lama   Tibetan monk

llama   animal native to the Andes

languid   weak or sluggish

limpid   clear or calm

last   final; exceptions: *last week, last month, last year*

latest   most recent, as in *latest letter* (not the final one)

past   most recent, as in *past three years* (not the final ones)

laudable   praiseworthy

laudatory   expressing praise

lay   transitive v., to set down; principal parts: *lay, laid, have laid, is laying*

lie   intransitive v., to recline; principal parts: *lie, lay, have lain, is lying*

lye   a strong alkaline solution

leach   to separate a solid from its solution by percolation

leech   n., bloodsucker; v., to suck blood

lead   n., metal; v., present tense of *lead*

led   past tense of *lead*

leak   v., to go through an opening; n., hole

leek   n., vegetable related to the onion

lean   to stand diagonally, as in resting against something

lien   the right to take or sell a debtor's property as security or payment on a loan

leased   past tense of *lease*

least   smallest

leave alone   to depart from by oneself; to allow someone to stay by him- or herself

let alone   to allow to be undisturbed

lectern   see *dais, podium*

legendary   Avoid as an overused adjective.

legislator   lawmaker
legislature   body of lawmakers

lend   verb. Past tense is *lent*, not *loaned*.
loan   noun. Some authorities permit this to be used as a verb if what is lent is money, but you should try to avoid that usage.
lone   adj., by oneself

less   see *fewer*

lessee   tenant
lesser   smaller
lessor   landlord or one who grants a lease

lessen   to make less
lesson   instruction

let's   contraction for *let us*
lets   allows

levee   riverbank
levy   n., an imposed tax; v., to impose a tax

liable   legally responsible; should not be used to mean likely (see *apt*)
libel   v., defame; n., defamation
likely   probable or probably

lichen   funguslike plant that grows on trees and roots
liken   to compare

lightening   making less heavy or dark
lightning   flash of light in the sky

like each other   two are alike

like one another   more than two are alike

linage   number of lines of printed material

lineage   descent from an ancestor

lion's share   all, not just most. In Aesop's fable, the lion got the whole thing, not just most of it.

liqueur   sweet, flavored alcoholic drink

liquor   distilled alcoholic drink

literal   actual

littoral   pertaining to a shore

literally   see *figuratively*

livid   Use to mean furious or black-and-blue. It is often misused to mean vivid or red.

load   v., to pack; n., a pack

lode   deposit of ore

loath   adj., reluctant; is followed by *to*

loathe   v., to dislike greatly

located   set

situated   set on a significant site

loose   v., to unbind; adj., not tight

lose   v., to fail to win; to fail to keep

luxuriant   abundant

luxurious   comfortable or self-indulgent

M

magnate   powerful person in business

magnet   metal object that attracts iron

Usage

majority   more than half

plurality   largest number but less than half

mall   shopping area

maul   to handle roughly

mania   abnormally intense enthusiasm for something

philia   tendency toward or abnormal attraction to something

phobia   abnormal fear of something

manikin   model of a human body with parts that detach

mannequin   clothes dummy

manner   way; see also *to the manner born*

manor   estate

manslaughter   see *homicide*

mantel   wood or marble structure above a fireplace

mantle   sleeveless cloak; region between Earth's core and crust

margin   the difference between two figures

ratio   the relation between two figures. If a committee votes 4–2, the *margin* is two votes and the *ratio* is 2-to-1.

marital   pertaining to marriage

marshal   v., to direct; n., title of an official in the military or in a police or fire department; the person leading a parade; sometimes, used capitalized as a name

Marshall   word as name only: *Marshall McLuhan, Marshall Islands*

martial   warlike; pertaining to the military, as in *martial law*

mask   n., a disguise; v., to disguise

masque   masquerade; amateur musical drama

masseur   man who gives massages; preferred term is *massage therapist*

masseuse   woman who gives massages; preferred term is *massage therapist*

masterful   powerful; fit to command

masterly   expert

material   thing out of which something is made

materiel   supplies of a military force

may, might   see *can, could*

may be   v., as in *it may be late*

maybe   adv., perhaps

meat   flesh of an animal

meet   v., to get together or be introduced; n., a gathering; adj., proper

mete   v., to distribute; n., a measure or boundary

medal   award

meddle   to interfere

metal   class of elements, including gold, iron, copper and so on

mettle   character

media   n., usually should be plural; adj., as in *media companies;* AP now also accepts, starting in 2016, *media* as singular when referred to as a monolithic group, as when a Republican says, "The mainstream media has become an arm of the Democratic Party."

medium   singular: *The medium is the message.*

meeting took place   not *meeting occurred.* Planned events take place; unplanned events occur.

meretricious   deceptive; attracting attention in a vulgar or gaudy way; deceptive or insincere

meritorious   deserving merit

might   conditional form of *may;* see *can, could*

mite   small arachnid; small object; small amount

militate   to work against

mitigate   to lessen

miner   one who mines

minor   adj., underage, lesser; n., one who is underage

minks   plural for the furry animal

minx   mischievous girl

mislead   present tense of the verb meaning to lead astray

misled   past tense of the verb meaning to lead astray

misnomer   This means an incorrect name for a person or thing, not merely any mistake.

misogamy   hatred of marriage

misogyny   hatred of women

mistake   see *error*

moat   ditch filled with water for protection (around a castle)

mote   speck, as of dust

momentary   short-lived

momentous   important

momentarily   Like the adjective *momentary*, this adverb means lasting only a moment. Some usage guides suggest it shouldn't be used to mean in a moment, although most consider that acceptable.

moot   open to argument

mute   speechless

moral   adj., virtuous; n., lesson

morale   confidence or spirits of a person or group

more important   not *more importantly*. The phrase is a shortening of *what is more important*.

more than   used with figures: *more than 60 people*

over   best used in spatial references, according to many editors, but AP dropped the distinction in 2012 and now allows *over* for either *above* or *more than*

morning   early part of the day

mourning   grieving

motif   main theme or repeated figure

motive   inner drive

motor   see *engine*

mucous   adj., secreting mucus: *mucous membrane*

mucus   n., liquid secreted

mull   Contrary to the use in many headlines, *mull* should not be used to mean consider. It is acceptable idiomatically, though, when followed by *over*, to mean ponder.

murder   see *homicide*

mutual   shared. Because it applies to a relationship between two, this adjective shouldn't be used in the broader sense to mean shared or common, which may refer to a relationship among more than two; exception: *mutual fund*.
reciprocal   interacting

myriad   a large indefinite number. *Myriad* should be used as an adjective, not a noun: *myriad ways*, not *a myriad of ways*.

N

nab   Use to mean grab, steal or snatch; don't use if something was earned.

nation   see *country*

nauseated   how you feel when your stomach turns
nauseous   what something is if it makes your stomach turn

naval   pertaining to the navy
navel   n., belly button or depression resembling a belly button, as in navel orange (an orange with such a depression)

negligent   careless
negligible   unimportant; small

neither   not either. Alone, *neither* is singular, not plural, so you would write, for example, *neither is*, not *neither are*.
nether   below

new   recent
novel   unusual

no body   adj., n.; no person's body
nobody   pro.; no one

nohow   Avoid this, using *instead* or *anyway*.

noisome   offensive

noisy   clamorous

nor   Some people use *nor* instead of *or* after any negative expression, but most grammarians say this is an overcorrection. *Nor* should be used after *neither* instead of *or*.

notable, noteworthy   worth noting

noted   famous

noticeable   capable of being seen; prominent

notoriety   a bad reputation

notorious   having a bad reputation

O

O   *O* is not followed by a comma and is used in addressing someone: *O Father, I have something to tell you.*

Oh   *Oh* is followed by a comma or an exclamation point and is used for exclamation rather than address: *Oh, my!*

oar   long paddle

o'er   over (poetic)

or   conjunction

ore   mineral deposit

observance   the act of paying heed to a custom or ritual

observation   the act of viewing

obsolete   Don't use this adjective as a verb.

obtuse   see *abstruse*

ocean   water between continents, the floor of which is made of dense basaltic rock

sea   narrower body of water than an ocean, the floor of which is made of lighter granitic rock of the continent

oculist   may be either an ophthalmologist or an optometrist

ophthalmologist   physician treating illnesses of the eyes

optician   makes eyeglasses (need not be a physician)

optometrist   measures vision (need not be a physician)

odious   hateful
odorous   fragrant

official   authorized
officious   meddlesome

older, oldest   see *elder, eldest*

omnifarious   of all kinds
omnivorous   eating any kind of food

on each side   not *on either side*

once in a while   not *once and awhile*

once removed   First cousins, once removed, are a generation apart; for example, your first cousin's child is your first cousin, once removed; your first cousin's child and your child are second cousins.

one another   see *each other*

ongoing   This adjective usually says nothing because the use of a present-tense verb alone means *still in existence.*

opaque   cannot be seen through

translucent   can be seen through but not clearly; allows light through
transparent   can be seen through clearly

oral   see *aural*

ordinance   law. An ordinance is adopted or approved, not passed.
ordnance   weapons and ammunition

other   adj., *Turn the other cheek. Other* is required in comparisons of the same class: *My car breaks down more than any other car I've owned.* Otherwise, omit.
otherwise   adv., *We should add more reinforcement to the wall, or otherwise it might collapse.*

over   see *more than*

over and over   Avoid this. Instead write *again and again*.

overdo   to do to excess

overdue   tardy

overly   Don't use. *Over* is already an adverb and should be used instead. Say someone is *overqualified*, not *overly qualified*.

own   Often redundant, as in *Do your own thing*.

P

paddy   swamp

patty   flat, usually fried, cake or piece of meat pressed together, such as a hamburger patty

pail   bucket

pale   adj., light

pain   n., hurt; v., to hurt

pane   sheet of glass

pained   receiving pain

painful   giving pain

pair   couple

pare   to trim

pear   a kind of fruit

palate   roof of the mouth

palette   board on which paint is mixed

pallet   small, hard bed; small platform for moving and storing cargo; tool for mixing clay; tool for applying gold leaf

parameter   a constant used for determining the value of variables. Avoid using to mean boundary or factor.

perimeter   the curved, outer boundary of an area

pardon   to release a person from further punishment for a crime

parole   early release of someone imprisoned

probation   the punishment received by one who is sentenced for a crime but not sent to prison

parity   equality
parody   comic imitation

parlay   to increase
parley   to talk

part   piece
portion   allotment

partake of   to share
participate in   to take part in

partially   to a limited degree; in a biased way
partly   part of the whole

passed   v., past tense of *pass*
past   n., history; adj., most recent (see *last*)

patent   adj., obvious or plain; n., a legal protection for a product
patented   adj., legally protected by a patent

patience   endurance
patients   people receiving treatment

peaceable   disposed to peace; promoting calm
peaceful   tranquil; not characterized by strife. Suspects surrender *peacefully*, not *peaceably* (unless they are antiwar demonstrators).

peak   n., high point; v., to reach a high point
peek   n., brief look; v., to look briefly
pique   n., transient feeling of wounded vanity; v., to provoke

peal   to ring or resound
peel   to pare

pedal   lever operated by the foot
peddle   to sell
petal   part of a flower

pediatrician children's doctor
podiatrist foot doctor

peer n., an equal, a member of the British peerage (nobility); v., to gaze
pier platform extending from shore over water (see *dock*)

penal pertaining to punishment
penile pertaining to the penis

penance act of repentance
pennants flags

pendant ornament worn around the neck
pendent hanging

penitence feeling of remorse
penitents people showing remorse

people *The AP Stylebook* prefers this as the plural for *person* in all instances.
persons Many usage experts argue that this should be used as the plural of *person* when an exact or small number of people is defined and that *people* should be used to refer to masses. *The AP Stylebook* prefers *people* for both meanings.

persecute to oppress
prosecute to take to court

personal private; individual
personnel employees; staff

perspective view
prospective expected

perspicacious having great insight
perspicuous easily understood

persuade see *convince*

petroglyph carving in stone
pictograph painting on stone

phenomena plural, things that are apparent to the senses
phenomenon singular, a thing apparent to the senses

physical   see *fiscal*

pidgin   combination of languages
pigeon   a kind of bird

pinch hitter   Don't use except in baseball; the pinch hitter is not a mere substitute but someone put in to do a better job than the regular batter.

pistil   part of a flower
pistol   handgun

pivotal   Use to mean crucial, not merely important.

plain   n., flat country; adj., not fancy
plane   n., airplane, type of tool; v., to shave level

plaintiff   person who sues
plaintive   mournful

plan to attend   not *plan on attending*

plead guilty of   not *plead guilty to*

pleased (at, by) a gift   not *pleased with*

plurality   see *majority*

podium   see *dais, podium*

pole   n., stick
poll   n., survey, voting place; v., to conduct a survey

police   need not be preceded by *the*

polite   see *courteous*

pompom   ornamental tuft carried by cheerleaders
pom-pom   weapon
pompon   a type of flower or the flower head

pomposity, pompousness   synonyms meaning self-importance

poor lacking

pore n., opening in the skin; v., to study carefully

pour to make a liquid flow

poorly Do not use for *badly*.

populace the common people

populous full of people

poring over looking over

pouring over emptying a liquid onto

portend to foreshadow

portent omen

possible for can be possible

possible that might be possible

practicable describes a thing that's possible

practical describes a sensible person or thing

practically This adverb means for all practical purposes. It should not be used to mean almost.

pray to worship

prey n., a hunted animal; v., to plunder or hunt

precede to go before

proceed to continue

precipitate to hasten; to bring on ahead of expectations

precipitous adj., steep

predominant adj., prevailing

predominate v., to prevail

premier n., prime minister; adj., outstanding. *The AP Stylebook* suggests, though, that you use *prime minister* unless the nation prefers the term *premier*, as in China, or *chancellor*, as in Germany and Austria.

premiere n., first presentation of a movie or play. Don't use as a verb or an adjective, although many authorities permit it.

prescribe   to order

proscribe   to prohibit or condemn

presence   act of being present; bearing

presents   gifts

presently   Despite widespread use to mean now, many editors prefer using it only to mean soon.

presumptive   founded on presumption

presumptuous   taking too many liberties

pretense   false or unsupported claim of distinction

pretext   what is put forward to conceal the truth

prevaricate   Use to mean to evade the truth or stray from it, not necessarily to lie. For example, an equivocation is a *prevarication* because it misleads, even though the statement may be literally true.

primer   elementary textbook; substance used to prepare a surface for painting. In America, the first meaning is pronounced like *primmer*, and the second is pronounced *prime-er*, as both meanings are pronounced in Britain.

primmer   more prim

principal   n., someone or something first in rank; adj., most important

principle   n., basic rule or guide

prodigy   something or someone extraordinary

protégé   someone guided or helped by someone more influential

profit   money made on a transaction

prophet   one who foresees

prohibit   see *forbid*

prone   lying face downward

supine   lying face upward

prophecy   n., a prediction of the future

prophesy   v., to predict the future

Usage

proposal   plan offered for acceptance or rejection

proposition   n., assertion set forth for argument, improper proposal; v., to make an improper proposal

prostate   male gland

prostrate   to lie prone

proved   v., past tense of *prove*

proven   adj., tested and found effective

purposefully   aiming at a goal

purposely   intentionally

put into words   not *put in words*

Q

quarts   plural of quart, the measurement

quartz   a kind of mineral

quash   to annul

squash   n., a fruit related to a gourd; v., to crush

quaver   to be tremulous (said of the voice)

quiver   to shake

quell   to suppress

quench   to satisfy thirst; to douse

queue   see *cue*

quiet   silent

quite   very. Avoid whenever possible. The word means entirely or all the way and shouldn't be used to mean considerably, rather or somewhat. It should never be followed by a noun.

quotation   noun; preferred noun form in more formal writing, especially when what's quoted is famous

quote   verb; also acceptable as a noun in informal usage and in referring to quotations in journalism

R

racism   the belief that some races are inferior to others, especially when associated with the idea that "inferior" races should be hated or discriminated against. See Chapter 7.

rack   n., stretching frame used for torture; v., to torture or strain

reek   to give off a strong, bad odor

wrack   damage brought about by violence, as in *wrack and ruin*; best avoided as a verb

wreak   to inflict, as in *wreak havoc* or *wreak vengeance*

wreak havoc   not *wreck havoc*. Considered by some a cliché, though, so another wording would be preferable.

wreck   to damage or destroy

rain   precipitation

reign   term of a sovereign's power

rein   strap to control a horse; used in *free rein*, meaning loosened control

raise   transitive v., *raise, raised, has raised*

raze   to destroy

rise   intransitive v., *rise, rose, has risen*

range of actions   not *range of action*

rappel   a descent by a mountain climber

repel   to drive back

rapt in thought   not *wrapped* (or *wrapt*) *in thought*

rare   in short supply all the time

scarce   in short supply temporarily

raring to go   not *roaring to go*. Means eager or enthusiastic.

ravage   to destroy

ravish   to rape; to seize and carry away by force; to enrapture

reaction   Don't use in place of *opinion*.

real   adj.: *The clock is real.*

really   adv.: *She is really tired.*

real good   Grammatically, this idiom should be *really good*. Better still, just say *good*.

reapportion   applies to state legislatures

redistrict   applies to congressional districts

rebound   to spring back

redound   to have a result

rebut   to answer a criticism or attack and deny or dispute it

refute   to disprove, not merely answer, deny, dispute or rebut.

reciprocal   see *mutual*

recourse   a resort; that to which one turns for help

resource   a supply

re-cover   to cover again

recover   to regain health or possession

re-create   to create again

recreate   to take leisure

redhead   AP accepts this for a person who has red hair, but many people object to being reduced to a hair color, depending on the context.

regardless   not irregardless

regretful   having regrets

regrettable   unfortunate; to be regretted

relaid   laid again

relayed   transmitted

reluctant   unwilling to act

reticent   unwilling to speak

remediable   capable of being fixed

remedial   intended as a remedy

rend   to split apart; to distress

render   to submit; to extract by melting

repairable   usually used with something physical that can be repaired

reparable   usually used with something not physical that can be repaired, such as a mistake

repellent   n., something that repels; adj., repulsive

repulse   to rebuff by discourtesy; to disgust

repulsive   offensive; disgusting

replica   a copy made by the original artist or under that person's supervision

reproduction   a copy made by someone else

reportedly   Use of this word is an excuse for laziness about looking up the facts and a way to try to avoid responsibility for a statement. Avoid it.

re-sign   to sign again

resign   to quit; to give up a job or an office

respectable   worthy of respect

respectful   showing respect

respective   in order

resume   to start again

résumé   a summing up, especially of a career; note both accent marks

reverend   This adjective always takes the article *the* in front of it except when directly addressing a member of the clergy. Don't write that someone *is a reverend*.

review   critical examination; scholarly journal

revue   theatrical production with skits, music and dancing

right   correct

rite   religious ceremony

wright   worker, as in *playwright*

write   to put down in words

risk averse   not *risk adverse*

Usage

sociable   enjoying company

social   pertaining to society

soldier   generally speaking, one member of the military. But U.S. Marines insist the term should be applied only to members of the Army.

troop   group of soldiers, police, highway patrol officers, scouts, people or animals. But *The AP Stylebook* also accepts it in the plural in relation to many military personnel, as in *About 40,000 U.S. troops were wounded in Iraq.*

trooper   cavalry soldier, mounted police officer or highway patrol officer

trope   figure of speech

troupe   company of actors, dancers or singers

trouper   member of a theatrical company; veteran performer

solecism   violation of grammar, usage or propriety

solipsism   belief that nothing is real but the self

solidarity   show of support

solidity   firmness, stability

soluble   capable of being dissolved; capable of being solved

solvable   capable of being solved

some   Don't substitute this adjective for the adverb *rather* or *somewhat.*

some time   adj., n.

sometime   adv., *former,* not *occasional.*

sort of   not *sort of a*

spade   shovel

spayed   past tense of *spay,* to sterilize a female animal by removing its ovaries

speak with   not *speak to*

specially   see *especially*

specious   deceptive; used to describe abstract things

spurious   counterfeit; used to describe concrete things

stable   n., animal shelter; adj., sturdy

staple   constantly used commodity

staid   sedate

stayed   past tense of *stay*

stake   n., a piece of pointed wood or metal; something bet; a share; v., to mark a location or furnish resources

steak   a thick cut of meat or fish; not used as a verb

stalactite   an icicle-shaped stone that hangs down from a cave ceiling

stalagmite   an icicle-shaped stone builds up on a cave floor

stamping grounds   not *stomping grounds,* although the latter is used perhaps more often now; either is now accepted in *Webster's New World;* AP, *American Heritage Dictionary* and *Oxford American Dictionary*

stanch   to restrain, as in *The nurse stanched the bleeding.*

staunch   firm in opinion

stationary   not moving

stationery   writing paper

stimulant   alcohol, drugs or agents such as caffeine

stimulus   incentive

straight   not crooked

strait   singular. Geographers prefer this term for a narrow passage connecting two bodies of water. But the expression is "strait is the gate" (not "straight is the gate") because here the word means *narrow* rather than *not crooked.*

straits   plural. This term is accurate when there is more than one strait, as in *Straits of Mackinac.* Note also the expression *dire straits.*

straight-laced   strict; severe

strait-laced   pertaining to confinement, as with a corset. Note also *strait-jacket.*

strikebreaker   someone hired to take the place of a striker, not just anyone who crosses a picket line, such as a manager or a union member who decides to work anyway

successive   see *consecutive*

suit   n., set of clothes, lawsuit; v., to please

suite   set of furniture, rooms or dance pieces

summon   v., to command, as in *Summon him to court.*

summons   a singular noun meaning an order to appear, as in *Give her a summons*; third-person singular verb meaning to order or to call to appear, as in *She summons a cab.*

summonses   plural noun: *Give them summonses.*

superficial   on or near the surface

superfluous   more than is needed

superior to   not *superior than*

supposed to   Note the *d.*

supposedly   not *supposably*

sure   adj.: *He is sure to attend.*

surely   adv.: *Surely she knows better.*

sustain a fatal injury   Avoid this phrase. An injury is not sustained if it is fatal.

systematic   methodical, having or showing a system

systemic   affecting the whole system

T

tack   course of action

tact   ability to do the kind thing in a delicate situation

talesman   person summoned to fill a jury

talisman   a charm

talk with   not *talk to*

taught   past tense of *teach*

taunt   to mock

taut   tight

tout   to praise or solicit

team   squad

teem   to abound

tempera   a method of painting
tempura   a method of cooking

temperatures   They should be described as *higher* or *lower*, not as *warmer* or *cooler*.

temporal   transitory; worldly
temporary   not permanent

tenant   person who lives in a rented house
tenet   doctrine

terminable   able to be ended
terminal   at the end

terrified   More than simply scared, *terrified* means paralyzed by fear.

that   *The AP Stylebook* says journalists should use *that* following these verbs: *advocate, assert, contend, declare, estimate, make clear, point out, propose* and *state*. Although *that* can often be cut from a sentence without loss of meaning, for clarity it should be used after *said* when a time element is involved. Also, use *that* rather than *as* after the verbs *feel, know, say* and *think*.

theft   see *burglary*

therefor   for it; for that; for this
therefore   for that reason

there's no admission   Say *There's no admission charge.* Better yet, just say it's free. (*There's no admission* means that nobody will be allowed to attend.)

think   see *feel*

thorough   complete

thrash   to beat an opponent. To thrash something out means to settle something with a detailed discussion.
thresh   to beat grain

threw   past tense of *throw*
through   preposition
thru   misspelling of *through* or *threw*

Usage

throne   seat

thrown   past participle of *throw*

thus   Change this conjunctive adverb to *so*, which is less pompous.

tic   twitch

tick   bloodsucking arachnid

til   sesame plant used in India for food and oil

till   prep., preferred shortened form of *until*; v., to plow; n., money tray

tinker's damn   not *tinker's dam*

to the manner born   not *to the manor born.*

toe the line   not *tow the line*

too   *Too* should be set off by a comma when at the end of a sentence.

tort   legal name for a wrongful act

torte   a kind of round layer cake

tortuous   twisting; complex; deceitful

torturous   pertaining to torture

transpire   Use to mean leak out or become known, not merely happen.

tread   v., to trample; n., the outer layer of a tire, the sound of someone walking

trod   past tense of *tread*

trek   Don't use as a synonym for *trip* or *journey*. A trek is a slow journey filled with hardships.

troop   see *soldier*

U

uncharted   unexplored, unknown, not on map or chart

unchartered   without a charter

under   see *fewer*

underway   There's no longer a distinction made starting with the 2015 *AP Stylebook* between the nautical use as a one-word adjective and the adverbial and other uses as one word. AP now suggests spelling it as one word in all uses.

unexceptionable   beyond reproach
unexceptional   common

unexpectedly   This form is preferred to *unexpectantly*, which is common but isn't in a number of dictionaries; in an unforeseen manner

uninterested   see *disinterested*

unquestionable   indisputable
unquestioned   something that hasn't been questioned

unthawed   There is no such adjective; use *frozen*.

up   Don't use by itself as a verb.

urban   pertaining to a city
urbane   sophisticated

used to   Note the *d*.

V

vain   possessing vanity
vane   device for showing wind direction
vein   blood vessel; streak

valance   short curtain
valence   an atom's capacity to combine

varmint   regional variation of vermin; plural: *varmints*
vermin   disease-carrying pest; plural: *vermin*

venal   corruptible

venial   minor

veracious   truthful

voracious   tremendously hungry

verbal   see *aural*

verbiage   excess words

wording   how something is said

very   Cut whenever possible. If you use it with a past participle, it requires an intervening word such as *greatly*, *highly*, *little* or *much*.

vial   small bottle

vile   evil

viol   a kind of stringed instrument

vice   corruption

vise   tool for gripping

viewpoint   *Point of view* is better.

viral   pertaining to a virus

virile   having masculine strength

virtually   Use to mean *in effect*, not *in fact*. In most cases, *almost* or *nearly* is better.

visible   able to be seen

visual   received through sight

W

waive   to give up or no longer require

waiver   the giving up of a claim

wave   n., a curve of something; v., to move back and forth

waver   to falter

wangle   to get by contrivance

wrangle   to bicker

want   n., desire; v., to desire

wont   n., custom; adj., accustomed

won't   contraction for *will not*

warranty   guaranty (see *guarantee*)

way   manner

weigh   to check for weight

weather   see *if*

well-heeled   not *well-healed*

wet   v., to moisten; adj., moist; you *wet your whistle* (that is, you moisten your mouth, not stimulate it).

whet   to sharpen, as in *whet your appetite* because you stimulate your appetite, not moisten it

wharf   see *dock*

when   at a particular time. Don't use to mean *by the time that*. Also, clauses introduced by an adverb shouldn't be used in place of a noun or pronoun: Rewrite "In tennis, 'love' is when your score is zero" as "In tennis, 'love' is a score of zero."

whenever   at any time

where   adverb. Don't use for *that*. Rewrite "I saw on the news *where* the vice president is coming to town" as "I saw on the news *that* the vice president is coming to town."

whether   see *if*

while   Some experts say that *while* should be used only to mean *simultaneously*, not *and, but, though* or *although*. If it's the first word in a sentence and it's meant to show contrast, change it to *although*. If it's meant to show contrast later in the sentence, use *though* or *but*.

whisky   Use this spelling only with Canadian whisky, Japanese whisky and Scotch whisky.

whiskey   Use this spelling in reference to bourbon, rye and Irish whiskey and others not listed above as specifically using the spelling *whisky*.

who's   contraction for *who is*

whose   possessive of *who*. This should be used only with people or animals, according to some editors. They would rewrite "The door, *whose* lock was broken, had to be replaced" as "The door, the lock *of which* was broken, had to be replaced." But because there is no possessive form of *that* or *which*, we say go ahead and use *whose* if the sentence would be awkward the other way.

worst way   Don't use to mean *very much*.

Y

yet   Some say this word should always have a comma after it, but we've seen plenty of places where we wouldn't put one. If *yet* falls at the end of a sentence, put a comma before it.

yoke   device or symbol for subjugation

yolk   the yellow part of an egg

yore   long ago

your   possessive of *you*

you're   contraction for *you are*

youth   singular; boy or girl age 13 to 18

youths   plural

Z

zoom   This word refers to upward motion or, in camera work, to move in closer. Don't use it to mean move speedily, as in *zooming down the highway*.

Associated Press Print and Web Style Summary

Style rules help avoid annoying inconsistencies. Without a stylebook, writers would not know whether the word *president* should be capitalized when preceding or following a name, whether the correct spelling is *employee* or *employe* (dictionaries list both, but AP says it's *employee*) or whether a street name should be *Twelfth* or *12th*.

Newspapers, magazines, websites, and radio and television stations use stylebooks to provide such guidance. For consistency, most newspapers and many magazines follow rules in *The AP Stylebook*, and radio and television stations often use a version of the AP guidelines modified to account for the spoken word. Many media outlets also make their own lists of exceptions to AP style, and some instead have their own stylebooks but mainly agree with AP's.

There often are good reasons for local variations. For example, AP style calls for spelling out *First Street* through *Ninth Street* but using numerals for *10th Street* and above. But if a city has only 10 numbered streets, for consistency it might make sense to use *Tenth Street*.

Although much of this book goes beyond the stylebook in providing help, this list instead goes the opposite direction and summarizes the main rules of AP style. (For more punctuation rules, see Chapter 15. For rules on radio and television style, see Chapter 4.)

This summary should be helpful even for those without a stylebook, but we provide it assuming that most users of this book have one. Why? Because the 2018 edition of the stylebook is 630 pages, which can be frightening, especially for someone trying to learn the rules for the first time. So, we try to help here by including only the rules used most often, arranged by topic to make them easier to learn. Only about 10 percent of the rules in a stylebook account for 90 percent of the rules you will use regularly, with the rest used only about 10 percent of the time. It makes sense, therefore, to learn first those rules you will use most often.

The rules we list here and throughout the book were up-to-date with or expanded beyond those in *The AP Stylebook* at the time of our writing in late 2018. But be aware that AP issues a new edition of its stylebook each June with around 200 changes each time (all but 20 or even less usually minor ones), whereas this book is published only every three years. It's possible, then, that some things might have changed by the time you read this. So, learn these and then consult the latest edition of AP as you write or edit. For quick lists of changes since this book came out, you could do a web search for "AP style changes" followed by a year.

Abbreviations and Acronyms

Punctuation

In general, abbreviations of two letters or fewer have periods:

> 600 B.C., A.D. 1066
>
> 8 a.m., 7 p.m.
>
> 8151 Yosemite St.

Exceptions include *AM radio*, *FM radio*, *35 mm camera*, *The AP Stylebook*, *D-Mass.*, *R-Kan.*, *IQ*, *TV*, *VR* (virtual reality) and *AR* (augmented reality), these last two when abbreviated on second reference.

In general, abbreviations of three letters or more do not have periods.

> CIA, FBI, NATO, mpg, mph

One exception is *c.o.d.* (preferred in all references to *cash on delivery* or *collect on delivery*).

Symbols

Always write out % as *percent* in a story, but you may use the symbol in a headline.

Always write out & as *and* unless it is part of a company's formal name.

Always write out ¢ as *cent* or *cents*.

Always use the symbol $ rather than the word *dollars* with any figure, and put the symbol before the figure. Write out *dollar* only if you are speaking of, say, the value of the dollar on the world market.

Dates

Don't abbreviate days of the week except in a table.

Don't abbreviate a month unless it has a date of the month with it: *December 2018*; *Dec. 7*; *Dec. 7, 2018*.

When a month is used with a specific date, abbreviate only *Jan., Feb., Aug., Sept., Oct., Nov.* and *Dec.* Don't abbreviate the five months spelled with five or fewer letters except in a table: *March, April, May, June, July*.

Never abbreviate *Christmas* as *Xmas*, even in a headline.

Fourth of July or *July Fourth* is written out when the holiday is meant.

Use *Sept. 11* or *9/11* to refer to the attacks on the U.S. on that date.

People and Titles

Few publications still use courtesy titles (*Mr.*, *Mrs.*, *Ms.*, *Miss*) on second reference in stories. Many publications use them only in quotations from sources. Others use them only in obituaries and editorials or on second reference in stories mentioning a husband and wife. In the last case, some newspapers prefer to repeat the person's whole name or, especially in features, use the person's first name. The Associated Press suggests using a courtesy title only in direct quotations or when a woman requests a specific title.

Use the abbreviations *Dr., Gov., Lt. Gov., Rep., Sen.* and *the Rev.*, as well as abbreviations of military titles, on first reference, but then drop the title on subsequent references. Note that *Rev.* should always be preceded with *the* because it is not an abbreviation for a noun.

Some titles you might expect to see abbreviated before a name are not abbreviated in AP style: *Attorney General*, *District Attorney*, *President*, *Superintendent*.

Use the abbreviations *Jr.* and *Sr.* after a name on first reference if appropriate, but do not set them off with commas.

Organizations

Write out the first reference to most organizations in full rather than using an abbreviation.

National Organization for Women

Exceptions include *CIA* and *FBI*. The abbreviation for these may be used on the first reference. *GOP* is acceptable on second reference when referring to the Republican Party.

You may use well-known abbreviations, such as *FCC* and *NOW*, in a headline even though the abbreviations would not be acceptable on first reference in the story.

Do not put the abbreviation of an organization in parentheses after the full name on first reference. If the abbreviation is that confusing, don't use it at all but rather call the organization something like "the gay rights group" or "the bureau" on second reference.

Use the abbreviations *Co., Cos., Corp., Inc.* and *Ltd.* at the end of a company's name even if the company spells out the word. Do not abbreviate these words if they are followed by other words such as "of America." The abbreviations *Co., Cos.* and *Corp.* are used, however, if followed by *Inc.* or *Ltd.* (and, by the way, *Inc.* and *Ltd.* are not set off by commas even if the company uses them).

Abbreviate political affiliations after a name.

Sen. Charles Schumer, D-N.Y., said . . .

Never abbreviate the word *association*, even as part of a name.

Appendix

Places

Don't abbreviate a state name except in a dateline, a headline or when giving a mailing address.

The names of the 50 U.S. states should be spelled out when used in the body of a story whether standing alone or in conjunction with a city, town, village or military base. In datelines, use the traditional state abbreviations, not the Postal Service's two-letter ones: *Miss.*, not *MS*.

But use the two-letter postal abbreviations when a full address is given that includes a ZIP code: *217 Ridgecrest St., Westminster, MA 01473*.

Here are the abbreviations used in datelines:

Ala.	Fla.	Mass.	Neb.	N.Y.	Tenn.
Ariz.	Ga.	Md.	Nev.	Okla.	Va.
Ark.	Ill.	Mich.	N.C.	Ore.	Vt.
Calif.	Ind.	Minn.	N.D.	Pa.	Wash.
Colo.	Kan.	Miss.	N.H.	R.I.	W.Va.
Conn.	Ky.	Mo.	N.J.	S.C.	Wis.
Del.	La.	Mont.	N.M.	S.D.	Wyo.

D.C. for *District of Columbia* is not normally used in AP style because *Washington* stands alone in a dateline or within a story.

Never abbreviate the six states spelled with five or fewer letters or the two noncontiguous states: *Alaska, Hawaii, Idaho, Iowa, Maine, Ohio, Texas, Utah*.

Note that the names of many large U.S. cities stand alone, even in datelines, without state abbreviations following. Examples include Atlanta, Philadelphia and Washington. See *The AP Stylebook* datelines entry for a list of cities that stand alone.

Some international cities (London, Mexico City and Toronto among them) also stand alone without country names following. See *The AP Stylebook* for a list.

Many publications add their own list of towns well-known in their state or region to AP's list of cities not followed by the state name.

Don't abbreviate the names of thoroughfares if there is no street address with them.

Main Street

West Boulevard

If the thoroughfare's name has the word *avenue, boulevard, street* or any of the directions on a map, such as *north* or *southeast*, abbreviate those words with a street address.

999 Jackson Ave.

1424 Lee Blvd. S.

In a highway's name, always abbreviate *U.S.*, but never abbreviate a state. In the case of an interstate highway, the name is written in full on first reference, abbreviated on subsequent ones.

> U.S. Route 63 or U.S. Highway 63
>
> Massachusetts Route 2
>
> Interstate 70 [first reference], I-70 [second reference]

Never abbreviate *Fort* or *Mount*.

Use the abbreviation *St.* for *Saint* in place names.

Exceptions include *Saint John* in New Brunswick, *Ste. Genevieve* in Missouri and *Sault Ste. Marie* in Michigan and Ontario.

You may abbreviate *U.S.* and *U.N.* for *United States* and *United Nations* whether used as a noun or an adjective. In headlines, drop the periods.

Miscellaneous

Abbreviations accepted in all uses, even on first reference include *CIA* and *FBI*; *IQ* (*intelligence quotient*); *TV*; and *UFO* (unidentified flying object).

Abbreviate and capitalize the word *number* when followed by a numeral: *No. 1.*

Write out *versus* or abbreviate it as *vs.*, except in the name of court cases, which use *v.*

Capitalization

Proper Nouns

Proper nouns are capitalized; common nouns are not.

Unfortunately, this rule is not always easy to apply when the noun is the name of an animal, a plant or a food or when it is a trademark that has become so well-known that people mistakenly use it generically. (See Chapter 11.)

When two or more proper nouns are combined and they share a word in common, the shared plural is lowercased.

> Missouri and Mississippi rivers
>
> Chrisman and Truman high schools

Geographic Regions

Regions are capitalized; directions are not.

> We drove *east* two miles to catch the interstate to the *West*.

Adjectives and nouns pertaining to a region are capitalized.

> Southern accent, Western movie, a Southerner, a Western

A region combined with a country's name is not capitalized unless the region is part of the name of a divided country.

> eastern U.S., North Korea

A region combined with a state name is capitalized only if it is famous.

> Southern California, southern Colorado

Government and College Terms

Government and college terms are not always consistent.

College departments follow the animal, plant and food rule: Capitalize only words that are already proper nouns.

> Spanish department, sociology department

By contrast, always capitalize a reference to a specific government department, even without the city, state or federal designator and even if it's turned around with *of* deleted.

> Police Department, Fire Department, State Department, Department of Commerce

College and government committees are capitalized if the formal noun is given rather than a shorter, descriptive designation.

> Special Senate Select Committee to Investigate Improper Labor-Management Practices
>
> rackets committee

Academic degrees are spelled out and lowercased, unless you are specifying the subject for which the degree has been earned

> Bachelor of Arts degree; bachelor's degree
>
> Master of Science degree; master's degree

Avoid the abbreviations *Ph.D.*, *M.A.*, *B.A.*, and the like, except in lists.

Always capitalize (unless plural or generic) *City Council* and *County Commission* (but alone, *council* and *commission* are lowercased). *Cabinet* is capitalized when referring to advisers. *Legislature* is capitalized even if the state's body is not formally named that. *Legislature* is capitalized, either with or without the name of the state in front of it, if it's the actual name of the state's legislature. *Capitol*, the building, is capitalized, but *capital*, the city, is not. Capitalize *City Hall* even without the city name but not *county courthouse* without the name of the county.

Numbers

Cardinal Numbers

Use cardinal numbers, or numerals, in the following cases:

- Addresses. Always use numerals for building numbers in street addresses: *7 Fifth Ave.*, *1322 N. Main St.*
- Ages. Always use numerals, even for days or months: *3 days old*; *John Burnside, 56.*
- Aircraft and spacecraft: *F-4, DC-10, Apollo 11.* Exception: *Air Force One.*
- Clothing sizes: *size 6.*
- Dates. Always use the numeral alone — no *nd, rd, st* or *th* after it: *March 20.*
- Decades: *the 1990s, the '90s, the 2010s.*
- Dimensions, heights: *the bedroom is 8 feet by 12 feet, the 8-by-12 foot bedroom; the 5-foot-6 guard* (but no hyphen when the word modified is one associated with size: *3 feet tall, 10 feet long*).
- Distances. Use figures for *10* and above; spell out one through nine: *She walked six miles; they walked 16 miles.*
- Highways: *U.S. 75.*
- Millions, billions and trillions: *1.2 billion, 6 million.*
- Money. Always use numerals, but starting with a million, write amounts like this: *$1.4 million.*
- Numbers: *No. 1, No. 2.*
- Percentages. Use numerals except at the beginning of a sentence: *4 percent.*
- Proportions. Always use figures: *2 parts water to 3 parts powder.*
- Ratios. Use figures and hyphens: *the ratio was 2-to-1, a 2-1 ratio.*
- Recipes. All numbers for amounts take numerals: *2 teaspoons.*
- Speeds: *55 mph, 4 knots.*
- Sports. Use numerals for just about everything: *8-6 score, 2 yards, 3 under par, 2 strokes.*
- Temperatures. Use numerals for all except zero. Below zero, spell out minus: *minus 6* (except in tabular data).
- Times: *4 a.m., 6:32 p.m., noon, midnight, five minutes, 16 hours.* Note that *12:00 noon* and *12 a.m.* are incorrect usages.
- Weights: *7 pounds, 11 ounces.*
- Years. Use numerals without commas. A year is the only numeral that can start a sentence: *2017 was a good year.*

Numerals With Suffixes

Use numerals with the suffixes *nd*, *rd*, *st* and *th* in the following instances:

- Political divisions (precincts, wards, districts): *3rd Congressional District.*
- Military sequences: *1st Lt., 2nd Division, 7th Fleet.*
- Courts: *2nd District Court; 10th U.S. Circuit Court of Appeals.*
- Streets. For *First* through *Ninth,* use words: *Fifth Avenue, 13th Street.*
- Amendments to the Constitution. For *First* through *Ninth,* use words: *First Amendment, 16th Amendment.*

Numbers as Words

Write out numbers in the following cases:

- Numbers less than 10, with the exceptions noted earlier in this section: *five people, four rules.*
- Any number at the start of a sentence except for a year or a numeral and letter combination: *Sixteen years ago . . ., 3D printing has . . .*
- Casual numbers: *a hundred or so.*
- Fractions less than one: *one-half.*

Other Rules for Numbers

Use mixed numerals for fractions greater than one.

$1\frac{1}{2}$

Use Roman numerals for a man who is the third or later in his family to bear a name and for a king, queen, pope or world war.

John D. Rockefeller III, Queen Elizabeth II, Pope Benedict XVI, World War I

Online Resources

Associated Press Style

The Associated Press Stylebook *apstylebook.com* The Associated Press provides both printed and online editions of its style-book, considered the journalist's bible. Requires paid subscription.

Editing

Several websites can be of use to journalists who need to sharpen their writing and editing skills for print, broadcast or the web. Among them are the following:

American Copy Editors Society *copydesk.org*

Copyediting *copyediting.com*

Dow Jones News Fund *newsfund.org*

EditTeach *editteach.org* A great website for learning and teaching copy editing.

The Slot (Bill Walsh) *theslot.com*

Fact Checking

The Center for Responsive Politics *opensecrets.org* Looks at political donations and lobbying.

FactCheck.org *factcheck.org* From the Annenberg Public Policy Center and winner of numerous awards as one of the best fact-checking sites on the web.

Great Books Online *bartleby.com* Free access to *Bartlett's Familiar Quotations, American Heritage Dictionary, Columbia Encyclopedia* and much more.

HeadlineSpot *headlinespot.com* Searches magazine, newspaper, radio, TV and wire-service websites.

Information Please *infoplease.com*

My Reference Desk   *refdesk.com*

PolitiFact   *politifact.com*   Pulitzer Prize–winning political fact-check site sponsored by the *Tampa Bay Times*, but sometimes criticized for leaning left.

Quackwatch.org   *quackwatch.org*   Guide to look up fraudulent medicine claims.

Snopes   *snopes.com*   Best guide, nonpartisan, to check out hoaxes, rumors, urban legends and false reports.

Washington Post's Fact-Checker   *washingtonpost.com/news/fact-checker/*

The Washington Post, along with *The New York Times*, is generally considered one of the nation's main newspapers of record, although both are also considered liberal. A third greatly respected paper is *The Wall Street Journal*, although it's considered conservative.

Grammar, Usage and Spelling Help

Grammar Girl (Mignon Fogarty)   *quickanddirtytips.com/grammar-girl* Website and podcast.

grammarNOW   *grammarnow.com/*

Guide to Grammar and Writing   *grammar.ccc.commnet.edu/grammar/index.htm*

The Online English Grammar   *ef.com/english-resources/english-grammar/*

Journalism Critiques

The best-known journalism reviews are the *Columbia Journalism Review* and the *American Journalism Review*, formerly print magazines but now websites. The Society of Professional Journalists website is another great source of information for reporters. Those sites offer critiques of journalism from within the field. On radio, a good weekly critique of journalism is available on National Public Radio's show *On the Media*. On TV, a good weekly critique is Fox News Channel's MediaBuzz. Check local listings for times and places.

In addition to those, realize that in these hyper-partisan times, many critiques of journalism come from partisan sources. Of course, they're promoting their own political agenda, but they're still useful for getting straight-from-the-horse's-mouth views rather than the stereotypes promoted by their opponents. Finally, there are some sites we'd classify as basically neutral, although partisans sometimes take issue, of course. There are also some sites particularly good at trying to summarize both sides of particular stories in the news or issues in the news.

American Journalism Review *ajr.org* Archives only—new content ceased in 2015.

Columbia Journalism Review *cjr.org*

Society of Professional Journalists *spj.org*

Left-Leaning Media Watchdogs

Fairness and Accuracy in Reporting *fair.org/*

Media Matters *mediamatters.org*

Project Censored *projectcensored.org/*

Right-Leaning Media Watchdogs

Accuracy in Media *aim.org/*

Media Research Center *mrc.org/*

Neutral Media Watchdogs

Annenberg *annenbergpublicpolicycenter.org* and its fact-check .org site

Center for Media and Public Affairs *cmpa.gmu.edu/* Sometimes criticized for leaning right.

Pew *pewresearch.org*

Sites Presenting Both Sides Fairly

All Sides *AllSides.com* Shows how each story is reported from the left, center and right.

Magazines

Ezine Universe *emailuniverse.com/*

Folio *foliomag.com* Magazine of the magazine industry.

Newsletter Access *newsletteraccess.com*

Specialized Information Publishers Association
siia.net/divisions/sipa-specialized-information-publishers-association

Media Law and Ethics

Ethics

American Society of News Editors *asne.org/asne-principles* Statement of principles.

The Poynter Institute *poynter.org/channels/ethics*

Society of Professional Journalists *spj.org/ethicscode.asp*

Law

First Amendment Center   *freedomforuminstitute.org/first-amendment-center/*

Media Law Resource Center   *medialaw.org/*

Reporters Committee for Freedom of the Press   *rcfp.org/first-amendment-handbook*

U.S. Copyright Office of the Library of Congress   *copyright.gov*

University of Iowa Library index to World Wide Web media law sites   *bailiwick.lib.uiowa.edu/journalism/mediaLaw/index.html*

Newspapers

American Press Institute   *americanpressinstitute.org*

American Society of News Editors   *asne.org*

National Newspaper Association   *nnaweb.org/*

The Poynter Institute   *poynter.org*

Society for News Design   *snd.org*

Non-Biased Language

American-Arab Anti-Discrimination Committee   *adc.org*

American Copy Editors Society   *copydesk.org*

Asian American Journalists Association   *aaja.org*

Association of LGBTQ Journalists, The   *nlgja.org*

Everyday Sexism Project   *everydaysexism.com*

Geena Davis Institute on Gender in Media   *seejane.org*

GLAAD (Gay and Lesbian Alliance Against Defamation)   *glaad.org*

International Women's Media Foundation   *iwmf.org*

Journalism and Women Symposium   *jaws.org*

Maynard Institute   *mije.org*

National Association for Multi-Ethnicity in Communications   *namic.com*

National Association of Black Journalists   *nabj.org*

National Association of Hispanic Journalists   *nahj.org*

National Center on Disability and Journalism   *ncdj.org*

Native American Journalists Association   *naja.com*

Religion News Association   *religionstylebook.com*

Society of Professional Journalists   *spj.org*

Southern Poverty Law Center   *splcenter.org*

Women in Media & News   *wimnonline.org*

Women's Media Center   *womensmediacenter.com*

Online Media

Internet Press Guild   *netpress.org*

Radio and Television

The Most Often Mispronounced Words in English   *alphadictionary
.com/articles/mispronounced_words.html*

National Association of Broadcasters   *nab.org*

The professional association for radio and television journalists.

Radio Television Digital News Association   *rtdna.org*

Strategic Communications

Public Relations Society of America   *prsa.org/*

Index

a/an, 125–26, 207–8
abbreviations
   in Associated Press style, 404–7
   in lists, 408
   on mobile media, 118
   on radio and television, 62
abundance, 200
academic degrees, 408
accident stories, 20, 32, 168
accuracy. *See* correctness
acronyms, 62, 404–7
active voice, 124
   for conciseness, 114
   parallel structure of, 201
   subjects in, 166
   verb tenses and, 183–84
adjectives, 125–26, 134
   appositives as, 213
   commas and, 224, 232
   comparative, 204–5
   confused with adverbs, 206–7
   correctness of, 204–5
   neutrality and, 28
   nouns and, 203
   positive, 204–5
   superlative, 204–5
   See also coordinate adjectives; modifiers
adopt/pass, 112
adverbs, 125, 134, 203–5
   comparative, 204–5
   confused with adjectives, 206–7
   conjunctive, 142–43, 144, 222, 231–32, 234
   correctness of, 204–5
   negative, 208
   neutrality and, 28
   positive, 204–5
   right form of, 125–26
   sentence, 132–33, 134, 216
   superlative, 204–5
   word order for, 217
   See also conjunctive adverbs; modifiers
advertising, 77, 80
advertising copywriting, 81
affect / effect, 112
African-Americans, 54, 101

ageism, 102–3, 241
ages
   hyphens and, 233
   on radio and television, 50
ago, 174
agreement, 192–202
   of plurals, 192
   with prepositional phrases, 200–1
   See also parallel structure; pronoun-
     antecedent agreement; subject-verb
     agreement
AIDS, 95
Alessandri, Steven M., 104
Alibaba, 93
all, 195
"all in the family" lead, 45
alleged/allegedly, 29, 39
also, 233
American Indians, 104
American Journalism Review, 414
American Society of Business Publication
   Editors, 77
American Society of Magazine Editors, 77
among/between, 112
an/a, 125–26, 207–8
analogies, 22
analytical journalism, 6
and
   at beginning of sentence, 46, 50
   commas and, 127, 223
   in radio and television, 50
   subject-verb agreement and, 192
   symbol for, 404
and/or, slashes for, 237
angle, for news writing, 32–33
animal names, 407
animation, in online media, 66
another, 195
antecedents. *See* pronoun-antecedent agreement
any, 195
anybody, 195
anybody's, 153
anyone, 195
anyone's, 153
anything, 195

apostrophes
    for compound words, 161
    for *contra*ctions, 128, 237
    for possessives, 128, 151, 161, 237
appositives, 134, 213
array, 200
articles, 125–26, 207–8
as a matter of fact, 46
as . . . as, 214
as/like, 122
Associated Press style, 403–12
    abbreviations in, 404–7
    acronyms in, 404–7
    for capitalization, 407–10
    for numbers, 411–12
    online resources for, 413
Associated Press Stylebook, 24, 131, 194, 272,
    403, 413
assumptions, objectivity and, 25–27
as well as, 154, 205
as/than, 122, 154
at, 174
at that time, 174
Atlanta Braves, 74–75
attributions
    dashes for, 236
    fairness and, 29
    for online media, 68
    for paraphrases, 46
    possessive form pronouns for, 155
    punctuation for, 228
    quotations and, 227–29
    on radio and television, 57–58
    word choice for, 39
    word order for, 228
audience
    analytics, 81
    angle for, 33
    correctness and, 23
    general, 19–20
    global, 91
    grammar and, 133
    for journalistic writing, 23
    as news value, 33
    purpose and, 23
    for radio and television, 50–51
audio, in online media, 66
authenticity, of quotations, 225
author, 112

balance, objectivity and, 25
BBC. *See* British Broadcasting Corporation
BBC News, 65
be it said, 189
be that as it may, 189

between/among, 112
biased writing
    modifiers in, 117
    terms in, 241–54
    See also isms; racism; sexism
Bible, 226, 235, 409
Bing, 72, 73
Black Friday, 93
blacks. *See* African-Americans
Blackstone, William, 100
Block, Mervin, 53
blogs, 69, 73–75
blurb, 236
both, 115, 195
both . . . and, 214
brand names, 323
Bremner, John, 194
British Broadcasting Corporation, 65
"Broadcast Standard English," 54
broadcast writing
    pronouns in, 198
    would/should in, 186
    See also radio; television
Brown, Michael, 92
bullets, 72, 235, 236
burglary/robbery, 112
Burke, Tarana, 96
Bush, George H. W., 95
but, 126
    at beginning of sentence, 46, 50
    in radio and television, 50
BuzzFeed, 72
by, 167

can/could, 124, 164, 186
capitalization
    after colon, 129
    Associated Press style for, 407–10
    proper nouns, 155
    quotations and, 230
    for radio manuscripts, 60
    for stressing words on radio and television, 62
cardinal numbers, 411
case
    of pronouns, 122, 152–55, 156
    suspensive, hyphens for, 236
Census Bureau, U.S., 68
centers around, centers on, 120
cents, symbol for, 61, 404
chunks, on online media, 71
civil rights, 100
Civil War, 100
clarity
    in journalistic writing, 18–23
    on online media, 67

on radio and television, 53
of words, 113–17
clauses, 134, 136–45
  essential, 123
  imperative, 222
  nonessential, 123, 148
  parallel structure in, 199
  in paraphrases, 229
  relative, 143
  restrictive, 123, 139–41, 147
  subordinate, 143
  See also dependent clauses; independent
    clauses
clichés, 43–45, 59, 117, 226
Clinton, Hillary, 95
c/o, 237
collective nouns, 147, 193–94, 197
college terms, 408–9
colons, 63, 129, 228, 234–35
Columbia Journalism Review, 414
come what may, 189
commas
  for adjectives, 232–33
  appositives and, 213
  conjunctive adverbs and, 222, 231–32
  for coordinating conjunctions, 127
  dashes and, 128
  for introductory items, 126–27
  for modifiers, 127–29
  for nonrestrictives, 140
  noun of direct address and, 212
  paraphrases and, 127
  for parenthetical items, 127–28
  problems with, 220–25
  quotation marks and, 224
  quotations and, 220, 228, 230
  semicolons and, 127, 129, 234
  subordinating conjunctions and, 231
  for two or more complete thoughts, 126
  when not to use, 223–24
  when to use, 220–23
  which and, 148
comma-splice sentence error, 126, 138
Commentaries on the Laws of England, 100
commentary, 7, 8
common nouns, 112, 151, 161
companion words, 120
comparative adjectives and adverbs, 204–5
complements
  infinitive, 160
  objective, 159
  predicate, 134, 143, 172–73
complete predicates, 170
complete subjects, 158
complete verbs, 172–73, 206

complex sentences, 144–45
compose/comprise/constitute, 112
compound-complex sentences, 145
compound modifiers, 207, 224, 232–34,
    236, 276
compound objects, 154, 224
compound sentences, 144, 145, 230
compound subjects, 153
compound words, 161, 210, 277
comprise/compose/constitute, 112
concealing identity, on online media, 77–78
conciseness, 113–17, 287–322
  clichés and, 117, 287–322
  helping verbs and, 114
  of online media, 67, 69–70
  phrases and, 114
  for radio and television, 52
  word choice for, 114–17
  words and phrases to cut, 287–322
conditional mood, 124, 171, 185–86
confidence, grammar and, 133
conflict, as news value, 33
confused words, 109–12, 329–402
conjugations, of verbs, 173, 183, 184, 187
conjunctions, 134
  commas and, 220, 224
  conciseness and, 115
  modifiers and, 231
  participles as, 213
  semicolon and, 234
  subject-verb agreement and, 192–93,
    199–200
conjunctive adverbs, 142–43, 144, 222, 231–32,
    234
connecting words, 134
  phrases as, 142
  problems with, 209–11
  See also conjunctions; conjunctive adverbs;
    prepositions
consistency
  grammar and, 133
  of verb tenses, 182–83
constitute/compose/comprise, 112
contact, 112
*contra*ctions, 50, 116, 128, 237
conversational style
  pronouns in, 155
  for radio and television, 48, 49–50
  split infinitives in, 218–19
  verb moods in, 190
  writing and, 130–31
convince that, convince of, 120
coordinate adjectives, 207, 223, 232–34
coordinating conjunctions, 126–27, 142,
    144, 211

copy editing. *See* editing
cornucopia, 200
corrections, on online media, 78
correctness
    of adjectives, 204–5
    of adverbs, 204–5
    of articles, 207–8
    of blogs, 69
    checklist for, 23
    in journalistic writing, 23–29
    on online media, 68–69
    political, 105
correlative conjunctions, 213–14
could have / would have, 165
could / can, 124, 164, 186
could / might, 165
couple, 193–94
creative writing, versus journalistic writing, 17–18
credibility
    grammar and, 133
    of online media, 68–69
crisis communication, 86
cultural shift, 92–93
Cyber Monday, 93

DADT. *See* "don't ask, don't tell"
dance companies, 226
dangling infinitives, 216
dangling participles, 212, 216
dashes, 235–36
    appositives and, 213
    colon and, 235
    commas and, 128
    for parenthetical items, 128
    on radio and television, 50, 63
    which and, 148
databases, 66
dateline, 235
dates
    abbreviation for, 404
    in hard-news leads, 39, 41
    in news leads, 35
    on online media, 69
day
    in hard-news leads, 39, 41
    in news leads, 35
debut, 112
decimal numbers, 63
Defense of Marriage Act, 92
definite articles, 207
delayed-ID who, in hard-news leads, 36
delayed leads. *See* soft-news leads
demographic shift, 92
dependent clauses, 136, 137, 143, 149
    commas and, 223
    in complex sentences, 144–45

on radio and television, 51
    subjunctive mood for, 188, 189
descriptive grammar, 132
details
    hard-news leads and, 40, 42
    in online media, 66
    soft-news leads and, 45–46
dialect, pronunciation and, 54
dialogue, 112
dictionary leads, 44
Dictionary of Offensive Terms, 241
different, 115
different than, *different from*, 120
direct objects, 134, 143, 159, 168, 169
direct quotations, 220
    interjections in, 209
    introductory clause or phrase for, 222
    titles in, 405
Dirksen, Everett, 22
discrimination. *See* ageism; biased writing; isms;
      racism; sexism
Disraeli, Benjamin, 22
dollars, symbol for, 61, 404
"don't ask, don't tell," 95
double negatives, 208
double possessives, 162
doubled prepositions, 115
drama
    in hard-news leads, 42
    as news value, 33
dramatic pause
    colon for, 235
    dashes for, 235
Drescher, Fran, 54

e, silent, 275
each, 195–96
each one, 195
e-commerce, 93
editing
    for online media, 74–75
    online resources for, 413
    for radio and television, 61
    symbols for, 49, 61
editorials, 8
effect / affect, 112
Eisner, Michael, 78
either, 196
either . . . or, 196, 214
either / or, 237
elderly, 110. *See also* ageism
"*Elements of Journalism, The*" (Kovach and
      Rosenstiel), 5, 10, 25
"*Elements of Style, The*" (Strunk and White), 94, 113
ellipses, 50, 63, 230
else, 125

empty expressions, in hard-news leads, 41
ending, on radio and television, 59–60
English as a second language (ESL)
   idioms and, 111
   perfect tenses and, 174, 175
   progressive tenses and, 176
   pronouns and, 155
   modifiers and, 206
   vocabulary and, 111
   word choice and, 111
equality revolution, 89, 96
essential clauses, 123
etc., 220
ethics, with online media, 76–78
ethnic groups, current reality of, 101–2.
      See also racism
euphemisms, 117
event planning, 81
everybody, 195
everybody's, 153
everyone, 195
everyone's, 153
everything, 195
excepting, 213
exclamation points, 126, 230, 237–38
   commas and, 224
   for interjections, 204, 209
   one-word leads with, 43
explanatory journalism, 6
extreme passive-voice sentences, 167

Facebook, 11, 66, 75
Facebook Subscribe, 75
fact-based journalism, 6
fact checking, online resources, 413–14
facts, objectivity and, 25–27
fair comment and criticism, 8
fairness, objectivity and, 25, 29
fake news, 7, 8
   political, 10–13
farther/further, 112
Faulkner, William, 139
feature leads. *See* soft-news leads
feet, 237
feminine pronouns, 152
few, 195
fewer/less, 112
fiction writing, 137, 138
   versus journalistic writing, 17–18
   run-on sentences in, 139
Finkel, Kenn, 238
first person, 119, 152
   for blogs, 74
   shall for, 177
   simple tenses and, 173
flashbacks, 182–83

Flaubert, Gustave, 109
Follett, Wilson, 217
food names, 407
for, 161
   indirect objects and, 159
   passive voice and, 167
Forbes.com, 78
forbid to, 120
formal style
   for audience, 23
   contractions and, 50
   grammar and, 129–35
   for news writing, 48
   predicate nominatives in, 158
formulaic writing, 31
Founding Fathers, 3
fractions, 63, 195, 237, 412
fragments, sentences and, 126, 137–38
frankly, 132
"funny thing" lead, 45
further/farther, 112
fused-sentence error, 126, 138
future perfect, 174, 181
future-perfect progressive, 176–77, 181
future progressive, 176–77, 181
future tense, 173, 181

gender
   of nouns, 150
   pronoun-antecedent agreement and, 119,
      152, 197–98
   of pronouns, 119
   revolution, 90, 96
   shifts, 92
   spelling and, 150
   stereotypes for, 104
   See also sexism; women
gender-neutral pronouns, 92
generalities
   in hard-news leads, 41
   on radio and television, 52
generics
   men as, 100
   trademarks and, 155, 323–27
geographic regions, capitalization of, 407–8
gerunds, 134, 160, 190
   adverbs and, 204
   commas and, 221–22
   nouns and, 157
   object of, 160
   objective form pronouns and, 154
   objects and, 157, 160
   possessive form pronouns and, 155, 156
   pronouns in front of, 123
God bless/God forbid, 189
Goethe, Johann Wolfgang von, 113

"good and bad news" lead, 44
good/well, 207
Google, 72, 73
Google Translate, 73
government terms, 408–9
graduate, 184
grammar, 118–35
    common problems of, 118–29
    confidence and, 133
    consistency and, 133
    correctness of, 23
    credibility and, 133
    descriptive, 132
    errors of, 132–33
    formal writing and, 129–35
    online resources, 414
    punctuation and, 126–29
    purpose of, 131
    for radio and television, 53
    traditional, 132
graphics, on online media, 72
Guide to Newswriting, 182

had/ought, 165
hanged/hung, 112
hard news, 6
hard-news leads, 34–42
    problems with, 40–42
    on radio and television, 56–58
hard-news stories
    impersonal tone in, 29
    inverted pyramid for, 42
    modifiers in, 117
    in present tense, 53
    on radio and television, 53
    soft-news leads for, 35
Hate Crimes Statistics Act, 95
have/of, 164
headings, for online media, 71
headlines
    commas and, 223
    quotations in, 231
    semicolon in, 234
hedging phrases, 28
helping verbs, 114, 165, 170–71

Hemingway, Ernest, 139, 410
here, 114, 197
her/him, 149
he/she, 149, 152
hidden information revolution, 91, 96
highway names, 62
him/her, 149
himself, 150
his/hers, 237

Hoffer, Eric, 136
Holtz, Shel, 71
homicide/murder, 112
homonyms, 52, 109, 111, 112
hopefully, 132–33
host, 112
how, 34
however, 46
hung/hanged, 112
hyphenated words, 255–71
hyphens, 233–34, 236–37
    for compound modifiers, 233, 236, 276
    compound words and, 277
    for modifiers, 128–29
    for phrases, 162
    possessives and, 162
    for prefixes, 236, 278
    for pronunciation on radio and television, 62
    spelling and, 276–79
    suffixes and, 277

I, 152
icons, on online media, 72
idioms, 117, 162
    ESL and, 111
    subjunctive mood for, 189
if, 188
If I were . . ., 124–25
if . . . then, 214
if/whether, 112
immediate-ID who leads, 35, 43
impact, as news value, 33
imperative clauses, 222
imperative mood, 185
impersonal tone, in hard-news stories, 29
implied passive voice, 168
imply/infer, 112
in, 115
Inc., 224
inches, 226
including, 213
indefinite articles, 207–8
indefinite pronouns, 195–96
independent clauses, 136, 137, 142–43
    colon and, 235
    commas and, 222, 224
    comma-splice sentence error and, 138
    in complex sentences, 144–45
    conjunctive adverbs for, 234
    fused-sentence error and, 138
    indicative mood for, 188–89
    in simple sentences, 143–44
Indians, 104
indicative mood, 184, 186, 187, 188–89
indirect objects, 134, 143, 159

infer/imply, 112
infinitive complement, 160
infinitive phrases, 216, 221–22
infinitives, 134, 160
    adverbs and, 204
    and and, 190
    commas and, 221–22
    nouns and, 157, 191
    object of, 160
    objective form pronouns and, 154
    present tense and, 174
    splitting, 191
    to and, 212
informal style, 23
    of blogs, 73
    predicate nominatives for, 158
    for radio and television, 49
    for social media, 118
    See also conversational style
Instagram, 66, 75
interaction for online media, 72
interjections, 134, 204, 209, 213
internet
    new standards of language for, 97
    See also online media; online resources
intervening nouns and pronouns, 196
intransitive verbs, 171–73, 206–7
introductory elements, commas and, 126–27,
    220–21
inverted order, of subject and verb, 197
inverted pyramid, 32, 35, 42
investigative reporting, 78
IQ, 407
irregular verbs, 165–66
Islam, 227, 248
isms, 88–105
    brief history of, 99–100
    Language Triangle, 94–97
    new players in new millennium and, 98–100
    new social change, 95–97
    new standards of language for, 97
    new video/content requirements for, 97
    up to date, ways to be, 104–5
it, 114, 152
it/its, 197
itself, 150
its/it, 197

Jackson, Andrew, 272
jargon, 19, 116
journalism, 3, 5–7, 15–16
    online resources, 414–15
journalistic objectivity, 10
journalistic writing, 17–30
    anticipating questions in, 20

collective nouns in, 194
versus creative writing, 17–18
versus fiction writing, 17–18
news writing, 31–46
objectivity in, 24–28
purpose of, 23
spelling in, 274
statistics in, 21–23
story formulas in, 24
in third person, 74
verb moods in, 186
verb-tense sequence and, 181–82
voice in, 29
word choice in, 19–20, 110–11
writing for eighth-grade-level readability, 30
Jr., 224

Ketterer, Stan, 68
Koran, 409
Kovach, Bill, 5, 10, 25
Kuralt, Charles, 60
Kurtz, Howard, 78

labels, stereotypes and, 104
language
    isms and, 97
    for online media, 73
    politically correct, 105
    See also English as a second language (ESL)
Language Triangle, 94–97
lay/lie, 112
lead/led, 124
leads. *See* hard-news leads; news leads; soft-news
    leads
led/lead, 124
left-leaning media bias, 9–10
legal concerns
    with online media, 76–77
    with proper nouns, 155
lesbian, gay, bisexual and transgender, 94, 249
less/fewer, 112
letters, apostrophes for, 237
Lewis, Michael, 104
LGBTQ. *See* lesbian, gay, bisexual and
    transgender
libel, 76
lie/lay, 112
like/as, 122
Lincoln, Abraham, 230, 231
linking verbs, 172, 191, 206, 212, 233
links, for online media, 71
lists
    abbreviations in, 408
    for online media, 72
little, 195

"little did she know" lead, 45
longevity revolution, 89, 96

MacArthur, Douglas, 177
magazines, 75
    Associated Press style for, 403
    online resources, 415
    quotations and, 226
Maidment, Paul, 78
main points, on radio and television, 51
main verbs, 170–71
majority, 200
Mandarin, 94
many, 195
many a, 195
marketing, 80
masculine pronouns, 152
may/might, 124, 164, 186
McCain, John, 95
McLuhan, Marshall, 109
meanwhile, 46
media
    bias, perceptions of, 9–10
    industry, 13–14
    online resources, 416
    relations, 81
Mehrabian, Albert, 130
metadata, 73
#MeToo Movement, 96
Mexicans, 96
Meyer, Philip, 25
microaggressions, 99
Middle Easterners, 95
Mies van der Rohe, Ludwig, 113
might/could, 165
might/may, 124, 164, 185
Milano, Alyssa, 96
Milton, John, 190
mine/my, 153
minorities, 102
minutes, apostrophes and, 237
misplaced modifiers, 215–16
misused words and phrases, 329–402
Mitchell, Richard, 167
mixed approach, news leads, 34
mobile media, 65–78
    abbreviations on, 118
    problems of, 67
    See also social media
"*Modern American Usage*" (Follett), 217
modifiers, 28–29, 134, 142, 143, 203–14
    in biased writing, 117
    commas for, 127, 128–29
    in complete subject, 158
    compound, 207, 224, 232–34, 236, 276
    conjunctions and, 211

    in hard-news stories, 117
    hyphens for, 128–29, 236
    misplaced, 215–16
    numbers as, 57
    punctuation for, 231–34
    squinting, 217
    vague, 114
    word order for, 197, 215–17
    See also adjectives; adverbs
mood. *See* verb mood
more, 195
more than one, 195
Morkes, John, 70
most, 195
most-important-element what, in hard-news
    leads, 37
much, 195
multiculturalism, 98
multiple-elements what, in hard-news
    leads, 37
murder/homicide, 112
musical group names, 194, 226
musical works, quotations and, 226
Muslims, 95, 96
my/mine, 153
myriad, 200
myself, 123, 150

names
    animal, 407
    brand, 323
    food, 407
    in hard-news leads, 40
    highway, 62
    musical group, 194, 226
    plant, 407
    proper, 147, 407
    on radio and television, 63–64
    team, 194
narrative writing, 7
Native Americans, 104
negative adjectives, 208
negative adverbs, 208
neither, 196
neither . . . nor, 196, 201, 214
neologisms, 110
neutrality, objectivity and, 27–28
New York, dialects of, 54
New York Times, The, 66, 75
news, 3–5
    fake, 7, 8, 10–13
    versus public relations writing, 84–85
    stories, 79–80
    websites, 11
news leads, 34–46
    hard-news leads, 34–42

for online media, 66
soft-news leads, 43–46
See also hard-news leads; soft-news leads
News Reporting and Writing, 3
news values, 33
news writing, 31–46
angle for, 32–33
formal style for, 48
inverted pyramid for, 32, 35, 36
news leads in, 34–46
for online media, 70–78
paragraphs in, 35
paraphrases in, 46
for radio, 47–64
for social media, 75–76
story formula for, 32, 45
for television, 47–64
transitions in, 46
newspapers, 14–15
Associated Press style for, 403
decline, 15–16
Facebook and, 75
hard-news leads in, 34
online media and, 65–67
online resources, 401
quotations and, 226
newsworthy, 4
Newsy, 72
Nielsen, Jakob, 70
"no comment" snapper, 59
no one, 195–96
nobody, 195
nominative absolutes, 216
nominative-case (subject form) pronouns, 122, 152–55
nonbias rule, 103–4
non-biased language, online resources, 416–17
noncountable nouns. *See* uncountable nouns
none, 195–96
nonessential clauses, 123, 148
nonrestrictive elements, 123, 139–41, 147, 223
not, commas and, 223
"not just for . . . anymore" lead, 45
not only . . . but also, 121, 199–200, 214
not so . . . as, 214
nothing, 195
nouns, 134
adjectives and, 203
adjectives for, 125
capitalization of, 156
collective, 171, 193–94, 197
common, 112, 151, 161
conciseness and, 116
gender of, 150
gerunds and, 157
infinitives and, 157–58, 191

intervening, 196
plurals of, 160–61, 195
possessives from, 151, 161–62
pronouns and, 119–20, 146, 157–58
pronouns in front of, 123
right form of, 122
singular, 160–61
uncountable, 193–94, 200
vague, 116
as verbs, 112, 169–70
verbs as, 114, 116, 170
nouns of direct address, 134, 140, 152, 112, 223
novelty, as news value, 33
number
Associated Press style for, 411–12
in hard-news leads, 40, 57
in journalistic writing, 21–23
prefixes to, 279
pronoun-antecedent agreement and, 119, 197–98
on radio and television, 62–63
subject-verb agreement and, 193
verbs and, 119
as words, 412
numerals
apostrophes for, 237
with suffixes, 412
nut graf, 36, 46

Obama, Barack, 95
obituaries, 35, 405
object pronoun, 122, 148–49, 154–55, 157
objective-case (object form) pronouns, 122, 152, 154–55
objective complement, 159
objectivity
assumptions and, 25–27
facts and, 25–27
fairness and, 29
in journalistic writing, 24–28
neutrality and, 27–28
rules for, 25–29
objects, 146–62
compound, 154, 224
direct, 134, 143, 159, 168, 169
gerunds and, 157, 160
indirect, 134, 143, 159
of infinitive, 160
infinitives as, 157–58
kinds of, 159–60
of participle, 159
phrases as, 141–42
of prepositions, 159, 209–10
problems with, 146–57
O'Brien, David, 74
oddity, as news value, 33

of, 115
"official" lead, 45
of/have, 164
on, 174
"On the Road," 60
one, 152
  only and, 201
"one thing is certain" ending, 59
"one thing's different" lead, 44
one's, 153
one-word leads, 43
online editorials, 8
online media, 65–78
  advantages of, 66
  advertising on, 77
  Associated Press style for, 403
  bullets for, 72
  chunks on, 71
  clarity on, 67
  concealing identity on, 77–78
  conciseness of, 69–70
  corrections on, 78
  correctness on, 68–69
  credibility of, 68–69
  editing for, 74–75
  ethics with, 76–78
  hard-news leads in, 34
  immediacy of, 71
  interaction for, 72
  isms on, 88–105
  languages for, 73
  legal concerns with, 76–78
  lists for, 72
  for *The New York Times*, 66
  news writing for, 48, 70–78
  newspapers and, 66
  photo manipulation on, 77
  privacy of, 76–77
  problems of, 67
  quotation marks in, 76
  for radio and television, 49
  versus radio and television, 48–53
  rewriting for, 70
  search engines for, 72, 73
  storyboards for, 70
  templates for, 70
  uniqueness of, 67–70
  updates for, 71
  word choice for, 71
  See also social media
online resources, 413–17
  Associated Press style, 413
  editing, 413
  fact checking, 413–14
  grammar, 414

  journalism, 414–15
  magazines, 415
  media law and ethics, 416
  newspapers, 416
  non-biased language, 416–17
  radio, 417
  spelling, 414
  strategic communications, 417
  television, 417
  usage, 414
only, 201
"only time will tell" ending, 59
opinion, 7–8
or, 193
organizations
  abbreviations for, 405
  punctuating Inc., 224
  websites for, 72
other, 195
"other side" snapper, 59
others, 195
ought/had, 165
ought/should, 165
ourselves, 150
overstatements, in hard-news leads, 42
ownership, possessives for, 161

Palin, Sarah, 95
paragraphs
  in journalistic writing, 19–20
  in news writing, 35
parallel structure, 119, 120
  for phrases, 192, 198–99
  of prepositional phrases, 210
  of verb voice, 201
paraphrases, 46, 127, 224, 225–26, 229
  quotation marks and, 225–26, 271
parentheses, 63, 148, 236, 238
parenthetical items
  commas and, 127–28, 223
  dashes for, 128, 235
  nonrestrictives as, 140
  subject-verb agreement and, 193
  which for, 147
partial quotes, 41, 225, 226, 229–30
participial phrases
  nominative absolutes and, 216
  on radio and television, 51
participles, 134, 159, 190, 204, 112
  object form pronouns and, 154, 156
  verb tenses and, 212
parts of a sentence, 134
parts of speech, 134. *See also specific parts of speech*
pass/adopt, 112

passive voice, 114, 124, 183–84
    avoidance of, 166–69
    parallel structure of, 201
past participle, 166, 177–79, 190
past perfect, 174–75, 179
past-perfect progressive, 176–77, 180
past progressive, 176–77, 180
past tense, 58, 179–80, 187–88
percentages, 195, 411
perfect tenses, 174–75
periods, 126, 224, 230, 237–38
person, 74
    pronoun-antecedent agreement and, 119,
        152, 197–98
    simple tenses and, 173–74
personalization, for radio and television, 50–51
persuade to, 120
persuasive communication, 79, 84
Pew Research Center, 75–76, 92
photo manipulation, on online media, 77
phrases, 134, 136–45
    clichés as, 117
    conciseness and, 113
    as connecting words, 142
    defined, 136
    for and, 161
    hedging, 28
    hyphens for, 162
    infinitive, 216–17, 221–22
    as modifiers, 142
    as objects, 141–42
    parallel structure for, 192, 199
    as predicate nominatives, 141–42
    prepositions as, 209–10
    restrictive, 139–41
    as subjects, 141–42
    as verbs, 142
    See also participial phrases; prepositional
        phrases
pictures, on online media, 72
Pilgrims, 100
place
    abbreviations for, 406–7
    in hard-news leads, 41
    in news leads, 35
plagiarism, 76
plant names, 407
plenty, 195
plurality, 200
plurals
    agreement of, 192
    apostrophe for, 128
    of common nouns, 151
    of nouns, 151
    of pronouns, 151–52

rules for making, 151
simple tenses and, 173
spelling of, 150–52
politically correct language, 105
positive adjectives and adverbs, 204–5
possessive-case (possessive form) pronouns, 128,
        152–55, 156
possessives
    apostrophes for, 128, 161, 237
    hyphens and, 162
    from nouns, 151, 161–62
    spelling of, 150–52
Poynter.org, 76
predicate adjectives, 134, 172, 206, 212,
        233–34
predicate complements, 134, 143, 172–73
predicate nominatives, 134, 141–42, 158, 172,
        197
predicate objective, 159
predicates, 119, 126, 134. *See also* verbs
prefixes
    hyphens for, 236, 277–78
    spelling of, 272–73
premier, 112
prepositional phrases, 134, 196, 209–10
    agreement with, 209
    parallel structure of, 210
    on radio and television, 51
    relative pronouns and, 200–1
prepositions, 121, 134, 218
    compound words and, 277
    dependent clauses and, 149
    doubled, 115
    at end of sentences, 211, 218
    object form pronouns and, 154
    object of, 159, 209
    participles as, 213
present participles, 177–79, 190
present perfect, 174–75, 180
present-perfect progressive, 176–77, 180
present-perfect tense, on radio and
        television, 57–58
present-progressive, 176–77, 180
present progressive tense, on radio and
        television, 57–58
present tense, 53, 57–58, 174, 188
    sequence of, 180
presently, 112
press releases, 79
print advertisement, 82
print media, versus radio and television, 48–53
privacy, of online media, 76–77
progressive tenses, 176–77
prohibit from, 120
prominence, as news value, 33

pronoun-antecedent agreement, 119, 146, 152, 192, 197–98, 201
pronouns, 122–23, 134
  adjectives for, 125
  antecedents and, 152
  apostrophes for, 237
  case of, 152–55
  in conversation style, 155
  ending in *self/selves*, 150
  in front of gerunds, 123
  in front of nouns, 123
  gender of, 119
  indefinite, 195–96
  intervening, 196
  nominative-case/subject form, 122, 152–55
  nouns and, 119, 146, 157
  object, 122, 148–49, 154–55, 157
  objective-case/object form, 122, 152–55, 156
  plurals of, 151–52
  possessive case/possessive form, 155
  relative, 143, 144, 147–49, 201
  right form of, 122–23
  singular, 152
  subject, 122, 148
  unclear references of, 146
pronunciation, on radio and television, 54–56, 61–62
proper names
  capitalization of, 407
  relative pronouns for, 147
proper nouns, 155
proximity, as news value, 33
public relations, 80
  versus news writing, 84–85
  quotation marks in, 226
pull quote, dashes for, 236
punch-line snapper, 59
punctuation, 219–38
  for abbreviations, 404
  for attributions, 228
  for compound modifiers, 233–34
  for coordinate adjectives, 232–33
  grammar and, 126–29
  of interjections, 204, 209
  for modifiers, 231–34
  for nonrestrictives, 140–41
  with quotation marks, 129
  for quotations, 129
  on radio and television, 63
  for restrictives, 140–41
  for sentences, 126–29
purpose
  of grammar, 131
  of journalistic writing, 23

question lead, 43–44
question marks, 126, 237–38
  commas and, 224
  quotations and, 230
questions
  anticipating, 20
  fragments as answers to, 138
  inverted order in, 197
  what/that/which in, 148
quotations and quotation marks
  attributions and, 227–29
  colon and, 234
  commas and, 220, 222, 224, 230
  exclamation points for, 238
  in hard-news leads, 41
  in online media, 76
  paraphrases and, 225, 287
  partial, 41, 224, 229–30
  in public relation, 226
  problems with, 225–31
  punctuation around, 129, 220
  on radio and television, 63
  what and how to quote, 225–26
  See also direct quotations; paraphrases
Quran, 235, 409

racism, 88–105
  biased term, 105
  current reality of, 100–2
  Language Triangle for, 94–97
  new players in new millennium and, 98–100
  new social change, 95–97
  new standards of language for, 97
  new video/content requirements for, 97
  up to date, ways to be, 104–5
radio, 47–64
  abbreviations on, 62
  Associated Press style for, 403
  audience for, 50–51
  clarity on, 53
  conciseness for, 52
  *contr*actions in, 50
  conversational style for, 48, 49–50
  copy-editing symbols for, 61
  editing for, 61
  Facebook and, 75
  grammar for, 53
  hard-news lead on, 56–58
  hard-news stories on, 53
  informal style for, 49
  manuscript preparation for, 60
  names on, 63–64
  news writing for, 47–64
  numbers on, 62–63
  versus online media, 48–53

online resources, 417
personalization for, 50–51
present tense on, 53
versus print media, 48–53
pronunciation on, 54–56, 61–62
punctuation on, 63
rewriting for, 52
sentences in, 48, 49
spelling on, 64
story formulas for, 59–60
style standards for, 60–64
timeliness for, 52–53
word choice for, 49
"rain couldn't dampen" lead, 44
raise/rise, 112
Rand, Ayn, 143
Ranly, Don, 20, 232
readability, 30
readability tests, 19
recipe lead, 45
redundancy, in time, 39
regarding, 213
regular verbs, 165
relative clauses, 143
relative pronouns, 143, 144, 147–49, 201
reliability, of online media, 67
Religious Organizations, 96–97
religious terms, capitalization of, 409
reported speech rule, 181
resources. *See* online resources
restatement snapper, 59
restrictive clauses, 123, 139–41, 147
restrictive phrases, 139–41
reviews, 8
revolves around, 120
rewriting, 52, 70
"*Rewriting Network News*" (Block), 53
"riding the elephant" ending, 60
rise/raise, 112
robbery/burglary, 112
Rosenstiel, Tom, 5, 10, 25
run-on sentences, 139

satire, 8
says/said, 220, 222, 227–28, 229, 235
scanning, on online media, 71
search engine optimization, 73
search engines, 71–72, 73
second person, 119, 152, 173
seconds, quotations and, 226
self/selves, 150
semicolons, 234
commas and, 127, 129
conjunctive adverbs and, 232
for independent clauses, 144

quotations and, 230
on radio and television, 63
semimodal verbs, 185
senior citizens, 110. *See also* ageism
sentence adverbs, 134
hopefully as, 132
nominative absolutes and, 216
sentences, 134, 136–45
attributions in, 228
common errors in, 137–39
conciseness of, 113
defined, 137
ending with prepositions, 211
fragments and, 126, 137–38
in journalistic writing, 19–20
parallel structure in, 120, 199
parts of, 134
with prepositions at end, 211, 218
punctuation for, 126–29
in radio and television, 49, 50
SEO. *See* search engine optimization
September 11, 2001, 95, 102
sequence-of-tense rule, 182
set/sit, 112, 172
several, 195
sexism, 88–105
biased term, 241
current reality of, 100–1
Language Triangle, 94–97
new players in new millennium and, 98–100
new social change, 95–97
new standards of language for, 97
new video/con*tent* requirements for, 97
in pronoun-antecedent agreement, 120
up to date, ways to be, 104–5
shall/should, 124, 186
shall/will, 177
she/he, 149, 152
should/ought, 165
should/shall, 124, 186
silent *e*, 275
simple predicate, 170
simple sentences, 143–44, 145
simple subjects, 158
simple tenses, 173–74
since . . . therefore, 214
single-element what, in hard-news leads, 37
singular nouns, 160–61
singular pronouns, 152
sit/set, 112, 172
slashes, 237
slavery, 100
Snapchat, 66
snapper, 59–60
Snoopy lead, 45

social media, 66, 113, 118
  new standards of language of, 97
  news writing for, 75–76
Society of Professional Journalists, 86, 414
soft news, 6
soft-news leads, 35, 36, 43–46
  for hard-news stories, 35
  stories, 80
somebody, 195
someone, 195
something, 195
"something came early" lead, 44
Sonderman, Jeff, 76
Southern Poverty Law Center, 102
Spanish, 94
specifics, in journalistic writing, 20–21
spell-checkers, 75, 236, 272
spelling, 23, 272–86
  gender and, 150
  hyphens and, 276–79
  in journalistic writing, 274
  list of commonly misspelled words, 280–86
  online resources, 414
  of plurals, 150–52
  of possessives, 150–52
  of prefixes, 272–73
  on radio and television, 64
  of suffixes, 273–75
split infinitives, 121, 218–19
sports scores, 62
squinting modifiers, 217
Sr., 224
state abbreviations, 406–7
statistics, 21–23, 200
  Hate Crimes Statistics Act, 95
stereotypes, 103
  dumping, 104
  ethnic groups and, 101
  labels and, 104
  racism and, 101
  sexism and, 101
stock index numbers, 62
story formulas
  for journalistic writing, 24
  for news writing, 32
  for radio and television, 59–60
storyboards, 70
strategic communication, 79–87
  legal and ethical issues, 85–86
  news release in, 84–85
  online resources, 417
  process, 81–83
strategic communicators, 83
  skills, 86–87
street addresses, 58, 63
strictly speaking, 132

Strunk, William, Jr., 94, 113
style standards, for radio and television, 60–64.
  See also Associated Press Stylebook; *UPI Stylebook*
subject form (nominative-case) pronouns, 122, 152–55
subject nominatives, 197
subject-predicate agreement. *See* subject-verb agreement
subject pronoun, 122–23, 148–49
subjects, 126, 134, 143, 146–62
  in active voice, 166
  clauses and, 136
  complete, 158
  compound, 153
  gerunds as, 157
  infinitives as, 157
  kinds of, 158
  nouns as, 157
  passive voice and, 166–68
  phrases and, 136, 141–42
  problems with, 146–57
  simple, 158
  subject form pronouns as, 153
  verbs and, 119
subjects of an infinitive, 134
subject-verb agreement, 119, 146, 192–7, 199–200
subjunctive mood, 124, 187–90
subordinate clauses, 143
subordinating conjunctions, 143, 144, 211, 231
substantives, 134. *See also* objects; subjects
subtitles, 235
such, 195
suffixes, 273–74, 277, 412
Sullivan, Margaret W., 104
summary what leads, 37
superlative adjectives and adverbs, 204–5
supposed to, 124
surfing, on online media, 71
suspensive case, hyphens for, 236
Swift, Jonathan, 110
symbols, 404
  for editing, 49, 61
  See also punctuation
synonyms, 111
  for *said/says*, 227

table of contents, for online media, 71
team names, 194
technical terms, 19, 30
technology shifts, 92
television, 47–64
  abbreviations on, 62
  Associated Press style for, 403
  audience for, 50–51

clarity on, 53
conciseness for, 52
contractions in, 50
conversational style for, 47, 49–50
copy-editing symbols for, 61
editing for, 61
Facebook and, 75
grammar for, 53
hard-news lead on, 56–58
hard-news stories on, 53
informal style for, 49
manuscript preparation for, 61
names on, 63–64
news writing for, 47–64
numbers on, 62–63
versus online media, 48–53
online resources for, 417
personalization for, 50–51
present tense on, 53
versus print media, 48–53
pronunciation on, 54–56, 61–62
punctuation on, 63
rewriting for, 52
sentences in, 47, 49
spelling on, 64
story formulas for, 59–60
style standards for, 60–64
timeliness for, 52–53
word choice for, 49
templates, for online media, 70
tenses. *See* verb tenses
terrorism, 95, 102
than/as, 122, 154
that
  for restrictive clauses, 147
  subjunctive mood and, 189
that/which, 123, 147–49
that/who, 123
the, 207–8
  phrases with, 115
theater troupes, 226
thee, 152
their, 119
  as singular, 198
their/theirs, 153, 197
their/there/they're, 112
them, as singular, 198
themselves, 150
then, 174
there, 114, 197
there/their/they're, 112
thesis, 38–39
they, 119, 197
  as singular, 198
they're/there/their, 112
third person, 74, 119, 152, 173

Thompson, Wright, 31
thou, 152
Thurber, James, 219
tightening, 109, 287–322. *See also* conciseness
time
  colon for, 235
  in hard-news leads, 35, 39, 41
  on radio and television, 58
  said/says and, 228
timeliness
  as news value, 33
  for radio and television, 52–53
titles
  abbreviations, 405
  capitalization of, 410
  in hard-news leads, 35–36
  on radio and television, 57
to
  dependent clauses and, 149
  hyphens for, 237
  indirect objects and, 159
  infinitives and, 212
  verbs and, 121
to be
  in hard-news leads, 41
  in linking verbs, 191
  object form pronouns and, 155
  passive voice and, 167
  present tense and, 174
  subjunctive moods for, 187–88
today, on radio and television, 58
too, commas and, 223
trademarks, 155, 323–27, 407
traditional grammar, 132
transitions, 138
  with conjunctive adverbs, 231
  with connecting words, 209
  in news writing, 46
transitive verbs, 169, 171, 206
truism lead, 45
Trump, Donald J., 6, 96
try and, 190
Twain, Mark, 113
Twitter, 66, 75

UFO (unidentified flying object),
  208, 407
unclear pronoun references, 146
unconscious bias, 104
uncountable nouns, 193–4, 200
underlining, for stressing words on radio and
  television, 62
undoubtedly, 46
units of measurement, 195
up, as verb, 211
updates, for online media, 71

UPI Stylebook, 182, 196
usage, 109, 328–402, 414
    correctness of, 23
    online resources, 414
    vocabulary and, 109
    See also word choice
used to, 124

vague modifiers, 114
vague nouns, 116
vague verbs, 116
value judgment, neutrality and, 28
variety, 200
verb mood, 124, 184–90
verb tenses, 58, 124, 173–91
    active voice and, 183–84
    consistency of, 182–83
    parallel structure of, 199
    participles and, 212, 213
    passive voice and, 183–84
    on radio and television, 53
    sequence of, 179–82
verbals, 134, 160, 190–91. *See also* gerunds;
        infinitives; participles
verbs, 134, 143, 163–91
    adverbs for, 125–26
    clauses and, 136
    complete, 172–73, 206
    conciseness and, 116
    conjugations of, 173, 183, 184, 187
    helping, 114, 164–65, 170–71
    intransitive, 171, 206
    irregular, 165–66
    linking, 172, 191, 206, 212, 233
    main, 170–71
    as nouns, 114, 116, 170
    nouns as, 112, 169–70
    numbers and, 119
    phrases and, 136, 142
    preferred use over nouns, 116
    problems with, 163–70
    on radio and television, 58
    regular, 165–66
    right form of, 124–25
    s at end of, 163–64, 174
    semimodal, 185
    subjects and, 119
    subject-verb agreement, 119, 146, 192–97,
        199–200
    to and, 121
    transitive, 169, 171, 206
    up as, 211
    vague, 116
    voice of, 124

video, on online media, 66, 72
vocabulary
    in conversational style, 50
    ESL and, 111
    usage and, 109
voice
    in journalistic writing, 29
    of verbs, 124
    See also active voice; passive voice

Wall Street Journal, The, 11, 45
Washington Post, The, 75, 78
wealth shift, 92
weasel words, 114
web writing. *See* online media
Webster's New World College Dictionary, 23, 131,
        272, 279
Webster's Third New International Dictionary,
        23, 279
well/good, 207
were, in subjunctive mood, 187
what
    for direct object, 159
    in hard-news leads, 34–35, 37–38
    infinitives and, 160
    in questions, 148
    on radio and television, 52, 57–58
    for subjects, 158
    who and, 38
"what a difference" lead, 44
"what it means" snapper, 59
what/which, 148
when
    in hard-news leads, 34–35, 39
    on radio and television, 58
    simple tenses and, 174
where
    in hard-news leads, 34–35, 40
    infinitives and, 160
    on radio and television, 52
whether . . . or, 214
whether/if, 112
which
    conciseness and, 115
    for nonessential clauses, 148
    for nonrestrictive clauses, 147
    for parenthetical items, 147
which/that, 123, 147–49
which/what, 148
while, 112, 211
White, E. B., 94, 113
who
    conciseness and, 115
    in hard-news leads, 34–36

on radio and television, 52, 57
  for subjects, 158
  what and, 37–38
whoever/whomever, 123, 147–49
whom, 159, 160
whomever/whoever, 123, 147–49
whom/who, 123, 147–49
whose/who's, 149
who/that, 123
who/whom, 123, 147–49
why, in hard-news leads, 34
will/shall, 177
will/would, 124, 186
wire-service credit, dashes for, 235
women, 92–93
  Trump and, 96
  See also sexism
word choice, 109–17
  for attributions, 39
  for companion words, 120
  for conciseness, 113–17
  for exact words, 116–17
  for fairness, 29
  for isms, 94–97
  in journalistic writing, 19–20
  list for, 329–402
  for neutrality, 27–29
  for online media, 71
  for racism, 94–97

  for radio and television, 49
  for sexism, 94–97
  for shorter words, 116
word order, 215–19
  for adverbs, 217
  for attributions, 228
  grammar and, 53
  for modifiers, 120, 215–17
  for participial phrases, 216
  for prepositions, 121
  for split infinitives, 121
would have/could have, 165
would/should, 124, 164, 186
would/will, 124, 186
writing
  for blogs, 73–75
  conversation style in, 130–31
  formal style in, 129–30
  versus journalism, 5–6
  See also specific types

Yahoo!, 72, 73
years, on radio and television, 63
yet, commas and, 223
"you might think" lead, 44
yourself, 150
yourselves, 150

Zarrella, Dan, 76

Copy-Editing Marks

Most editing has been done on computers for decades now, but editing symbols are still used to edit manuscript copy—whether your own or someone else's. Examples could include corrections on a printout of your own work, submissions sent to you by mail or broadcast copy to be read off of paper.

Here are some of the most commonly used manuscript markings. Technically, there are differences between copy-editing marks and proofreading marks, but increasingly these have been merging. Keep this list handy when editing or reading a manuscript or proof, but adapt your marks to how you see them made where you work.

Indent for new paragraph

(no) ¶ No paragraph
(in margin)

Run in or bring
copy together

Join words: week end

Insert a *single* word or phrase

Insert a mising letter

Take out anm extra letter

Transpose words two

Transpose tow letters

Make Letter lowercase

Capitalize columbia

Indicate italic letters

Indicate small capitals

Indicate bold face type (bf)

Abbreviate January 30

Spell out abbrev.

Spell out number 9

Make figures of thirteen

Separate runtogether words

Join letters in a word

Insert period ⊙

Insert comma ⌄

Insert quotation marks " "

Take out some word

Don't make this correction *stet*

Mark centering like this

Indent copy from both sides
by using these marks [

Indent copy on left

Spell name Smyth as written

or

Spell name Smyth as written (f.c.)

There's more story: (MORE)

This ends story: # (30)

Do not obliterate copy; mark it out with a thin line so it can be compared with editing.

Mark in hyphen: =

Mark in dash: ⊢⊣